BYZANTIUM BRITAIN & THE WEST

THE ARCHAEOLOGY OF CULTURAL IDENTITY
AD 400–650

BYZANTIUM BRITAIN & THE WEST

THE ARCHAEOLOGY OF CULTURAL IDENTITY
AD 400–650

ANTHEA
HARRIS

TEMPUS

Cover photograph, *Byzantine silver fluted basin with a depiction of a female head from Sutton Hoo mound 1.* Copyright the Trustees of The British Museum
First published 2003

PUBLISHED IN THE UNITED KINGDOM BY:
Tempus Publishing Ltd
The Mill, Brimscombe Port
Stroud, Gloucestershire GL5 2QG

PUBLISHED IN THE UNITED STATES OF AMERICA BY:
Tempus Publishing Inc.
2 Cumberland Street
Charleston, SC 29401

© Anthea Harris, 2003

The right of Anthea Harris to be identified as the Author of this work has been asserted by her in accordance with the Copyrights, Designs and Patents Act 1988.

All rights reserved. No part of this book may be reprinted or reproduced or utilised in any form or by any electronic, mechanical or other means, now known or hereafter invented, including photocopying and recording, or in any information storage or retrieval system, without the permission in writing from the Publishers.

British Library Cataloguing in Publication Data.
A catalogue record for this book is available from the British Library.

ISBN 0 7524 2539 0

Typesetting and origination by Tempus Publishing.
Printed in Great Britain by Midway Colour Print, Wiltshire.

CONTENTS

ACKNOWLEDGEMENTS   6

1 INTRODUCTION   7
   THE END OF THE ROMAN EMPIRE IN THE WESTERN PROVINCES

2 CONSTRUCTING THE OIKOUMENÊ   21
   EAST-WEST DIPLOMACY IN LATE ANTIQUITY

3 TRADING & EXCHANGE   41
   BETWEEN THE BYZANTINE EMPIRE & THE WEST

4 ROYAL TOMBS, TEXTILES & GOLD COINAGE   73

5 THE ROLE OF THE CHURCH   105
   IN EAST-WEST CONTACTS

6 BRITAIN & BYZANTIUM   139

7 CONCLUSION   189
   A BYZANTINE COMMONWEALTH IN LATE ANTIQUITY?

BYZANTINE EMPERORS   195

NOTES & BIBLIOGRAPHY   196

INDEX   221

ACKNOWLEDGEMENTS

I have incurred debts to several people during the preparation of this book. Some have generously spent time discussing aspects of the argument with me and answering my questions, others have gone out of their way to help me obtain photographic and other materials. In both these respects, I would particularly like to thank Susanne Bangert, Lise Bender Jørgensen, Gabriella Bijovsky, Terry Bloxham, Simon Buteaux, Roger Collins, Ken Dark, Simon Ellis, Philip Grierson, David Griffiths, Hallberg Håkan, Melanie Holman, Jonathan Harris, Zoë Harris, Katie Hinds, Jeremy Huggett, Sean Kingsley, Elena Kosmopoulou, Janet Larkin, Françoise Le Saux, Peter Lorimer, Michel Martin, Philip Mills, Rebecca Naylor, Robert Philpott, Paul Reynolds, Joanna Richards, Andrew Richardson, Ian Riddler, Vanessa Sercombe, Sovati Smith, Elma Sutanto, Tania Watkins, Peter Weddell, Sally Worrell and Susan Youngs. For guidance and encouragement at a much earlier stage of this work, I would like to thank David Buckton, Jonathan Franklin, Hero Granger-Taylor, Edward James, Jeremy Knight, R.J. Barry Jones and Jack Spence. The errors within the book remain, of course, my own responsibility.

    The Scouloudi Historical Foundation provided me with financial help, for which I am very grateful. I am particularly indebted to the Economic and Social Research Council (ESRC), whose award of a Post-Doctoral Fellowship enabled me to write this book. I therefore wish to thank the ESRC, and to extend my thanks, too, to colleagues and friends at the University of Reading (where I held the Fellowship) for their many kindnesses to me. My final thanks must be to my family, who have supported me throughout.

1

INTRODUCTION

THE END OF THE ROMAN EMPIRE IN THE WESTERN PROVINCES

In the fifth century AD, the Roman Empire in Western Europe fragmented into many competing 'barbarian' (that is, non-Roman) kingdoms. By about 500, in many areas of the West the great Roman monuments were in disrepair, if they still stood at all. It is usually supposed that this represented both the end of Roman political influence in the West, and that the 'barbarian' kings were wholly independent of the Roman Empire. Moreover, it is claimed that where Roman culture did survive in these kingdoms, it was simply as a residue of former generations. *Romanitas*, it has been said, was evoked by the new 'Germanic' élites ruling the West as a form of 'legitimation' – a political ploy to bolster their tenuous hold on those lands and peoples newly under their sway. However, this assumption is not as clear-cut as it initially seems. In part, the emphasis that has been placed on understanding 'the end of the Roman Empire' has obscured other strands running through this period. Historians and archaeologists alike have been anxious to determine when exactly the Roman Empire ended in the different areas of the West, or have wanted to clarify the way in which Roman authority declined. This is, of course, a legitimate and important concern, but it has meant that the same scholars have often overlooked the ways in which the Roman Empire in the East was forging new links with the West in the latter half of the fifth century. These links would, in some cases, continue through until the sixth, or even seventh, century. It still comes as a surprise to some to discover, for example, that those areas of the British Isles with the least evidence of an official Roman presence in the third and fourth centuries, may have been those with which the Eastern Roman Empire ('Byzantium') had the most links in the fifth and sixth centuries.

No contemporary written text gives a definite and unambiguous statement of the political realities of the immediately 'post-Roman' West. In particular, textual sources seldom even allude to the precise political relationships between Western barbarian kingdoms and what remained of the Roman

Empire in the Eastern Mediterranean. However, what is certain is that when the West passed under barbarian rule the East remained ruled by the Roman state. The Eastern Roman Empire, usually today termed the 'Byzantine Empire' (or 'Byzantium') after the collapse of the West in the fifth century, survived largely intact in political, military and economic terms throughout the whole of the fifth and sixth centuries, before undergoing a crisis of its own in the seventh century. This Empire, which included modern Turkey, Greece, Syria, the Holy Land, Egypt and parts of Italy, co-existed with the barbarian kingdoms of the West, but since most texts are ambiguous about even how Western kingdoms were organised, ascertaining the precise nature of their foreign relations is difficult, to say the least.[1]

The relationship between the Eastern Mediterranean and the West is, therefore, an important question for archaeologists, historians and art historians studying the fifth to seventh centuries, and it is this question that forms the central theme discussed here. This book builds on the work of many previous scholars who have pointed out ways in which contacts between the Eastern and Western halves of the Roman world continued between the 'fall' of the Western Roman Empire in the fifth century and the mid-seventh century. Some of these scholars have considered the way in which individual themes linked East and West (for example, trading patterns and religious negotiation) and specific types of material culture (such as architecture and metalwork). However, it is rare for these categories of evidence to be brought together to investigate the composite role that the Eastern Mediterranean played in shaping the cultural world that emerged in the West after the fifth century. This is the goal that this book seeks to achieve.[2]

It should be stressed at the outset that this is not a complete survey of all those categories of material that may point to East-West contact; far from it. On the contrary, the central subject matter of the book is explored with reference to a selection of the material that might be employed in this way. Specific themes are pursued with the intention of setting out a hypothesis that allows for the synthesis of evidence from both East and West. It is to be hoped that future work will use these and other categories of evidence to explore the questions raised in this book in more detail and to shed light on the validity (or otherwise) of this hypothesis.

Throughout the twentieth century, archaeologists and historians came increasingly to realise the centrality of the fifth to seventh centuries for understanding much more wide-ranging themes relating to the Roman world and the origins of medieval Europe and the Middle East. It is in these centuries that we see the growth of identities, cultures and religions that still play a central role in the modern world. As a consequence, what was commonly and misguidedly known as the 'Dark Ages' has become the subject of intense investigation and re-evaluation and is now more often referred to as 'Late Antiquity'. The current wave of debate dates from the 1930s when the Belgian historian, Henri Pirenne, published his justly famous book, *Mahomet et Charlemagne*, in which he argued that the 'Roman world' did not come to an end in the fifth century, but continued until the so-called 'Seventh Century Transformation'. In his view, the growth of Islam and the resultant expansion of the Arabs into the Byzantine Holy Land, then through the Mediterranean to Sicily, North Africa and finally Spain (with brief forays into southern France), shattered what was left of the Roman economic system, and gave the Carolingian, Anglo-Saxon and Scandinavian world of north-west Europe the impetus to became the economic and political focus of the former Roman West.[3]

Despite severe and fair criticisms, Pirenne's hypotheses still dominate thought about Late Antiquity, and especially the question of how the period came to an end. Pirenne's appeal has been long-lived because it extends across several disciplines, and to scholars studying both the Ancient and the Medieval worlds. His work has now inspired several generations of historians and archaeologists to study the ways in which large-scale and long-lasting transformations have taken place in world history and in European history in particular. Moreover, to a great extent, the current generation's interest in the 'Pirenne Thesis' has been stimulated by the vast quantities of new data that were generated by archaeological research during the second half of the twentieth century. This has re-opened many debates regarding the nature and scope of Late Antiquity, and has placed archaeologists at their forefront. When Pirenne wrote his magisterial work, the study of Late Antiquity had to be primarily historical. Few material remains appeared to survive from that period compared, say, to the wealth of evidence from earlier Roman centuries. But today the situation has changed dramatically: the vast majority of the available evidence is archaeological, and this has provided us with radical new perspectives on the material culture of the many peoples of late antique Europe and the Mediterranean world more generally.[4]

It is archaeological material that forms, therefore, the main source of evidence used in this book. Of course, it is important not to neglect the value of those written sources that survive as contemporary witnesses to the late antique West, but these often newly-available data, and the sophistication of the methods developed for their analysis, sometimes yield a very different picture to that envisaged by Pirenne or inferred from texts.[5]

Economic continuities between the Late Roman period (prior to *c*.400) and Late Antiquity were the principal foci of Pirenne's work. These can also be re-examined in the light of archaeological evidence. Patterns of production, distribution and exchange can be identified using material evidence and these can illuminate economic relations between the Eastern Mediterranean and the barbarian kingdoms of the West. For example, evidence available from maritime archaeology – especially the study of shipwrecks in the Mediterranean – has enabled archaeologists to reconstruct a picture of the cargoes and vessels commonly involved in East-West trade.[6]

Objects, structures and burial practices have more than a utilitarian role. They can also be symbols of status and identity. As such, they have the potential to contain information about past ways of thought, beliefs and values. This gives them an even greater role in investigating the nature of contacts between the Byzantine Empire and the West, for they can – in principle – tell us about what was understood by such links. Obviously, this sort of information is extremely hard for us to 'access' today, but archaeological theory has pointed to ways in which this is not an impossible task. It is an aspiration that becomes more easily achieved when, as in Late Antiquity, particular types of material were strictly controlled by governments and religious authorities. As such, the presence in the West of specific materials, such as porphyry (a type of purple-coloured stone) and silk, which were under the control of the Byzantine court and its officials, may indicate not merely trade, but the 'archaeology of diplomacy'.[7]

Although full of new and perhaps surprising information as we shall see, material data are, nonetheless, restricted by practical considerations. The archaeology of Late Antiquity is constrained by both the quality of the data and by the variability of its study and publication. Archaeological research does not have a standardised set of procedures and techniques universally applied across the whole of Europe and the Mediterranean, so regional differences 'structure' the data and limit or enhance how it can be analysed. For example, if a site has not been stratigraphically excavated, the ability of any scholar to extract a sense of chronological sequence from it will be hugely impaired, no matter how well it has been published. Similarly, if objects are only known out of context, then the information that can be derived from them is severely limited.[8]

Neither are all parts of the late antique world equally studied by archaeologists, nor with reference to the same questions. There is far more archaeological research of all sorts on the period c.400-c.650 in Britain than, for example, in Spain. In the Eastern Mediterranean, while the fascination of 'Roman archaeology' has long been in evidence, 'Byzantine archaeology' is still in its infancy, and for most of the Empire we know far less than would be true of the same area in the Roman period. This creates a very uneven distribution of data across the area with which this book is concerned and constrains what can be said about it even when material is plentiful.

It is a common misconception among archaeologists and historians working on other periods that the data for the fifth to seventh centuries are exceptionally sparse in general. This is not at all true, notwithstanding these limitations. For example, many thousands of excavated and published graves, containing 'grave-goods' (objects buried with the body) are known from across Europe. Moreover, in the very areas where the evidence might be the most difficult to recognise in less than state-of-the-art excavations and surveys, such as western Britain, the standard of archaeology has been particularly high. Readers familiar with the (sometimes seemingly intractable) archaeology of western Britain will be aware that interpretations that might seem tenuous when applied to material elsewhere in the former Roman world have been extremely helpful in establishing patterns of social change in the fifth to seventh centuries. Problems arising from variations in methods impose limitations, therefore, rather than render the whole subject beyond reach.

Methodological matters are not the only ones that need to be clarified. Scholars often dispute when the Byzantine Empire came into existence. The Eastern Roman Empire was created by the constitutional reforms of Diocletian at the end of the third century when the Empire was divided into two administrative parts. Some thirty years later, Constantine I set in place some of the most important features that modern scholars associate with the Byzantine Empire. During his reign, Constantinople became the Eastern capital, and that city was elaborated and subsequently developed in a way that reflected the esteem in which the Christian religion was now held at an official level. The move of political authority to Constantinople also facilitated the dominance of Greek – the main language of the Roman East – over Latin, although Latin remained a language of government until the mid-sixth century (**colour plate 1**).

However, it would be misleading to use the terms 'Byzantine Empire' and 'Eastern Roman Empire' as synonyms from the 330s onward. Although Diocletian had governmental divisions in the Roman Empire, his successors did not always adhere to these and under Constantine and his sons the Empire was reunited. The final division between the Eastern and Western Empires in terms of government did not come until the death of Theodosius I in 395. Moreover, despite the intense programme of church building in Constantinople, Rome and elsewhere, and the role of Constantine at the Council of Nicaea during the second quarter of the fourth century, the Christian Church was not yet integrated into the life of the state in the way that it later became. For example, it was not until 383 that the Altar of Victory was removed from the Senate in Rome.[9]

By the beginning of the fifth century, then, the Roman Empire had been divided for the final time. The Empire had adopted not simply a new religion, but a new set of principles, codes and standards of practice that would change its direction for the rest of its history. The most important characteristics of the 'Byzantine' Empire had been set in place.

The Western Roman Empire also remained in existence at the beginning of the fifth century, and it, too, became officially Christian. For people living at the turn of the fifth century it would not necessarily have been apparent that a different political and cultural unit was emerging in the East. Even so, change occurred very rapidly, given that Western Europe had been part of the Roman Empire for centuries before the fifth century. In 406 the Rhine froze, allowing perhaps thousands of Germanic migrants to enter the Empire, and eventually settle throughout the Continent. In 410 the city of Rome was sacked, after several attempts, by the Goths, led by Alaric and, in the same year, the provinces of Britain were ordered to carry out their own defence. By the 440s,

Gaul was also operating as a separate political entity from the Empire, followed shortly afterwards by Spain. Yet, during the mid-fifth century there was regular communication between the Eastern government and what remained of its Western counterpart. Moreover, there remained a 'Roman' Emperor in the West who was acknowledged by Constantinople, a situation that persisted until 476 when Romulus (the infant son of the Emperor Julius Nepos, who had been deposed the previous year) was removed from office by the Germanic general, Odovacer.[10]

While the Western Roman Empire was still in existence, however enfeebled, it is legitimate to describe it as part of a larger entity, the 'Late Roman Empire'. This was an entity that included, of course, its Eastern counterpart, the Eastern Roman Empire. During the fifth century, the East began to develop new characteristics, ones that, with the benefit of hindsight, we might call 'Byzantine'. The Byzantine Empire originated in the fifth century, therefore, but exactly when in that century remains uncertain.

The geographical context

The changes that took place at the end of Roman rule in the West also need to be understood in a geographical perspective, since physical geography constrained and facilitated the shape of the new pattern of relationships and structures that emerged. In about 350 the Roman world was a single, unified state, with one Empire-wide network of land, river and sea communications. By about 450 the political fragmentation of the former Roman world, first through the division between the Eastern and Western Empires after the death of Theodosius I, and then the emergence of a series of seemingly independent kingdoms across the former Roman West, had disconnected this communications system throughout most of that area. Thus, travel – especially by land – was impeded by a series of boundaries and risks that had not existed during the Late Roman Empire.

The most important physical feature of this region was (and remains) the Mediterranean Sea, connecting the main coastal or near-coastal cities of the Early Byzantine Empire – Constantinople, Ephesus, Sardis, Pergamon, Antioch, Alexandria, Carthage, Thessaloniki and Athens – with Italy, southern Gaul and the eastern and southern seaboard of Spain. Lining the Mediterranean and its subsidiary seas, such as the Sea of Marmara, the Aegean and the Adriatic, were numerous ports where large ships could safely shelter, off-load and load up, or areas from which naval attacks could be launched, as at Sicily in 536 when the Byzantine general Belisarius made his attack on Rome (**1**).[11]

Always important during the Roman period, the Mediterranean arguably became more significant after the political fragmentation of the fifth century. Sea routes came to represent the fastest form of long-distance transport, especially when some military roads were abandoned and others became too dangerous to traverse regularly. The situation was compounded by international political developments in the sixth and seventh century. Safe passage through the Balkans could not be guaranteed at any point during Late Antiquity, while security in the mountain ranges north of the Italian peninsula depended upon who controlled the area at any given time. The Alpine passes that provided important thoroughfares for monks such as Columbanus in the seventh century, and boosted the fortunes of monasteries at St Gallen and Geneva, were not necessarily as secure in the fifth and sixth centuries. Conversely, by the mid-seventh century, and the end of the period under investigation here, the rise of the Arabs as a political force had begun to close off the Holy Land and Egypt to Western and Byzantine travellers alike.[12]

Even within the former Roman West, long-distance travel was often difficult. Stories abound of travellers in Gaul who experienced attempts to delay them on either leg of their journeys to and from the East, sometimes on suspicion of being associated with a rival king, at other times simply for theft of their belongings. Wholly overland long-distance journeys remained risky and fraught with danger, especially in the face of the decline of both Late Roman customs of hospitality relating to aristocratic residences and the *cursus publicus*, a system that provided regular stations for refreshment and lodgings. Yet, this is not to imply that the Mediterranean, by contrast, could be traversed at whim, although it was the principal means of long-distance travel. Its treacherous tides and winds meant that from November to the end of March very few ships took the risk of sailing any significant distance. Indeed, the Theodosian Code (380) stipulated that sea travel should only take place between mid-April and mid-November. Even when shipbuilding technologies permitted the construction of stronger and more sea-worthy vessels, the midsummer months of June and July remained the peak time for sea travel and, despite the difficulties and expense involved, many people still preferred to travel overland.[13]

As sea travel became more important, so too did major rivers running from inland areas down to the coast, the Mediterranean especially, but also the Atlantic. Such routes became critical means of overseas and long-distance communication, although safe passage through a river system still required good relations with all parties who controlled its various tributaries, and river and road systems were often closely linked. So, although located in central Spain, the important late antique city of Mérida could be accessed by the Guadiana River, for example, while other central Spanish towns were also suitably provisioned by rivers running to the interior. Similarly, it was still possible in the sixth and seventh centuries to travel by sea and river from the Eastern Mediterranean to Lyon in the heart of southern Gaul, sailing up the Rhône, potentially with bulk cargoes, after stopping at Marseille or Fos-sur-Mer, before travelling west to the Loire or east to the Rhine. Notwithstanding the changing political relationship between those groups that controlled the Po Valley in northern Italy,

1 *Map of Europe showing selected places mentioned in the text*

vital for passage across the Alps to the Rhine, the Rhineland itself could be reached quite easily by travellers coming from the Byzantine Empire. The northern city of Cologne and the towns in its vicinity were a key part of the Frankish kingdom in the seventh century, thus increasing the relevance of the Rhine for regional and long-distance transportation. In this way, the arrival of the Lombards in northern Italy in 568 had implications that far outreached politics in that region, even if it was the home of the Byzantine administration at Ravenna. Relations between the Lombards and their allies also determined the extent and range of long-distance contacts between the Rhineland area and the Eastern Mediterranean and, potentially, with Britain as well.[14]

Conversely, areas away from the coast and major rivers (those suitable for sea-going ships) were far less likely to come into contact with people from distant parts of what had been the unified Roman Empire. This suggests that one should focus on coastal and riverine zones in order to gauge the extent and nature of links between the Eastern Mediterranean and the former Roman West, and that relative linear distances are not necessarily good indicators of the closeness of relations between East and West.

The role of islands is obviously important here, both because they are so easily accessible by sea and because they have frequently served as staging posts where sea-going ships might shelter or take on water and provisions. Consequently the archaeology of islands, whether off-shore islands, such as Lérins or Port-Cros (southern France) and Bréhat (Brittany), or larger island groups, such as the Scillies or Channel Islands, may deserve special attention in exploring East-West contacts during Late Antiquity. It also highlights the importance of the British Isles in early post-Roman networks of contact. This might be taken to suggest that the decline of overland transport and the cessation of Roman imperial boundaries could have benefited the west and north of Britain and the south and east of Ireland by eliminating differences in access between these and many Continental destinations.

Further inland, however, beneath the mountains and throughout the whole area, was a densely settled agricultural landscape that had been thickly studded with farms since at least the Iron Age. Whilst the Roman littoral of the Mediterranean may have been a network of towns, even in the fourth century much of the north and west of Britain, Spain and Gaul was predominantly rural, with few large urban settlements. There were some exceptions, even in Britain. The *Life* of St Germanus of Auxerre implies that *Verulamium* (modern St Albans) was still an important place when the saint visited the former Roman town in 429. Moreover, in those areas that had been heavily urbanised in the fourth century, notably southern Gaul and the Rhine valley, urban life survived in some form throughout the fifth, sixth and perhaps even seventh centuries, as at Marseille, Lyon, Trier and Cologne. Italy seems to have fared better than most of the former Roman West and several towns survived, albeit in reduced form. Across Gaul, Spain and Italy (albeit to varying degrees) there is evidence for the survival of Roman-style villas to the end of the fifth century and sometimes beyond.[15]

In such environments, classical education and literacy in Latin often also persisted, as did other aspects of Late Roman culture, such as the burial of the dead in stone sarcophagi and the erection of sub-Roman memorial stones (with epitaphs in Latin). Some belt buckles and ceramics continued to be produced in Roman forms, as in the Rhine valley, where Mayen ware was produced from the Roman period until long into the post-Roman period. The glass industry also remained in operation in the Rhine valley in the first part of the fifth century and a sub-Roman form of coinage was maintained in some places. Partly as a result of this continuity, some of the most helpful textual sources for the fifth- and sixth-century West were written by the descendants of upper class Roman provincials still living in what had been Roman-period towns or villas, such as Sidonius Apollinaris, Cassiodorus and Gregory of Tours.

By the sixth century, these patterns had been developed in a more explicitly Christian context, and it is no coincidence, for example, that these three 'sub-Roman' aristocrats played important roles in the life of the local Church. As the landscape became overlaid with a series of rural Christian churches and monasteries some 'new' towns, as at Tours or at Xanten, sprang up in the immediate proximity of what were, at the beginning of the fifth century, major Roman towns. At such sites the focus of settlement often shifted beyond the Roman walls into what had been extra-mural cemetery areas. This was where the graves, and later churches, of saints and martyrs were located, providing a focus for first veneration and then settlement. Alongside this 'Christianization' of town and countryside, rural temples and other pagan religious foci rapidly declined, and many villas were converted into monasteries. Likewise, we see the desertion of Roman military sites, although some former Roman forts were used for aristocratic and religious settlements, sometimes with new churches being founded within their Roman walls. In Italy, post-Roman hill-forts were constructed and some continued to function into the seventh century.[16]

Routes from Constantinople to the West

From a Constantinopolitan perspective, the first task in making a journey to the West was to decide which route to take out of Constantinople. The main routes to the West from the Byzantine capital city passed either through the Balkans or along the Danube, or both. Precarious throughout the fifth- to seventh-century period due to the incursions of Huns, Avars, Goths, Lombards and others into the region, these routes functioned with varying and intermittent degrees of safety during Late Antiquity. The most northern of these passageways linked the imperial capital in the East to northern Italy through the Danube valley, either by the road from Ptuji (Poetovio) to Constantinople – what Dimitri Obolensky termed the 'Belgrade to Constantinople highway' – or by the river itself. Consequently, the disruption of the Danube basin and its tributaries as a means of transportation was undoubtedly one of the most significant barriers to late antique East-West communication.[17]

Nevertheless, the Danubian route was not the only means of getting from East to West across the Balkans. The Via Egnatia is perhaps the best-known of the two main alternative routes, and probably functioned until the Bulgar migrations into the eastern Balkans made it too difficult to negotiate with any safety. This military road is often seen as the main highway linking Constantinople and the great city of Thessaloniki, in many ways the political and military key to what would today be termed northern Greece. From Thessaloniki it proceeded through the southern Balkans via Ohrid to Durazzo (Dyrrachium), from where it was a short sea voyage to Bari on the east coast of Italy. The third principal route to the West was predominantly undertaken by sea. Travellers taking this sailed from Constantinople to the Gulf of Corinth, where ships were dragged over the narrow strip of land separating the Peloponnese from the mainland, and then onwards to southern Italy. Thus, at least in principle, these routes offered travellers from the capital an option to take each of the main forms of long-distance transport known in Late Antiquity: horse-driven vehicle along a well-made road, river boat or sea-going vessel (**2**).[18]

The question of 'Romanization'

This is the landscape against which the cultural developments and long-distance linkages discussed in this book need to be understood. However, there remains the question of 'Romanization' and the part it played in facilitating East-West relations during the fifth to seventh centuries. As we have seen, many parts of the West retained aspects of 'Romanization' during Late Antiquity, particularly in the earlier part of the period. The term 'Romanization' has been maligned, rightly in some cases, as a descriptive tool for analysing the culture of the fifth- and sixth-century West, often because it is used to give the impression that there was either a uniform Roman provincial culture or an unbroken line of cultural continuity from the Roman Empire, with very little or even no contribution from other groups.[19]

The intention here is to imply neither an uninterrupted 'romanization' deriving from the Late Roman Empire nor a total lack of indigenous cultural innovation. The subject matter of this book is those aspects of fifth- to seventh-century cultural life that might be said to derive from the Eastern Roman Empire specifically, notwithstanding their adaptation, refinement and application in what was often a radically different cultural context. Of course, new cultural contexts might also render redundant the meanings inherent in the Eastern prototypes: that is to say, such prototypes might be interpreted in the West in a completely different way. In other words, there was no transmission of a composite Eastern Roman culture to the West, assuming that one even existed in the East. Instead, there was a transmission of different aspects of the culture of the Byzantine Empire that, together, helped to shape the cultural identity of Western Europe during Late Antiquity. This is not to say that Eastern cultural attributes were so changed in their Western interpretation that their source had become irrelevant. On the contrary, as we shall see, many of

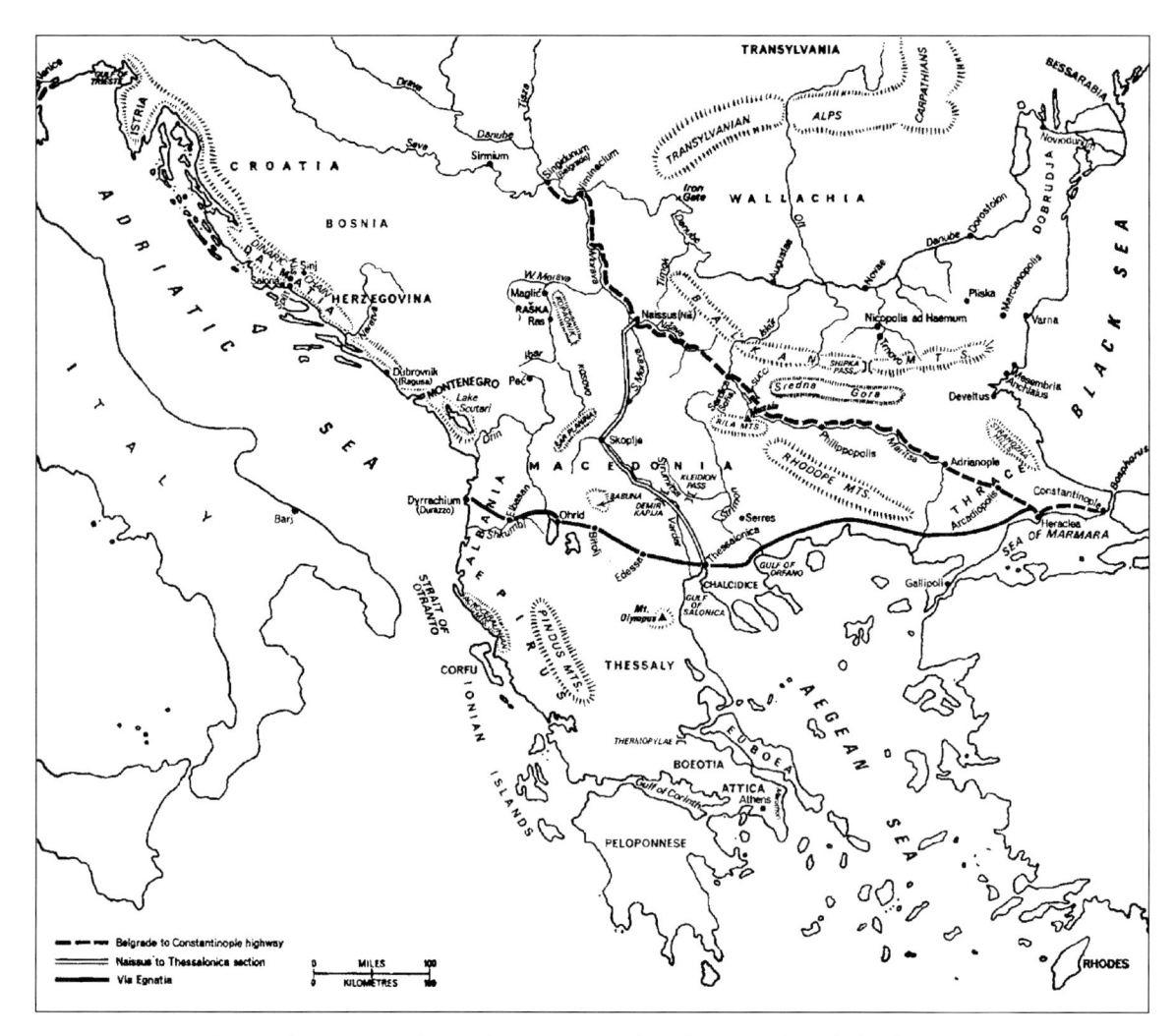

2 Map showing principal routes from Constantinople to the West. After Obolensky (1971)

these can be interpreted as an expression of a common identity with the East, or as the material manifestation of a direct link with the Byzantine world.

In many other ways, of course, the Byzantine Empire retained a cultural legacy from the Late Roman Empire, and so many aspects of its social, political and economic life were derived directly from its predecessor. The Byzantines, after all, thought of themselves as *romaoi*: in other words, 'Romans', and not 'Byzantines' or 'Greeks'. Late Roman culture was expressed, for example, in representations of Byzantine emperors on coinage and official portraiture. These retained a distinctly 'Roman' and secular style until the seventh century, when more explicitly religious contexts were depicted. Thereafter, profound changes occurred, but these are outside our remit here.

The geographical and chronological scope of this book

The scope of this book encompasses the whole of what had been the Roman West north of the Mediterranean. However, a combination of the availability of evidence and shifting patterns of formal Byzantine control prevent a wholly uniform coverage of the region, and so various emphases will become evident. Italy's close relationship with the Byzantine Empire, to the extent that there was an imperial presence there throughout the period, means that evidence for contacts between 'non-Byzantine' Italy and the Eastern Mediterranean are not as surprising as, say, evidence for similar contacts between northern Gaul and the Byzantine East. The methodological problems involved with the examination of links between Italy and the Byzantine Empire are also, for this reason, more prohibitive. Similar issues are faced in the interpretation of the evidence from Spain, which was also subject to the Justinianic Reconquest in the mid-sixth century. Here, however, the Byzantine presence was less long-lived and perhaps less intrusive in terms of material culture. It was long claimed that the Reconquest was largely a military occupation, although advances in Spanish archaeology have rendered this less certain. The evidence for Byzantine contacts with 'non-Byzantine' Spain is sometimes rather weaker than for other areas of the late antique West, but this might be a function of our sources, in particular the distribution and character of archaeological research, rather than late antique realities. For these reasons, therefore, Italy and Spain are given less emphasis in this book than other areas of the West.

The opposite is true of Britain, where any trace of Byzantine contact is surprising, given its distance from the Mediterranean and lack of Roman-period relations with the Eastern Roman world. The principal focus of this book is Britain and, as such, the evidence for Byzantine contacts with Italy and with the Iberian peninsula is less important than the evidence for links with Gaul, which for the latter part of our period might more accurately be termed 'Frankia' (both terms are employed here). A discussion of Byzantine contacts with Britain might imply a focus on Gaul, which was often – but not always – the facilitator of late antique British communications with the Eastern Mediterranean. The nature of contacts between Gaul and the Byzantine Empire is, therefore, of considerable importance to a study of the contacts between Britain and the East, and of great interest in themselves. It is in Gaul that we have the richest written evidence for Byzantine-Western contacts. It might be thought that Ireland would be included in a study of this nature, for Byzantine objects (especially pottery) have been found on several Irish sites. The island of Ireland and, by the same reasoning, the Isle of Man, are excluded simply on the basis of their location outside the former Roman West. Also on this basis, the whole of Scotland and those parts of England north of Hadrian's Wall are not considered here.

There are several reasons for choosing the period *c*.400–*c*.650 as the chronological remit for this book. At the beginning of the fifth century, as we have seen, the Roman Empire had been divided for only five years, and yet almost immediately witnessed changes that brought about the collapse of the Western Roman Empire as a unitary polity, beginning with the crossing of the Rhine in 406. In 409 Britain may have experienced a 'revolution', the culmination to a series of uprisings by usurpers and various rebels, and the *civitates* of Britain were, the following year, told to look to their own defences in the so-called 'Rescript of Honorius'. As noted above, the fifth century as a whole marked the transition from Roman to barbarian rule in Gaul, Italy and Spain, symbolised most dramatically in the Goths' sack of Rome in 410. This was accompanied by the rapid spread of Christianity in the countryside, for although imperial financial support for the public cults of Rome had been permanently halted some seventeen years before the start of our period, Christianity did not become the majority religion immediately. It only took firm hold outside the towns in the first part of the fifth century, facilitated enormously in Gaul by the evangelism of St Martin of Tours. A similar pattern for the spread of rural Christianity is documented elsewhere in the West, even in Britain, where the first evidence that the majority of the population was Christian comes from the fifth century, not before.[20]

At the other end of the period, the mid-seventh century was equally a time of transition, again in political, military, social and economic terms. Several scholars have pointed out that new trade patterns only become clearly visible in the second half of the seventh century, as the regeneration of a long-distance maritime trading network occurred. The mid-seventh century also saw the collapse of Byzantium as the principal political and military force in the Eastern Mediterranean, a change that particularly affected those Western kingdoms with Mediterranean coastlines, to a large extent cutting Spain and southern Gaul (Frankia) off from North Africa, and from a shared religion and culture. Religious change in the form of the rise of Islam in the East was mirrored in the West by the widespread conversion of the Anglo-Saxons to Christianity. Thereafter, the cultural world of the Anglo-Saxon kingdoms also underwent rapid change, focusing increasingly on ecclesiastical developments in Italy and on the Continent more generally. This coincided with a reversal of the relative positions of the British and Anglo-Saxons, for by *c*.650 the Anglo-Saxons had become the dominant political and military force in what had been Roman Britain, while the territories controlled by the indigenous Britons were confined to the western fringes of the island.

This book will explore a new interpretation of relations between the Byzantine Empire and the West in the period *c*.400–*c*.600, with some recourse to the following century. As we shall see, these might be used to support a very different understanding of Byzantine-Western contacts in this period than that usually proposed.

2

CONSTRUCTING THE OIKOUMENÊ
EAST-WEST DIPLOMACY IN LATE ANTIQUITY

Introduction

Late Roman intellectuals sometimes described the *Orbis Romanus* ('Roman world') as the *oikoumenê*, a term derived from the root word *oikos*, meaning 'house' or 'home'. To speak of the *oikoumenê* in Late Antiquity was to allude to the civilised world (literally, it means 'the inhabited') and, after the establishment of Christianity as the Roman state religion in the fourth century, the term acquired additional associations with the 'Christian world'. The *oikoumenê* was not conceived of as extending across the entire 'inhabited world', as a literal translation of the term might suggest, but contained self-defining limits. Byzantine knowledge of global geography included large parts of Asia, and yet it seems that the imperial government made no attempt to incorporate lands such as India and China into its political or religious orbit, according to texts such as the sixth-century *Christian Topography of Cosmas Indicopleustes*, although economic transactions took place between them. It was the 'Christian world' and the 'Roman world', often regarded as equivalent to each other, that seem to have comprised the *oikoumenê*, and the view that this was the case permitted the claim that the ruler of the 'Roman world' was also the ruler (in temporal terms) of the 'Christian world'. Thus, the term had political content: it suggested an area over which the rule of the Roman Empire, and its successor in the East, the Byzantine Empire, held sway.[1]

Unfortunately, *oikoumenê* evades a more precise definition, not least because the Byzantines themselves were reluctant to define the term more specifically. This may have been a deliberate measure on the part of the imperial government, which was otherwise often very precise in its use of terminology. Its love of ambiguity in foreign relations was well-known in the Late Antique and medieval periods, and was usually characterised in negative terms by non-Byzantines. To Cassiodorus, the secretary of state in early Ostrogothic Italy, such practices were 'cunning' and not to be encouraged. However, for the Byzantines themselves ambiguity allowed them changes in the minutiae of foreign policy while the broad sweep of policy objectives was kept relatively constant.[2]

Despite this, the concept of the *oikoumenê* provides a useful starting point for an analysis of Byzantine-Western European relations during Late Antiquity. In a fifth- to seventh-century world where, especially outside the Eastern Mediterranean, political authority was often tenuous, areas of the former Roman Empire could perhaps be seen as being permanently 'Roman'. Justinian I alluded to this theme when he claimed in the prelude to his *Digest* that the Empire had an integrity amounting to more than its territorial aspect, being rooted in a unified Christian society. It is possible, on this basis, to put forward a hypothesis that the *oikoumenê* was more than simply a political ideal. It was also a geopolitical construct with three defining characteristics: cultural (particularly religious) commonalities, a perception of a shared 'Roman' past and an implicit acknowledgement that the Byzantine Emperor was the supreme political authority. Then, as now, perceptions of the past, as well as the political realities of the present, were often used as indicators of legitimacy. In this case, enduring memories of the *Pax Romana* structured relations between East and West during Late Antiquity, with the potential to create a distinctive 'international order' that transcended explicit political authority.[3]

It should not be thought that this 'international order' was comprised simply of a continued sense of *romanitas* amongst sub-Roman populations, and the continued adherence in some quarters to a 'Roman' way of life. While drawing on residual *romanitas*, particularly the belief that the Empire was somehow more than the sum of its constituent parts, the shared material culture that emerged was distinct from 'Late Roman' culture, often having its origin in the fifth- to seventh-century Eastern Mediterranean world. Whether the distinctions between 'Late Roman' and 'Byzantine' culture were apparent to contemporaries is another question. After all, as far as they were concerned, the Roman Empire had not 'died'. It still existed in the East and so there was no reason to call anything deriving from that area by any other name. Thus, it is probable that what we might call 'Byzantine' objects were accorded a 'Roman' identity by some Westerners, even in the seventh century. It should be recognised, therefore, that the distinction between 'Late Roman' and 'Byzantine' is principally an analytical one.[4]

It may also be anachronistic to imagine that the Western Roman Empire looked 'dead' to all Westerners, for substantial sub-Roman populations remained, often surviving into the sixth century. From the 530s onwards, Rome was once again an imperial city and remained so throughout the period, despite the growing importance of the Papacy. At other towns across the West, Roman-period structures survived in substantial form, as did aspects of Roman administration. Even the Western use of Latin may have been seen as an expression of shared identity with the East, for Latin remained a language of government in the Byzantine Empire until the mid-sixth century. Some Western contacts with the Byzantine Empire may have taken place in a cultural context, therefore, where the Roman Empire was perceived to have an enduring reality in both East and West, albeit now with the focus of authority in Constantinople (**3 & 4**).

Of course, if we applied this approach to the discussion here, it may seem that a pan-Mediterranean identity, based on *romanitas*, was extremely widespread. We must bear in mind, then, that this may have been the perception of contemporaries. However, to adopt such an approach would render an investigation of Byzantine-Western relations very difficult. Instead, this study shall attempt to trace Western relationships with the East through the importation and use of objects that *we* would term 'Byzantine', bearing in mind that contemporaries may have seen them differently. In order to avoid confusion, and to draw attention to specifically fifth- to seventh-century linkages between Byzantium and the West, we shall not focus on those aspects of late antique culture that were 'so ubiquitous in the late Roman world that to imagine any close connections with the East may be quite misleading'. Rather, aspects of culture deriving from the fifth to seventh centuries shall form the principal components of the investigation.[5]

An example may illustrate this juxtaposition. Sidonius Apollinaris, a fifth-century writer and administrator living most of his life in post-Roman Gaul, wrote in Latin in the style of a Roman aristocrat, whilst living in a way that might have been admired by his ancestors a century earlier. Many of his extant works, including the letter that he wrote to his friend 'Count' Arbogast in *c*.477, point to a continuing identification with the customs of the Late Roman Empire in the face of sometimes dramatic social change:

> You have drunk at the well-spring of Roman eloquence, and no draughts from the Moselle can take away the taste of the Tiber from your mouth . . . you permit no barbarism to pass your lips; in eloquence and valour you equal those ancient generals whose hands could wield the stylus no less skilfully than the sword . . . while you live and preserve your eloquence, the Latin tongue stands unshaken. As I return your greeting, my heart is glad within me that our vanishing culture has left such traces with you; continue your assiduous studies, and you will feel more surely every day that the man of education is as much above the boor as the boor in his turn is above the beast.[6]

As Peter Heather has pointed out, Sidonius used imagery alluding to the civilising power of Rome, and his habit was to make barbarian rule palatable by portraying it in terms of its 'Roman-ness'. The perceived accommodation in his mind was between barbarian and (Western) Roman. There is nothing here to suggest any explicit identity with the Empire now based in the Eastern Mediterranean.[7]

In other cases, however, aspects of 'Roman' and 'Byzantine' cultures converged, and it is here that difficulties in interpretation arise. For example, public displays of respect for the Emperor had been a common feature of political life throughout the Roman Empire, and we might reasonably expect

3 *Roman walls at Tongeren, Belgium.* Photograph by Anthea Harris

The physical remains of the Roman Empire would have dominated life in some areas of Western Europe during Late Antiquity.

4 *Roman baths at Paris.* Photograph by Anthea Harris

some aspects of this phenomenon to have continued into the post-Roman West. Yet, subtle differences in the way in which respect was expressed in a given situation might permit us to interpret it either as an expression of shared identity with the East or as a wholly Western development. To give a hypothetical example, on the one hand, indigenous authority might be respected (the 'barbarian' King being treated *as if* an Emperor); on the other hand, the Byzantine (or 'Roman') Emperor might be honoured over and above the Western rulers. The latter might, in this case, be seen as evidence of a shared identification with the Roman Emperor in Constantinople, while the former might suggest the transference of an idea from the Roman past into a new political context. Of course, even this may be too simplistic, for, as we shall see, the concept that Western kings ruled with authority delegated to them by the Byzantine Emperor may have had a real political expression in Late Antiquity.

Formal political linkages between the Byzantine Empire and Western polities, therefore, provide a useful starting point for investigating Byzantine relations with the West. The precise nature and formality of such exchanges, as well as the fact that they were often (but by no means always) recorded by at least one of the parties involved, means that they are important tools for understanding Byzantine-Western contacts in this period.[8]

The Byzantine government developed an, albeit irregular, network of full-time diplomatic contacts between itself and its neighbours. This was comprised of envoys, ambassadors and possibly even intelligence gatherers. As late as 669, the Franks were suspicious enough of the papal envoys, Theodore and Hadrian, to detain them on their way north through Frankia to Kent. Hadrian, who came from Byzantine Egypt, was suspected of being an imperial spy. While there is no evidence to corroborate this, Hadrian and Theodore's detention on these charges might imply, as Brian Brennan has suggested, that imperial spies had previously operated in the West.[9]

Although texts do not directly state that permanent diplomatic embassies from the Byzantine Empire were established in the West, the network of long-distance communication between political representatives was not necessarily as casual as might be imagined. There was a large imperial bureaucracy, much of it overseen by the *magister officiorum*, whose responsibility it was to maintain the smooth running of the system. There were also specific circumstances in which diplomatic missions were organised. Evangelos Chrysos has argued, for instance, that the Byzantine court notified the rulers of the sixth- and seventh-century Western kingdoms every time a new Emperor succeeded to the throne, just as it did with the Persian rulers. Embassies were also probably sent to the West every time a new Western ruler succeeded or was appointed. The purpose of such a high-level mission was, in these circumstances, merely to confirm ongoing relations between the Empire and the other kingdom, despite changes in government composition. As Paul Barnwell has pointed out, by the seventh century developments in the concept of Western kingship and, in particular, its theocratic tendencies, tend to support the idea that direct communications involving statements of political ideology took place between Eastern and Western rulers. Changes such as royal marriages, the birth of children to a reigning Emperor, or victories over particular enemies, could also be deemed to be of political significance and were accordingly marked by the sending of embassies.[10]

On occasion, the Byzantine government is attested as having intervened in the civil conflicts of other polities, or disputes between rival dynasties, an action that we would not expect if principles of state sovereignty had applied. We hear, for example, of the Frankish king, Chilperic I, sending envoys to the East. Presumably, they were charged with securing Byzantine support of some undetermined nature in the insecure world of late sixth-century Merovingian (Frankish) politics, where the rulers of Burgundy, Provence and the northern Frankish kingdoms vied for territory and authority. The diplomatic expedition took Chilperic's envoys three years, and they were shipwrecked and robbed on their arrival back in Frankia, but nevertheless they managed to deliver large amounts of treasure sent to Chilperic by the Byzantine Emperor. Gregory of Tours, who describes the event, singles out for special attention a quantity of gold medallions, each weighing a pound, and with the image of the Emperor Tiberius Constantine and the inscription 'TIBERII CONSTANTINI PERPETVI AVGVSTI' on the obverse, with the inscription 'GLORIA ROMANORVM' and the image of a chariot and charioteer on the reverse. Chilperic, and any literate person who saw the coin, would have been left in no doubt as to who occupied the imperial throne, and of that throne's continuing authority. Although it is unclear what Chilperic intended to do with the gold pieces, his possession of them may have enhanced his standing in Frankish politics, and possibly served as tangible evidence of his contact with the imperial court, as well as a reminder that superior 'Roman' authority was still very much alive and operating from its Eastern base.[11]

Diplomatic envoys were used in several other types of negotiations, such as the negotiation of trade agreements and of peace treaties. If Chrysos is correct in suggesting that the extant records of Byzantine embassies to the West and North Africa are vastly incomplete, as seems likely, the written record represents only the 'tip of the iceberg' of Byzantium's diplomatic activity. Most of this could have been carried out unobtrusively and may have taken place so regularly as a matter of routine that officials may not have considered it worth recording and, in any case, writers such as Sidonius or Gregory may not have had access to the relevant details.[12]

The transfer of authority in the West

The deposition of the last Western Roman Emperor, Romulus Augustulus, in AD 476 has often been seen to mark the end of the Roman Empire in the West.

This said, although most scholars now prefer to envisage a process of political and constitutional change taking place throughout the fifth century, rather than a cataclysmic collapse of political and economic institutions. In terms of events and contemporary experience, the trauma of the sack of Rome at the hands of the Gothic chieftain, Alaric, and his army, in August 410 was not easily forgotten. For Easterners of the period, usually hearing of events in the West second-hand and perhaps long after they took place, it was difficult to assess the impact of the changes. Marcellinus *comes*, for instance, writing some one hundred years after the event, and from the Eastern Mediterranean, saw the murder of Aetius in 454 as marking the end of Roman authority in the West. Aetius was the Western *magister militum*, and thus the military commander of Gaul and Italy. With the help of his ally, Theodoric II, who controlled a Visigothic enclave around Toulouse, Aetius had recently defeated Attila the Hun in the Danube area, but in 454 he was murdered in Rome. With his death, in Marcellinus's view, the way was open for the demolition of Roman authority.[13]

It was over twenty years, however, before the Emperor Julius Nepos was finally deposed from power and exiled to a palace on the Dalmatian coast. Nepos's infant son, Romulus, was proclaimed as the new Emperor, but his youth meant that he was unacceptable to the military. A power vacuum emerged in the Italian territories, but was filled the following year when a soldier of Germanic origin, Odovacer, came to power in a military coup. However, rather than proclaiming himself Emperor, as he might have done had he followed military and political tradition, Odovacer continued to acknowledge the theoretical position of Romulus whilst ruling in Rome in his stead. This is reflected in the numismatic evidence, as John Moorhead has suggested: 'the early coinage of Odovacer has been interpreted as allowing an uneasy acceptance of the claims of Nepos, who only died in 480.' This marked a significant change in Italian and other Western politics. For the first time, the *position* of Western Emperor, as opposed to the holder of that office, was discredited and ignored, as if military and political Western élites no longer had aspirations to holding it.[14]

It was not that the *idea* of imperial authority was under threat. The new ruler of the Italian territories, Odovacer, sent embassies to the Eastern Roman Emperor, Zeno, requesting his authority to rule in the West without a Western Emperor, to which Zeno replied that he should welcome the return of Nepos. Odovacer did not reject the sentiment behind Zeno's suggestion, although Nepos was not restored. Instead, he maintained Roman methods of government, ensuring that a Western consul was nominated and appointed each year between 480 and 490, an act that may represent an attempt to conciliate sectors of the Roman population. Given that the Eastern government actually accepted Odovacer's nominations for consul without equivocation, this may also represent Constantinople's (partial) acceptance of the political situation in Italy. Although, from his sixth-century Byzantine perspective, Marcellinus may have thought that Roman authority was no more, Odovacer's use of the existing political resources in Italy, and his respect for imperial authority based in Constantinople, implies a less traumatic interpretation of fifth-century events than traditionally depicted. Odovacer may even have been related to the imperial family in Constantinople (as the brother of the *magister militum*, Armatus), although this is unclear. If so, this would have made him the nephew of Basiliscus, who usurped the imperial throne in 475-6 and, therefore, a not wholly inappropriate candidate for ruler in Italy.[15]

If this last is true, it is all the more curious that Odovacer did not attempt to take the Western Roman throne for himself. Given the actual (and perceived) greater wealth and stability of the East in the fifth century, it may be that élites living in Italy in the last quarter of that century saw no necessity for a Western Emperor. Instead, they may have believed that the existence of an Eastern Emperor was quite sufficient for them! Perhaps, too, they believed that the reunification of the Roman Empire was the solution to its long decline. From a fifth-century perspective, the separation of the Empire into two political units in the reign of Theodosius may have been seen as the start of several generations of troubles. Might this not be the reason for the adulation of Constantine I in the fifth century, as much as for his conversion of the Empire to Christianity?

While Odovacer's rule proceeded with mixed successes, a child named Theodoric was being held hostage at the imperial court in Constantinople. The son of an Ostrogothic chieftain, Theodemer, he was to have an immense impact on Italian politics and Western-Byzantine relations. The Ostrogoths had allied themselves with the Huns in the early 450s, but after the death of Attila in 453 had separated from them and come to an arrangement with the imperial authorities that enabled them to settle peacefully on the periphery of imperial territory in Pannonia. The young son of the Ostrogothic chief was taken to Constantinople as security, where he was educated and given access to the imperial court for the next decade.[16]

At the age of 17 or 18 Theodoric was sent back to his parents in Pannonia with gifts from the Emperor Leo. Shortly afterwards, some of the Ostrogoths moved west into Gaul, where they joined forces with the Visigoths. The rest (including Theodoric and his family) moved east, initially to Thessaloniki and the surrounding area. During these years, Theodoric assumed the Ostrogothic leadership, and earned himself the approval of the Emperor Zeno by supporting him against the usurper, Basiliscus, while at the same time defeating his rival in the Ostrogothic leadership, Theodoric Strabo. For his services to the Emperor, Theodoric was made *patrician* and adopted as Zeno's 'son-at-arms'.

However, in 478 Theodoric reversed his loyalties. He joined forces with his former rival in the Ostrogothic leadership, and made demands on the Emperor Zeno for land and grain. Zeno seems to have interpreted this as a threat to the security of his government, and offered Theodoric large payments of money and a marriage to the daughter of a former Western Emperor on condition that he turn against his rival, Strabo. Although Theodoric declined the marriage, it is interesting that the offer was made at all. It would have placed Theodoric in a good position from which to acquire the Western throne; indeed, in later centuries several men would inherit the Byzantine Empire through marriage to a daughter of the Emperor. Zeno's readiness to make the offer suggests that he would have been happy for Theodoric to accede to the Western throne: presumably nothing had been seen in his long exile that made the Byzantines wary of him. In more general terms, it indicates that the Eastern Roman government was willing to continue to delegate imperial authority to the Goths up to the level of Western Emperor. That the offer was declined is also significant, and seems to confirm the suggestion that the Western throne was no longer of especial relevance for politically-aspirant Western élites.[17]

In 483, Theodoric reached a truce with Zeno, and agreed to divert his troops from the East by turning against his Ostrogothic rival once more. He murdered the son of Strabo and, around the same time, possibly immediately afterwards, he was given further gifts by the Byzantine government, granted the title of *magister militum* (roughly equivalent to senior general) and made consul for the year 484. However, such bounty did not buy Theodoric's loyalty. Two years later in 486 he attacked Thrace and marched (unsuccessfully) on Constantinople. Yet, it is not clear that Theodoric wanted specifically to acquire the imperial throne at any point in these proceedings. When he eventually turned his attentions to Italy and the West, the Ostrogothic leadership showed every sign of seeking to work within the pre-existing Roman framework of authority. By the end of 489 Theodoric controlled part of Italy, but he had made sure both to seek authority from Zeno and to issue 'his' coins in the name of the Eastern Emperor, first from the Milanese mint, and later from Rome.

Odovacer, on the other hand, made the curious unilateral move of declaring his son, Thela, to be the *caesar*, implying that he himself was the *augustus*, which as far as we know he was not. He then alienated himself further from the Byzantine government by minting coins that bore the representation of Rome and Ravenna, rather than the image of the Eastern Emperor. Although this drew upon 'Roman' symbols of power and authority, his actions earned him no support from the imperial government in Constantinople. Despite, or perhaps because of, Odovacer's possible links with the imperial family, Byzantine hopes and diplomatic efforts thenceforth focused on Theodoric as the new ruler in Italy.

By the summer of 493 Theodoric had defeated and disposed of Odovacer. Theodoric's rule was soon recognised by the Eastern court. It is not clear exactly what title he was known by in the East, but thereafter Theodoric styled himself 'king' and an equestrian statute of him was erected in central Constantinople. Such a move suggests that the Byzantines now accepted Theodoric as a legitimate candidate to rule in the West, but only under the authority of the Eastern Emperor. The imperial administration was not unrealistic in expecting Theodoric to act as a client ruler in a 'Byzantine' context. He had after all spent his youth as an exile at the imperial court in Constantinople, and was thoroughly *au fait* with Byzantine customs although, notably, he did not convert to Christianity, but remained an Arian. He probably visited Constantinople three other times, perhaps on one occasion in the company of his sister, but visited Rome only once, despite it being much nearer to his base in Ravenna. Roman-style games were encouraged in the circus and amphitheatre – for which Theodoric is said to have become known as 'Trajan' and 'Valentinian', after former imperial patrons of these sports. He may have sponsored the applied arts, including the commissioning of the production of the *Codex Argenteus* ('Gothic Bible') and, as is well-known, Byzantine prototypes were frequently employed in the construction of monumental architecture in Theodoric's Ravenna (**colour plate 2**).[18]

Perhaps more importantly, Theodoric's government continued to maintain the Roman method of administration. Members of Roman aristocratic families, rather than Goths, were appointed as government administrators. The civil service continued to operate on its previous 'Roman' lines, with senatorial families intrinsic to its day-to-day running, and the Gothic 'king' was careful not to interfere with Roman legal codes. By the reign of Justinian I, Eastern Mediterranean views of Theodoric emphasised these qualities above all else. The Byzantine historian, Procopius, wrote of his reign:

> We have preserved both the laws and the form of government as strictly as any who have ever been Roman Emperors, and there is absolutely no law, either written, or unwritten, introduced by Theodoric or by any of his successors on the throne of the Goths.

Theodoric's apparent absorption of Roman ideas of government and rule later caused Procopius to comment again: 'he invested himself with all the qualities which appropriately belong to one who is by birth an Emperor'. These were remarkable words indeed, especially given that as an Arian Theodoric was the antithesis (in religious terms) of what the Byzantine Emperor might have hoped for in the governance of the Christian Empire.[19]

From his own perspective, however, Theodoric was not simply a 'client' of the Emperor. The letters of Cassiodorus (his secretary of state) show a manipulation of the relationship between the imperial court and Theodoric's government, as well as the perceived position of the Ostrogothic territories within the Empire. The first of the published letters, a document addressed to the Emperor Anastasius I, is a clever piece of diplomacy, which makes a favourable comparison between the Eastern Empire and the kingdom of Theodoric: 'Our royalty is an imitation of yours, modelled on your good purpose, a copy of the only Empire'. The second published letter concerns the preparation of special purple dye from the shell of the *Murex trunculus* sea snail for the robes of Theodoric.

This shows, as Moorhead has suggested, how important it was for Theodoric to be seen as a wearer of the purple, a privilege associated with holders of the imperial office. The production of this dye may have been strictly controlled in the East. In the light of his earlier refusal to marry into the imperial family, this suggests either that Theodoric had changed his mind about the position of Western Emperor, or that he was anxious to be perceived as Emperor in Italy at least, without the incumbent duties this would entail elsewhere.[20]

As his reign continued, Theodoric became increasingly involved with Western political developments outside Italy. Despite various attempts to deter war amongst the various Western political élites, the Ostrogoths, along with the Franks, the Burgundians and the Visigoths, were drawn into a series of armed conflicts in southern Gaul and northern Spain at the beginning of the sixth century. Perhaps dismayed that the Ostrogoths appeared to be becoming too powerful in the West, and aiming to disrupt their necessary and fragile trading routes, the Emperor Anastasius sent a fleet of 100 Byzantine ships and 100 *dromones*, carrying 8,000 soldiers, to attack the Italian coast at Apulia in 507 or 508. Nevertheless, and without the expected help from their Vandal allies against the Byzantine fleet, the Ostrogothic army pressed north into Gaul. They relieved the Frankish and Burgundian sieges at Arles and Carcassonne, and re-established Gothic control in these territories, thereby making important strategic and territorial gains.

Whatever the reason for the naval expedition to Italy, the Byzantine government did not follow it up with military action, but diverted its energies into diplomacy with the West. While a neutral diplomatic relationship appears to have been achieved with the Ostrogoths, the evidence suggests that the Franks now became the main focus of Byzantine diplomacy. In many ways, this initiative appears to have been successful. The Frankish élite largely relished its relationship with the Eastern court although, of course, its response to Byzantine overtures was made partially in the context of their precarious situation vis-à-vis the Ostrogothic and Visigothic territories to the south. Sigismund of Burgundy (incidentally, Theoderic's son-in-law through Sigismund's marriage to his daughter) maintained a detailed correspondence with the Emperor in Constantinople and was later rewarded with the title of *patricius* by the Emperor and, possibly, also *magister militum per Gallias*.

Like the Ostrogothic rulers of Italy, the new Merovingian Frankish dynasty now sought to legitimise itself by reference to the Emperor in Constantinople. Childeric, for instance, is said in one text to have been sent to Gaul from Constantinople by the Eastern Emperor, bearing gifts, and with the Emperor's permission to rule there. Although the story is probably fictional, it confirms – at the very least – the perception in seventh-century Frankia that Constantinople had been a legitimising standard in late fifth- and sixth-century Frankish politics. Such an impulse was implied by the Byzantines themselves in the sixth century, when Procopius claimed that 'the Franks never considered that their possession of Gaul was secure except when the Emperor had put his seal of approval upon their title'. The need to have imperial consent, or at least to be seen to have imperial consent, is also reflected in Theodebert's (the great-grandson of Childeric) curious claim that he was the son of the Emperor Justinian. This is also unlikely to be true, and more likely to be a reference to a symbolic 'family of kings' with the Emperor at its head. Nevertheless, it emphasises that the Frankish establishment sought to legitimise itself and its position by reference to its relationship with the imperial throne in Constantinople. It is possible that Theodebert did have a relationship with the Byzantine Emperor, albeit not one of literal sonship, for he may, in fact, be the same ruler mentioned in Procopius's description of a Frankish King sending envoys to Constantinople, to persuade Justinian that he (the Frankish king) was the *de facto* ruler of *Brittia*, Britain.[21]

Childeric's son, Clovis, enjoyed a more securely attested relationship with the Byzantine court. In 507, at Vouillé, he defeated and killed the Visigothic ruler, Alaric II, largely driving the Visigoths out of Aquitaine and south beyond the Pyrenees. For this Clovis was richly rewarded by the imperial government. In an oft-quoted chapter of Gregory of Tours' so-called *Historia Francorum*, he is described as having been granted the consular codicils from the Emperor Anastasius I in a ceremony in the church of St Martin in Tours. It was an imperial title (albeit an honorary one) intended to convey great honour upon the holder and to proclaim that he enjoyed a close relationship with the imperial court. It is significant, too, that the title was conferred upon Clovis in a church, not only because the Western Church still recognised the authority of the Emperor at Constantinople at that date, but because this drew upon a wholly 'Byzantine' understanding of Roman authority, rather than a Late Roman one. Moreover, in the first decade of the sixth century the Church was a self-evidently more stable institution than Clovis' own kingdom.[22]

Clovis responded to his appointment by donning the costume which was the consul's right in Roman tradition – a purple tunic – parading through Tours on horseback, munificently scattering gold and silver coins to the assembled people as he made his way to the church. His respect for Roman tradition was further demonstrated by his observation of the 'Adventus', the imperial arrival ritual, and his subsequent reference to himself as *ex consule*. Although he had only been made a consul, Clovis' behaviour suggests that he saw the appointment as highly significant, and used it to show that he was the inheritor of a Roman imperial tradition. The purple robes, diadem and scattering of gold and silver coins suggest that he saw himself, as Gregory suggests, as *augustus* as well as consul. While this perception was wholly false, as anyone picking up and examining the image and inscription on one of his scattered coins would have realised, the episode yet again shows the Frankish élite attaching great importance to its relationship with the Eastern Emperor. By the end of his life, Clovis appears to have had 'most favoured ruler' status at Constantinople, for he was also the Western *magister militum*, a position for which his son had to petition the Byzantine Empire on his father's death.[23]

By giving these and other titles and ranks to Western élites the Byzantines drew upon and emphasised a shared 'Roman' identity. They encouraged its development for their own purposes, but were pragmatic enough to recognise at the same time the transfer of political power (but not ultimate authority) at an everyday level. The underlying implication is that the imperial government worked on the assumption that the Eastern Emperor exercised hegemony (potential or otherwise) over both East and West and, accordingly, chose aspects of the Roman past (and Byzantine present) with which it knew the Franks would identify.

In order for this relationship to operate to the advantage of the Byzantine government, it was necessary that the recipient of the title – in this case, Clovis – believed that he belonged to, or at least might belong to, a 'Roman' community, with the Byzantine Emperor at its head. Whether this idea was couched in terms of Late Roman titles or Byzantine pretensions of 'kinship' is not necessarily relevant. Such diplomatic initiatives should be seen as part of an ongoing relationship, where it was mutually accepted that the Frankish rulers regarded themselves as part of an undivided 'Roman' Empire with its capital at Constantinople. This was the context in which the Burgundian king, Sigismund, informed the Emperor that 'our homeland is [part of] your world and my royal administration does not reduce your sovereignty in your provinces'. The sentiment was still evident in the seventh century when the author of the *Chronicle of Fredegar* reported that the Emperor Heraclius, in a letter to the Frankish king, Dagobert, 'decreed that the same [that is, baptism of the Jews] be done through all the provinces of the Empire'. While not necessarily implying that Dagobert's kingdom was a 'province' of the Empire, this level of strategic coordination suggests, to say the least, that a very close political relationship between the Byzantine Emperor and the Frankish rulers extended into the seventh century.[24]

It is important to note, however, that the Byzantines did not confine the use of this tactic to the West. It can be seen more clearly in John Malalas's description of imperial relations with the Lazi (a group from the eastern end of the Black Sea). This group appears also to have had 'client' ruler status with the Empire in the same period under investigation here. When Ztathius, the King of the Lazi, visited Constantinople in 520 the Emperor Justin received him graciously, and his membership of the *oikoumenê* was affirmed by the receiving of both Christian baptism and a Byzantine wife. These necessaries completed, Ztathius was elevated in the imperial hierarchy, but with symbolism that made it clear he remained subordinate to the Emperor. Justin himself placed a crown on Ztathius's head and a white silk robe around his shoulders, but instead of the purple border reserved for the Emperor, the silk robe had a border of gold. A 'true purple' portrait of Justin was embroidered on the front of the garment. The accompanying tunic also carried a portrait of Justin, in gold imperial embroideries, so that anyone approaching the King would have been left in no doubt as to where he derived his authority. Thereafter, the Lazi continued to acknowledge the role of the Eastern Emperor in their system of government, to the extent that 'whenever the royal throne of Lazica was vacant, the legitimate heir would come to Constantinople to express his loyalty and receive from the Emperor the insignia of his dignity'. This description may form a background to the less well-documented evidence of formal diplomacy with Western rulers, especially where these, too, hint at 'client' relationships.[25]

While the Franks, at least north of Aquitaine and Burgundy, seemed increasingly drawn into the Byzantine political orbit, the Ostrogoths continued their 'advance' into the West. In about 511, Theodoric established his grandson Amalaric as King in Spain, after defeating the man the Visigoths themselves had raised as King at Narbonne. The Iberian peninsula was drawn tighter into his control. Both the Visigothic territories there and in southern Gaul had to pay 'tribute' to Theodoric: money and goods that were then used to support the Ostrogothic army. At the same time, although he himself was not an orthodox Christian, Church councils in Spain were dated in accordance with 'the year of King Theodoric'. Among Western rulers of this date, Theodoric's power was unsurpassed.[26]

The Emperor Anastasius came to distrust Theodoric, but his successor, Justin, apparently acquiesced in Theodoric's 'foreign policy'. In 519, the second year of his reign, Justin made Theodoric's Visigothic son-in-law, Eutharic, the consul for the West and adopted him as 'son-at-arms', while he, Justin, served as the consul for the East. Eutharic, as the husband of Theodoric's only legitimate child, Amalasuintha, was in line to inherit the Ostrogothic territories in Italy and elsewhere. Such a warm renewal of diplomacy suggests that Justin was seeking to bring Theodoric and his immediate relatives into the Eastern circle of government, probably to neutralise any potential threat they posed, just as Zeno had attempted to do several years before. Evidently, Justin was prepared to overlook Theodoric's ambivalent track-record in relation to Eastern authority.[27]

Alternatively, and perhaps more plausibly, the Eastern Emperor may have recognised that the political situation in the West was now greatly changed from that of the mid-fifth century. He had, therefore, to seek to 'contain' the situation by harnessing the goodwill of the Western protagonists, rather than exerting his authority more overtly. In the event, however, Eutharic died before both Theodoric and Justin, and Athalaric, his son by Amalasuintha, succeeded Theodoric. Byzantine diplomacy now had to take a turn in a different direction.

The role of royal marriage in late antique diplomacy

Theodoric made stringent efforts to create links with the major Western élites and a key strategy in this was the formation of marriage alliances. He himself was married to the sister of Clovis, whilst his three daughters, Theodegotha, Amalasuintha and Ostrogotho, were married to Alaric, the Visigothic King defeated at the hands of Clovis, Eutharic a Visigothic aristocrat and Sigismund the Burgundian ruler respectively. Theodoric's sister, Amalafrida, was married to the Vandal king, Thrasamund.

'Marriage diplomacy' is, of course, well-attested in international diplomatic practice throughout history. Strategic marriage alliances brought tangible benefits to both parties. The Byzantines gave generous gifts of money, jewels and titles (which sometimes came with a salary or additional privileges), and the other party usually reciprocated with only slightly less ostentation. Through such transactions, the Byzantines gained a foothold in foreign courts, which often afforded them political influence and other advantages for several generations, not to mention enhancing communications between the two courts. The Byzantines were careful not to give away land as a marriage gift, and when they themselves received land as a dowry it usually remained part of the bride's private property. Dynastic marriage contracts usually had objectives other than territorial expansion.[28]

Given these benefits, it may, at first, seem curious that during Late Antiquity there was a reluctance to permit Byzantines of imperial blood to marry into the families of Western rulers, especially as many Western Emperors before $c.400$ had themselves been of 'barbarian' origin. Given, too, that other forms of 'kinship' (such as baptismal sponsorship of infants) posed logistical problems, one might expect dynastic marriages to take place more regularly. Yet, no Byzantine princesses were married abroad before the end of the ninth century and only three sets of marriage negotiations between Byzantines and Westerners took place at all before $c.800$.

Dynastic marriage involving a male member of the imperial family was equally rare during our period. Yet, a brief look at how royal marriage was used in the eighth century shows how valuable this could be as a policy option, usually reserved for occasions when the security of the Empire was at stake. For example, in 705, Emperor Justinian II married a Khazar princess in an overtly political act, repaying a debt to the Khazar government – then ruling a formidable Empire to the north of the steppe. The asylum it had provided him in exile afforded him invaluable assistance in later regaining the imperial throne from a usurper. Even then, however, the imperial court took extensive measures to transform Justinian's bride into a 'Byzantine'. On her marriage she converted to Christianity and adopted the Greek name, Theodora, thus achieving her 'Byzantine' credentials. Twenty-seven years later, in 732, Justinian's descendant, Emperor Constantine V, also married a Khazar princess.

This woman, the daughter of the Khazar ruler, was also given a new name – Irene, meaning peace – symbolising her honorary Byzantine status. As Empress, she did retain her own 'fashion sense': for a while Khazar costume became *de rigueur* in Constantinopolitan court culture. However, this was a passing trend probably confined to court circles and did not herald a new sympathy to all things Khazarian.[29]

In this later period, marriages between the Byzantines and the Western ruling élites were contemplated when the Byzantines perceived the political *status quo* to be in danger. So, in 754, when a rapprochement between the Pope and the Frankish King threatened Byzantine interests, the imperial government began marriage negotiations with the Franks, presumably attempting to drive a wedge between them and the Papacy. The suggested marriage – between the future Leo IV and Gisela, the daughter of Pippin III of Frankia – never took place, but the rare negotiations illustrate the seriousness with which the Byzantines considered the Frankish-Papal alliance.

The scarcity of Byzantine-Western dynastic marriages before *c.*650 is, therefore, in marked contrast to the Middle Byzantine period. Moreover, following the coronation of Charlemagne in 800, an event that shocked the Byzantine world, a flurry of Byzantine-Western marriages were negotiated – ten sets of negotiations being completed before 952. In other words, the Byzantines used dynastic marriage to alter, rather than maintain, the political situation and remind other rulers of their subordinate position vis-à-vis the imperial government. The notable *lack* of Byzantine marriages with Westerners in the fifth to seventh century might, therefore, imply a degree of contentment with the state of the formal relationship between these élites.

Interestingly, the emergence of the Franks as the dominant political force in the former Roman West was mirrored in their own marriage alliances. By the second quarter of the sixth century the rulers of the Frankish kingdoms, by now gaining political prominence in the West, were cautious in the way they used this tool. The Merovingian dynasty made little effort to export brides to their Ostrogothic and Visigothic neighbours, although it was less wary when it came to accepting foreign women as marriage partners.[30]

As the Byzantines would come to do in the eighth and ninth centuries, the Franks only negotiated diplomatic marriages for royal women at times when they were especially anxious to retain their position in Western politics. Three Frankish diplomatic marriages were negotiated when, arguably, this was the case. The first was that between Chlodoswintha, the daughter of King Chlothar I and Queen Ingundis, and the Lombard king, Alboin. This is explicable in the context of Frankish-Lombard politics of the mid-sixth century. Between the 530s and the 560s, the Franks were anxious to incorporate themselves into the Lombard monarchy, presumably because the Lombards were emerging as potentially important leaders in Italy. About twenty years later, the King of Austrasia (the eastern Frankish kingdom), Theodebert II, was careful to have ambassadors present when Chlodoswintha's son, Adaloald, was made King of the Lombards and he later betrothed his young daughter to the new Lombard king. Plainly, regional politics now cast the Lombards as a force to neutralise and marriage was a useful way of doing this.[31]

In 579, another Frankish marriage took place, this time between the Frankish princess, Ingundis, and Hermenigild, the heir to the Visigothic throne. Ingundis was the sister of Childebert II, the Austrasian king. These were years during which the Visigothic kingdom of Spain was undergoing rapid consolidation and it is possible that the marriage was seen, from the point of view of the Franks, as helping to secure an alliance with a potential regional 'power', or to harness a possible threat. Once again then, the same strategy can be recognised: marriages involving Merovingian women were only conducted when political security, and regional stability in particular, was at stake.[32]

Finally, Bertha, the daughter of King Charibert and Queen Ingoberg, was married to King Æthelberht of Kent some time before 581. The presence of the Christian Bertha was, of course, to pave the way for Augustine's evangelisation of the Anglo-Saxons in 597 and the conversion of Æthelberht. This must be seen as a special case, for it is by no means certain that Kent can be seen as 'external' to Frankia in the sixth century. Ian Wood has proposed that Kent was part of the Frankish kingdom, or at least subordinate to it, during this period. Certainly, the Franks asserted some claim to Kent, even if this was based more on aspiration than actual events: in the 550s a Frankish envoy was sent to Constantinople, informing the Byzantine Emperor of Frankish authority over the south-eastern part of Britain.[33]

Further research is necessary on this issue, but whether Kent turns out to have been part of sixth-century Frankia, or whether this was Frankish 'wishful thinking', it is significant that dynastic marriage was used to further these interests.[34] In summary, it would seem that as Frankia emerged as the dominant polity in the West its rulers started to adopt the Byzantine mode of marriage diplomacy, showing that Byzantine diplomatic practice had an enduring impact in the West beyond actual Byzantine-Frankish contacts.

Of course, as we have seen, the Byzantine Empire maintained an active interest in Western political affairs, despite the lack of Byzantine-Western royal marriages. Justinian's Reconquest of Italy and southern Spain, along with Vandal North Africa, was the consequence of intense military planning, and was also preceded and accompanied by diplomatic and economic initiatives. In fact, in both Italy and Spain the initial Byzantine entry was brought about by an invitation from within rather than being the result of an arbitrary military attack.

The Reconquest has been the subject of so much debate in recent years that it is impossible to do justice to it here: that would require a book all of its own. In briefest form, the Vandal kingdom in North Africa was defeated in 533 and 534 under the direction of Belisarius, Justinian's chief general. A series of attacks on Italy followed, first in Sicily in 535 and simultaneously in Dalmatia. Despite early successes, the Byzantine expedition was soon faced with stiff opposition from the Gothic forces. Nevertheless, Naples fell in 536, Rome in 538 and Ravenna in May 540. Gothic counter-attacks in the following years resulted in a series of gains and in the re-taking of Rome by the Goths in 546, only for it to pass once more into Byzantine hands in 547. In 550 it was eventually re-taken by the Goths, along with Sicily. Justinian had not finished with Italy, however, and in 552 his army, under Narses, marched through the Balkans to northern Italy. At the same time, a fleet attacked the south-eastern coast of the Italian peninsula. This strategy was ultimately successful, for between 558 and 560 imperial authority was successfully re-established in Italy. Indeed, as late as 665, Constans II actually considered moving the capital of the Empire back to Rome, although in the event this did not happen.[35]

The Byzantine intervention in the Iberian peninsula was facilitated by struggles between the Visigothic élite and sections of its sub-Roman population, as well as intra-élite rivalries. These were instrumental in permitting the Byzantines to set up an administration in 554 that stretched across the entire south and south-east of the peninsula. Seville, Cadiz, Córdoba, Málaga and Cartagena were effectively 'Byzantine' until 624, when the Visigothic monarchy, under Swintila, was sufficiently well-organised to take them back into Visigothic control.

Throughout the second half of the sixth century, the Byzantines took an active interest in events further north. When the Visigothic heir, Hermenigild, led an uprising against his own father, Leovigild, in 582, the generals of Emperor Tiberius gave him support. When Hermenigild was eventually killed in Tarragona, the child of his marriage to Ingundis was taken to Constantinople and placed in custody there. The 'sponsoring' of the children of foreign rulers was favoured in the Byzantine Empire for much of its history. By holding them as half-hostage, half-guest, the imperial government could attempt to educate these children in the 'correct' manner and inculcate views that would make them less likely to turn against the Empire in later life. Needless to say, the policy had a mixed success rate.[36]

The Franks were spared from Justinian's military attacks in the mid-sixth century, and diplomatic contacts were maintained between the two polities until at least 629 (when the textual sources largely become silent). Consequently, Frankish-Byzantine relations remained warm while the Reconquest foundered to the south. Indeed, during the latter part of the sixth century, the Byzantines seem to have seen the Franks as potential agents of their policy in the West, especially after the Lombard invasion of northern Italy in 568. Gregory of Tours describes how the Frankish king, Sigibert I, sent envoys to Constantinople in about 571, although he does not tell us exactly why they went there, only that they went to secure peace. Given that Sigibert had been on the throne for some time in 571, it is unlikely that they went to proclaim his accession. Perhaps they were in Constantinople as a mutually acceptable intermediary, to mediate between other Westerners and the Byzantine armies still in the West.

In 578, as we have seen, Chilperic I also sent envoys to Constantinople, to Emperor Tiberius I, where they stayed for three years, presumably as guests of the imperial court, until they journeyed home with gifts from the Emperor to the king. In the 580s Childebert II 'received fifty thousand *solidi* from the Emperor Maurice to get rid of the Lombards from Italy', and he plainly was prepared to invade Italy on behalf of the Emperor (although not without benefit to himself as well). However, unfortunately for the imperial government, its investment in the Franks was misplaced. Hearing that the Lombards had submitted to the Franks, the Emperor asked for the money to be returned, but Childebert, by now confident of his own authority and political standing, did not, as far as we know, meet with the Emperor's request (**colour plate 8**).[37]

Squabbles in internal Frankish politics also sometimes spilled over into Byzantine affairs. The author of the *Chronicle of Fredegar* records that a neighbouring and rival King to Childebert, Guntram (who was also his uncle), sent a representative to Constantinople in 586, namely 'Count' Syagrius. The antagonists obviously thought it advantageous to appeal to the Emperor for approval. Once in Constantinople we are told that Syagrius was 'fraudulently appointed patrician'. Quite why this was fraudulent is not clear, although (assuming he meant patrician of Provence) it may have been because someone else, Leudegisl, had already been appointed to the post. In any case, if true, it is remarkable that political office in the West could still meaningfully be bestowed by Constantinople toward the end of the sixth century.[38]

While partially successful in his manipulation of the Byzantine Emperor, Guntram was also nervous of others using Byzantine authority for their own ends. When Duke Guntram Boso, Sigibert's military commander, was travelling home from a diplomatic visit to Constantinople (in the late 570s or early 580s) Guntram captured him and accused him of going to the Eastern Mediterranean in order to persuade the Byzantine government to intervene in Frankish politics. If this was impossible in practice, it is unlikely that Guntram would have felt so threatened. At the very least, Guntram believed that it was possible that the Byzantines would intervene in Frankia. In fact, there was some substance in Guntram's accusation. Boso had probably been to Constantinople to negotiate for the return of another would-be ruler of the Franks, the 'pretender', Gundovald, who landed at Marseille in 582 and duly demanded his share of the kingdom. Gundovald, apparently the illegitimate son of Chlothar II, had spent over 30 years of his life as an exile in Constantinople, presumably as a 'hostage-guest' at the imperial court.[39]

Another dimension of Frankish-Byzantine diplomacy was facilitated by shared religious affinities and aspirations. Radegund, former wife of King Chlothar I and abbess of the nunnery at Poitiers after her estrangement from her husband, was a key diplomatic agent in the second half of the sixth century. Yet, all without leaving her nunnery. For instance, her correspondence with the Empress Sophia, wife of Justin II, resulted in a piece of the True Cross being sent to Poitiers in an elaborately decorated Byzantine reliquary. The Patriarch of Jerusalem also sent Radegund a precious relic – the finger of St Mammes – again at her own request. Her contacts in the Eastern court enabled Réoval, a doctor from Poitiers, to go to Constantinople to improve his medical knowledge. These links with the Byzantine Empire were not arbitrary, for Radegund was one of the most astute political negotiators of this period. She was instrumental, for example, in the appointment of Gregory, our main source for sixth-century Frankia, to the bishopric at Tours in 573 and, in 584, she successfully dissuaded Chilperic, the King of the Frankish kingdom of Neustria, from marrying his daughter to a Visigothic prince. The following year, Radegund's diplomatic skills were demonstrated again when she was asked to arbitrate in Gundovald's war with his rival, Guntram, part of the civil wars that rent Frankia apart after the death of Clovis in 511. Her position in Frankish society made her a desirable target for Byzantine diplomacy, whilst her contacts with the East, in turn, must have increased her status and influence in Frankia itself.[40]

Conclusion

It seems then that East-West diplomacy in the fifth-seventh century was far more substantial than the gift-exchange and content-less title-giving often imagined. Byzantine diplomatic initiatives involved direct attempts to influence Western politics, a capacity for Byzantine rulers to grant offices and appoint officials in the West and a Western acceptance of Eastern suzerainty, at least in theory. The imperial government could, on occasion, align the policies of apparently independent kingdoms with their own and, at least potentially, intervene in Western affairs against the wishes of incumbent rulers. This suggests more than token acknowledgement of the imperial past or the meaningless acquiescence to Byzantine forms of address and titles. Moreover, this is not likely to be a mere residue of Western Roman political structures, two centuries after effective Roman rule had ceased, for it took place in the context of ongoing relations with the Byzantine Empire.

This does, however, raise a series of other questions. One must ask to what extent did Byzantine rulers have authority in the West, especially after the fifth century, and what use did they make of it? Were Byzantine representatives resident in the West on a regular basis and can we identify a system of consistent linkages instead of opportunistic or occasional points of contact? To what extent were political activities bound up with other matters: social, religious and economic? If we are to move towards answering questions such as these, we must consider the archaeological evidence. The starting point for this is trade.

3

TRADING & EXCHANGE
BETWEEN THE BYZANTINE EMPIRE & THE WEST

Introduction

It is still not clear what happened to economic life in the West after the end of the fifth century, despite decades of debate about Pirenne's famous hypothesis that pan-Mediterranean trade continued until the seventh century. What is clear, and has become especially so in the light of extensive archaeological research, is that there was variation in what happened and that the complexities of economic life in the Mediterranean and beyond have been hugely underestimated. While some areas of the former Roman West flourished, others declined; while some types of goods continued to be traded, the demand for others dwindled. The question of whether the lack of a particular commodity at a given site signifies that people at that site lived at a lower economic threshold, or merely that they had no taste for that particular product, highlights just one of the theoretical problems involved in reconstructing late antique commercial life. Much work remains to be done on the economic structures and trends of Late Antiquity, rendering discussions of trade and trading links somewhat provisional. Nevertheless, some preliminary remarks can be put forward here.

Eastern commodities in the West

Eastern products continued to be shipped to the West, until the seventh century in some areas, just as they had been since the Late Roman period, although not necessarily via the same distribution networks. For example, the famous Gaza wines make several appearances in texts and the amphorae in which they may have been carried appear in the archaeological record. These and other foodstuffs transported in amphorae were often to be found at the tables of ecclesiastical and secular élites, from Classe and Ostia (the ports of Ravenna and Rome respectively) in Italy, to Tintagel in Cornwall and Reask in County Kerry. Fish sauce and olive oil, commodities well known and widely exported in the Roman period, continued to be imported by the West, although often from ports on the North African coast, as opposed to the eastern provinces of the Byzantine Empire. Papyrus, a luxury that by the seventh century was in short supply north of the Alps, was exported from Egypt during the fifth and sixth centuries and reached the ports of southern Gaul, whence it was transported up the Rhône. The extent of trade in some other items, such as spices, nuts and textiles, is more difficult to trace, although it is occasionally mentioned in texts. It should not be forgotten, either, that even a spice as common today as pepper, could form the basis of a substantial diplomatic gift. Alaric I, for example, is said to have requested three thousand pounds of pepper, a sign of wealth, in the negotiations to restore peace to Rome in 408.[1]

Building materials and manufactured goods were also exported from the Byzantine Empire. Carved stone capitals from Byzantium have been attested in Italy and in Gaul, as at Arles, and may even have been part of large consignments of building materials shipped from the East (**colour plate 4**). The well-known 'church' shipwreck (Marzamemi B) off the coast of Sicily, dating to between about 500 and 540, was carrying a cargo of Byzantine roof tiles and church fittings, probably destined for Italy or southern Gaul. They included architectural pieces in white Proconnesian marble, mined from the island of Proconnesus in the Sea of Marmara. It was not, of course, that such materials were unavailable in the West in every case – marble quarrying continued in northern Spain, for example – so the shipping of Constantinopolitan stonework to the West may reflect taste as much as a lack of fine stone at source.[2]

Manufactured metal goods were also taken to the West, although the Germanic expertise in metalworking was almost without parallel in Late Antiquity. Fine brooches and other jewellery continued to be manufactured in the barbarian world, suggesting that some mines and metal-producing sites may have remained open, although reused materials were probably widely employed. The mining of metal is frequently given as an explanation for Byzantine relations with western Britain in the late fifth and sixth centuries, although this is by no means certain, as we shall see. What is clearer is that from about 400 onwards, metal goods travelled in the opposite direction: from the Empire to the West. Copper-alloy (usually bronze) items were increasingly exported from the Byzantine world, many of which were used as grave-goods in the West and thereby have become preserved as part of the archaeological record. Others, doubtless, were melted down and transformed at some later point, especially if they were composed of silver or gold.[3]

The increased importation of Byzantine copper-alloy objects would appear to mirror the decline in metal production in the West, and it has even been suggested that the Byzantine authorities raised the rate of their production in order to respond to this decline, hoping to exploit the 'barbarian' desire for metal objects for their own ends. Certainly, copper mining in the East seems to have continued into at least the late sixth century in some areas, and perhaps later. Indeed, when fire destroyed large areas of Sardis in the first half of the seventh century, large quantities of copper-alloy items were strewn around in the debris and were not retrieved, even when the army of Constans II camped at the city in the 640s. By contrast, when the same Emperor visited Rome in 663 his men stripped the metal roof off the Pantheon and robbed the city of its metal statues, perhaps suggesting that the availability of some metals, especially in the West, had declined drastically in the space of decades.[4]

The ceramic evidence

Pottery forms the most important category of evidence for studying late antique trade, and Byzantine-Western linkages in particular. It is virtually indestructible and yet since it is extremely brittle, it has a relatively short period of usefulness and so is often helpful in establishing precise chronologies. Moreover, pottery sherds are ubiquitous on many archaeological sites and provide vital diagnostic evidence for reconstructing the daily activities of life in the past. It is fortunate then that Eastern ceramics were favoured in the West, either for their own sake or, in most cases, for the commodities that they contained. As a result, a great amount of research has been done in recent years on the numbers of amphorae exported to the West during Late Antiquity, and on the possibilities of reconstructing pan-Mediterranean and further trading patterns during this period.

Eastern fineware — that is, good quality pottery designed for use in the preparation and serving of food — forms part of the Byzantine assemblage found in the former Roman West in the fifth to seventh centuries. Typically, Byzantine fineware comprises red-slipped, unglazed, wheel-made pottery, produced in large quantities and widely traded within the Empire on a regional basis. Whereas amphorae were principally containers for food and wine, and did not necessarily originate in the same place as the commodity they contained, fineware plates, cups, bowls and other vessels were specific to regions within the Empire and unlikely to have been primarily traded as containers. They are more straightforward as a category for establishing trading routes and distribution patterns, therefore, since there is less likelihood of them having been re-exported away from their general area of origin. Mediterranean shipwreck archaeology shows that amphorae could be used more than once, potentially to carry different commodities.[5]

The principal fineware that the Byzantine Empire exported to the West was Phocaean Red Slip Ware (hereafter PRSW, formerly known as 'Late Roman C'), although there were several red-slipped wares in use in the Byzantine East. PRSW was produced at Phocaea on the western coast of

Anatolia. Other red-slipped wares are also often referred to today by terminology reflecting the regionality of their production. For example, Egyptian Red Slip Ware was produced in Byzantine Egypt, Cypriot Red Slip Ware in Cyprus, and Sagalassos Red Slip Ware was manufactured at the southern Anatolian town of that name. It is interesting that of all these regional classes only PRSW has been found in any quantity in the West and it is even doubtful whether any of the other finewares were imported into the West at all from the fifth century onwards. This in itself suggests something of the origins of Byzantine contacts in this period.[6]

Finewares were also produced in North Africa, principally that known as African Red Slip Ware (hereafter ARSW), throughout the fifth- to seventh-century period. ARSW finds are more problematic in terms of discussing Byzantine contacts with the West for two main reasons. First, the pottery was produced from the second century onwards and may therefore reflect Roman-period trading routes instead of late antique pathways of exchange and, second, until the mid-sixth century North Africa was under barbarian, rather than Byzantine, control. Although, therefore, ARSW was manufactured in a territory under Byzantine administration from the mid-sixth century until the fall of Carthage in 698, it cannot be relied upon to tell us about East-West contacts during the period that concerns us here (**5**).[7]

5 *African Red-Slipped Ware bowl with internal decoration.* Reproduced with the kind permission of the British Museum

TRADING & EXCHANGE

Amphorae – used to transport food stuffs, wine and other commodities – were manufactured in many parts of the Eastern Roman world, including those that also produced finewares. Anatolia, the Holy Land, and Egypt all had distinctive regional classes of amphorae and these vessels were traded widely in the Eastern Mediterranean. Both finewares and amphorae were also imitated across the Empire, so that classes specific to one region were often imitated in another. So far as is known, none whatsoever of these imitations reached the West, but Byzantine amphorae were widely imported into all parts of what had been the Western Roman Empire in the fifth to seventh centuries. The only area that may have been for the most part an exception to this generalisation was the east of Britain, where only a few sherds of Byzantine amphorae or, for that matter, finewares, have been found.[8]

In form and colour the Byzantine imports of the fifth to seventh centuries are analogous to Late Roman ceramics. Both PRSW and ARSW have orange-red-coloured fabrics, covered in an orange-red slip. The slip on PRSW appears slightly darker in relation to the colour of the fabric itself, whereas the ARSW slip appears the same colour as the fabric. Both types of fineware often have stamped decorations such as animals and Christian motifs on the interior, sometimes with rouletting on the rim. The rim itself is usually vertical with a shallow flange, and the wares tend to have a low foot rim.

Late Roman 1 (hereafter LR1, also 'British Bii') are buff-coloured cylindrical-shaped amphorae, with asymmetrical twisted handles and tegulated ribbing over most of the body. They were produced in vast quantities from what is today northern Syria, south-western Turkey and Cyprus, probably for the purposes of transporting olive oil. Late Roman 2 (hereafter LR2, also 'British Bi') are squat globular-shaped amphorae, buff-red-coloured, and may have been associated with olive oil or wine transportation. They have smoother bodies than the LR1 amphorae and have distinctive combed ribbing around their shoulders. They are thought to originate from the Argolid region of the Peloponnese and the island of Chios in the Aegean (**6** & **8**).

Late Roman 3 (hereafter LR3, also 'British Biv') amphorae are usually described as 'carrot-shaped' vessels. Like LR1, they have tegulated ribbing, but are smaller and have a very micaceous red-brown-coloured fabric. They are thought to have been produced in the Sardis area, but it is not clear what commodity was carried in them, and they may not have been intended for any particular product. These almost always occur in a context with either LR1 or LR2 amphorae, or both. Late Roman 4 (hereafter LR4, also 'Gaza') amphorae are brown in colour and long and cylindrical in form, with D-shaped upturned handles. They are usually associated with the export of Gaza wines. Late Roman 5/6 (hereafter LR5/6, also 'Palestinian') amphorae are buff-orange or grey and are sometimes described as 'bag-shaped', having a squat body and a ribbed fabric. Their principal association is with Palestinian wine exportation, and they have a limited distribution in the West, mainly in

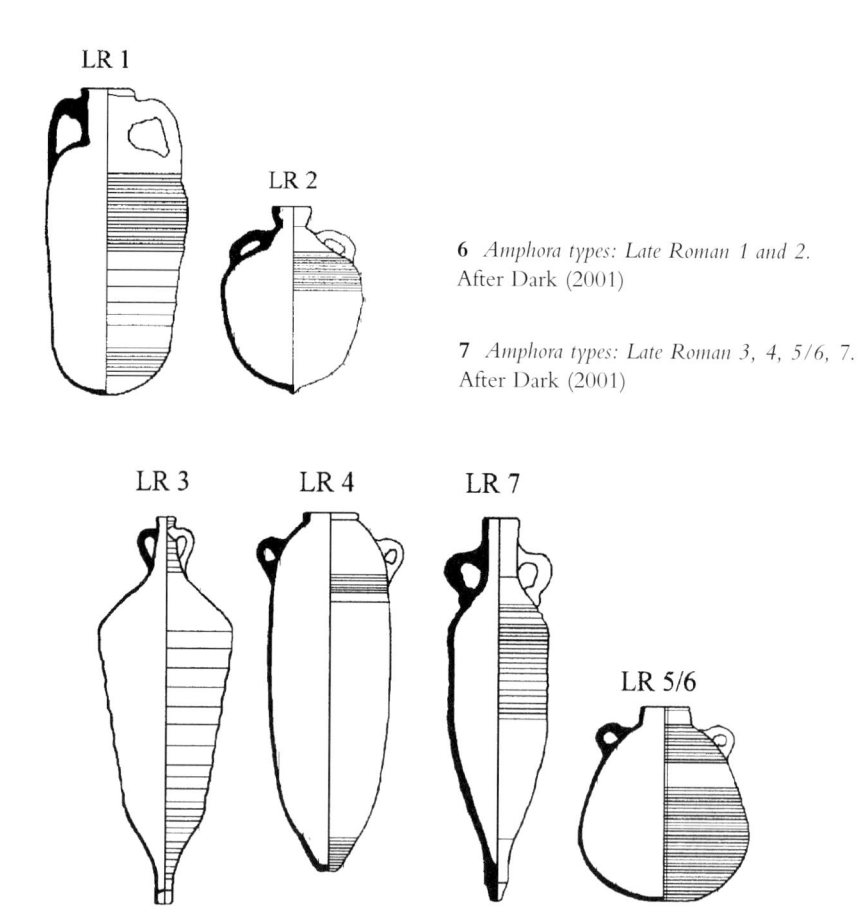

6 Amphora types: Late Roman 1 and 2. After Dark (2001)

7 Amphora types: Late Roman 3, 4, 5/6, 7. After Dark (2001)

southern Gaul, eastern Spain and at Rome. Late Roman 7 (hereafter LR7, also 'Egyptian') amphorae are buff-coloured vessels, cylindrical in form and probably produced in the Nile region, and also elsewhere, such as modern Tunisia, but are generally rare in the West (**7** & **9**).[9]

However, there are many limitations with pottery evidence. With the exception of fineware, it tells us mainly about the origin of various containers that were used in the world of late antique shipping. As noted above, the contents of the vessels may have originated elsewhere, and the date of an amphora's manufacture need not relate precisely to the date of its deposition, or even to the last exchange in which it was used, for an amphora could be reused several times. Moreover, the pottery evidence only yields information – and this only potentially – about the proportion of traded goods that were transported in amphorae, and objects carried in more organic types of container are often lost to the archaeological record. Grain, for example, would have been transported in sacks or poured directly into the ships' holds. Crates or barrels would have transported many other types of commodities, such as fruits and some types of wine, and others may not have needed any container whatsoever. The slave trade, attested in literary sources, has left little or no archaeological evidence; neither has trade in textiles.

Moreover, the pottery evidence available from any given site is only a sample of the pottery that might have been recovered had excavation strategies been different, or had larger areas been uncovered. The sample need not be representative either of relative proportions of different forms, or of overall quantities. So analysis of the sample can, at most, yield information about relative not absolute quantities of material. New data on pottery itself can also alter understandings of trading routes. To give but one example, LR1 amphorae were previously thought to originate in Egypt, and so their presence on sites in Italy, southern France and Spain was initially interpreted as evidence of a 'north-south' Mediterranean trading link. However, Jean-Yves Empereur and Maurice Picon have demonstrated – on the basis of an archaeological survey of kiln sites – that this pottery was manufactured in the north-eastern corner of the Mediterranean around Antioch, including both northern Syria and Cyprus. As a result of their work, it is now accepted that LR1 amphorae derive from the far east of the Mediterranean, and some material that might previously have been seen as evidence for north-south trade is now interpreted as evidence for exchange on an 'east-west' axis. Given, for example, that at Marseille 30 per cent of amphorae from the second quarter of the fifth century are composed of LR1, this would suggest a more directly east-west exchange during these years than had previously been recognised (**8**).[10]

Notwithstanding these limitations, pottery remains one of the most important categories of evidence for reconstructing Byzantine-Western contacts and so warrants an examination in more depth.

The role of North African pottery in East-West 'exchange'

Despite the methodological problems with using ARSW as evidence for Byzantine trade, the presence of more unambiguously 'Byzantine' wares in the Western archaeological record cannot be understood without reference to the African export market. In the fifth and sixth centuries, and sometimes even into the seventh century, the occurrence of ARSW on many sites in Italy and Spain may imply large-scale importation and distribution. ARSW was also used in the eastern provinces of the Byzantine Empire, sometimes into the seventh century. Although production continued under Byzantine administration, the North African export market began to shrink, and in fact had begun to do so even before the Reconquest. In some areas (for example, southern Italy), quantities of African fineware and amphorae had already fallen by the end of the fifth century, and locally-produced amphorae dominated the regional and local economy.[11]

8 *Late Roman 1 amphora, produced in Syria, Cyprus or Cilicia. Sherds from similar amphorae are found on many sites throughout Continental Western Europe and Britain.* Reproduced with the kind permission of The British Museum

9 *A Byzantine 'Palestinian' LR5 amphora, probably used for the export of wine.* Reproduced with the kind permission of Sean Kingsley

Excavations at Carthage, the capital of Byzantine North Africa after the Reconquest, support this analysis, showing that the North African export market contracted drastically in the late sixth century. By early in the seventh century, African amphorae had almost disappeared from the overseas market. After *c*.600, there are no African sherds in the assemblages from the port of Ravenna at Classe and only a very few sherds from the eastern Byzantine provinces. Klavs Randsborg has interpreted this sequence as a 'regionalisation' of the local economy, perhaps as north-eastern Italy started to become independent of Byzantine political control. At other Italian sites, such as Naples, the numbers of African imports also declined.[12]

Various views have been put forward as to the cause of the decline of the North African export market. In the early 1980s it was suggested that producers had been almost crippled by taxes imposed on them by the incoming Byzantine administration, which needed to recoup its military and administrative costs. This view has been widely supported ever since, although the evidence from Marseille and Tarragona has presented a serious challenge to it in recent years. In the Iberian peninsula, for example, North African goods continued to be imported, at Tarragona and elsewhere, until about 600 or slightly later, albeit in smaller quantities than in the sixth century. Most North African pottery found in late sixth- and early seventh-century Iberian contexts comes from sites on the eastern Spanish coast, but North African amphora sherds have now been found in central Spain in a seventh-century context. Sonia Gutiérrez Lloret has suggested that these may represent 'old' amphorae that had originally been imported into Byzantine-controlled Cartagena, and then later redistributed in central Visigothic Spain. This need not necessarily be the case, especially since North African amphorae were still being exported to Marseille in the early seventh century.[13]

The situation at Marseille and southern Gaul in general has been the subject of much discussion in recent years. The region plainly played an important and long-lasting role in both late antique Mediterranean trade and in Merovingian politics, and the two are, of course, related. Extensive excavations at Marseille indicate that the town remained a focus of local, regional and even long-distance trade until the seventh century. Indeed, the fortunes of the town, which were already good during the Roman period, actually improved between the fifth and seventh century. Rather than shrinking, as most other towns in Gaul did in this period, the latest archaeological research suggests that Marseille expanded, especially in the extra-mural suburb nearest to the port itself.[14]

There was, on the face of it, no specific reason at Marseille for importing fineware from overseas. From the fifth century onwards, the local pottery, *paléochrétienne grise* and *orange*, was extremely popular in southern and western Gaul, and was also exported as fineware to Spain and Italy. Yet, despite its wide distribution, the port of Marseille continued to import large quantities of ARSW finewares, as well as North African amphorae. Indeed, North African tableware was shipped into Marseille in greater quantities in the sixth century than it had been in the fifth century. More surprisingly still, numbers of North African amphorae actually rise from the late sixth century onwards, from 47 per cent of the assemblage from the main excavation area in the period *c*.575-625, to 90 per cent of the total assemblage by the seventh century itself. At nearby Saint-Blaise a similar pattern is evident. North African fineware and lamp imports continued into the early seventh century and, although Eastern Mediterranean amphorae were also present in the sixth century, by the final phase of occupation it was North African amphorae that dominated. Elsewhere in Western Europe, imports of African finewares and amphorae had rapidly declined by this date, but plainly in southern Gaul the market for African exports was still active.[15]

Why should southern Gaul have continued to be the recipient of North African amphorae, when other parts of Western Europe ceased to import North African goods after the mid- to late-sixth century? Marseille was an important political, ecclesiastical and commercial centre, and this may offer part of the explanation. R.B. Hitchner has suggested that trade involving ecclesiastical properties in North Africa and episcopal centres in southern Gaul may also be relevant here. A precedent for this type of exchange is found in Sicily and Sardinia, from where the managers of Papal estates sent goods to Rome.[16]

Gregory of Tours tells an instructive story about the Merovingian King Theudebert I lending 7,000 gold coins to the Bishop of Verdun, who promised to repay it 'as soon as the men who are in charge of the commercial affairs in my city have reorganised their business'. The account suggests that both the King and the ecclesiastical authorities were actively concerned about the operation of the local economy, and confirms the involvement of the bishop in civic affairs. Interestingly, the bishop refers to Verdun as 'his' city.[17]

The evidence remains inconclusive, but if Hitchner is correct, his suggestion would shed light on several textual references to a relationship between ecclesiastical authorities and commercial exchange, including Gregory of Tours' well-known comments about the Bishop of Marseille importing cargoes of oil. Indeed, this form of ecclesiastically-sponsored exchange may have been even more widespread than the archaeological evidence presently suggests: another sixth-century writer, Cassiodorus, noted that the Bishop of Salona imported sixty vessels of oil to fill the lamps of his church. It is reasonable to suppose that the source of this oil was also North Africa, given that this was where the largest quantities of olive oil were produced.[18]

Perhaps the most important way in which this North African material provides a background to Byzantine contacts is that it highlights the relative chronology of the Byzantine and African imports. It was only after the decline of Vandal control in North Africa that Byzantine products made a significant impact on trade patterns in the Western Mediterranean. Between about 400 and 500 the Vandals exported amphorae extensively in the Mediterranean world, but thereafter, with the exception of southern Gaul, numbers of African amphorae rapidly decline in the archaeological record. There are some other exceptions: African *spatheia*, very small narrow amphorae, are often found in the graves of Lombard women, where they are thought to have been receptacles for perfume or spices. What may be important to note is that as the North African export market went into a general decline, exports in amphorae from the Byzantine Empire 'proper' underwent a sharp increase. This may suggest that the absence of African products left a demand for similar products that could not be fulfilled through local production. This, in turn, might have created a series of opportunities for Eastern Mediterranean traders to market their wares more widely in the West than was hitherto possible.[19]

Amphorae and fineware imports from the Eastern Mediterranean

The ceramic evidence shows that Eastern Mediterranean imports reached the entire Mediterranean littoral during the fifth and sixth centuries, with average numbers of imports actually rising in the latter part of this period. The British-directed excavation at Carthage has revealed that 25-30 per cent of the amphorae deposited there around the time of the Reconquest were from the Eastern Mediterranean. At the Italian excavation in the same town 50 per cent of mid-sixth-century amphorae were of Eastern Mediterranean origin. At Byzantine-controlled Ravenna and Naples about 65 per cent of the sixth-century amphora assemblages were Byzantine. A similar pattern may be adduced from the Iberian evidence, where more Byzantine amphorae have been found from sixth-century than from fifth-century contexts. The same is true for Gaul, where Eastern Mediterranean amphorae were shipped to its southern shores, and then distributed more widely inland, mainly to urban centres such as Tours, Lyon and Bordeaux. A sherd has even been found as far north as Brittany. Taken together, this evidence represents, as Simon Keay has argued, 'a powerful upsurge in the presence of Eastern Mediterranean amphorae on sites in the Western Mediterranean during [and after] the later fifth century AD'. Such a statement might be applied to Britain as well, as we shall see in a later chapter.[20]

The work carried out at Marseille has revealed that products brought in Eastern Mediterranean amphorae continued to reach the town even after *c*.600. In one early seventh-century deposit they may account for up to 10 per cent of the entire amphora assemblage for this period, showing that Marseille had not been completely cut off from exchange with the East. This conclusion is supported by shipwreck evidence: the early seventh-century shipwreck (Saint-Gervais II) at nearby Fos-sur-Mer contained, amongst other items, PRSW finewares and a Gaza amphora (LR4). These objects were not necessarily intended for exchange. They were probably ships-stores and the main cargo was grain. Nevertheless, the ship's Eastern Mediterranean origin shows that Byzantine traders still maintained an interest in Gaul in the early seventh century. As noted above, the presence of African amphorae on this ship might suggest that North Africa remained an integral part of the exchange system at the beginning of the seventh century.[21]

Interestingly, the distribution of PRSW in the Western Mediterranean does not correlate exactly with the distribution of Byzantine amphorae. This might enable us to see different networks of supply in operation, although it should be noted that finewares were unlikely to have been the sole or even principal cargo. Carthage received almost no imports of PRSW and despite the high percentages of Byzantine amphorae at Rome and Ravenna, these sites, too, yield very little PRSW, although higher quantities have been identified in southern Italy and along the Adriatic littoral. In southern Gaul, PRSW is found principally at Marseille (**10**).

By contrast, these finewares are widely distributed along the south-eastern Spanish coast, at Barcelona, Rosas and Ampurias, with a particularly large concentration at Cartagena ('New Carthage'). This is not surprising, given that the south and south-east of the peninsula was under Byzantine administration in the second half of the sixth century. What is perhaps more noteworthy is that the four Portuguese sites to have yielded PRSW are all along the coast, suggesting an Atlantic littoral network of distribution for these ceramics.

It should be noted that the Portuguese assemblages do not represent a mere 'trace' of PRSW. Excluding the areas that were under actual Byzantine control in this period, they yield the highest number of PRSW sherds found on the entire Iberian peninsula. Indeed, this represents the largest assemblage of PRSW found in the West (again excluding areas under Byzantine administration) after south-west Britain. Taken together, this evidence might imply that different mechanisms of exchange operated in Italy and, perhaps, southern Gaul (with the exception of Marseille), where demand for PRSW vessels was not high, to those mechanisms that operated in the Iberian peninsula. Perhaps more importantly for our purposes, the evidence from PRSW highlights the unique case of Britain in relation to Eastern Mediterranean imports. However, that is a matter for another chapter.[22]

Motives for Byzantine-Western 'exchange'

The question remains of what the Byzantines hoped to receive in exchange for their goods, but this has not yet been resolved. Unfortunately, many items that may have been the object of late antique trade are invisible archaeologically. Wheat has been suggested as the 'price' for Byzantine wine and oil at towns in the Iberian peninsula, although as elsewhere in the West this cannot be verified archaeologically. Given that Egypt was the largest grain-producing area in the Mediterranean and that this was readily obtained as part of the *annona*, the tax

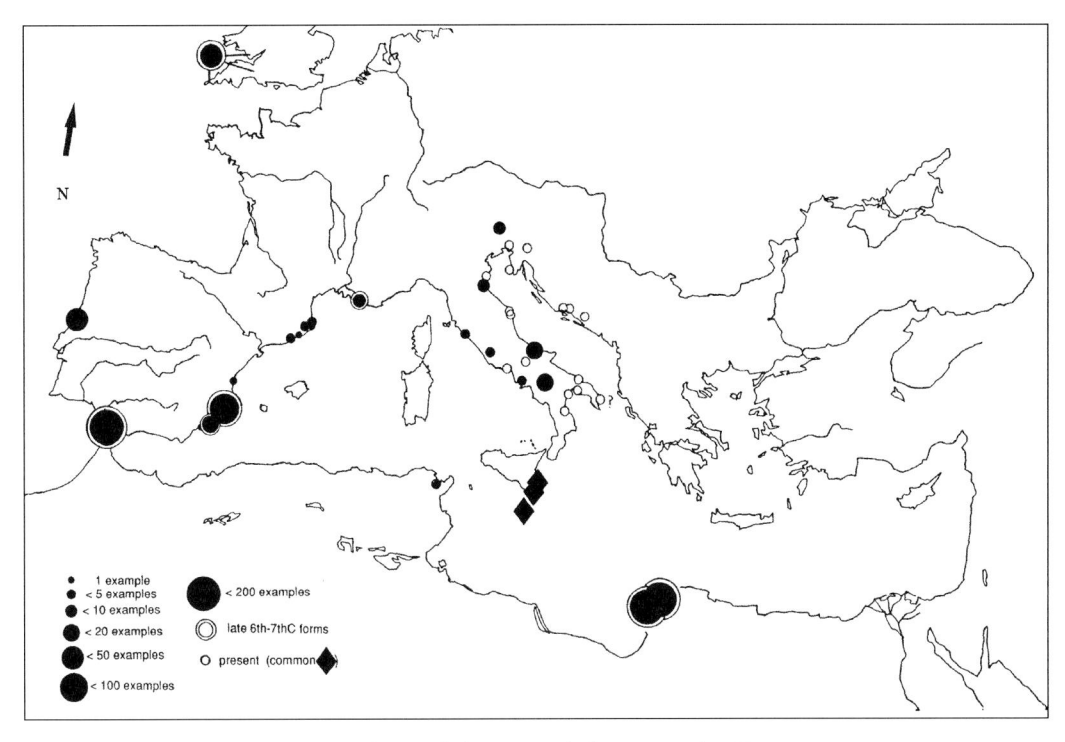

10 *Distribution of Phocaean Red Slip Ware in the West.*
Reproduced with the kind permission of Paul Reynolds

that was raised by the imperial government to meet military and administrative costs, it is unlikely that the Byzantines required wheat from Spain. What is more likely, is that Eastern Mediterranean sailors delivering these goods may have stayed in the West for some considerable time, for the sailing season was relatively short and such a journey would need careful provisioning.[23]

Whether or not Byzantine merchants, or even the Byzantine state, were consciously responding to the decline of the North African export trade from the mid-sixth century onwards, is not clear. The evidence is also rather more complicated than first meets the eye. For example, the combined presence of PRSW, ARSW and North African amphorae in the cargo of a seventh-century shipwreck at Marseille might suggest a continuing role for Carthage in Eastern Mediterranean trading patterns. Moreover, to suggest that the Byzantine state deliberately stifled North African exports, so that it might open up new markets for its own merchants, may also be to assume that trading initiatives were part of a deliberate and long-term Byzantine 'economic policy'.[24]

While there may indeed have been a relationship between merchants and representatives of the state, there is little evidence to suggest that this was part of an 'economic policy', although there may have been political objectives at stake. Indeed, several scholars have suggested that Byzantine merchants operating overseas were also acting as political agents, although we must be aware of the limitations of the sources for dealing with this question. If there were comprehensive economic or political objectives in international trade it is not necessarily the case that these would have been written down by our informants, or even alluded to in texts. Furthermore, even if such material was committed to writing, there is no reason to suppose that there would have been any incentive for its preservation in, for example, monastic archives of later centuries. Saints and emperors may have been of enduring interest, but it is unlikely that merchants were afforded similar attention. Archaeology, once again, provides most hope of moving towards a resolution of this matter.[25]

The vast distances involved in direct trade between the Byzantine East and Gaul or the Iberian peninsula suggest possible motives for the exchange. One can imagine that the incentive for merchants (if this is what they were) to trade across such distances was the scale of the potential returns, especially if relatively common or cheap items in the East could generate greatly increased profits when transported to the West. Such a trade might be expected to take material unobtainable in the West, but commonplace in the East, in large quantities across the Mediterranean and sell it at inflated prices. Seen from a Byzantine viewpoint, it would not look like a 'luxury' trade, but rather a trade in 'everyday objects'.

Yet, this is not what we find in ceramic terms. With the exception of amphorae, Byzantine coarsewares, almost certainly the lowest cost ceramics in the East, are extremely scarce in the West. It is surprising, given that they would have been superior in technical standard to most, if not all, coarsewares produced in the West during this period, with the exception of the *paleochrétienne grise* and *orange* of Gaul. If Byzantine traders were intent on exploiting the differences in availability and technical competence between the East and West, one would expect coarseware vessels to be much more strongly represented in Western assemblages than they actually are. With the exception, again, of Marseille, the only sites to have yielded Byzantine coarseware bowls and plates are those that were anyway under Byzantine administration. Indeed, it is possible that all known Byzantine coarsewares in the West could represent the presence of merchants themselves, and not traded goods at all.[26]

An alternative is the possibility of a genuine two-way trade, in which Western products were also taken back to the Eastern Mediterranean. But this, too, is unattested. Apart from a few possible sherds of *paleochrétienne grise* and *orange* at Corinth, and possibly Athens, no Western imports have, to my knowledge, been reported across the Eastern Empire from stratified contexts. The only other reflex of a Western product in the East relates solely to Britain. This is the possible presence of British in the Byzantine East, a point to which we shall return in a later chapter. Otherwise, there is no reason to believe that Western products travelled to the Eastern Mediterranean as payment for the Byzantine artefacts found in the West.[27]

Of course it is possible that Western exports took a form not easily identified archaeologically. Western slaves, or animals (such as hunting dogs), or foodstuffs, such as honey, might have been shipped to the East, but we have no textual or archaeological reason to suppose that this actually happened. It is not permissible to use Roman-period or pre-Roman textual references to reconstruct late antique trade patterns and we have no evidence for slave-trading between Byzantium and the West during the period discussed here. Slaves were traded between Western kingdoms, as famously evidenced by Gregory the Great's encounter with Anglian slaves in Rome during the 590s. The extent and pattern of this slave trade is nonetheless unclear and it is possible that it was on a more limited scale than in earlier centuries, not least because of the political fragmentation of Western Europe.

This leaves two possibilities: a directional East-West trade in luxury goods, presumably directed at Western élites, and a politically motivated network of diplomatic exchanges. In fact, these may have been combined, as has been suggested in relation to Byzantine mercantile activity in Western Europe. There are two ways in which this might have occurred: either ceramics may have been given as diplomatic gifts or those involved in long-distance trade for economic motives might have had official subsidies or grants to act as agents of the state. This latter possibility would have offset the risks and variable profits of very long-distance commerce and so stimulated the trading patterns evidenced by pottery.

There is textual evidence to suggest that those who undertook long-distance state business sometimes exploited their journeys for private commercial concerns. In 409 a law was issued to forbid this, but this does not mean that the law was adhered to. Instead, it might actually point to the state's inability to regulate this aspect of official life. The pottery might also have been attractive as diplomatic gifts either because the ceramics contained intrinsically valuable or desirable substances, such as spices or perfume, or because such pottery was itself especially valuable in the West. It is possible that Byzantine red-slipped wares could have been perceived as 'higher-status' tableware than any products available locally in Gaul and Spain.[28]

The main objection to this last point is that there is little evidence from shipwrecks that wholly fineware cargoes were ever traded; rather, finewares were a supplement to bulk cargoes carried in amphorae and perhaps in organic containers. This suggests that amphorae contained the principal object of trade, or for that matter, the principal gifts represented by this pottery. This has the surprising consequence that Byzantine amphora sherds might represent the presence of higher-status goods at a site than might fineware from the Byzantine Empire. After all, finewares similar to PRSW were already being imported into the West in much larger quantities from North Africa in the fifth and sixth centuries. This suggests that it was the contents of the amphorae, not the finewares, which constituted the most important products represented archaeologically by this pottery. Nevertheless, the patterns evidenced by the distribution of PRSW in the West remain a useful tool for identifying the different networks that might have supplied these goods.

Unfortunately, as we have seen, it is not possible to make a simple correlation between amphorae, or even a specific class of amphora, and any single product. However, it is likely that there was a relationship between some classes of amphora and particular products, and the assumption that these were connected may even have motivated some producers to 'copy' these classes. In this way, they could pass off their, possibly inferior, products as valuable alternatives. The best known of these correlations is between amphorae from the Gaza area and the famous Gaza wines, popular in Western élite circles in Late Antiquity. The majority of Gaza amphorae may well have carried Gaza wines, but it is important to recall that amphorae may have been reused in carrying a very wide range of products. Even Gaza amphorae were copied elsewhere; for example, in Egypt. Therefore, without scientific confirmation of the source of an amphora sherd it is not possible to be absolutely sure of an association with an area of production, let alone a given substance.[29]

One cannot even be certain in many cases of who was undertaking the transportation of these goods to the West. Ships might be owned by guilds of merchants, individuals, the state, or even the Church. According to the seventh-century *Life* of the Patriarch John (known as 'the Almsgiver'), the Patriarchate of Alexandria owned a fleet of 13 large sea-going vessels. As Marlia Mango's recent discussion of this text has highlighted, there was also a tendency for ships to carry mixed cargoes, which prevents us from assigning overall importance to any one commodity. Some impression of precisely how 'mixed' a late antique cargo could be is indicated by the description given in two fifth-century Alexandrian horoscopes. These tell us that ships left Egypt with cargoes composed of a mixture of small birds, papyrus, camels, high-quality textiles, objects of bronze and kitchen utensils, silver, dried goods (perhaps pepper and other exotic items imported from the Far East). Identifying the components of such cargoes in archaeological terms would be extremely difficult. It is salient that in this example only the bronze and silver (and possibly the 'kitchen utensils', assuming that these were not wooden) would be visible in the archaeological record. This is a sobering thought, especially as the organic material may have been the most valuable and considered to be the principal cargo. For example, the high-quality textiles carried by the ships described in these texts 'may have been as expensive as the luxurious bed covering (*gonachion/pallion*) that John was given by a well-wisher, which cost 36 *solidi* or half a pound of gold . . . . Silk garments owned in the mid-sixth century by the widow of a *cubicularius* at Constantinople were worth twice as much, namely one pound of gold (72 *solidi*) each; 100 such garments would have been worth 100 pounds of gold'.[30]

With these important caveats, it may nevertheless be possible to suggest an association between a few classes of amphorae and imperial supply. In an important study, Olga Karagiorgou has recently argued convincingly that LR2 amphorae (from the Argolid of Greece and Chios) were shipped to military sites along the Danube *limes* as part of the Byzantine state's military *annona*. LR2, which are often associated with finds of LR1, are not only found in higher numbers on sites with military associations, but (together with LR1) carry more *dipinti* (markings sometimes interpreted as capacity indications) than other amphorae types on these sites. This, it is argued, suggests that their distribution was highly controlled, perhaps by the state. For instance, the excavations at Nicopolis ad Istrum show that between 450 and 600, when the city was under threat from first the Huns and then the Goths, it became more reliant on imports of commodities brought to the site in LR1 and LR2 amphorae. Similarly, at the military *limes* fort at Independenta, there are unusually high levels of LR1 and LR2 in the layers from the late sixth and early seventh centuries, a period when the military situation might reasonably have been expected to be especially tense.[31]

The higher incidence of LR1 and LR2 amphorae at these sites in relation to others is interpreted as 'an imperial initiative introduced in order to meet the deficiencies in local agricultural supply'. If this is true, it would seem that officially-commissioned ships carrying LR1 from Syria (and perhaps Cilicia) stopped in the Aegean to take on LR2 consignments, before putting back to sea for their final destination. Karagiorgou's study may, therefore, offer strong evidence for an association between LR1 and LR2 and government supply originating in Syria and passing through the Aegean.

This may have implications for the study of East-West relations more generally. If LR1 and LR2 are associated with the *annona* in the Danube area (and possibly other sites in the Eastern Mediterranean), the possibility is raised that there is also an association between these classes of amphorae and the *annona* in the West. Following Keay and others, Karagiorgou sees the presence of LR1 and LR2 amphorae on Western Mediterranean sites as the result of 'free market' trade, probably the 'trading-on' of amphorae that were surplus to requirements. This may well be true in some – even most – cases, but it seems unlikely to explain all LR1 and LR2 found together on Western sites.[32]

LR1 occurs frequently on sites in the Western Mediterranean area throughout this period, but it usually forms the largest single class in the amphora assemblage in towns that were under Byzantine administration in the sixth century. These include Rome, Carthage, Cartagena, and the nearby sites of Alicante and Benalúa (Spain). Yet again, Marseille forms an exception. It, too, imported large quantities of LR1, despite not being under formal Byzantine control. Elsewhere, the statistics yield quite different information. At Gallic sites other than Marseille, classes of Byzantine amphorae other than LR1 formed either the dominant import or were imported in equal numbers to LR1. For example, at Lyon, LR3 and LR4 were predominant in the late fifth-century levels, and remained the most popular Eastern Mediterranean import in the sixth-century levels, too, when these are taken as a whole.[33]

LR2 appears at these and other Western Mediterranean sites, but quantities are usually low in relation to quantities of LR1, especially in the late fifth century and the first half of the sixth century. However, what is most interesting is that during the course of the sixth century the relative importance of LR2 in the overall amphora assemblages often increases sharply. This can be seen most clearly, for example, at Rome, Naples and Marseille (**11**).

The most plausible explanation for the rise in LR2's relative importance at Rome and Naples is that it represents the activation of an official supply route from the Byzantine court after the Reconquest. However, it is less clear why relative quantities should have risen at Marseille. The town was plainly an exceptional case in Late Antiquity, as extensive archaeological work there is revealing, and more work needs to be done before its ceramic evidence can be interpreted with confidence. However, the possibility remains that the Byzantines had a quasi-governmental, or even governmental, interest in Marseille during the period of the Reconquest. Why this should be the case is an interesting question, but not one for which we can, at this stage, give an answer.

The increasing coalescence between relative quantities of LR1 and LR2 in the second half of the sixth century raises the possibility that other amphora classes were associated with 'official' Byzantine activities in the West. Assuming

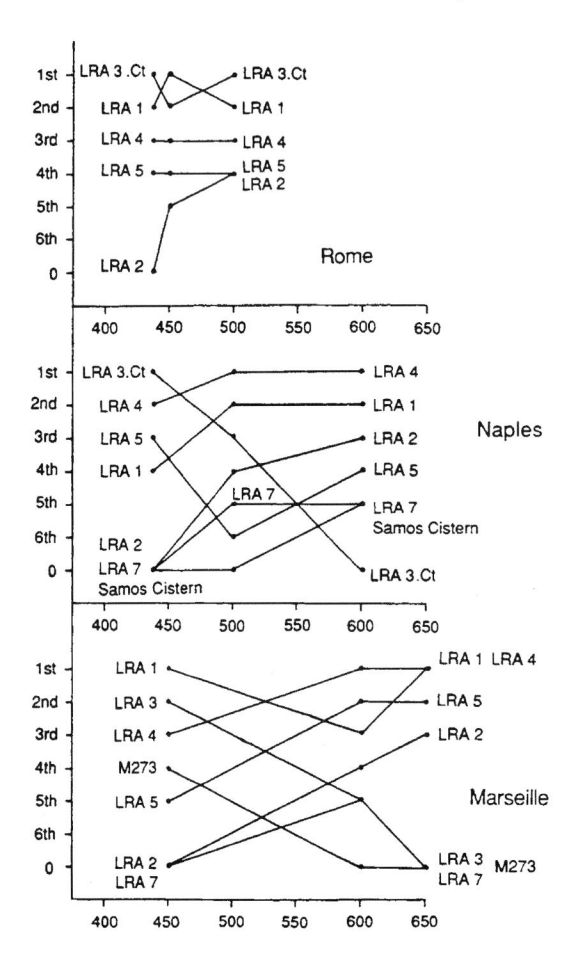

11 *Graphs showing relative quantities of Eastern amphora types at Rome, Naples and Marseille.* Reproduced with the kind permission of Paul Reynolds

that LR1 and LR2 were carried together, as seems likely, the presence of LR1 (without LR2) in sixth-century deposits on Western sites might reflect either internal redistribution networks or the 'entrepreneurial' activities of Eastern sailors whose principal purpose in the West was to deliver official supplies from the Byzantine government. This latter suggestion does not rule out the possibility that these supplies, too, were somehow delivered in an 'official' capacity.

In this context it is interesting that Western texts frequently connect contacts between the Eastern Mediterranean and the West with 'Syrians' (sometimes described as 'merchants'). Syria and the surrounding region was, of course, the same area in which LR1 amphorae were produced. It might reasonably be expected that Syrian merchants engaged to service supply routes to the Western Mediterranean would stock spare areas in their holds with other local amphorae perhaps containing other local products.[34]

The possible re-activation of official supply routes to the West in the second half of the sixth century provides a potential context for the Portuguese ceramic evidence. As we have seen, PRSW has been found on the Atlantic littoral (including Conimbriga) in large quantities relative to other deposits in the West. A purely commercial explanation for the presence of these finewares is out of the question. As we have seen, the relative values concerned would make it economically unviable and finewares were, in any case, not usually the principal commodities carried on long-distance voyages. In contrast to the situation at Gallic sites along the Mediterranean littoral, where it is unclear whether the Byzantine imports arrived there in a commercial or political context, the very directionality of this Portuguese exchange system suggests that it was not governed by entirely economic concerns. Why, if the desire was merely to pass on surpluses, should Byzantine shippers make their way up the Atlantic coast to Portugal when they could sell their products within the Mediterranean area itself?

We may be seeing, then, ceramic evidence for Byzantine official engagement with both Marseille (and perhaps southern Gaul more generally) and modern Portugal. This may help resolve the problem raised earlier in relation to the profitability of shipping amphorae westwards. If the reason was official supply, profitability might well have been of secondary importance. Certainly, we know that the organisation of the fleet administering the *annona* (both *militaris* and *civica*) was a very large-scale operation indeed. Cyril Mango has estimated that the yearly responsibility of paying the *annona* required some 3,600 shiploads of 10,000 *modii*, and some scholars have suggested more. Even so, Mango's figure would seem to justify entirely the alleged eye-witness statement of a resident of Constantinople who described the sight of the ships in the Sea of Marmara as being so dense as to appear to turn the sea into dry land. Michael McCormick has suggested, on this basis, that there must have been between about 1,200 and 1,800 state-subsidised ships operating out of Constantinople in any one year during Late Antiquity, even allowing for multiple voyages being made. Such figures explain the evidence, from Egyptian papyri, for the widespread ownership of sea-going vessels among wealthy individuals, including ownership as their sole occupation. While a few people captained their own ships, it is presumed that most simply managed them as an asset.[35]

Of course, this raises the question of whom exactly this costly and wide network was intended to supply. Karagiorgou interprets the Balkan evidence as a component in military provisioning; that is to say, the contents of the amphorae were used to feed the troops stationed there. Unless texts have been remarkably silent about Byzantine involvement in the West, a substantial military presence seems inconceivable. One can see evidence for Byzantine traders and ecclesiastics, but not for the army. No archaeological evidence for Byzantine forts in the Western kingdoms can be adduced until the Reconquest and, even then, only in the areas directly under Byzantine control. If we base our interpretation of this evidence on those sites that received Byzantine goods, then it would seem that this exchange system was supplying Western élites. To a lesser extent, this is also what texts may suggest about the activities of 'Syrian merchants'.[36]

It may even be possible that the luxury Eastern foodstuffs stored in the royal warehouses at Fos-sur-Mer and Marseille (and redistributed as part of Merovingian largesse) actually had their origin in this system. Whether or not this was the case, the existence of any imperial supply network might explain the existence and role of these 'Syrian merchants', their ethnic identity and even seventh-century fears that they were agents of the Byzantine state. But it would also suggest that Byzantine diplomacy with the late antique West took place on a larger scale than previous studies have envisaged. A network of this size would have involved substantial imperial organisation and the redirection of part of the *annona*, for diplomatic purposes. It is hard to imagine that this can have been anything less than a major part of Byzantine diplomacy in the fifth and sixth centuries and, in particular, it forms a new perspective on the background to the Justinianic Reconquest, as well as on the end of the system of large-scale government subsidies at the beginning of the seventh century.

The role of Byzantine merchants in the West

Such a hypothesis highlights the role of Byzantine mercantile communities in the West. The precise role of these groups is still unclear, but in general they were comprised of concentrations of Easterners, principally merchants, in prominent Western settlements. Although their exact location within these settlements is uncertain, Byzantine merchants had houses and churches of their own in several former Roman towns. They also seem to have been organised on a guild basis, with an internal structure and probably with a hierarchy. Such communities sometimes seem to have played a very visible role in the life of their 'host' towns. For example, Syrians in Marseille were accused of being a 'mob' that dominated the life of the port, and defrauded local people. Similarly, in Vandal-controlled Carthage, Eastern traders were incarcerated for allegedly inciting war, and Greek dealers were expelled from Rome in the early fifth century. It is reasonable to suppose that these allegations could not have been substantiated unless there were sufficient numbers of Eastern traders resident in these cities.[37]

Several other former Gallo-Roman towns – Bordeaux, Lyon, Orléans, Paris, Arles, Nice, Autun, Tours, Poitiers, Vienne, Narbonne, Toulouse, Nîmes – are said to have played host to communities of Eastern merchants. Salvian wrote disparagingly of the 'crowds of Syrian merchants who have occupied the greater part of nearly all cities'. According to Gregory of Tours, when Guntram arrived at Orléans he was greeted by 'citizens' speaking at least three different languages. 'The speech of the Syrians', we are told, 'contrasted sharply with that of those using Gallo-Roman and again with that of the Jews'. At Narbonne, similarly, the population had a distinctly multinational character. Meeting in 589, the Church Council there declared that the population of the city was made up of 'Goths, Romans, Syrians, Greeks and Jews'. In Italy, Como, Pavia and Venice may have had Byzantine communities, and larger groups of 'Syrians' were, unsurprisingly, to be found in the Byzantine-controlled cities of Naples, Rome and Ravenna. In the Iberian peninsula, Eastern merchants are textually attested at the ports of Cartagena, Seville, Málaga and Córdoba, as well as the important Roman and late antique city of Mérida, and may have been present in other towns, such as Ampurias, Denia, Elche and Rosas. In 589, Byzantines (described as 'Syrians' and 'Greeks') are said to have been present in Visigothic Septimania, many of whom were probably traders.[38]

The distribution of Byzantine communities mentioned in texts suggests that these were especially concentrated near the south coast of Gaul and along the major river networks leading inland from it. This is hardly surprising, and the presence of Byzantines in Italy and Spain is even less remarkable, but outlying communities in Gaul seem to have been positioned in the most important political and ecclesiastical centres, such as Paris, Tours and Orléans. This may go some way towards confirming the close relationship with Western élites that is hinted at in some of the textual evidence, such as the Gaza wines enjoyed by the Bishop of Tours, or the large quantities of coins that Clovis scattered amongst the people on his processional route (**12**).

Whilst maintaining their connections with local élites, as we have seen, these communities sometimes had an awkward relationship with other members of the population. Eufronius, a Byzantine resident in Bordeaux, had his house burgled by men acting on behalf of the bishop. The underlying cause of discontentment is unclear, but can perhaps be attributed either to the perceived 'foreign-ness' of Byzantines, or their behaviour towards local people. Perhaps they were also perceived to wield undue influence, or to be overly wealthy in relation to most Westerners, a charge that was levied against the Eastern community in sixth-century Bordeaux, for instance.[39]

In summary, then, it is possible to identify organised and sizeable Byzantine groups in political and economic centres across the late antique West. These communities sought influence and exhibited great wealth, as well as performing a useful commercial role. The diplomatic role of Byzantine merchants has been suggested elsewhere, but this can be re-emphasised on the basis of the ceramic finds: classes of amphorae associated with imperial supply. The amphorae support the suggestion that Byzantine communities in the West were in some way operating on behalf of the imperial administration. This is not to say that the network in question was supplying simply the mercantile communities, for the relevant amphorae are found far more widely than the known distribution of these communities, as recent work attests. It is likely that some were used as vehicles of trade, either by Byzantine merchants themselves, or in the course of secondary distribution. If the former were the case, this might suggest that the trade itself was wholly or partly state-sponsored.[40]

How genuine is the Syrian connection?

Many, although by no means all, of the Easterners attested in the West are described as 'Syrians'. Some scholars have argued that this is a generic term for people hailing from the Byzantine Empire, rather than Syria specifically. If this is the case, it raises the question of why Westerners believed these people to be

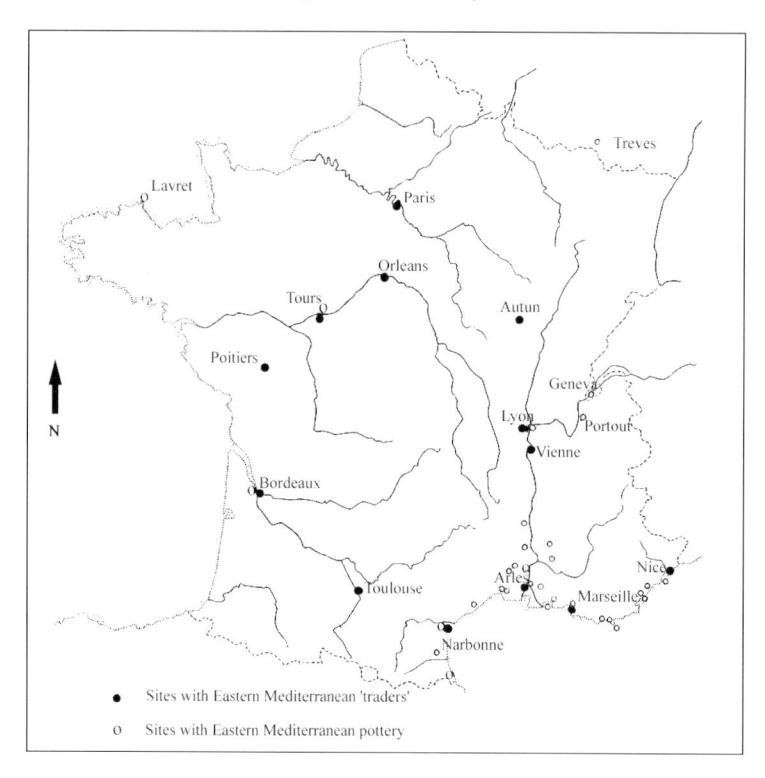

12 Distribution of imported pottery and Byzantine 'traders' in Gaul. After Bonifay and Villedieu (1989)

'Syrians' in the first place. It may be that most Byzantine merchants *were* Syrians, and this led to 'Syrian' becoming a commonly-accepted term for an Eastern merchant.[41]

Yet Western writers who used the term 'Syrian' were not ignorant of other regional identities within the Byzantine Empire. We hear in textual sources, for example, of a marble-dealer from Syria and a silk-maker from Antioch (the biggest city in Syria) being present in Rome, and these people are discussed in the midst of many other nationalities. From Gregory of Tours we learn of an 'African', someone 'of Asiatic decent', someone 'from the Euphrates region' and references to Egypt, in addition to 'Syrians'. Given that most 'real' Syrians would have spoken their own language and would, therefore, have been readily distinguishable from Constantinopolitans, Anatolians, Egyptians and other Byzantines, it seems likely that Westerners, particularly those on whose writing we now rely, used the term 'Syrians' advisedly. Thus, without evidence to the contrary, a provisional acceptance of these people as 'Syrians' is credible.[42]

If it is accepted that there might be a connection between 'Syrians' and imperial activities in the West via the importation of LR1 and LR2 ceramics, the question is then raised of why this specific group of people was chosen to act on behalf of the Byzantine state. One reason, of course, is that Syrians were already active in the West as traders, and the imperial government could simply utilise existing modes of communication and transport, as well as local knowledge. Jerome's late fourth-century comments on Syrian merchants, which verge on caricature, suggest that this was a real possibility:

> The Syrians have, up to the present day, an innate tendency for trade. Their love of profit takes them all over the world, even in these times when the Roman world has been invaded. Their passion for trade pushes them in the search for wealth among swords and into the killing of the innocent, and to flee from poverty, coming face to face with danger . . . [and] they are businessmen and the most greedy of mortals.[43]

In addition, Syria's importance to the functioning of the fifth- to seventh-century Byzantine Empire should not be underestimated, despite some evidence – in house construction rates, for instance – for relative decline from the mid-sixth century onwards. As the manufacturing centre for both LR1 amphorae and the initial centre for the production of raw silk, as well as silk-weaving, Syria was linked to the heart of both the Byzantine political and economic worlds. Moreover, its links to important cities such as Edessa, Mélitene and Chalcis made it a vital focus for trading activities throughout the period. Fifth- and sixth-century Antioch was one of the Empire's most important cities, as evidenced by heavy imperial investment in its monumental architecture and other buildings. The urban life of Syria was apparently so flourishing that Chinese texts of the period betray a tendency to confuse Antioch with Constantinople, suggesting that the former city was almost of as much vital political and economic importance (at least in their eyes) as the capital itself.[44]

Other forms of evidence also support this view. Bricks bearing indication stamps from the recent excavation of a baths complex at Berytus (present-day Beirut) can probably be sourced to Antioch, providing archaeological evidence for an imperial interest in the functioning of the city and its economy, specifically its brick-making industry. Many roof tiles from Beirut are petrologically identical to LR1 amphorae from the Cicilia and Antioch region, indicating that these, too, were produced in Antioch and then exported elsewhere. Combining this range of archaeological and textual evidence, then, the case for Syrians being involved in organised activities in the West, probably with the sponsorship of the imperial government, seems increasingly likely.[45]

However, it is unlikely that Syrian merchants travelled to the West directly from Syria, carrying cargoes comprised only of goods deriving from that region. As we have seen, when appearing on Western sites, LR1 amphorae are often found in the context of ceramics from other areas of the Eastern Mediterranean. We might infer from this that other Eastern Mediterranean cities were integrated into this network. In particular, the well-attested links between Syria and Constantinople might mean that ships sailed first to the eastern Aegean and the Sea of Marmara and the capital, picking up mixed cargoes of PRSW, LR4, and other items as they went, perhaps in exchange for Syrian commodities, such as textiles.

The African ceramic evidence might also be relevant here. It is possible that the 'Syrian' route to the West was somehow coordinated with the north-south trade between North Africa and the northern shores of the Mediterranean. To reiterate, this brought a mass of North African products across the Straits of Gibraltar and the Mediterranean into Spain and Gaul, most notably at Marseille and Tarragona. These products include ARSW finewares and a range of distinctive amphora classes. This north-south network might now be understood as an adjunct of the 'Syrian' east-west network, and explained in terms of ease of access and continuing demand in Spain and Gaul, especially for African oil and finewares. The relatively small quantity of African imports at non-Mediterranean Western sites, such as in Britain, argue against the African component of this trade being the most important motivation for 'Syrian' involvement in the West. It may be the case that the North African network was quite separate from East-West exchange with the Byzantine Empire itself, but further work is necessary before this can be understood in more detail.[46]

A second Byzantine-Western trading axis?

A trading network can be discerned that appears quite separate to this apparent 'Syrian' system. The second trading axis is not so visible in pottery evidence, but is associated mainly with a distinctive range of metalwork, particularly the so-called 'Coptic' copper-alloy vessels. These vessels, although undoubtedly Byzantine, were not necessarily produced in Egypt and so the nomenclature is rather misleading. It is possible that they were not all produced in the same city or even the same region, and various possibilities have been suggested for each class of vessel.

The network by which they were brought to the West employed some of the same routes used by Syrian merchants, especially in southern Gaul (Frankia), but focused on the northern Italian, Alpine and Rhine route to north-west Europe. Whereas the pottery evidence covers the entire fifth- to seventh-century period, by contrast, the copper-alloy vessels were exported in a reasonably narrow window between the late sixth and early seventh century. Joachim Werner, whose work on these objects is still unsurpassed, classified them into eight types (A1, A1a, A2, B1, B1a, B2, B3 and B4), with a 'Class C' made up of anomalies. This classification was later added to by Peter Richards, who identified another class within the 'B' group of vessels: the bowl type sometimes now known as B5, which was previously part of the 'C' group. These Byzantine vessels include bowls, basins, ewers and other domestic utensils, most of which have been excavated in burials from the Rhineland and Alpine regions (where over 40 examples are known), and from Lombard Italy (where over 30 examples are known). Other Western examples come from northern Spain and, as we shall see in a later chapter, from Anglo-Saxon England as well (**13**).[47]

Although less well provenanced, several other categories of artefact share a similar distribution and may, therefore, have arrived in Western Europe via the same route. These include amethysts, cowrie shells and elephant ivory rings – all transported from India or Africa, almost certainly via the Byzantine Empire and probably up the Rhine, perhaps from northern Italy, depending upon who had political control of the Po Valley at the time. Working from their distribution, such objects seem to have been transported along the same routes as the 'Coptic' copper-alloy vessels. The largest concentration of cowrie shells, for example, is from the areas of southern Germany that correspond to the Alamannic lands.[48]

It is not clear where in the East this second network originated, or if indeed it truly was a separate network. The copper-alloy vessels could have been produced in several major cities of the Empire. In Constantinople, for example, the bronze workers were sufficiently large in numbers so as to have their own district of the city and discrete organisation. We must consider, too, the limitations of burial evidence, which we are reliant upon in identifying this postulated second network. Assemblages that include these vessels, cowrie shells and other exotica simply reflect the burial practices of a given community. Another community with exactly the same range of goods available to it may have chosen not to deposit them in graves, but to use them in ways which are now archaeologically invisible. However, in this case, the

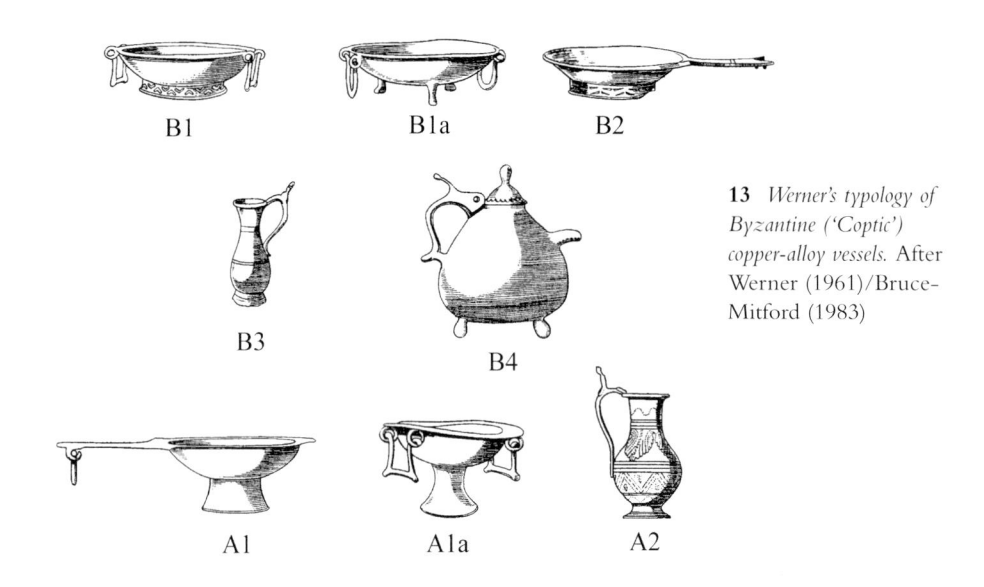

13 *Werner's typology of Byzantine ('Coptic') copper-alloy vessels.* After Werner (1961)/Bruce-Mitford (1983)

corresponding lack of relevant ceramic evidence in the same areas where the copper-alloy vessels were found would tend to diminish this possibility. If pottery and copper-alloy vessels had been carried together we might reasonably expect to see evidence of this in the archaeological record. However, this is not the case, for Byzantine pottery is only noticeable for its absence along this second route to the West (**14**).

Moreover, apparent correlations between the two postulated networks might not be as significant as they might at first appear, a point that has sometimes been missed in previous scholarship. The presence of 'Coptic' bowls in Spain might lead to suggestions of an overlap between the two networks. Yet, a closer examination reveals that this assemblage is comprised principally of a class that is much less common in northern Italy and the Rhineland than other classes of vessel. Whereas the majority of 'Coptic' vessel finds elsewhere are comprised of classes B1 and B2, the Spanish assemblage is comprised mainly of class B3 vessels. These come from Calonge, on the far north-east Mediterranean coast of Spain, from further south at La Grassa (Tarragona), from the Ávila area in central Spain, from Léon and from Mallorca. Two more examples are unprovenanced.[49]

Besides, Spain is an anomaly in terms of reconstructing links with the Eastern Mediterranean because of the Reconquest and the subsequent presence of a Byzantine administration in the south of the peninsula. It seems possible, too, that the typological differences between the Rhineland and Spanish assemblages reflect the presence of other networks of distribution in east-west exchange. It may be relevant that almost none of the Spanish vessels were found in cemetery contexts, in contrast to virtually all examples from elsewhere in the West. Where they have a provenance, the Spanish vessels are

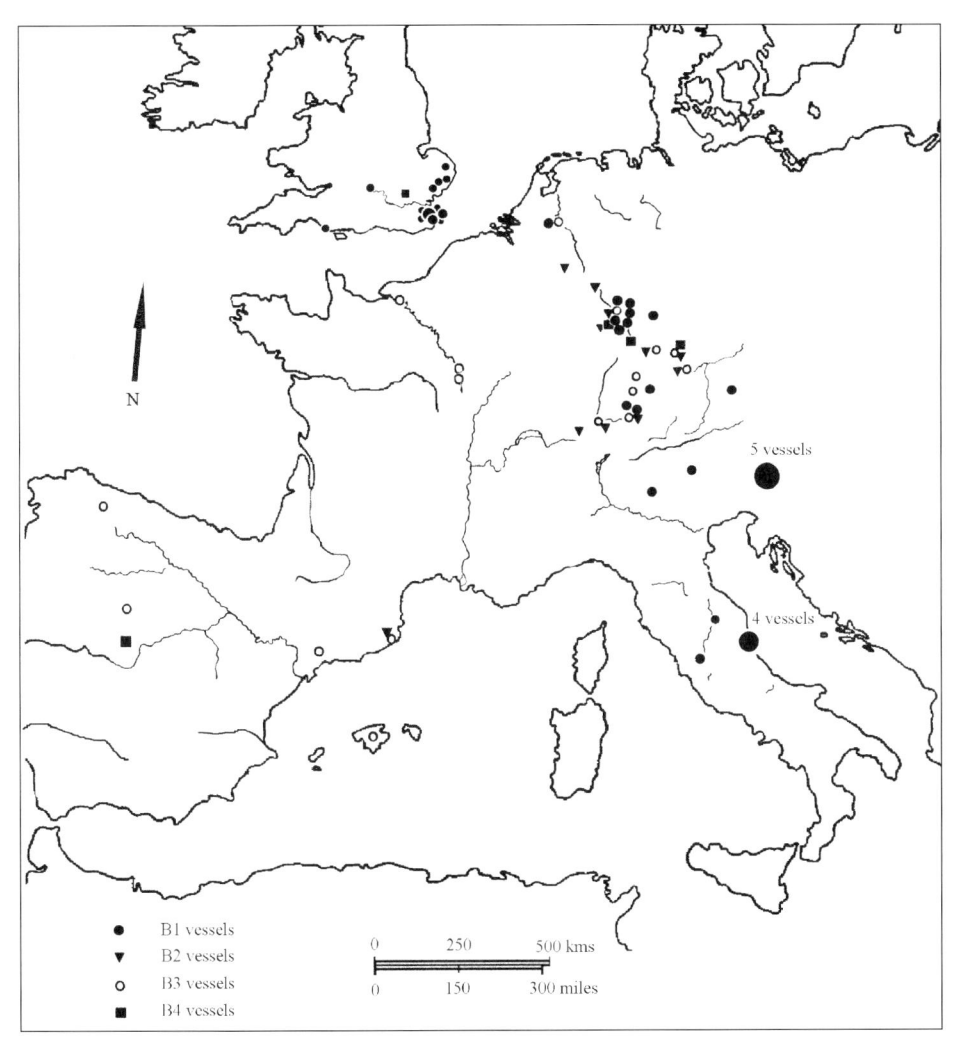

14 *Representative distribution map of Byzantine ('Coptic') copper-alloy vessels in the West.*
After Richards (1980)/Périn (1992)

usually from church contexts, leading to the suggestion that they were intended for some sort of ecclesiastical use. This is especially likely given that several late seventh-century Spanish imitations of the vessels are recognised, most of which have inscriptions indicating an ecclesiastical function.

Moreover, another Byzantine copper-alloy vessel – a goblet-shaped censer from an entirely different range of objects – found in the Balearics also comes from an ecclesiastical context, reinforcing the idea that ecclesiastical, not commercial, networks had some hand in its arrival there. Confirmation of this may come from the Cape Favaritx shipwreck in Minorca, where the range of material recovered suggests that the ship was involved in the transportation of liturgical objects to the Balearic Islands, or further west. Within the assemblage were several copper-alloy and other metal objects, all of an Eastern

Mediterranean origin. Incidentally, as we shall see in another chapter, this might also be employed as supporting evidence for a prominent Byzantine role in Iberian ecclesiastical life (outside the Byzantine territories) before the conversion of the Visigothic monarchy from Arianism at the end of the sixth century.[50]

Once the Spanish evidence is set aside, the case for the existence of two separate 'trading' networks is strengthened. This in itself does not shed light on the second network's origin. Yet, although 'Coptic' vessels do not necessarily have an Egyptian provenance, Egypt still presents itself as a possible point of origin. Egypt, and the port of Alexandria in particular, was another principal economic centre in the late antique Mediterranean. Given its geographical position, much of the Eastern exotica found in Western burial contexts – such as the (African) elephant ivory rings and the cowrie shells – are more likely to have been traded through Alexandria than through other Byzantine commercial centres.[51]

As we have seen, even the Alexandrian Church had a fleet of sea-going ships and an interest in trade-related activities. The 'Miracles' of St Artemius documents merchants sailing from Egypt to Gaul and recent archaeological research has highlighted evidence for bone and ivory carving. Papyrus was exported to the Frankish world from Egypt throughout the period, and we hear of Egyptian textiles being used in the Church at Tours, as well as a hermit who ordered herbs from Egypt. The numismatic evidence from Alexandria – bronze coins were minted throughout the period – indicates large-scale copper-alloy production; indeed, there was even a bronzeworkers' guild there.[52]

Again, Egyptian links with the capital, Constantinople, are well attested, even after the Monophysite controversies of the fifth century. As Peter Sarris has recently argued, Egyptian élites maintained an active presence in Constantinople, often pursuing commercial and other interests there, whilst travelling back and forth between Egypt and the capital. It would be logical for a wealthy city with a strong maritime tradition and with strong links to officialdom in Constantinople to initiate such a 'trade', if this is indeed what it was.[53]

The evidence provided by St Menas *ampullae* might also support this hypothesis. These pottery flasks were produced in association with the Egyptian pilgrimage site dedicated to St Menas. Insofar as their distribution in Western Europe can at all be ascertained, it fits more closely with this second north-south network than with the east-west network described earlier in this chapter. Furthermore, it is interesting that, apart from those already discussed, neither 'Coptic' vessels nor St Menas flasks are widely found in Spain. This might suggest that the network that carried them did not venture through the Straits of Gibraltar, but confined itself to the Rhône/Rhine or Northern Italian/Rhine route. Whether or not every so-called 'Coptic' copper-alloy vessel is a genuinely Egyptian product, which seems unlikely, these distributions nevertheless connect the Byzantine metalwork with artefacts and exotica likely to have been brought to the West through the south-eastern Mediterranean Byzantine ports, rather than Constantinople or even Antioch.

The inclusion of St Menas flasks may suggest that it was, at least in part, a route with its origins in Egypt, as may the few sherds of late antique Egyptian amphorae that have been identified in Western Europe (**15**).[54]

Even if St Menas flasks were brought to the West by returning pilgrims, this does not impede the hypothesis that Egypt was the source of this second network. It may only imply simply that pilgrims returning from Egypt were able to use a well-established trading route, and travel alongside merchants carrying goods from the Byzantine East. It is possible, of course, that Egyptian merchants used the same Gallic riverine route as their Syrian counterparts, or that these artefacts, too, were carried by the Syrians. We must not overlook the possibility that pilgrims may have travelled from Egypt to Syria, before boarding ships to Italy and elsewhere in the West. If the claim that St Symeon Stylites in Syria was visited by merchants en route from Egypt to Gaul is to be believed, the relationship between Egyptian and Syrian traders may be more interdependent than the distribution of objects would in itself suggest. This may explain, for example, the postulated presence of Syrian fabrics in graves and cemeteries that otherwise suggest they were linked to a possible 'Egyptian' network of trade. E.D. Hunt may, therefore, be correct in describing the route between Antioch and Alexandria as the principal 'coastal artery' in the midst of a new network of communication linking the main routes of the Empire.[55]

Motives behind the operation of the second 'trading' axis

It is intriguing to note that a wide range of artefacts that could have been traded through these routes have *not* been found in Western contexts, even when they might have been expected to survive and to have been recognised in archaeological work. For example, Byzantine glass vessels are very rare finds in the West, although Syria was a major glass-manufacturing region of the Empire. Similarly, neither finewares nor amphorae (other than LR1) from Cyprus have been found widely in Western contexts. The range of Byzantine metalwork found in the West is also somewhat restricted although, as noted above, shipwreck evidence is now bringing more variety of metalwork to light. It is clear that the material exported to the West was a deliberate selection of the range of possible exports. Thus, it is legitimate to investigate the rationale behind this selection as a means of understanding these patterns.[56]

To recapitulate, amphorae may have been the main cargo of the 'Syrian' exchange constituting the principal east-west axis. We have already seen that fineware bowls and glass vessels might be interpreted as space-fillers in bulk cargoes of this sort. Such space-fillers need not have been low-value items; they could have been the most intrinsically valuable part of the cargo. On the basis of the association between LR1/LR2 and official supply, the motivation for the range of goods apparently carried by this network (as far as they can be identified archaeologically) is, therefore, comprehensible in terms of the transport of the cargoes they contained. This may, then, have been an official supply route, albeit one that also transported smaller quantities of luxury goods, such as fineware. It is even possible that the luxury goods might have been diplomatic gifts or derived from an understanding of local élite tastes in the West. On this basis, it comes as no surprise that a wider range of luxury goods is, to date, absent from the zone encompassed by this trade network.

An official and directional system such as this could have also delivered payments in coin or bullion. However, Byzantine coin finds in the West are notoriously difficult to interpret because many of the higher denomination coins are chance finds and have no archaeological context and others were reused in jewellery. Lower denomination coins have been retrieved – such as from the 'Grazel B' shipwreck near Gruissan, off the southern French coast, where the 101 copper-alloy coins yielding a *terminus post quem* of 631 for the voyage, are mainly of Constantinopolitan origin. As low denomination coins, these are unlikely to have been intended for diplomatic purposes and are more likely to represent private funds, perhaps payments to sailors on board. Thus, the numismatic evidence for East-West contacts remains a highly problematic area and more work is necessary before it can shed light on the motives for east-west exchange.[57]

The second major route of Byzantine contact with the West, that which ran along the Rhine Valley, is more strongly associated with items that were probably perceived, at least by many of their recipients, as 'luxury' goods. This is most visible archaeologically in the copper-alloy vessels, many of which were found in high-status Germanic graves. This second route lacks a link with artefacts carrying official connotations, although it has been suggested that the uniformity of the vessels might imply state control in their manufacture. The repeated presence of the copper-alloy vessels in probable high-status contexts might suggest that these objects were used in diplomatic exchanges, but not necessarily ones involving Byzantines.

With the exception of the copper-alloy vessels, many of the goods that travelled this route may have arrived in the West in the form of raw or unfinished materials, such as garnets and other semi-precious stones, albeit perhaps already cut. This seems more like a classic long-distance luxury goods trade, although not necessarily strictly speaking what anthropologists would term a 'prestige goods network'. Exchange of this sort is extensively attested around the non-Western periphery of the Byzantine Empire, both in Late Antiquity and in the Middle Byzantine period. It may be the case that these goods were transported from the Eastern Mediterranean to a major trading centre in the West, perhaps Byzantine-controlled Ravenna or Rome, where Byzantine merchants are attested. From there, they could have been traded northwards through a series of transactions involving local and/or Italian merchants and the well-trod Alpine pathway, before finally reaching the much smaller-scale markets or courts of the northern Frankish territories.[58]

TRADING & EXCHANGE

15 Pilgrim flask from the shrine of St Menas (Egypt) with a depiction of a ship. Reproduced with the kind permission of The British Museum

Conclusion

Seen in this way, the difference between the apparently 'Syrian' system and what we might, for convenience, call the 'Egyptian' system is easily explicable. Consequently, it is possible to reconstruct the main trade routes, the identity and motivation of the traders, and the rationale behind the selection of the objects of trade – albeit to varying levels of reliability. Surprisingly, the patterns identified here have not always been recognised in other work but this is probably because these trade routes have been homogenised in terms of site-finds and examined regionally, rather than understood as broad networks with shared characteristics.

Here, of course, the most important facet of this re-interpretation of late antique trading networks in Western Europe is what may be evidence of directional diplomatically-motivated trade, between Constantinople and parts of the West. If this evidence is credited, it might suggest that the Byzantine Empire maintained diplomatic links with political centres and ecclesiastical and royal élites across the whole of Western Europe during the late fifth and sixth centuries, and possibly into the seventh century in some areas.

The lack of evidence for this extensive network in textual evidence need not count against its existence. Written evidence for Byzantine diplomacy in the fifth to seventh century usually only mentions overseas relations, which is when problems were felt to have arisen. It rarely focuses on the day-to-day work of communicating with foreign dignitaries in the capital, or the rather tedious task of ensuring the smooth running of the provinces and the hinterland. The absence of references to this system might, therefore, suggest that it was seen to be operating successfully, whatever its precise objective.[59]

However, we know that the role of the *annona* declined after the recurrence of plague from the second half of the sixth century onwards and the fall of Alexandria to the Persians in 617. It is possible to imagine that, in the light of the failure of the Reconquest, the imperial government had decided to cut its losses with this strategy in the West and to cease state-sponsored exports in the early seventh century. This is consistent with McCormick's observation that, by the first part of the seventh century, Eastern Mediterranean imports are found mainly at 'outposts' still held by Constantinople, such as Naples, Rome and Ravenna in the West.[60]

If it is the case that imports of LR1 and LR2 represent deliberate targeting of particular towns in the West, it is interesting that Marseille continued to receive Byzantine imports into the seventh century. Plainly it was not under Byzantine 'control' as such, but perhaps there was a continued diplomatic interest there, despite the failure of the overall strategic and diplomatic programme. One possibility suggests itself: as the capital of Provence, the first Roman outpost in Gaul (*Provincia*), it may have held special significance in the East, perhaps making the imperial government reluctant to halt the supply of subsidies there. After all, the historian, Agathias, writing during the reign of Justinian, described it as the most important city in Gaul – on exactly these grounds.[61]

Finally, it is important to ask what Western élites hoped to gain from the contacts represented by this evidence. They might have had any of several aims: the creation of formal connections (real or illusory) with the Byzantine court, the desire to obtain exotica, which could be used in ceremonial and gift-exchange, the attraction of obtaining information about the wider world from traders, or even simply the acquisition of luxuries for their own use and consumption. The desire to link themselves with the Byzantine court is suggested by the imitation of Eastern Mediterranean artefacts by Western élites and by the long-term residence of 'Syrians' in strategic political and economic centres in the West. The incorporation of Eastern traders in the ceremonial and institutional life of Gaul supports the view that these people were far from transient or peripheral figures, of use only as vendors of exotic objects. All of these motives may have played some part in the Western acquisition of Byzantine goods.

4

ROYAL TOMBS, TEXTILES & GOLD COINAGE

Introduction

Having looked at 'trade' routes and diplomacy, the next logical step is to look at the Western beneficiaries of those exchanges. This may enable us to examine their consequences in terms of material culture. As the networks facilitating these interactions seem to have been directed towards élites, and possibly ruling élites in particular, it is to the archaeology of these groups that we should first turn. In effect, this links the archaeology of long-distance exchange to the archaeology of Western kingship. The question is then raised of whether concepts of kingship in the post-Roman West developed in the context of links with the Byzantine Empire, or whether these were principally independent phenomena. Exactly how the development of Western kingship might be explored has been problematic for archaeologists and, as we shall see, the evidence is often ambiguous.

There is surprisingly little settlement archaeology that we can associate confidently with Western rulers of the fifth and sixth centuries. Leaving aside Britain, the only site at which we have much indication of the physical form of royal courts in barbarian Europe is Ravenna, where a depiction of Theodoric's palace might be glimpsed in one of the mosaics at San Apollinare Nuovo. This may have been modelled on the Great Palace at Constantinople, with a vestibule 'copied' from the Chalkê gate that marked the entrance to the Constantinopolitan palace. However, the extent to which this was the case is uncertain. Consequently, if we are to address the question of kingship and Byzantine-Western relations, we have to look at royal burial and artefacts possibly associated with kingship. In practice, this requires this chapter to focus on tombs, gold coins, textiles and gift-exchange – categories of evidence that might be helpful in investigating this question.[1]

Gift-exchange

Gift-exchange is well-known from other historical settings and anthropological evidence and is attested in Late Antiquity by contemporary written sources. For instance, we saw in chapter 2 how Radegund of Poitiers received gifts from the imperial court such as a jewelled reliquary cross and other devotional items. We saw, too, how the Frankish king, Chilperic, received gifts of coins and precious metal vessels from the Emperor Maurice Tiberius. There may have been a well-developed ideology behind such activity. Whilst gift-exchange could represent simply the transfer of considerable wealth, the transaction was usually more complex. God, the ultimate authority, was perceived as a giver of gifts, and the Byzantine Emperor was obliged to follow this model. Reciprocity was a key feature of formal relationships between rulers and gift-exchange was used to convey implicit messages about the relationship between the two parties concerned. If unable to repay the giver in full for the gift immediately, the recipient remained indebted until the gift was repaid. This was probably the intention behind some of the imperial court's more excessive displays of gift-giving.[2]

Contemporary depictions of gift-giving, therefore, such as that seen on the base of the Theodosius obelisk in the Hippodrome in Constantinople (390), do not allude to mere sentimentality. They served as a physical reminder of a relationship that was encoded in an equally material manner. Gift-exchange was important in an ecclesiastical context, too: Radegund, it will be recalled, received a gift from the Patriarch of Jerusalem and, in 597, Augustine took gifts to his hosts in the Merovingian towns he travelled through on the way to Canterbury – plainly his passage was not guaranteed by goodwill alone (**16** & **17**).[3]

It might be supposed that the subject of gift-exchange would be adequately evidenced in texts, but this is not the case. As shown in chapter 2, diplomatic activities probably went unrecorded for the most part, and this might be expected to include instances of gift-exchange. Moreover, the 'superior' partner in such exchanges laid less emphasis on recording and describing the gift than the 'inferior' partner. This being the case, gift-exchange with Western élites might be expected not to have been afforded much attention in Byzantine texts, while the Western written evidence is often variable in its coverage and, at best, weak on the detail of Byzantine-Western political relationships.[4]

Unfortunately, identifying diplomatic gifts in the archaeological record is also extremely difficult. The evidence rarely yields any information on how an object was acquired. A scattering of seventh-century reliquary crosses and precious metal vessels in cathedral treasuries across Europe may have been acquired as contemporary diplomatic gifts – in either secular or ecclesiastical contexts – but it is not possible to be sure. Once within Western kingdoms, one might expect these objects to have been dispersed over time, especially in

16 *The obelisk of Theodosius in the Hippodrome, Istanbul.* Photograph by Anthea Harris

17 *Detail of a relief from the obelisk of Theodosius, Istanbul, showing barbarians giving gifts to the Emperor.* Photograph by Anthea Harris

donations to churches and monasteries. Finding a direct association in an archaeological context between a Byzantine import and material relating to Western élite groups is intrinsically likely to be rare, even if the association was once common.

Furthermore, the purpose to which an object was being put at the time of its final usage did not necessarily signal whether it had, at any time, been used in gift-exchange. By this point, much time may have elapsed and the object passed through the hands of several owners. The most that can usually be suggested is that a particular object is more *likely* to have been the subject of diplomacy than of trade. Moreover, it should not be forgotten that wood, textiles, foodstuffs and other organic items, such as papyrus, that might have been the subject of diplomatic gift-exchange would not usually survive on a typical Western European site. As few relevant waterlogged sites are available for excavation and analysis, it seems reasonable to suppose that we have 'lost' the visibility of these components in the archaeological record, although occasionally we might see their reflection in more durable materials, where these have been 'copied' from organic exemplars.

However, some diplomatic gifts may survive. The well-known votive crowns from Visigothic Spain present themselves as rare objects whose component parts, or even their composite whole, may have been acquired in a diplomatic context (**colour plate 6**). It is worth noting that the Byzantine court gave lavish gifts of richly- and symbolically-decorated crowns to their neighbours, the Hungarian rulers, in the eleventh century, when it was interpreted as part of the protocol surrounding the so-called 'family of princes'. It is not out of the question that an analogous Byzantine practice may have taken place in relation to Visigothic Spain.[5]

Twenty-two crowns (14 copper-alloy and 8 gold) were found by chance in 1858 and constitute the famous 'Guarrazar Treasure'. Four more were found in subsequent excavation. They appear to have been hastily buried in close proximity to a church, and are generally interpreted as having been hidden in advance of the invading Arab armies at the beginning of the eighth century. However, their votive deposition cannot be ruled out. One example, now lost, spelled out the inscription 'King Swintila gave this' (+SU[IN]T[H]IL[A]NVS REX OFFE[RE]T) which, given that Swintila reigned between 621 and 631, provides a *terminus post quem* of 621 for its manufacture. The most famous and elaborate of the remaining crowns, the 'Recceswinth crown', probably dates from later in the seventh century, Recceswinth having reigned between 653 and 673. It is so-called because gold cloisonné letters, attached to delicate chains hanging from small loops in the gold band of the crown itself, spell out the statement, 'King Recceswinth gave this' (RECCESVINTHUS REX OFFERET).[6]

The Recceswinth crown lies outside our period, but taken as a whole, the group provides an important insight into mid- to late seventh-century kingship in Spain, suggesting that concepts of kingship developed in the context of élite-level relations with the Byzantine Empire. Most of the gold crowns are highly-decorated with garnets, pearls, sapphires and coloured glass cabochons, set in gold against a background of very fine open-work gold filigree. In this way, they are reminiscent of the jewelled crowns worn in the mid-sixth-century mosaics of Justinian and Theodora at San Vitale, Ravenna, although this is not to say that they are actually Byzantine. Stylistically, the crowns have antecedents in other Visigothic and Germanic metalwork. However, components of the crowns, such as the cut gems and jewelled crosses, may have arrived at the Visigothic court as gifts from the imperial court at Constantinople. A third votive crown, now in the Musée de Cluny in Paris, with a Latin-style cross suspended from it, has parallels with gem-studded Byzantine jewellery: Katherine Brown has suggested that the practice of suspending a gemmed cross from a votive crown can be traced to Constantine I (**colour plate 7**). Byzantine or Byzantine-style gem-studded crosses were also used as jewellery in Western contexts, for they have been found in burial assemblages (such as grave 23 at Saint-Dénis), again pointing to links with the East.[7]

The Spanish votive crowns were probably used in an ecclesiastical context, possibly a funerary one, perhaps in emulation of the Byzantine emperors at Hagia Sophia and elsewhere. The giving of votive crowns was not uncommon in Byzantine ruling circles; usually these were exchanged between secular élites, but sometimes they were bestowed upon an ecclesiastical foundation. For example, Justinian deposited a crown on the altar of Hagia Sophia, while a sixth-century pilgrim's account of the Holy Sepulchre, Jerusalem describes 'emperors' crowns' hanging in the church as votive offerings, along with other jewellery and precious stones. This is consistent with documented Visigothic practices, for Recceswinth is said to have presented the Church in the Iberian peninsula with a gold crown, dedicated to the memory of the martyr, St Felix of Girona. It is instructive, then, that the only objects that can be directly linked to the Visigothic monarchy have explicitly 'Byzantine' associations, even if they themselves are not Byzantine. It is even more interesting that these items may once have constituted part of public displays of royal identity. As such, they provide a material expression of the importance of the Visigothic monarchy's relationship with the imperial court (**colour plate 12**).[8]

Burial evidence

A potentially more fruitful, but just as problematic, source for exploring Byzantine links and the development of kingship is burial evidence. This is one of the most extensively studied areas of late antique archaeology in the West and has yielded a vast array of information on social and economic life in the fifth to seventh century, including the development of hierarchy, culture and identity in the barbarian kingdoms. It is largely through the excavation and analysis of literally tens of thousands of burials across Continental Europe and Britain that we are now in a better position to identify culturally-distinct strata and social change within late antique society. It is unfortunate then that there has, as yet, been no systematic study of all Byzantine objects found in Western European graves and no investigation of the question of their possible 'meaning'. Such a study cannot be attempted here, but this remains a useful category of evidence that might illuminate the relationship between East-West contacts and Western kingship.[9]

There was no commonly accepted rite of burial in Western Europe during Late Antiquity. In about 400, most social groups within the Roman Empire practised inhumation, although cremations still took place. In very general terms, people gave up cremation either when they converted to Christianity or as a result of fashions in burial practice within the Roman period. Barbarians generally abandoned cremation when they migrated into former Roman territory. Among fifth-century sub-Roman communities, people still tended to be buried according to Late Roman practices, which usually meant inhumation without grave-goods but, by contrast, Germanic groups, particularly the Franks, continued to use grave-goods even after they became Christians. This practice survived into the seventh century, thus providing us with a useful source of information about their material culture and, potentially, its links with the East. The oft-presumed correlation between 'accompanied burial' (graves containing objects) and paganism of any sort is fallacious but, equally, not every 'unaccompanied' burial signifies a Christian grave. The relationship between religious identity and burial customs may have been much more complex and is not yet well understood.[10]

Where late antique graves do contain artefacts, these can usually be divided into two categories: personal attire and non-dress items. The interpretation of personal attire is usually fairly straightforward. This mainly consists of clothes fastenings – brooches and belt buckles – and jewellery and, very occasionally, traces of organic substances such as textiles. However, the 'meaning' of the other artefacts raises more questions and remains a largely unresolved issue. What are usually understood as 'Germanic' groups tended to use grave-goods to a greater extent than non-Germanic ones, although this, too, is far more problematic than is sometimes appreciated. Grave-goods could have carried ethnic associations, but how commonly this was the case is unclear, as is the question of how this information was conveyed to contemporary observers of the burial. Determining social position or religious affiliation from burial evidence may be far more difficult than was until recently assumed. This, of course, raises the question of how fixed and unitary any ethnic (or other) identities were – could one be both a 'Frank' and a 'Roman', for example? Our attention is then turned to the matter of who precisely comprised the intended audience of burial customs. Was it simply the family, or a far wider social group, who assembled at the grave to see the dead lie in their best clothes surrounded by their most treasured objects, for how long did they assemble, and for what reason? But even a sentence such as this contains many preconceptions and assumptions about what was taking place in late antique funerary practices.

In the fifth and sixth centuries most burial took place in cemeteries away from churches, even where that burial seems to have been conducted in a Christian context. By the sixth century most Franks, Goths and sub-Romans buried their dead in inhumation cemeteries. In Gaul these usually took the form of *Reihengräberfelder*, or 'row grave cemeteries'. Very high-status, presumably 'aristocratic', graves have been excavated in these cemeteries, attesting to increased social stratification in late fifth- and early sixth-century Gaul. However, it is still unclear how these are to be interpreted, despite much scholarly attention over the last century. To give an example, it is not known what 'meaning' the owner or depositor attached to the well-known copper-alloy jug from the Germanic cemetery at Lavoye (grave 319). This is impressed with scenes of the Evangelists, but the extent to which this object may have had Christian (or any other) meanings attached to it remains elusive. The same problems of interpretation apply to many other objects, including the ivory comb, possibly of Egyptian origin, that was found at Griesheim in Darmstadt-Dieburg (grave 285). This was decorated with relief carving depicting the wedding at Cana, but it is unclear whether it was deposited in the grave of a Christian.[11]

The Krefeld-Gellep cemetery in Nordrhein-Westfalen, dating from approximately 480 to about 520, also yielded 'aristocratic' graves with grave-goods apparently signalling high status. As at Lavoye and elsewhere, high-status graves sometimes yield weapons decorated with garnet and gold cloisonné work (**colour plate 9**). These have been extensively studied by Birgit Arrhenius, who argues that the high-quality gold and garnet jewelled swords occasionally found in Germanic graves of the late fifth and early sixth century were produced in a central workshop in Constantinople. A Byzantine origin can be posited for some other weapons fittings from Germanic burial contexts prior to the mid-sixth century, especially those produced with the 'cement cloisonné' technique. Even where the garnets were not actually set into the gold cells in the Eastern Mediterranean, they were almost certainly cut there. Arrhenius and others have pointed out that these objects are related to Late Roman military and imperial regalia and probably allude to the perceived adoption of Roman authority by the barbarian élites. Their Byzantine origin could suggest that the Roman authority upon which they relied was one that was current and based in the Eastern Mediterranean, rather than one that related solely to the memory of the Late Roman Empire.[12]

During the course of the sixth century, a small number of high-status individuals founded churches for the express purpose of their own burial. The group of resulting burials – often richly furnished – are referred to as 'founder's graves', even when it is not absolutely clear whether the occupant of the grave was responsible for the founding of the church in which he or she lay. Examples include those at Flonheim in Rheinhessen and Arlon in the Belgian province of Luxembourg. Unfortunately, many were robbed of their artefacts and their archaeology destroyed, sometimes even in Late Antiquity and within days of the funeral. However, where they have been excavated they often provide an excellent archaeological resource in the form of elaborate grave-goods and a detailed knowledge of their depositional context. Here, in the context of our wider theses, we shall confine ourselves to four well-studied examples of graves that have been – with differing degrees of confidence – identified as 'royal'.[13]

The grave of the Frankish king, Childeric[14]

The best-known of these 'royal' graves is not a church burial, and took place in what has traditionally been seen as a pagan context. Yet it is perhaps the most useful in illuminating the question of Byzantine-Western relations in the late fifth century. This is, of course, the grave of the Frankish king, Childeric (d. c.481/2). Childeric was the father of Clovis, the King usually accorded with the unification of the northern Frankish kingdoms and converting the Merovingian dynasty to Christianity. Childeric's grave was, famously, discovered by antiquaries in 1653 at Tournai in Belgium. The tomb yielded particularly spectacular grave-goods, including a seal-ring with the inscription 'CHILDERICI REGIS', which was used to identify its occupant. Although most of the metal (including gold) grave-goods were stolen and melted down in the nineteenth century, careful records made of them before this event suggest that Childeric plainly regarded himself as the inheritor of Roman authority in Gaul. For example, the grave contained a large gold crossbow brooch, commonly seen as the symbol of Roman authority, and used in the Late Roman period as a badge of imperial office. There were also thirty gold and garnet bee motifs, the Roman symbol of eternal life, now sometimes interpreted as having been part of the decoration of a horse harness. Other grave-goods included a bracelet, a large belt buckle and a purse fastener, the latter all fashioned in gold and highly-decorated with cloisonné work of garnets and other semi-precious stones. The tomb was, typically, a 'weapons grave', and so included a range of weapons, among them a throwing axe, a spear, scramasaxe and a sword (**18**).

At first sight, most of this would seem unrelated to the late fifth-century Byzantine East. The 'Roman' symbolism of the grave might be supposed to either be for the consumption of the king's sub-Roman subjects or to hark back to an imagined Roman past. But this is once more thrown into a different light by evidence of contemporary Byzantine contacts. Some of the jewellery

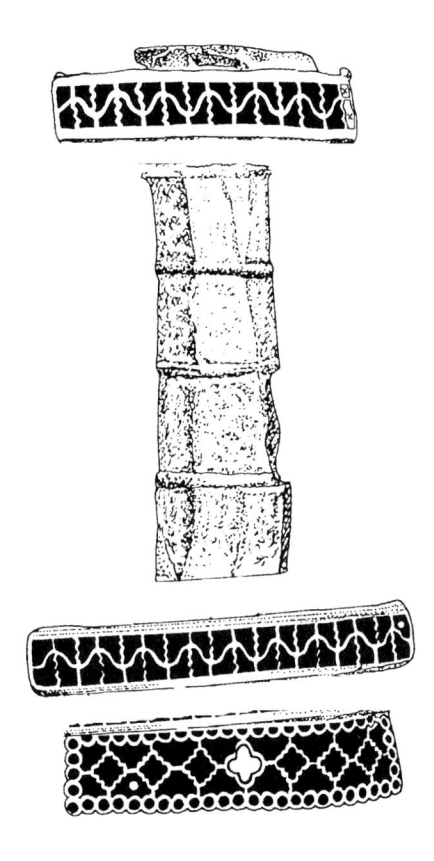

18 *Gold and garnet weapon fittings from Childeric's grave.* After Arrhenius (1985)

may have been of Byzantine origin: the *opus interrasile* gold patterning on the crossbow brooch has been likened to Byzantine jewellery of the late fifth century, and the stepped cloisonné garnets were held in place by a gypsum-based cement that is only attested at Alexandria (and possibly Syria) in this period. In fact, Arrhenius has argued that the gold and garnet fittings in Childeric's grave were not only manufactured in Constantinople, but that they may have been gifts from the imperial court. Michel Kazanski has recently supported a Byzantine origin for them, whilst suggesting that they may have been produced at a workshop associated instead with the imperial court at Ravenna. However, it is unclear how the chemical analysis would fit with this last suggestion. The grave and the area associated with it also yielded 100 Byzantine gold coins and 200 Byzantine silver coins dating from the reign of the Emperor Zeno. That these must have arrived in Frankia during Childeric's reign shows contact, whether direct or indirect, with the Byzantine East and suggests, at the very least, that Childeric's ideas of kingship were framed in the context of these links.[15]

Three hundred coins of the same Emperor can hardly be a chance accumulation and this is an exceptional group in fifth-century Gaul. Other Merovingian graves from the same cemetery yielded nowhere near the same quantity or quality of grave-goods. In fact, it is interesting that even those graves in immediate proximity to that of Childeric were not at all dissimilar – in terms of the range of grave-goods deposited – from many thousands of Germanic inhumations excavated on the Continent. This would suggest that Childeric's burial and the symbolism associated with it could be seen as the archaeological representation of a distinct and discrete Frankish élite.[16]

The Byzantine coins are unlikely to be the product of trade alone and the composition of the assemblage is dissimilar to the diversity usually seen in analogous Western assemblages, insofar as these exist. The coins might, therefore, be seen as a hoard representing a gift to Childeric, presumably from a Byzantine governmental source, for this is a unique grave find and might reasonably merit an exceptional explanation. Clearly, that explanation must encompass a diplomatic initiative from the Byzantine authorities to Childeric in the late fifth century. Given, too, that there are textual references to late fifth-century diplomatic relations with the Franks, as we saw in chapter 2, Childeric's place in the Byzantine political orbit seems secure. In this context, as Malcolm Todd has recently pointed out: 'It is not fanciful to view the imperial overtones evident in this burial as indicative of Byzantium in the politics of the West. It is a short step further to suggest that Childeric had been the recipient of imperial recognition as an allied ruler'.[17]

The royal mausolea of Clovis and Theodoric

It is interesting that Childeric's links with the Eastern Empire seem not to have been facilitated by the Church. Whatever Childeric's religious beliefs, his burial took place in an ostensibly pagan context, including the sacrifice of several horses as part of the funerary ritual. Childeric's son, Clovis, was buried in an entirely different context, marking a clear social change in Frankish society. Indeed, Clovis may have been the first Germanic ruler to be buried in a church: in his case the Church of the Holy Apostles, Paris (later St Geneviève), which he had founded for this express purpose. The church was not built on 'secular' land, but over the tomb of the much-venerated Gallic saint, Geneviève (d. *c*.502), which was already a focus for religious activity. The choice of this church dedication may be far from coincidental: the Byzantine Emperors were buried at the Church of the Holy Apostles in Constantinople from the fourth to the eleventh century, and their church, too, was a focus for the veneration of saintly relics. So Clovis might have established a funerary church with the same dedication in *his* capital to signal that he inhabited a similar cultural and religious world to that of the Byzantine Emperors. More than this, the church and its dedication may have been intended to convey his respect for the imperial throne, whilst ensuring his prestige and status in Gaul by the use of symbols that would be understood as having imperial associations. As we shall see in the following chapter, the Byzantines themselves erected 'copies' of the Holy Apostles church, so Clovis' building activities would not have been interpreted as a usurpation of imperial authority.[18]

Emulation in monarchical architecture was not confined to the Franks. The Ostrogothic élite in Italy was also interested in 'copying' Byzantine imperial funerary models. Theodoric (known as 'the Great'), Clovis' near contemporary in Ostrogothic Italy, was commemorated in a rotunda mausoleum at Ravenna that may have emulated the rotunda mausoleum of Constantine the Great at Constantinople. It is not clear whether the mausoleum was built shortly before or shortly after the death of Theodoric in 526, but it is likely that he had a hand in its design. Still standing, it uses stone to synthesise Late Roman, Gothic and Byzantine architectural models in a way that Richard Krautheimer suggested may have been accomplished by builders brought in from the Byzantine East. If the building depicted in a mosaic at San Apollinare Nuovo in Ravenna is indeed Theodoric's palace, then his preference for employing Eastern architects and builders is all the more likely.[19]

Possibly the two greatest fifth- to sixth-century barbarian kings in Western Europe were, therefore, laid to rest in a fashion appearing to emulate the Byzantine Emperor. One of these may have also lived in a palace having parallels with the imperial palace at Constantinople, built in the same capital city as his mausoleum. So there is little doubt that Western élites could use burial practice to stress their association with the Byzantine court. It has sometimes been assumed this was the empty aping of Byzantine practice, but these signals of association have to be understood in the context of actual diplomatic links with the imperial government, whether or not direct communication took place between these courts on a regular basis. Barbarian rulers, however great, might want to be seen by their subjects as part of the Byzantine world.

Connections with the Byzantine Empire were still being expressed in royal burial at the end of the sixth century. After the reign of Clovis, the Frankish ruling élite was usually buried in churches, where the contexts in which Byzantine objects were placed in graves suggest that they remained symbols of prestige. Thanks to research in the late 1950s and 1960s, there are some excellent examples of royal or princely burials available for study from Cologne and Paris.

The 'Aregundis burial' at Saint-Dénis, Paris[20]

The so-called 'Aregundis burial' was excavated at Saint-Dénis in Paris, an ecclesiastical site with textually-attested Merovingian royal connections. Clovis's Holy Apostles did not attract his successors as a place of burial and the cathedral church of Saint-Dénis became the 'official' burial place of the kings of Frankia after the reign of Dagobert I (d. 639). The Aregundis burial (grave 49) is somewhat earlier, probably dating to the last third of the sixth century. It was interpreted as the grave of the Frankish queen, Aregundis, on the basis of a seal-ring bearing both the name 'Arnegundis' and a monogram that was interpreted as 'REGINA'. There is some doubt over this interpretation, because quite apart from the fact that 'Arnegundis' is not the same as 'Aregundis', 'REGINA' is not the only reading of the monogram inscribed on the ring. Textual evidence places the death of Aregundis – the second wife of Chlothar I (511-561) and the mother of Chilperic I (561-584) – in the 560s, rather earlier than the apparent date of this grave.

This raises the question of how we identify a 'royal grave'. In principle, the ring could have been a gift from the Queen, if indeed its inscription relates to Aregundis at all, and it might have signified the bestowal of royal favour to a trusted kinswoman. Other very high-status graves excavated at Saint-Dénis have yielded 'luxury' items such as silk (see below) and a Byzantine-style buckle. Yet, these have not been interpreted as 'royal'. It is salient to remember here that another high-status barbarian in contact with Constantinople – Attila the Hun – chose to express his royal status by drinking from a wooden cup while those around him drank from gold and silver goblets, and by wearing the simplest costume amongst members of his entourage. Expressions of late antique royalty could plainly be subversive (**19**).[21]

19 *Byzantine-style belt buckle from Saint-Dénis, Paris, sixth century.*
Photograph by RMN, J.G. Berizzi

Moreover, it may be incorrect to make such a direct association between royal status and mortuary practice. Extrapolating from modern preconceptions about royalty and the symbolisation of royal status can easily prompt misleading interpretations. This is succinctly illustrated in a nineteenth-century assessment of the significance of the grave-goods of Childeric. As a result of a series of assumptions about the symbols of monarchy, the bee motifs that may once have decorated a horse harness were embroidered onto the coronation outfit of Napoleon. Napoleon, like the barbarian kings, wanted to emphasise the legitimacy of his rule with reference to an established source of political authority and probably thought that these items had been worn by Childeric himself.[22]

Whoever the occupant of the grave might have been, she was clearly a high-status individual and could well have been a queen. Her grave contained, *inter alia*, two gold pins, a silver gilded pin with inlaid cloisonné garnets, gold earrings, a pair of circular brooches decorated in gold cloisonné with inlaid garnets, a glass bottle, silver belt buckle, again with inlaid garnets, and shoe clasps. The woman was, it seems, buried in a dress of 'violet-blue' silk, with a covering cloak of 'red-brown' silk, which was lined with linen and decorated with red satin and gold braid.

The textile evidence is of special interest here, because the presence of so much silk can only indicate a high level of access to 'luxury' Eastern Mediterranean imports, and the gold braiding reflects some knowledge of Byzantine contemporary design, even if it was not itself of Byzantine origin. Silk was not produced in late sixth-century Frankia, or indeed anywhere else in the West. It is, therefore, more than likely that the fabric was imported via the Byzantine Empire, and probably actually woven there. Whether it had been imported in a trading context or whether it had arrived in Paris as a diplomatic gift cannot be known. Nevertheless, it demonstrates that the Eastern Mediterranean connections visible in the grave of Childeric in the late fifth century were still in evidence in Frankish royal burials over one hundred years later.[23]

The royal graves at Cologne Cathedral[24]

Analogous evidence comes from Cologne. Here, two slab-lined graves were found in 1959 under the choir of the present cathedral. Probably dating to the first half of the sixth century, a *solidus* of Justin I (518-527) in one of the tombs gives a *terminus post quem* of 518. Later excavation demonstrated that these formed part of a small group of graves, although only two still held their contents. Both graves were richly furnished, indicating – along with their location – that their occupants were of extremely high rank, despite one of them having been a child at the time of death, and were likely to have been of royal status.

The contents of grave 808 (that of a woman) included a head-band of gold thread, garnet earrings, a chain, rings for each hand, bracelet, and cloisonné brooches – all worked in gold. A multi-pendant necklace was partially comprised of seven mounted gold coins. Four of these were *solidus* issues of the Emperors Anastasius I and Justin I, while the remaining three were issues of fourth-century Late Roman emperors. On and around the body itself there were more brooches with garnet and gold cloisonné decoration, a silver belt buckle, richly decorated knife, a crystal ball on a gold mount and a spherical silver-gilded pyxide. However, the grave-goods around the coffin were comprised of, arguably, less 'personal' items, such as glass and pottery vessels, a copper-alloy banded wooden bucket, wooden bowls and a class B1 'Coptic' copper-alloy vessel – holding hazelnuts – similar to several found in the Rhineland region. This is, it might be noted, an example of a B1 vessel employed in an explicitly high-status context and with reference to the 'offering' or 'display' of food. The British parallels for this will be discussed in chapter 6.

Grave 809 (interpreted as that of a young boy) was unique insofar as it contained a chair and a bed, both of turned wood, as well as several full-sized weapons, including a sword, lance, shield, bow and arrows, and axes. A child-sized helmet was also found in the tomb, perhaps signalling that its occupant was of 'royal' or near-royal status. It was apparently hanging on the back of the chair. Metallurgical tests on this object showed it to be of Byzantine origin, while Lise Bender Jørgensen has demonstrated that its ring-mail neck guard was lined with a tapestry that also came from Byzantium, possibly Egypt. Tests on the costume from grave 808 have established that this was produced from Byzantine silk and a similar provenance can be posited for the cloak accompanying it.[25]

Although both the Cologne and Saint-Dénis sites yield evidence of Byzantine contacts, in these cases the significance of those contacts is harder to assess without entering into speculation about what may or may not have been intended as a representation of the deceased's royal status. As we shall see in chapter 6, the short necklace worn by the woman in Cologne grave 808 may reflect some knowledge of contemporary Byzantine styles. However, most of the grave-goods cannot be used as evidence of direct Byzantine-Western contacts, let alone the development of 'royal' status in the context of such links. Neither can the use of Byzantine and Late Roman coins as pendants be given any special association, for coins were often employed in this way in the fifth to seventh centuries and not always in overtly high-status contexts. Furthermore, the cloisonné jewellery from these graves was probably produced in a Western workshop, although there are Byzantine parallels with some pieces. In any case, cloisonné work was extremely popular from the mid-sixth century onwards, and so it is difficult to interpret it as having explicitly 'Byzantine' or 'royal' connections. The presence of silk in both female burials and the 'Coptic' tapestry from the tomb of the boy opens what may be a more useful line of enquiry: the circulation of Byzantine textiles in the West.

Tombs and textiles: the importance of silk

The significance of silk in the tombs of the Western late antique élite should not be underestimated. Before about 1200 there were no silk weaving centres in the West and, therefore, silk and silken goods were among the most highly prized items from the East. Even in the Eastern Mediterranean the production of silk was closely regulated and, arguably, a relatively recent innovation. Procopius claims that the silk industry in the Byzantine Empire dated from about 552 when Nestorian monks smuggled some silkworms across Asia and into the Empire. According to his account, traders from 'the East', probably China, had introduced silk production, and thenceforth the Emperor ensured that it remained an imperial monopoly. Within a few years, silkworms were being raised in rural Syria, apparently with successful results, for Justin II is said to have shown Byzantine-produced silk to visiting Persian ambassadors in 568.[26]

This account is often repeated in the scholarly literature but, as Anna Muthesius has pointed out, silk production almost certainly existed in Byzantium before this. The famous description of the embassy to Attila the Hun in about 449 claims that the Emperor Theodosius II sent 'silk garments and Indian gems' from Constantinople to the ambassadors of Attila. Although the gems are accorded an Indian origin, no origin is given for the silk, perhaps permitting us to infer that it was produced 'at home'. This inference may be legitimate, for another source claims that when the Persian ruler, Shapur II, invaded the Syrian provinces of the Empire in 360, he took as hostages the weavers and dyers who worked in the silk industry. This would seem to confirm Hirth's identification of Syria as the mysterious country of 'Da Qin' referred to in some Imperial Chinese annals as having a thriving silk-producing industry, and to suggest that Byzantine silk-production did not have its origins in the reign of Justinian. Rather, production may have increased under Justinian.[27]

It is not merely the rarity of silk in the West that makes it useful evidence for considering Byzantine-Western relations. Byzantine silk production was subject to a state monopoly and, therefore, silks were not supposed to leave the Empire without passing through the hands of official bureaucracy. Moreover, silks dyed in the special imperial 'purple' were subject to an even stricter monopoly. Imperial purple, as we have seen, was produced from the shells of deliberately crushed *Murex trunculus* sea snails, and was closely regulated by the provisions of the Theodosian Code.[28] At least in theory, all silks that were intended as diplomatic gifts were stamped with the seal of the Emperor before they left the Byzantine Empire, although it is possible that some smuggling took place, and evidence of 'clandestine dyeing operations' is enshrined in an edict of 436.[29]

Whether such illegal activities continued is unknown. On the one hand, the stringency of the government investigation into this offence suggests both that it was not a 'one-off' and that there may have been a deterrence value in mind, perhaps to curb a problem of increasing magnitude. On the other hand, it may be that the edict had the intended outcome, and that the purple dye industry was more closely regulated in the fifth and sixth centuries than it had been in the fourth. Justinian I's refortification of the town of Berenice, in Cyrenaica, where imperial dye works were stationed, may suggest continuing imperial interest in controlling the dye industry, especially given that there is little evidence of surplus production for general export. State-sponsored dyeing activities may have continued into the sixth century elsewhere in the East, as in the fifth- to seventh-century 'shops' at Sardis. Recent excavations at Aperlae in Lycia suggest that the town achieved 'moments of prosperity well beyond mere subistence' as a result of the demand for the *Murex trunculus* sea snail that was found in its local waters. Purple dye was also produced at Diaspolis and Dor in the Palestinian provinces.[30]

In this respect, the 'violet-blue' silk dress in the so-called grave of Queen Aregundis is particularly intriguing. One wonders whether this choice of colour was an allusion to the royal connections of the woman or her family, perhaps even to suggest an association with the imperial court in the East. It is not impossible, although it is unlikely, that the dress was made of genuine 'purple' from the imperial weavers at Constantinople and, if so, it was probably in origin a sixth-century diplomatic gift from the Constantinopolitan court. Unfortunately, we cannot know which of these possibilities, if any, was the case. What is better attested, and yet has seldom been commented upon, is the resemblance borne by the 'frieze motifs' on the sleeve of her gown to Byzantine exemplars. This frieze took the form of a series of adjacent roundels, each containing what might be interpreted as a six-pointed star or six-petalled flower. As we shall see in the next chapter, analogous designs are known in the contemporary Eastern Mediterranean, and this might strengthen the case for the gown itself being a Byzantine import, possibly a gift.[31]

This is a rare example of a surviving silk. The fragility of the fabric means that there are few extant silks pre-dating the ninth century, let alone ones retrieved in such a favourable condition. Where they are still available it is difficult to identify them as diplomatic gifts especially where there is no accompanying historical record. Nevertheless, texts make it clear that silk was a highly-prized commodity in the fifth- to seventh-century West, and was often used in ceremonial contexts, such as for altar coverings or other church furnishings, or in religious ceremonies, as at Mérida and Tours. For example, the 'purple silk' curtains at the palace of the mid-fifth-century Visigothic king, Theodoric II, are singled out for praise by Sidonius Apollinaris, although these might not have been made from genuine imperial 'purple'.[32]

Texts also describe silk being used in Byzantine diplomacy with the West, albeit slightly after the end of our period. When the Emperor Constans II travelled to Italy in 662-3 with the intention of re-establishing Byzantine authority there, he presented the Pope with a gold silk *pallium*. In the political and ecclesiastical climate of seventh-century Italy, the meeting with the Pope would have been one of his most important encounters, and it is in this context that the gift should be interpreted. Plainly, it was intended to impress the Pope and encourage him to acknowledge the authority of the Emperor, not least in the face of the Lombard threats to Byzantine-Italian security that were then approaching crisis point. As one of the most prestigious items that the Emperor could bestow, a gift of silk would have emphasised to both parties involved that the imperial court was far superior to any of its Western counterparts. It would have underlined the recipient's subordinate position in relation to the Byzantine Emperor, whilst making it clear that he or she enjoyed the favour of the Emperor (**20**).[33]

Unfortunately, tests for demonstrating whether or not a silk was 'purple' dyed according to this process are not yet advanced, and what fragments of fifth- to seventh-century silk remain from Western contexts have usually not been subjected to them. One should also be aware that some textiles appear

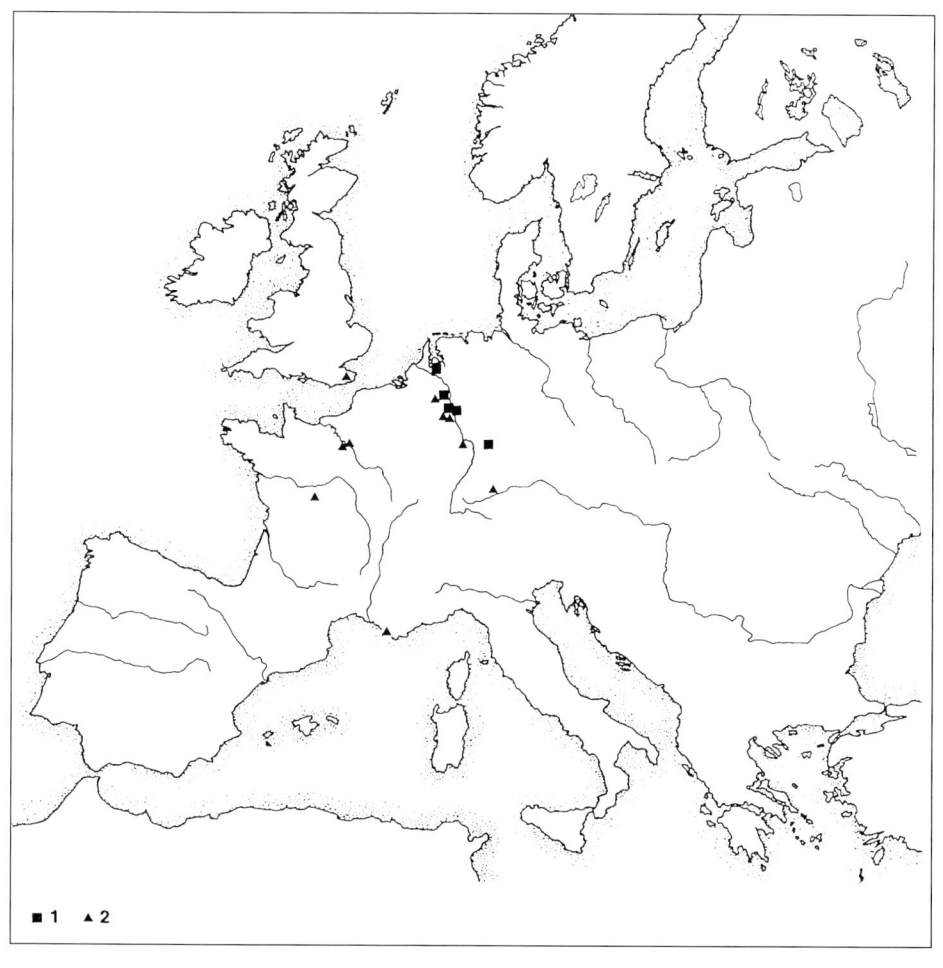

20 *Distribution of Coptic tapestries and Byzantine silks in the fifth- to seventh-century West.* Reproduced with kind permission of Lise Bender Jørgensen

purple when excavated – a result of chemical changes in the ground. In any case, very few silks of this period have been identified archaeologically at all. Bender Jørgensen's research has revealed five from Germany: one, as we have seen, from the 'royal' female grave at Cologne Cathedral, and three others from princely graves at Bedburg-Morken-Harff, Niederstotzingen and Planig. These last three graves all contained helmets and other artefacts indicating that their occupants were of very high rank indeed. A grave from St Severinkloster, also at Cologne, reportedly contained silks.[34]

There is less evidence from France, but in part this must be a reflection of fewer burial context textiles having been analysed and possibly of widespread destruction of cathedral treasuries during the French Revolution. Another grave at Saint-Dénis, in addition to that of 'Aregundis', contained silk, as did a late sixth-century grave (grave 6) at the cemetery at Perruson (Indre-et-Loire). Unusually, the grave of a young woman at St Victor's Abbey, Marseille (grave 20), yielded remarkably well-preserved textile evidence. She had been buried in a long silk tunic, with gold braiding around the collar and the front of the tunic; she also had a silk cloth with fringes and a silk taffeta veil around her head. The body had been wrapped in linen cloth before being placed in the sarcophagus. Associated with the body (indeed, lodged in the bone), was a small Byzantine gold pendant cross with flared arms and jewels, which has been identified as Syrian. It is not clear in all these cases whether the silks are Byzantine or Persian in origin, but the weight of the other evidence renders a Byzantine origin more likely. Anyway, they would probably have arrived in the West through the hands of Byzantine intermediaries even if they had been produced in Persia (**21**).[35]

Muthesius's extensive work on the silks in Western cathedral treasuries has revealed more Byzantine silks that may have been in the West before about 650. In general, these are distributed among cathedral treasuries in Germany

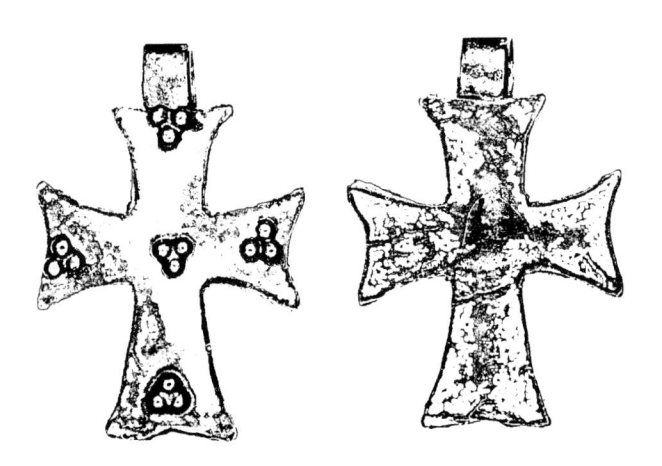

21 *Byzantine ('Syrian') cross from Saint-Victor, Marseille (grave 20). After Boyer et al. (1987)*

22 *'Daniel in the lions' den' silk, sixth- or seventh-century Byzantine. This shows a figure with arms raised, a fluted column and two lions. Byzantine textiles may have provided a template for artistic and architectural styles in the West.* Reproduced with the kind permission of the Victoria and Albert Museum

and Switzerland, and there is a faint but intriguing correlation with the Rhine-Alpine route from the East that went through eastern Gaul. Some of the silks have Early Christian motifs, such as the 'Daniel in the lions' den' silk (previously in Germany) and the 'Joseph' silk from Sens Cathedral. The silks with pastoral scenes, such as those from St Maurice and Sitten, both in Switzerland, and the so-called 'Dancer silks' from Sens and St Maurice have also been dated to the sixth to seventh century (**22**).[36]

A similar range of dates may be appropriate for the low number of silks with small-scale foliate, geometric and animal designs. These are found in the cathedral treasuries at Chur and St Maurice in Switzerland, and also at Sens. A silk from St Maurice depicting horses feeding has been likened to the horses on the Great Palace mosaic in Constantinople. Chur was an important town in Late Antiquity insofar as it stood at a crossroads for travellers crossing the Alps and it is quite plausible that the textiles in the cathedral treasury there had arrived in the locality by the mid-seventh century. So-called 'Achmim' silks, such as the one from the shrine of St Servatius, Maastricht, with characteristic fragile foliage designs, may also date from this period, but since they were probably produced up until the tenth century they cannot be considered here as evidence for Byzantine-Western relations. 'Antinoe' silks, whose defining characteristic is a synthesis of Classical and Sassanian motifs, may be of Byzantine – possibly Egyptian or Syrian – origin and of a seventh-century date, but this is unclear. Several examples of this type have been found at Sens (**23**).[37]

Tombs and textiles: other Byzantine textiles in Western graves

We have already noted the 'Coptic' tapestry in the grave of the young boy from Cologne Cathedral. While this was once thought to be the only example of such a textile from a fifth- to seventh-century Western context, Bender Jørgensen's work has now identified a small number of other sites with similar tapestries. One important grave at St Severinkloster (Cologne) yielded a 'Coptic' tapestry, the two possible silks already mentioned, an 'Oriental carpet', and a gold brocaded band and string, all of which may have come from the Byzantine Empire. A piece of fabric from grave 1351 at Krefeld-Gellep on the lower Rhine has been tentatively identified as similar to the Cologne cathedral tapestry, although the piece is so small and fragile that this cannot be confirmed. Grave 40 at Niedernberg (Bavaria) and (outside the former Roman world) a grave from Rhenen (Utrecht) also yielded textiles identified as tapestries originating in the Byzantine Empire. Finally, the well-known so-called

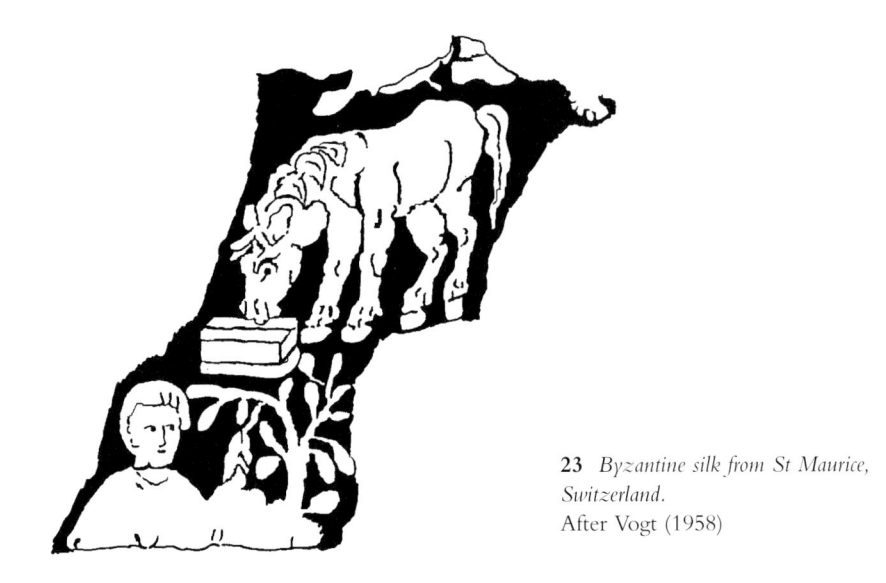

23 *Byzantine silk from St Maurice, Switzerland.*
After Vogt (1958)

'Chemise de Sainte-Balthilde' from Chelles uses silk thread to embroider a Byzantine-style cross 'pendant' on the front of the garment. This is thought to date between 640 and 665 and has been used, by Hayo Vierk and others, partly as a basis on which to suggest the emulation of Byzantine court fashions on the part of the Frankish élite in the mid-seventh century.[38]

The textile evidence is particularly interesting in the light of Anthony Cutler's work on gift-exchange in the Middle Byzantine period. He has recently demonstrated that in their diplomacy with the Arab kingdoms the Byzantines used gifts of clothes as part of their negotiations to a far greater extent than Byzantine written sources might lead us to expect. These could acquire added significance in diplomatic exchange if they had previously been worn by a person perceived to be of particular importance, whether it be a prince or a monk. In such a case, the item of clothing in question might not, at first glance, appear 'high-status', yet would, to all intents and purposes, be an extremely valuable artefact. It is likely that similar attitudes prevailed in Late Antiquity.[39]

There is, in summary, some evidence for the export of Byzantine silk and other textiles to the West, perhaps as diplomatic gifts rather than as traded commodities, at least in the case of silk. Yet, it is instructive that the numbers of silks in the West before about 650 are few compared to the evidence for silk exportation in the latter part of the seventh century and all of the eighth and ninth centuries. This is probably not merely a reflection of Byzantine trading practices, for silk exports to the West increased at the very same time that the export of other Byzantine objects, such as copper-alloy vessels, declined. The presence of Byzantine silks in the West after *c.*650 may be a reflection of increased Byzantine-Western diplomatic activities, either secular or religious. As noted in chapter 2, diplomatic marriage negotiations – to give but one example – became more plentiful in the eighth and ninth centuries than they had been in the fifth to seventh centuries, and this may reflect increased insecurity in the Byzantine-Western relationship. So the evidence gained from silk might also point to a qualitative change in contacts between the Byzantine Empire and the West after *c.*650.[40]

The numismatic evidence for East–West contacts

Although textiles add further evidence of Byzantine contacts with Western élites, by far the most plentiful evidence for the links between Western kingship and the Byzantine court is provided by gold coinage. As élite objects (the majority of the population would not have had to make transactions involving gold coins), these were a material expression of late antique kingship. Gold coinage is, therefore, another potential source for illuminating Western attitudes to the Byzantine court.

Coinage served both economic and propaganda purposes, as Richard Reece's extensive work on Roman and post-Roman coinage has emphasised. During Late Antiquity, coinage was used in a variety of ways: as payment for goods, to pay taxes, and as grants to 'client' rulers. It was also, of course, used as bullion. The golden salver encrusted with gems that Chilperic proudly showed Gregory of Tours and which he had had made 'for the greater glory and renown of the Frankish people' may have been made from melted down gold coins. Joachim Werner demonstrated that the melting down of coins took place in Late Antiquity by pointing out that the weight of barbarian gold bracelets often corresponds to a precise number of *solidi*, suggesting that these, too, were produced from melted down gold coins. In this way, the bracelets would have become the material representation of a person's wealth.[41]

Coins were also hoarded as an indicator of wealth and prestige, and placed in graves for the same purposes – witness the many Byzantine coins in Childeric's grave at Tournai – and the practice of converting Roman coins into jewellery, particularly pendants, continued into the fifth and sixth centuries. Similarly, unless this social purpose is recognised, it might seem curious that between 430 and 450 the Huns, who had no use for currency in their indigenous economy, accepted payments from the Emperor Theodosius II in the form of nearly 40,000 pounds of gold coin. The Huns had no intention of putting this coin into circulation for trading purposes, and buried it for future security. Remarkably, a hoard of 1,437 coins was discovered in Hungary in 1963, thought to be an almost intact tribute payment from Emperor Theodosius II, just three coins short of the original number (1,440).[42]

Plainly, gold coins served both economic and social purposes. Coin design, however, as well as the question of where it was minted and in whose name, is also readily linked to political considerations. The design of a coinage served both to set a kingdom apart from its neighbours and to emphasise the commonalities between them. It had implications, too, for domestic politics. This is seen, for example, in the civil conflict in Visigothic Spain that ensued in *c.*579 when the position of the Visigothic ruler, Leovigild, was challenged by his son, Hermenigild. One of Hermenigild's first actions was to mint coins in his own name, suggesting that this would legitimise his royal authority. Leovigild responded to his son by issuing new coins, each with *his* own name on them. The haphazard manner in which Leovigild's name is stamped on these coins suggests that this measure was undertaken with some urgency. Not to be outdone, Hermenigild then issued another coin, this time with an inscription according divine sanction to his actions. Again, the message is clear: coinage was an important vehicle for conveying messages about the source of political authority and legitimacy.[43]

It is also of interest to this argument – although outside its chronological remit – that the Empress Irene (797-802), whose hold on the Byzantine throne was decidedly tenuous, not least because she was female, chose to put an image of herself on both sides of imperial gold coins. This was a radical departure from the contemporary Byzantine practice, where Christ's image was usually placed on the obverse, and suggests that the imperial mint was attempting to reinforce perceptions of the Empress's legitimacy. Interestingly, Irene used the masculine term *basileus*, rather than the feminine *basilissa*, almost certainly for the same reasons.[44]

Some 80 years before the events in Visigothic Spain, in 498, the Emperor Anastasius I implemented a far-reaching change in the coinage system, creating what is generally regarded as the 'Byzantine' currency. It was based closely on the old Roman system and Constantine I's *solidus*, but with lower denomination coins produced in greater multiples, and the weights of the high denominations approximately doubled. The next denomination down from the *solidus* (called *nomisma* by Greek-speakers) was the *semissis* (half a *solidus*) and the *tremissis* (one third of a *solidus*). These coins were minted only in gold until the seventh century, when the Emperor Heraclius re-introduced silver (615), but throughout the period smaller denominations were minted in bronze. These included *nummi* and theoretically there were about 7,200 *nummi* to the *solidus*, although this was never strictly enforced. Forty *nummi* made up one *follis*. The monetary system instituted by Anastasius remained remarkably stable until the tenth century, providing a basis for international trade across the Empire and even beyond. Cosmas Indicopleustes, a former merchant operating out of sixth-century Alexandria, wrote: 'All the nations, from one end of the Earth to the other, trade with Roman money. This money is appreciated by all men, whatever the kingdom to which they belong, because no currency like this exists in any other country of the world'. Although obviously not true – the Persians and other empires minted their own coins during the sixth century – Indicopleutes's words evoke an impression of the importance of Byzantine coinage during these centuries (**24** & **25**).[45]

The West had access to Roman coinage throughout the traumatic fifth century and specifically Eastern Roman coinage from 476 onward. Apart from in Britain, gold coinage appears to have been relatively plentiful until the seventh century when silver became the dominant metal for the production of currency. However, the status of the *solidus* as the premier unit of currency remained high, even outside the former Roman world, and there are numerous references in texts to barbarian kings and other élites giving and receiving large sums of money in cash. For example, an archdeacon at Marseille was fined 4,000 *solidi* for stealing oil and fish sauce from a merchant there, although it is unclear whether we should assume that the archdeacon had this sort of money available to him. Yet, when the King heard of the incident, the governor of Provence (who had heard the case) was himself fined 16,000 *solidi*, because he had arrested the archdeacon as he took the Christmas Day service.[46]

Clovis gave a more 'realistic' 200 *solidi* to the poor via the church of St Martin in Tours when he returned from defeating Alaric and crushing the

24 Solidus *of Justinian I (527-565)*. Reproduced with the kind permission of The British Museum

25 Tremissis *of Justinian I (527-565)*. Reproduced with the kind permission of The British Museum

Visigothic kingdom of Toulouse in 507. The following year when he received the *ex consulate* title there, he apparently had enough gold and silver coins to 'shower' them on the people of Tours. Clovis was almost certainly distributing Byzantine (or imitation Byzantine) coins, perhaps acquired in Bordeaux, where he had spent the preceding winter, and where there was a community of Byzantine merchants. It is possible that he had acquired the coin specifically from this group, either in commercial exchange or as part of a political payment. In distributing coin to the people, Clovis was acting against the imperial legislation of 452 that forbade consuls from distributing silver in their processions. The distribution of gold was also strictly prohibited, this being the prerogative of the Emperor. Yet, this does not appear to have been a conscious violation of the Emperor's position for, as we saw in chapter 2, even Gregory of Tours did not comment on it.[47]

1 *Porphyry statute depicting the emperors and their deputies after the division of the Empire. Fourth century, from Constantinople, now in Venice.* Reproduced with the kind permission of Zoë Harris

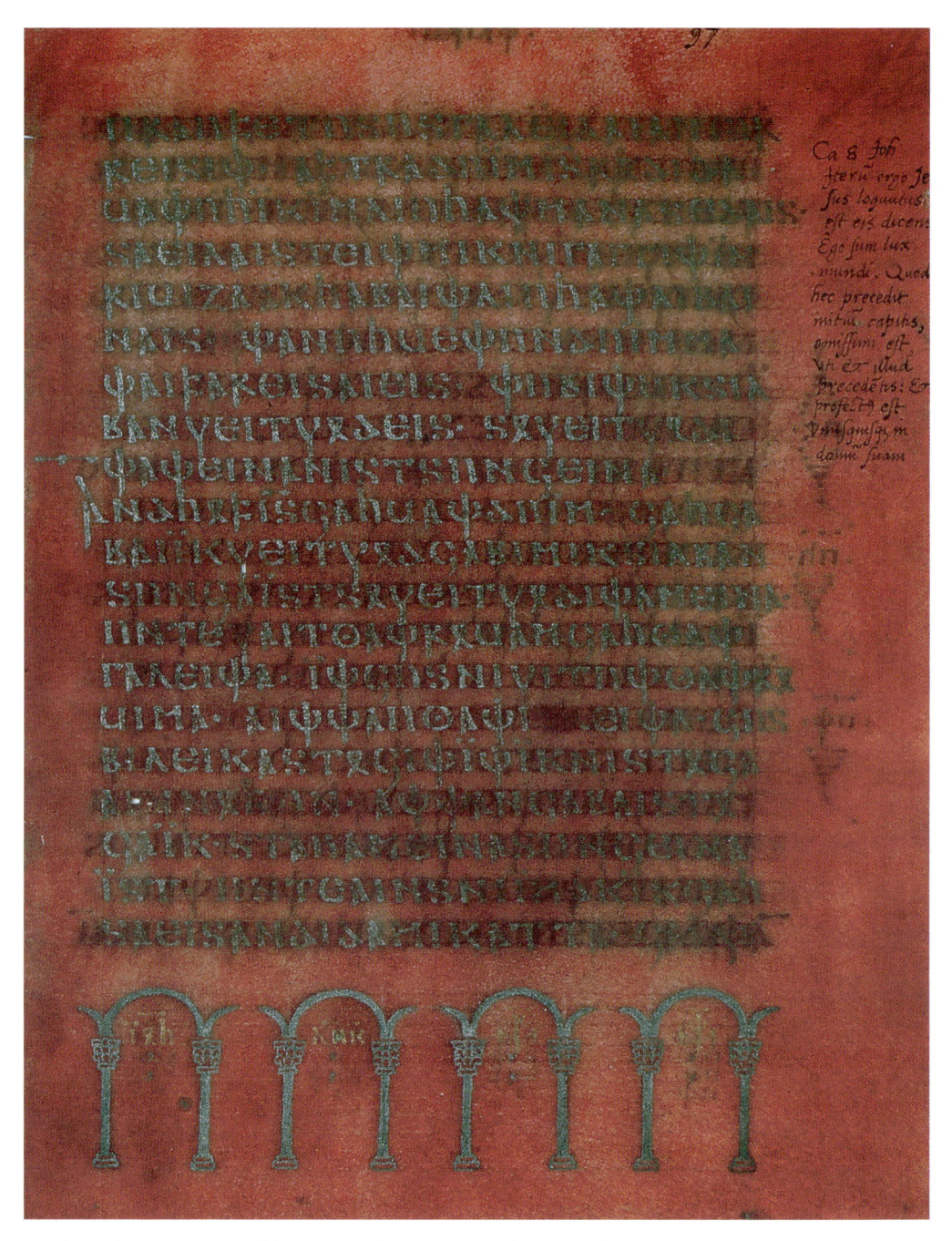

2 The Codex Argenteus, *a fifth-century Bible in the Gothic language. This folio is John 7:52 and 8:12-17 (Folio 97r). The Ostrogothic king, Theodoric, may have commissioned this manuscript.* Copyright Uppsala University Library

3 *Stylites' column base at Qal'at Si'man*. Reproduced with the kind permission of Stuart Whatling

4 *Byzantine column capital from Arles, southern France.* Copyright Musée de l'Arles Antique

5 *Sixth- or seventh-century St Menas flask from Arles in southern France.* Copyright Musée de l'Arles Antique

6 *Crowns from the Guarrazar Treasure, Spain. The giving of votive crowns shows the Visigothic monarchy drawing on Byzantine concepts of authority.* Copyright Archivo Fotográfico, Museo Arqueológico Nacional, Madrid

7 *Seventh-century jewelled gold cross from the Guarrazar Treasure, which would have been suspended from a votive crown. Richly decorated objects like these may have been used as diplomatic gifts by the Byzantine court.* Photograph by RMN, Franck Raux

8 *Sixth-century Byzantine solidus, found at Famars, northern France (obverse and reverse).* Photograph by RMN, R.G. Ojeda

9 *Gold and garnet fittings from a 'chiefly' grave at Lavoye (grave 319). 'Luxury' objects found in high-status barbarian burials often have associations with Roman military regalia, but to a sixth-century Western ruler* romanitas *may have meant identifying with the Byzantine East.* Photograph by RMN, Gérard Blot

10 The late fourth-century Church of San Nazaro, Milan, formerly the Church of the Holy Apostles and a possible 'copy' of the similarly dedicated church in Constantinople. Photograph by Anthea Harris

11 The late fourth-century church of San Simpliciano, Milan, another example of an early cruciform building. Photograph by Anthea Harris

12 *Hagia Sophia, Istanbul. Built by Justinian I in the mid-sixth century, it was the focal point of Christian worship and ceremonial in Constantinople.* Photograph by Anthea Harris

13 *Decorated stone capital from San Pedro de la Nave, Zamora, Spain. The depiction of animals on capitals and the use of filled roundel motifs have parallels in the fifth- to seventh-century Byzantine Empire.* Reproduced with the kind permission of Roger Collins

14 *Santa María de Quintanilla de las Viñas, Lara, Spain. The decorative frieze has parallels with sculpture in late antique Syria.* Photograph Scala, Florence

15 *Late Antique stone structures at Tintagel, Cornwall.* Reproduced with the kind permission of Ken Dark

16 *Detail of sculptured roundel with chi-rho/alpha and omega monogram, from the monastary of St Symeon Stylites.* Reproduced with the kind permission of Stuart Whatling

17 *Fourth-century glass flask from an Anglo-Saxon inhumation at High Down, Ferring. The deposition of this object may have been intended to express identity with the still existing 'Roman' world in the East, rather than a long-gone Western Roman Empire.* Copyright Worthing Museum and Art Gallery

18 Sixth-century 'Buckle of Saint-Césaire', from Arles, southern France. The buckle depicts the Byzantine church of the Holy Sepulchre at Jerusalem. Copyright Musée de l'Arles Antique

19 Pilgrim flask from the shrine of St Menas (Egypt), found at Meols, Wirral. Pilgrims travelling from Britain to the Eastern Mediterranean are attested in contemporary texts. Reproduced with the kind permission of David Griffith

20 Tintagel, Cornwall. Many thousands of sherds of Byzantine pottery, including amphorae and finewares, have been excavated here. Reproduced with the kind permission of Ken Dark

21 Possible eremitical site at Lavret (Îles de Bréhat, Brittany). A sherd of Late Roman 1 amphora was recovered here. Reproduced with kind permission of Ken Dark

22 *Mosaic depicting Classe Harbour at the sixth-century Byzantine church of San Vitale, Ravenna. Ships similar to these probably sailed as far as Britain.* Photograph by Scala, Florence

23 *Reconstructed neck and shoulders of a Late Roman 1 Byzantine amphora from Bantham, Devon. This and similar amphorae would have probably brought oil and wine from the Eastern Mediterranean to British shores.* Copyright Exeter Archaeology

24 *Bantham Bay, south Devon. Many sherds of fifth- and sixth-century Byzantine ceramics have been excavated here.* Copyright Tim Stanger/Devonscapes

25 *'Pseudo-imperial' solidus of Anastasius I (491-518) from Hampshire. Late Roman and Byzantine coins were often made into pendants during Late Antiquity.* Reproduced with the kind permission of Hampshire Portable Antiquities Scheme

26 *Byzantine copper-alloy 'bucket' (situla), found in a high-status Anglo-Saxon grave in Hampshire.* Reproduced with the kind permission of Hampshire Portable Antiquities Scheme

27 *Gold and garnet buckle from the Taplow mound burial.* Reproduced with the kind permission of The British Museum

28 *Seventh-century gold and garnet disc pendant with filigree gold cross, from the Anglo-Saxon cemetery at Lechlade (grave 95/1). Gold and garnet jewellery may have had associations with the 'Roman' world that was still flourishing in the Eastern Mediterranean.* Reproduced with the kind permission of Oxford Archaeology

It might be expected that the barbarian élites would develop their own coinage systems in the late fifth and early sixth centuries, or continue to produce copies of (Western) Late Roman *solidi*. However, this was not the case. Instead, coins were produced that were often remarkably similar to those being produced in contemporary Constantinople. In design, notably, both barbarian *tremisses* and *solidi* of the late fifth and early sixth century appear to have been produced in direct emulation of Byzantine coins. The Western versions were often – but not always – lighter than their Eastern prototypes, and closer to the Byzantine *tremissis* in weight. Yet, this should not cause us to doubt their similarity with their Byzantine prototypes. The Byzantine Empire itself issued 'lightweight' *solidi* from the reign of Justinian, a fact that has sometimes caused some confusion in the identification of these coins.[48]

Theodoric the Ostrogoth, one of the most important figures in Western politics of this period, minted *solidi* that conformed very closely to Eastern Roman models. These bore the Emperor's name on the obverse, together with a facing bust of the Emperor, while the reverse bore a left-facing depiction of Victory carrying a cross. When found today, they are distinguishable from actual Byzantine coins only by the monogram of Theodoric that is carried on the reverse. Even this is absent from issues of gold *tremisses* of his reign, which are distinguishable from Byzantine *tremisses* only by small stylistic differences. Theodoric's silver coins (the Ostrogoths were unusual in this period in issuing their own silver as well as gold currency) also carry his personal monogram.

In addition, Theodoric minted – in about 509 – a gold coin (or, more accurately, a medallion) bearing an image of himself. He is portrayed as long-haired and with a moustache, very much as the 'Gothic', rather than the late antique 'romanized', ruler. On the reverse is a depiction of Victory and the title 'REX'. The issue of this coin would appear to be inconsistent with his 'client' status of the Byzantine Emperor, but the coin was probably not intended to circulate outside Italy and, therefore, it should not be invested with too much importance in this respect. Moreover, it is not entirely clear how the inscription 'REX' would have been perceived by the Byzantines; after all, at least one Byzantine text also refers to him in this way. The term was sometimes used to indicate the *augustus*, or Emperor, and its use in a Byzantine context is somewhat curious, to say the least. Whatever the reason for the employment of this terminology, the coin is probably irrelevant for our purposes here, because the issuing of medallions was a Late Roman tradition, carried on far into Late Antiquity and, arguably, Theodoric was merely standing in this tradition as an expression of his 'Roman' affinity with the East.[49]

The gold coins of Theodoric's successors in Italy do not include the monogram of the king. Instead, these were minted in the Byzantine style and are, to all intents and purposes, 'pseudo-imperial'. Theodoric's successor and grandson, Athalaric, did put his monogram on the reverse of silver coins, but given that the Byzantine Empire did not mint silver coins in the sixth century, this, arguably, was consistent with the Ostrogothic kingdom's position as a 'client' of the Empire.

Like the Ostrogothic 'pseudo-imperial' *solidi*, other equivalent Western-minted *solidi* usually carry a facing bust of the Eastern Emperor on the obverse, as well as his name. The reverse carries a left-facing personification of Victory and appropriate inscription, as well as the Constantinople mint mark. With few exceptions, they do not carry the monogram of the ruler in whose territory they originate, and are often difficult to distinguish from genuine Byzantine *solidi* of approximately the same date. *Tremisses* were also minted in the name of the Eastern Emperor and these may have been more common than *solidi*, which would only have been used for large transactions. They carry the name and bust of the Emperor on the obverse (either facing to the front or the right), while the Victory depicted on the reverse either faces left or to the front. Again, they also bear an acronym for the Constantinople mint.

Ironically, what sometimes renders 'pseudo-imperial' Western gold coins identifiable in the archaeological or numismatic record is their acronym for the Constantinople mint, which is often erroneous. Rather than bearing the acronym 'CON' or 'CONOB' (the stamp of the mint at Constantinople), the Western coins often bear the distortion 'COMOB' or 'COHOB'. There has been some discussion as to whether 'COMOB' stood for *comes obryzi* (Treasury Official), but Philip Grierson and Mark Blackburn have argued that this is unlikely to have been the case.[50]

Given that even during the Roman period there had never been a centralised imperial mint, the phenomenon of the 'pseudo-imperial' coins is a unique expression of Byzantine cultural – and perhaps political – influence. In fact, under Roman rule there had been at least 18 urban centres where coins had been minted, about half of which were in the West, although they were not all in use simultaneously. They included Arles, Trier, Lyon, Milan, Aquileia, Rome, Ravenna (after 402) and Barcelona in the West; Carthage in North Africa; Siscia, Sirmium and Thessaloniki in the Balkans; and Heracleia, Constantinople, Nicomedia, Cyzius, Antioch and Alexandria in the Eastern Mediterranean. As the fifth century progressed, however, the imperial mints throughout the Western Roman Empire were gradually closed – for example, Trier, Arles and Aquileia were shut down in the early fifth century, and as early as 441 Frankish *solidi* were minted in the name of the Emperor Valentinian III with the mint mark, 'COMOB.' The same erroneous mint mark appears on a *tremissis* of the penultimate Western Roman Emperor, Julius Nepos, recently found at Oxborough in Norfolk. By the end of the century, 'genuine' imperial gold coins were minted at Constantinople alone and, it would seem, Western élites were still anxious to use coin that purported to originate from the Eastern capital, even if it meant passing by an opportunity to advertise their own authority.[51]

Had Western élites been drawing on some notion of past *romanitas* in order to legitimise their monetary systems, they would probably have chosen the mint marks of Western Roman, not Eastern Roman, mints. Indeed, this may well have been the easier thing to do, given that Late Western Roman minting technologies may have been more available to them than contemporary Eastern ones. The many finds of misshapen 'pseudo-imperial' coins, usually with blundered inscriptions, attest this. That élites chose to use the mint mark of Constantinople and the image of the Eastern Roman Emperors indicates that they were looking not only to an extant tradition of *romanitas*, but one that was consciously focused on the Eastern government, for pragmatic reasons or otherwise. In choosing to align themselves with the Byzantine capital, Western élites were acknowledging it as the ultimate source of political authority even in the West. In other words, they looked to Eastern Roman – Byzantine – traditions to express *romanitas*, rather than wholly pre-fifth-century legacies.

Of course, if 'pseudo-imperial' coins had simply been intended for use in 'international' trade, issues of *romanitas* would be irrelevant. If their design aided their commercial usefulness one could argue that an attempt to produce coins exactly like those minted in Constantinople was motivated purely by economic concerns, and that political considerations played no (or very little) part in their design. That is to say, it would have been easier for Westerners to participate in the international economy if their coin was accepted as legal tender in Byzantium.

However, this does not seem to have been the case. Grierson has argued that coinage was not extensively used in long-range commerce in Late Antiquity. Commercial exchange usually took place in kind, and *solidi* were only used to make very large purchases, such as land (and to make tax and salary payments). Moreover, Byzantine archaeological sites have not, to my knowledge, yielded any Western 'pseudo-imperial' coins, despite hundreds of thousands of other coin finds from across the region. Of course, there is a danger that Western imitation *solidi* and *tremisses* have been mistaken for the very Byzantine coins they purport to be, and excavators on Eastern sites must be aware of the existence and distinguishing marks of these Western coins. However, as noted above, very many 'pseudo-imperial' coins are distorted and their inscriptions blundered, features that should quickly draw attention to them were they to be found on Eastern sites.[52]

It is instructive then, that a brief survey of the coin finds from over ten Byzantine sites, including major settlements such as Constantinople, Sardis, Pergamon, Ephesus, Corinth, Antioch, Beirut and Athens reveals no identified finds of Western 'pseudo-imperial' coins (*solidi* or *tremisses*). This would, again, suggest that these were not intended for international trade. No 'pseudo-imperial' Western coins have been found in Israel either, although coins with the mint marks of Ravenna and Rome have been found in post-fifth-century deposits, such as at Sumaqa (Carmel). Indeed, only four out of the 960 *solidi* for this period registered in the collection of the Israel Antiquities

Authority are from Western mints, and these are not from mints further west than northern Italy. It is hardly surprising that Italian coins should be represented on Israeli sites, since Ravenna, Rome and their hinterlands were effectively 'Byzantine' for much of this period. On the contrary, given how much the Byzantine territorial holdings in the West were linked to other parts of the former Roman West, it is surprising that they do not appear on late antique Eastern Mediterranean sites in greater quantities.[53]

In economic terms, therefore, the 'pseudo-imperial' coins were probably intended for circulation in the West alone, mainly for transactions between Western élites, including salary and tax payments. Perhaps, too, they were intended to serve a social and political purpose as much as an economic one. The most likely explanation for their peculiarly 'Byzantine' design is that they reflect a Western belief that the only *legitimate* mint for the minting of *solidi* was in Constantinople. That is to say, the legitimating political authority for the coinage was not represented as the Western kings, but as the imperial mint at Constantinople. These were not simply 'Western' coins, but Western coins purporting to be Byzantine coins supporting the authority of Western élites. In other words, the authority of the Western kings was being projected as deriving from the authority of the Byzantine Emperor.

A 'political' explanation of this kind might also go some way towards explaining why Western coins were sometimes minted in the name of a particular Emperor when that Emperor's reign had already ended. This phenomenon is known as 'type immobilisation'. In early sixth-century Burgundy, for example, before the territory passed into Frankish rule, Gundomar II minted coins in the name of the Emperor Justin I, and continued to do so, even though Justin died early in Gundomar's reign (527). This would suggest that the Burgundians were not in close contact with the Constantinopolitan court and, therefore, not under imperial pressure to mint coins in the Emperor's name. That is to say, it would appear that the primary impetus for the minting of these coins came from Burgundian internal political dynamics, rather than the need to participate in a Byzantine-dominated economic system. Although they may have encountered Byzantine traders at Lyon, the lack of Burgundian coins on Byzantine archaeological sites suggests that the coins were probably of no great importance when trading with the Eastern Mediterranean, directly or otherwise.[54]

In the second quarter of the sixth century, one Frankish King usurped the implicit authority of the Eastern Emperor by minting a gold *solidus* in his own name. The King in question, Theodebert I (534-548), had just attacked Byzantine-controlled areas of northern Italy, and it may have been in order to make a political point that his coin carried epithets appropriate only to the imperial office (including 'VICTOR'). It is notable that Theodebert went to some lengths to mint this *solidus*, for Frankish rulers of the period did not appear particularly anxious to monopolise the minting of coin. Minting rights were usually shared with other regional authorities and moneyers.[55]

Theodebert's *solidi* are an anomaly, for almost all other Frankish gold coins in the first half of the sixth century and until after the reign of Justinian are 'pseudo-imperial', with no indication of the Frankish ruler responsible for its issue. Curiously, Procopius, hearing of Theodebert's coin issue, made an impassioned response to his actions, and condemned them as 'illegal'. Why Procopius should have accused Theodebert of having broken Byzantine law – presumably this is the law to which he refers – when by the mid-sixth century the Franks were no longer under Byzantine jurisdiction is unclear. The accusation would suggest that Procopius, who was after all close to the Constantinopolitan court, believed Theodebert to have challenged the position of the Emperor and that this was outside the acceptable limits of behaviour. We do not know whether he thought the Frankish King was claiming to govern the whole 'Roman Empire', the former Roman West or some other territorial entity. Either way, however, Procopius implied that the constitutional position of the Western kingdoms in the mid-sixth century was unambiguously the business of the Emperor in Constantinople.[56]

By the 570s and 580s, most Western rulers had begun to develop so-called 'national' coinages – with the exception of Britain where an indigenous coinage system was not developed until much later and is, therefore, irrelevant to the argument presented here. The new 'national' coins were stamped not only with the names or monograms of their issuer, but the mint at which they were produced. In many cases, especially in Frankia, this meant the name or monogram of the moneyer rather than the local ruler. The name of the Emperor was quietly dropped.

With few exceptions, most élites adopted the *tremissis* as the centre-piece of their currencies, although large sums of money were still valued in *solidi*. For example, when the early seventh-century Frankish king, Dagobert I, was refused the precious gold platter he had been promised by the Visigoth, Sisenand, in return for help in deposing Swintila from the Spanish throne, he apparently accepted instead the sum of 200,000 *solidi*. The author of the *Chronicle of Fredegar* tells us that Dagobert 'weighed the amount carefully' (**26 & 27**).[57]

However, the rulers of Provence continued to mint 'pseudo-imperial' *solidi* until about 613, and thereafter minted *solidi* in their own names. The special position of Marseille as a port city receiving goods – and revenue – from all over the Mediterranean may partly explain its rulers' reluctance to forgo minting *solidi*. In any case, the *tremissis* appears to have been the main unit of monetary exchange in seventh-century Provence and this was now minted in the name of the king. Nevertheless, it retained its typological similarities to Byzantine *tremissis* for several years. The reverse of the new coins carried the mint mark of the city in which they were minted – including Vienne, Valence, Viviers and Marseille – as well as the Byzantine-derived symbols of a cross and a globe, while the obverse carried the image of the King and his inscribed name. Ironically, the bust on most seventh-century Provençal coins was the

26 Tremissis *issued in Spain from a Visigothic mint.*
Reproduced with the kind permission of The British Museum

27 Solidus *issued by the Frankish king, Chlothar II (584-628/9).*
Reproduced with the kind permission of The British Museum

same as that which had hitherto accompanied the name of the Emperor, suggesting that, if the bust had been modelled on a true likeness of the Byzantine Emperor, then Frankish coins continued to carry a portrait of the Emperor, even after their 'nationalisation'![58]

The Visigoths had, by the late sixth century, also developed a coinage that both acknowledged the wider authority of the Eastern Emperor and emphasised the importance of the Visigothic monarchy. Indeed, Leovigild of Spain was the first Western European ruler to develop a 'national' coinage; that is, to put his own name on the coinage in place of the Emperor's. He also standardised the weight of his coins against that of the Frankish coinage, rather than the old 'Roman' standard. While the significance of this development in the consolidation of the Visgothic state should not be underestimated, it must also be seen in the context of Leovigild's domestic troubles vis-à-vis his son Hermenigild, and his need to secure his political position, and may not wholly be a reflection of change in Byzantine-Western relations.

Like most other Western ruling élites, Leovigild continued a form of deference to Constantinople insofar as he stopped minting *solidi* at all, rather than mint them in his own name. Given that the Byzantine Empire retained the *solidus* as a basic unit of exchange until far beyond the end of our period, it cannot be said that the *solidus* had become meaningless in economic or political terms. Western rulers' failure to copy it cannot be interpreted as an indication that it was no longer relevant to Western society, especially as long as the rest of the coinage remained based on another unit of the Byzantine monetary system, the *tremissis*. Neither can it be seen in terms of the cessation of the *solidus's* circulation in the barbarian kingdoms. Coin hoards demonstrate that Byzantine *solidi* were available in the West until at least the early 640s, some 60 years after 'national' coinages first started to emerge. However, it cannot be seen straightforwardly as an adherence to imperial monopoly either. From the seventh century, a stricture in the gold supply meant that silver became more important in the Byzantine monetary system and so adjustments in the Western system must also reflect this.[59]

Nevertheless, it would seem, as Grierson has suggested, that the right to mint *solidi* was, and remained, an implicit monopoly of the Byzantine Empire. Although the Western kingdoms were outside *de facto* Byzantine jurisdiction, the rulers of Germanic kingdoms did not presume to infringe this Byzantine right. That lower denomination 'national' coins were minted in abundance only serves to highlight the assiduousness with which non-Byzantine élites sought to avoid the minting of *solidi*. Incidentally, until as late as 562, even Persian rulers officially recognised that the minting of *solidi* was a Byzantine monopoly. In this light, it is perhaps not surprising that in most of the former Roman West the imperial monopoly was recognised for at least a century longer. Western élites were apparently under no imperial pressure to do this, although Procopius' indignation suggests that their actions were closely monitored by the Eastern government. Here, again, therefore, we have evidence of an asymmetrical political relationship between Byzantium and the West, with the perceived advantage on the side of the Byzantines.[60]

An admiration for other Byzantine modes of governance can also sometimes be detected in coins. The new 'national' coinage of Visigothic Spain placed Leovigild's two sons with him on the coins, a distinctly Byzantine practice. It could be that they had been appointed 'co-rulers' with their father, in the same way that Byzantine Emperors often nominated their sons as 'co-emperors'. After all, the Lombards adopted this practice around the same time. The Lombard king, Agilulf, had his son made 'co-ruler' with him by the early seventh century. This was a practice otherwise reserved for the Byzantine

Emperors, although Theodoric's daughter, Amalasuintha, drew upon this tradition when she issued a coin whose reverse depicted herself, her father and her son, Athalaric. The obverse of Amalasuintha's coin featured the name of the Byzantine Emperor. Both of these practices drew on contemporary symbols of *romanitas*, that is, specifically 'Byzantine' symbols of kingship. This was not, then, the *romanitas* of the Late Roman Empire, but the emulation of a contemporary court culture based in Constantinople.[61]

Conclusion

The numismatic evidence is fascinating and yields the clearest picture yet of the development of kingship in the post-Roman West. Yet, taken as a whole, this chapter might be said to have drawn attention to the difficulties of investigating the relationship between the development of Western kingship and Byzantine contacts. Where we can with any certainty identify high-status artefacts in the archaeological record, it is rarely possible to associate them with formal political exchange, even when they are found in extensively studied archaeological contexts. The most we can arrive at through archaeological analysis is an impressionistic view of formal relations between the imperial government and the West. What might more confidently be stated, is the existence of a distinct 'transnational élite', seen when the burial evidence from Tournai, Cologne and Saint-Dénis is compared to contemporary Germanic inhumation graves – in the case of Tournai those even in the same cemetery. The latter rarely show evidence of links with the Eastern Mediterranean, yet the former display several indications of such contacts.

Whatever 'meaning' may be attached to them, very high-status Germanic élites of the fifth to seventh century were often buried in association with Byzantine or Byzantine-derived artefacts, several of which (such as the gold brocade and the helmet) may have been employed in similar ways in the Byzantine East. The emergence of this apparently transnational élite, distinguished by its shared modes of expression, took place then in the context of wide-ranging contacts with the wider Byzantine world. Those who belonged to it were both constrained and enabled by their relationship with the imperial state and its concomitant economic and political structures, as is amply demonstrated in the numismatic evidence. Here, the pre-existing monetary system of the Eastern Mediterranean was adopted, maintained – when there was no commercial need to do so – and eventually re-evaluated when its period of usefulness had passed. By that seventh-century point, the barbarian kingdoms were well-established polities and the foundations of a distinctly 'medieval' world had been set in place. Yet, it was not merely the 'secular' interactions of élites that permitted the development of shared cultural preferences at the highest stratum of society; as we shall now see, the role of the Church may also have been vital.

5

THE ROLE OF THE CHURCH
IN EAST-WEST CONTACTS

Introduction

Aside from burial evidence, the vast majority of the archaeological material for late antique communities in the West comprises structures and artefacts coming under the general heading of 'Church archaeology'. Often, these have been recovered with relatively little detailed stratigraphical control, although in the last few decades many churches have been excavated according to modern archaeological methods. For sites examined earlier, the most that is usually known is an outline plan of any stone-built or brick-built structures, mosaics or other solid floors, and sculptural finds, frequently architectural fragments. Detailed evidence from sites excavated according to normal archaeological principles enables this poor quality database to be interpreted more reliably than might otherwise be the case. This is assisted by the work of architectural and art historians, who have collected a wide range of comparative evidence in their studies to set alongside excavated evidence. Their work has extended over a longer time period, but focused mostly on still-standing or well-preserved buildings.

Combining these sources enables us to investigate the relationship between church architecture in the West and that of the Byzantine Empire. Such an investigation has to work from the shared architectural heritage of the Roman Empire and of the Christian Church. It also needs to take into account the possibility of wholly Western or wholly Eastern innovations, including those that produced parallel, but in fact unrelated, developments under similar circumstances (such as liturgical requirements) and based on a shared architectural repertoire. However, even with these limitations in mind it is possible to recognise examples of the apparent Western emulation of Byzantine church architecture that cannot simply be explained by occasional pilgrims or the movement of ecclesiastical texts.

First, it may help to sketch in briefest form the fourth-century architectural innovations that produced a common church architecture for the Roman Empire before 400. The monumental building programme initiated by Constantine I and his immediate successors in Constantinople, Rome and the

Holy Land, gave rise to several new developments in ecclesiastical architecture, and renewed impetus to other, existing, designs. As is well-known, the earliest Christian (that is to say, purpose built) churches had been based on the plan of the Roman basilica, or public meeting hall: a rectangular east-west orientated building, sometimes with an apse at the eastern end, and possibly with side aisles. The, usually tiled, roof was normally wooden-framed, with lower roofs for the side aisles, so that the weight of the main roof rested on semicircular arches, in turn resting on columns separating the nave from the side aisles. Churches of this sort could be constructed in virtually any part of the Roman Empire in the early fourth century and what may be basilican churches are even known from Roman Britain.[1]

It should be noted at the outset that baptisteries are not considered here because their plans, although plausibly derived from Eastern models, may also have been based on Roman-period buildings. In general, baptisteries became standard features of episcopal complexes in the fifth century, when the octagonal shape was often adopted in both East and West. While octagonal baptisteries were common in Syria and Constantinople, they are nevertheless particularly well-known from northern Italy (such as at St Tecla, Milan), south-east Gaul and Rome, so it is likely that Italy played a direct role in the appearance of this plan-type elsewhere in the West (**28**).[2]

In the fifth century, the range of church plans rapidly diversified. While non-basilican churches had been constructed before 400, the fifth century was a period of vigorous architectural experimentation in relation to ecclesiastical structures. The process had begun in the fourth century, when church architects and builders of the new monumental churches were given relatively free rein to develop their plans. Elaborations on the basic apsed basilica plan included the addition of a clearly-defined chancel just west of the apse, or multi-apsed churches, usually with the central apse flanked by two smaller ones. Sometimes, especially in the East, the apse was internal; that is to say, it was enclosed within the rectilinear exterior walls of the church, or 'boxed in' by additional walls built around the east end of the church. The concept of the 'twin cathedral' was also instituted, at first in the provinces on the eastern shores of the Adriatic, and then further to the west, as at Trier and Geneva. Here, large halls or churches were built directly parallel to each other, usually adjoining, for purposes that are not wholly understood. Other churches were organised around a central plan, usually a circle or a polygon, probably derived from Late Roman mausolea, and lending themselves to several architectural variations, including the addition of apses, triconches and atria. Constantine I himself was buried at Constantinople in a domed rotunda mausoleum with an apse, standing slightly to the east of the area where the Church of the Holy Apostles was later erected by Constantius II.[3]

28 *Fourth-century octagonal baptistery at St Tecla, Milan.* Photograph by Anthea Harris

The cruciform church

Holy Apostles itself (later re-built by Justinian I in 536), was one of the first of a group of very large funerary churches, constructed with imperial patronage in the fourth century, as for example at St Peter's in Rome or the Church of the Holy Sepulchre in Jerusalem. These churches had north-south transepts with arms extending to a greater or lesser extent outside the line of the nave, thereby providing space for the large numbers of pilgrims expected to come and pay homage at the shrine of the saint or martyr, and to view their relics. At Holy Apostles, a cruciform plan was achieved by the juxtaposition of a transept and a chancel area that extended past the east end of the transept. Although this plan later became the standard church plan throughout medieval Europe, during Late Antiquity it was but one of a diverse selection of plans and, therefore, other contemporary occurrences of it are noteworthy in this context.[4]

Holy Apostles, Constantinople, with its cruciform plan, was 'copied' in the design of other fourth- and fifth-century churches in the East, most famously at St John, Ephesus (also later rebuilt by Justinian), but also in the Holy Land and Egypt, including the pilgrimage church at Abu Mîna. The supposed meeting point of Christ and the Samarian woman at the well, at Sichem, was marked by a cruciform church known only from a later plan and, interestingly, the description of the seventh-century Frankish traveller, Arculf, who later journeyed as far as Iona to relate his experiences.

Incidentally, given that knowledge of church plans and other architectural features often travelled 'by memory', we would not expect late antique churches to be exactly the same as their possible counterparts, whether at Constantinople or elsewhere. As Krautheimer first pointed out, Arculf's description of the Church of the Holy Sepulchre, Jerusalem, is inaccurate: it does not mention eight piers of the church.[5]

Other prominent cruciform churches, possibly 'copies' of Holy Apostles, include the martyrium of St Babylas, built just outside Antioch in 379, and another Syrian martyrium, Qal'at Si'man. This was an imperially sponsored foundation, built in *c.*490 by the Emperor Zeno to enclose the column of the famous stylite, St Symeon the Elder, and more impressive in scale. As a late fifth-century monument, it was also some 100 years older than the Antioch church. It is, therefore, logical to investigate whether Western copies of the building were also constructed during Late Antiquity, especially as the distinction between martyrial and regular churches faded in the fifth century (**29**).[6]

It is in Italy that one may begin to look for Eastern cruciform designs in Western church architecture that may imply the direct emulation of this Byzantine prototype. Although cruciform church plans remained uncommon even into the fifth and sixth centuries, a handful of major cruciform churches were constructed in the fourth century, as at Holy Apostles and San Simpliciano, which are both in Milan and still standing (**colour plates 10 & 11**). Less prominent transepts were built at the churches of St Peter and, in the fifth century, San Pietro in Vincoli (St Peter in Chains), both in Rome. Imperial rotunda mausolea were built next to the church of St Peter in the late fourth century, in the same way that a rotunda mausoleum had been constructed for the body of Constantine I. Yet, it is important to recall that Milan and Rome (along with Trier and Cologne) were major imperial residences in the fourth-century Roman West, so the occurrence of this plan-type there is not surprising. While some of these churches, especially Holy Apostles

29 *Qal'at Si'man, Syria.* Reproduced with the kind permission of Stuart Whatling

(now San Nazaro) and San Simpliciano, Milan, may well have been intended as 'copies' of the Constantinian church of the Holy Apostles at Constantinople, their construction within a Late Roman context renders them less relevant to the study of Byzantine contacts with the West in the fifth to seventh centuries.[7]

The existence of a Western Church of the Holy Apostles with a cruciform plan also urges caution about too readily assigning every other cruciform church in the West, even those with the same dedication, the label of 'copies' of the Constantinopolitan original. In point of fact, it serves as a reminder that individual categories of archaeological and architectural evidence must always be understood in the context of other categories of evidence if they are to be interpreted with any accuracy. The 'special case' of Italy may mean that cruciform churches here are less likely to have been built in emulation of Byzantine prototypes than they are in places where the cruciform plan is rarer, although these might, in turn, have been copying Italy.

The model for cruciform-planned churches appears to have spread from Milan to other towns in the north of Italy: the 'Princes of the Apostles' church, Como (on the site of the later Sant' Abbondio), Santa Croce in Ravenna and San Stefano in Verona. Given the importance of Milan, both as an imperial capital and as the seat of the influential fourth-century bishop, Ambrose, these churches remain most reasonably interpreted as the local imitation of the Milanese Church of the Holy Apostles. Yet, the cruciform plan was still popular in the early seventh century when northern Italy was under Lombard occupation. Queen Theodelinda constructed a church in the shape of 'a perfect Greek cross' at Monza, whilst other Lombard cruciform churches included Santa Euphemia at Como and St John the Evangelist at Castelseprio. The latter has been compared with a late antique church at Jerash, as well as other, sixth-century, churches in the East. Such a parallel would be perfectly plausible, especially given the extensive 'Byzantinization' of aspects of northern Italian culture after the Justinianic Reconquest.[8]

After the Reconquest, of course, Ravenna, and to a lesser extent Rome, was a major Byzantine cultural centre, famously celebrated in the mosaics of a very 'Constantinopolitan' church in that city, San Vitale, and also at San Apollinare in Classe (**colour plate 20**). Yet, it would be incorrect to underrate Byzantine ecclesiastical links with northern Italy in the period before Reconquest simply because of the historical and cultural importance of Milan. Indeed, the Emperor Zeno's well-documented enthusiasm for the patronage of ecclesiastical architecture may have informally extended to the region. Column capitals at Theodoric's church of San Apollinare Nuovo, Ravenna, built in about 490, are almost identical to high-quality capitals from the Nea-Anchialos church in Greece. There is textual evidence for Zeno's involvement in the architecture of Apulia – Bishop Laurence of Siponte (modern Manfredonia), requested that Zeno send artists to come and decorate his new episcopal complex – so an imperial role in northern Italy might also be possible. Rather than Milan being an architectural role-model solely in its own right, it could be the case that its continuing prominence in this way was, at least in part, due to northern Italy's links with the East (**30**).[9]

The cruciform church gained in popularity outside Italy in the fifth and sixth centuries. Although often assumed to be another reflex of the Milanese Holy Apostles – Milan having become a crossroads for people and ideas travelling between East and West – this is not nearly as certain. At the cruciform church at Grenoble, the half-domes have been likened to scalloped half-domes in the East, namely at the church of Sts Sergius and Bacchus, Constantinople, and churches in Byzantine North Africa. The presence of other distinctly 'Eastern' architectural elements in south-east Gaul, such as the internal apse and lateral chambers at Cimiez and Riez, and the internal apse at La Cadière-d'Azur, might also point to a genuinely Eastern point of contact. To some extent, these – including the cruciform church of St Laurent at Aosta – might be interpreted in the light of the Reconquest, for late antique churches on Corsica (occupied in the Reconquest) sometimes display similar features.[10]

While churches in south-east Gaul and the Alpine regions might have been built to emulate those of northern Italy, the overall distribution of cruciform churches in Gaul suggests that by no means all of these churches north of the Alps necessarily emulated Italian, rather than more distant, models. Cruciform churches were built at Clermont, Tours and Nantes between the fifth and sixth centuries. Clovis' Church of the Holy Apostles at Paris, a funerary basilica like

30 San Vitale, Ravenna, built by Justinian I in the mid-sixth century.
Reproduced with the kind permission of Zoë Harris

its namesake in Constantinople, was also probably cruciform, as was the early sixth-century church of St Vincent (later St Germain-des-Prés), founded in the reign of Childebert I, and the cathedral at nearby Orléans, of disputed date.[11]

The mid-fifth-century cruciform churches at the southern Gallic town of Lyon could simply be another reflex of the Milanese churches. However, we must remember that Lyon lay on the Rhône, a major route to Marseille and the Mediterranean, the entry point for goods and people coming from North Africa and the East. The town also occupied an important position for traders using the Rhône-Rhine route and the route west to the Loire. A community of Byzantines is attested at Lyon – both in textual and epigraphic evidence – during Late Antiquity, and this may be archaeologically supported by Byzantine imports. It might be the case, therefore, that the tripartite cruciform churches in the town, St Laurent-de-Choulans (begun in the late fifth century) and St Just, reflect contact with the East just as much as they reflect contact with northern Italy. At St Just, Phase Two alterations (probably early sixth-century) rendered it cruciform and provided it with an apse with a polygonal exterior, along with lateral chambers communicating with the apse, a feature with Eastern origins, as we shall see below (**31**).[12]

Interestingly, the southern Anatolian coast (whence some members of the Byzantine communities in the West may have come) had, to use Krautheimer's term, a 'surprising' number of late fifth-century 'tripartite transept' churches. This was in contrast to western Anatolia, and even Constantinople. It would be tempting to suggest that this renders it more, not less, likely that analogous churches in the West, particularly where 'Syrians' (who may also have been associated with southern Anatolia) are attested, were built using Eastern, rather than Italian, models. Whatever the case, there is not a complete correlation between the use of the cruciform plan and geographical proximity to northern Italy. What several western and northern Gallic cruciform churches have in common is that they are in locations where 'Syrian' merchants are documented as having lived.[13]

However, the possibly cruciform sixth-century cathedral at Nantes, dedicated to the apostles Peter and Paul, allegedly had two features resembling the Church of the Holy Apostles at Milan. On these grounds it might be supposed that it counts against an association between western and central Gallic cruciform churches and the Constantinopolitan church of the same dedication. Yet on further investigation it seems that this might not be the case. The Nantes cathedral is only known from a textual description and the alleged similarities are relatively minor details: a column bearing a silver cross and arcading under the tower. Moreover, as Philippe Guigon and Jeremy Knight have both pointed out, it is uncertain whether Nantes cathedral was cruciform at all. It may have had a nave terminating in three apses, rather than an actual transept.[14]

Another possibility is that although these details were based on Milan, the rest of the building at Nantes was modelled on what was known of the

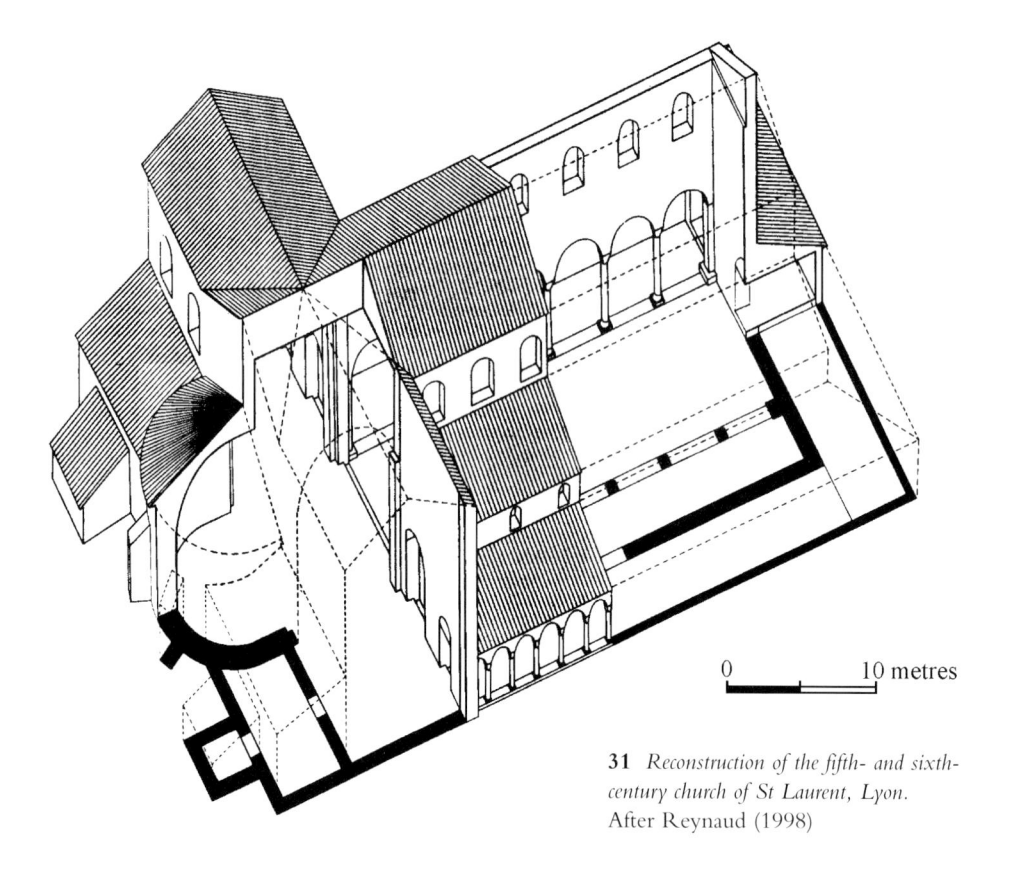

31 Reconstruction of the fifth- and sixth-century church of St Laurent, Lyon. After Reynaud (1998)

Constantinopolitan church – the synthesis being seen as appropriate to features derived from two churches of the same dedication. In this sense, we might expect to see a mélange of Eastern and Western features, rather than a straight 'copy'. As a result, the cathedral at Nantes may be stronger evidence for the weakness of relying on textual accounts of church architecture alone than it is against the hypothesis that these other churches were based on the Church of the Holy Apostles at Constantinople. There is some, albeit limited, additional evidence to suggest Byzantine links with Nantes. Gregory of Tours describes how, in response to a Breton siege on the town, a procession of men in white garments carrying candles was seen to emerge from the cathedral and move around the town until the enemy was disorientated and fled in confusion. The description of this event seems to draw upon distinctly 'Eastern' traditions of religious ceremony.[15]

Other churches in Gaul were dedicated to the Holy Apostles, but were not necessarily cruciform. They may have emulated the dedication rather than the design of the original Constantinopolitan church or have been 'copied' from Holy Apostles, Milan, or even Clovis' church at Paris. So this is evidence of a lower grade than that afforded by cruciform churches in places with Byzantine mercantile communities and at some distance from Italy.

However, the extra-mural Church of the Holy Apostles at Le Mans cannot be a 'copy' of Clovis' Parisian building, at least, since it was constructed at the end of the fifth century by Bishop Victuris, who intended it for the remains of his predecessor, Liborius. Equally, the Church of the Holy Apostles at the *civitas* capital of Viennensis (modern-day Vienne) cannot be a 'copy' of Clovis' church. This was built by Bishop Mamertius in about 475 as a mausoleum for the tombs of the city's bishops, and later rededicated to St Peter alone.[16]

Vienne was an important trading centre during Late Antiquity and yet another town playing host to a community of Byzantine merchants. In this context, therefore, the plan of the late fifth-century phase of this church is particularly interesting. It is a rectilinear building, with an eastern apse, flanked by two rectilinear rooms. Directly to the east of the apse was a rectilinear mausoleum that was reached by a door through the eastern apse of the church. Although not a rotunda in plan, the position of the mausoleum in relation to the church echoes the situation at Holy Apostles, Constantinople, where the possible Constantinopolitan model also had a door in its apse leading to the mausoleum. Any similarities the church at Vienne bore to Holy Apostles, Constantinople in this phase were enhanced in the sixth century when an additional burial chapel was added in the junction of the north transept and the apse. It may or may not be significant that the mausoleum of Justinian I was built at Constantinople in exactly this relative position, also in the sixth century. Admittedly Justinian's mausoleum was cruciform, but it is nevertheless striking how the relative positions of the mausolea, the plan of the church and the door in the apse all have parallels with the church at Constantinople (**32**).[17]

These examples of Holy Apostles churches in fifth- and sixth-century Gaul had two important shared characteristics. They were built to serve as funerary churches for ecclesiastical élites, in former *civitas* capitals where both secular and ecclesiastical authority was often in the hands of the bishop. It would be reasonable to suppose that they symbolised that authority in those towns, suggesting that the choice of dedication was meant to assist this. That these towns were either some considerable distance from Milan or had attested Byzantine links might also permit the possibility that the authority symbolised (in political and ecclesiastical terms, rather than doctrinally), lay in Constantinople, rather than elsewhere.

It is important, too, that the later popularity of the transept in the Carolingian period, plus the list of cruciform churches given here, must not be allowed to obscure the relative rarity of the transept in the fifth century, and even the first part of the sixth century. Its presence in the late antique West is indicative of a variety of links and relationships, not all of which must have been mediated through Rome or northern Italy. Several surely originated in the Byzantine world. Krautheimer alluded to this when he pointed out that: 'Cross-shaped martyria, with four arms of equal length or nearly so, whether aisleless or basilican are clearly variants on Constantine's own martyrium, the Apostoleion in Constantinople'.[18]

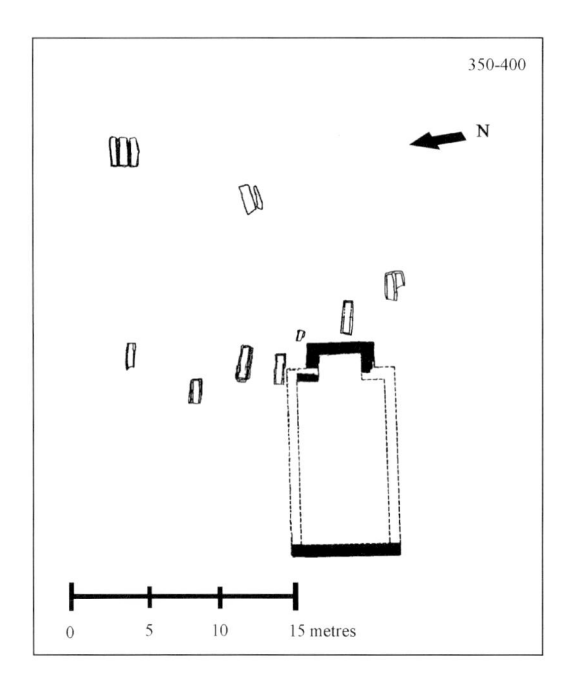

32 (a, b, c) *Plan of Holy Apostles, Vienne, showing fourth- to sixth-century phases of activity, with suggested reconstruction. The apse partially underlies the present cathedral apse.* After Knight (1999)/Jannet-Vallat *et al.* (1986)

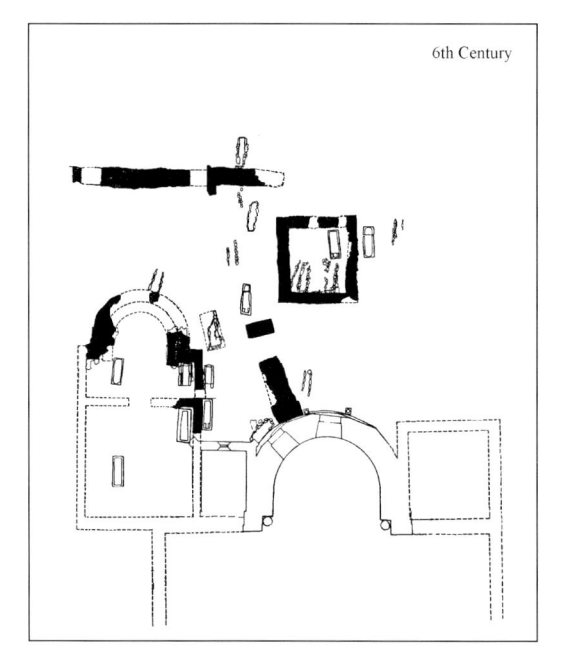

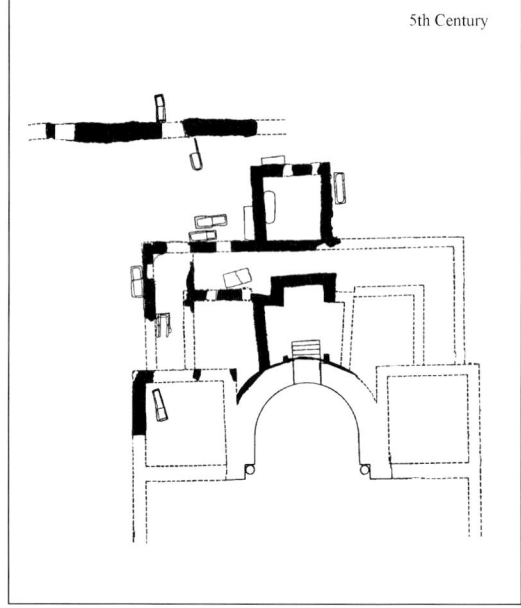

Other Eastern church dedications in the West

Not only 'Holy Apostles' dedications, but dedications more generally may be relevant as categories of evidence for Byzantine-Western contacts in the fifth and sixth centuries. As Knight has pointed out, it was not always necessary for cathedral churches to have dedications: they were often simply known as the 'cathedral of' the particular city in which they were built. Dedications for churches, especially cathedral churches, became more common in the late fourth and fifth centuries when the cult of martyrs (and their relics) became popular and urban communities came to have more than one church. Martyr cults, and the closely associated veneration of relics, flourished first in the fourth-century East, where members of the House of Constantine, inspired by the Empress Helena's 'discovery' of the True Cross in Jerusalem, ensured the gaining of important relics for their churches.

St Augustine of Hippo spoke out against the excesses of the cult of martyrs in North Africa, but the storage and veneration of relics of saints and martyrs was rapidly incorporated into Christian worship. Relics were even deposited in the small chapel adjacent to the base of the Column of Constantine during the ceremonies to inaugurate the city of Constantinople in 334. The ceremony was preceded by a solemn procession with both ecclesiastical and secular dignitaries present. Once in place, relics were believed to protect the town in which they lay, and for this reason were brought out and paraded around the walls in times of danger. Ceremonies surrounding objects such as relics gradually came to provide a focal point for people across the former Roman world, promoting a sense of themselves as inhabitants of a particular town and reinforcing the late antique Christian identity of that town.[19]

In much of the West, and particularly in Gaul, the cult of martyrs was active from the latter part of the fourth century and associated with St Martin of Tours. Its archaeology is mainly represented by wooden structures – *cellae* – which were placed over the graves of the saints, often later replaced by stone *memoriae* and, later still, by churches. Churches located outside the walls of the city commonly originated in the fourth and fifth centuries with the tombs of particularly venerated Christians, usually martyrs or bishops. Understandably, from a late antique perspective, the cult of the True Cross was popular in both the West and the East. The mid-fifth-century Bishop of Astorga brought back a piece of the True Cross from the Holy Land, while in Tours a Syrian man was treated with great respect when it was discovered that he, too, had a piece of it in his possession. Tours may have been a particular focus of Eastern-style devotional behaviour, perhaps facilitated by its association with St Martin and his ascetic tradition. In addition to Byzantine imports and textually attested Easterners, the Bishop of Tours at the time that Clovis received the consulship there, Licinius, had travelled widely in the Eastern Mediterranean and might reasonably be expected to have brought back ideas and knowledge about Byzantine ecclesiastical practices.[20]

St Martin and other Gallic martyrs remained intensely popular, both in Tours and elsewhere, but the relics of Syrian and Anatolian martyrs were also collected. At Langres (Haute-Marne), the relics of some Cappadocian martyrs, Mammetis, Speusippos, Elisippos and Melasipplos, were received in the fifth century. A popular local devotion to them existed until the early seventh century when the relics of a local man, St Didier (or Bishop Desideratus), were also translated there. Subsequently, their cult diminished. Relics of other Eastern saints were also much sought after, particularly Sergius and Bacchus, and the Syrian 'brother-doctors', Cosmas and Damian. Even in mid-seventh-century Toledo, for example, the local archbishop composed a mass in honour of the latter pair of saints.[21]

Gregory of Tours described how the people of Bordeaux came to hear of 'a certain King in the east' who had benefited from wearing the relics of St Sergius on his right arm. The relics were said to possess the power to disperse the enemies of the Eastern King if he would only raise the arm on which they were bound. When the Frankish king, Gundovald, heard the account, he sought to obtain relics of St Sergius for himself and, hearing that a Syrian man named Eufronius was in possession of some (St Sergius had also been a Syrian), he sent one of his men and the Bishop of Bordeaux to take them by force. Plainly a wealthy man, Eufronius offered first 100 and then 200 gold coins to the men to go away. However, they refused to leave and eventually found the relics 'hidden in a casket in the top of the wall facing the altar', where they were then broken up, divided and taken away.[22]

According to Gregory, the same Eufronius, who we have already encountered in chapter 3, had 'made his house a church'. This provides some evidence – along with a certain Leocadius from Bourges who also transformed his house in this way – that house-churches were still in use, and perhaps not out of the ordinary, in sixth-century Gaul. Such a 'house-church' probably had an ambiguous relationship with the ecclesiastical authorities in Bordeaux, and this may have lain behind the grudge that the bishop bore towards Eufronius. The story illustrates that Easterners could find themselves in wealthy positions in the West, well-known in high-status circles and with their personal belongings the objects of desire, yet rather isolated from the ecclesiastical establishment and seemingly without immediate means of protection and support.[23]

St Stephen was probably the most popular Eastern saint in Gaul as far as church dedications of the fifth and sixth centuries were concerned. Relics thought to be those of St Stephen, the first Christian martyr, were found in Palestine in 415 and transported to Gaul shortly afterwards, where they were distributed between several churches. The event prompted ecclesiastical authorities in Gaul and elsewhere to dedicate cathedrals and churches to St Stephen throughout the period. One of the most notable of these is San Stefano Rotondo in Rome, which Krautheimer suggested could have been modelled on the Church of the Holy Sepulchre at Jerusalem. In western and central Gaul, dedications to St Stephen were particularly popular, in part probably because the region had so few indigenous martyrs for whom to dedicate churches. The cathedral at Bourges, which was part of a complex with a baptistery and a bishop's palace, was dedicated to St Stephen, as was the cathedral at Valence until its demolition in 1094. St Stephen at Bordeaux may have been an early cathedral and at Le Mans, again, the cathedral was dedicated to St Stephen.[24]

Dedications to St Stephen were given to churches, as well as cathedrals. For example, at Clermont in central Gaul an extra-mural church was dedicated to him, the decoration of which was supervised by the Bishop's wife herself. Vienne had its own martyr in the form of St Ferreolus, who had been martyred at Lyon in 177, and might be expected to have ignored faraway Eastern saints. Furthermore, St Martin had added to its 'indigenous' martyrial focus by adding relics of Gervasius and Protasius, the Italian martyrs. Yet, Vienne, too, had a sixth-century church dedicated to St Stephen: an extra-mural church, lying on the north side of the river d'Outre Gére. There may have been another extra-mural church of St Stephen at Marseille – Gregory of Tours describes it as being 'next to the city' – while Metz, Valence and Lyon also had ecclesiastical monuments dedicated to the saint. There was a church of St Stephen at the monastery of Choisy-au-Bac by the eighth century, when it became the burial place of Childebert III, but it is unclear whether this was of fifth- to seventh-century origin.[25]

If ecclesiastical authorities in Gaul were intent on 'copying' Italian prototypes, we might expect more churches and cathedral churches to be dedicated to St Laurence than St Stephen. The cult of St Laurence (who was martyred in Rome in 258) grew rapidly in Italy after 410 and several important churches, including the burial place of the bishops of Rome, were dedicated to his memory. St Stephen, by contrast, was a more popular church dedication in the Eastern Mediterranean where, during the reign of Anastasius I, the church of St Stephen was probably one of the ten most important churches in Constantinople, and played a prominent role in imperial ceremonies. In Jerusalem, a church of St Stephen was erected by the Empress Eudocia in the mid-fifth century and this, too, was an important monument throughout Late Antiquity. That dedications to St Stephen were so popular in Merovingian Gaul may, in the context of other evidence, be suggestive of the known ecclesiastical links between East and West in the fifth and sixth centuries.[26]

The interiors of Merovingian churches

When it comes to examining the interior decoration of Merovingian churches, there is little archaeological evidence available, and Gregory of Tours is yet again our mainstay. Notwithstanding the problems with this as evidence – Gregory's agenda in describing these buildings is not entirely clear to us – we may nevertheless infer that church design and decoration shared elements in common with the Byzantine East. Whereas Roman monumental buildings were usually extravagantly decorated on the exterior, the builders of Merovingian churches, like their Eastern Mediterranean counterparts, often saved such displays of skill and craftsmanship for the interior. A few examples will suffice. Gregory's comments on the fifth-century church at Clermont evoke an ambience especially reminiscent of Eastern ecclesiastical contexts: 'In it . . . those at prayer are often aware of a most sweet and aromatic odour which is often wafted towards them. Round the sanctuary it has walls which are decorated with mosaic work made of many varieties of marble'. The use of incense, mosaic work and, to a lesser extent, marble all point to possible Eastern contacts and, indeed, the incense itself could have been an Eastern import. The church of St Antolianus, also at Clermont, was said to have had a domed roof, as well as 'curved arches on columns of Parian marble and Heraclean stone'. Taken together with the marble columns, the presence of the dome might suggest a degree of Byzantine emulation, conscious or otherwise.[27]

Not all of these churches were necessarily of political as well as religious importance, but they were almost certainly all built by high-status men and women with the desire to display their wealth, status and good taste, in addition to their piety. The church of St Martin at Autun, a royal endowment of the late sixth century, is documented as having marble and mosaic work in its design, and also had a tripartite apse. The interior walls of a sixth- (or possibly fifth-) century church at Toulouse were covered in gold mosaic work, depicting Biblical figures and angels. The iconographic cycle of the now destroyed church is known in some detail from a description made in 1633. Mosaic-producing was a highly skilled task, and by the sixth century most master mosaicists probably resided in the East or in the 'Byzantine' cities of Italy: Rome and Ravenna. It is possible, therefore, that Eastern craftsmen were sent for in order to assist in church building, especially outside of Italy.[28]

The evidence from marble decoration is rather more problematic in exploring East–West contacts. The marble used in these and other buildings could, of course, derive from the Pyrenean quarries in south-western Gaul, most notably St Béat. It could also be *spolia*, pieces of marble reused from redundant Roman buildings. It might, too, have been shipped to Frankia from Italy, particularly in the case of the Merovingian sarcophagi of the Arles and Marseille area. The quality of sculptural ornament, particularly in relation to the sarcophagi of south-west Gaul has attracted much scholarly attention. It is possible that the marble-carving workshops were in some way linked to developments in the Eastern late antique world, but we cannot be sure of this. Both Merovingian and Visigothic sculpture, while displaying many elements in common with sculptural designs in the contemporary Byzantine East, relies too heavily on motifs current in the Late Roman Empire and presumably still circulating in the fifth- to seventh-century period to permit detailed stylistic affinities with the East to be identified. The vast range of sculptural evidence must reluctantly, therefore, largely be abandoned as a means of investigating East-West contacts.[29]

However, it is possible that some marble was shipped to southern Frankia from quarries in the Eastern Mediterranean region. The identification of a sixth-century Byzantine marble from Arles renders this possible, as does the evidence for the export of 'prefabricated' churches from the Empire to the West by sea (**colour plate 4**). The Marzamemi shipwreck off the Sicilian coast had a cargo of 200-300 tons of prefabricated marble fittings that included columns, a choir screen, a pulpit and an altar, all deriving from the Byzantine Empire. Sidonius Apollinaris may have alluded to an East-West trade in marble when he wrote wryly to his friend, Domitius, that his villa in Clermont did not have marble from Proconnesus, Phrygia, Numidia and Sparta. He suggested, instead, that his new *piscina* made up for this, but the implication is that other contemporary buildings *were* sometimes constructed with such materials. This was only to be expected, for exotic marbles would have been highly desirable.[30]

Western churches and the veneration of images

The Eastern practice of the veneration of images is often assumed to have been absent from Western ecclesiastical life in the fifth to seventh centuries. As Pope Gregory the Great put it, religious images were 'not for adoration, but for the instruction of ignorant minds'. However, this was probably not the case. We know that images were used in the churches of Marseille at the end of the sixth century, much to the disgust of the local bishop, who condemned the practice. In Gregory of Tours' descriptions of various sixth-century Merovingian churches, several appear as having contained paintings depicting the human figure: saints and apostles in particular. It is not clear how much these were 'venerated', although the reference from Marseille suggests that this was the case there at least. Religious paintings were sometimes associated with miracle stories and, as Robert Markus has pointed out, Gregory uses the same word – *iconia, icona* – for describing sacred images as that used in the Eastern Mediterranean. Even as 'Roman' a priest as Augustine walked with an icon ahead of him as he came ashore in Kent in 597, an action that may have been motivated more by Eastern (and possibly popular Frankish) conceptions of sacred images than by conservative Roman ones.[31]

The image of Christ on the Cross was also employed more widely than official sanctions would allow. Depictions of the Crucifixion were not officially sanctioned by the ecclesiastical authorities until the Council of Trullo in 692 and previously the Crucifixion was often symbolised by the Greek letters alpha and omega. However, 'realistic' depictions of the Crucifixion were used in religious art from the fifth century. The image was more popular in the East, but appeared in the West from an early date, as on the doors of Santa Sabina, Rome. Its presence in Western contexts cannot, therefore, be used to point to links with the East in every case, but it may provide supplementary evidence for contacts with the Byzantine Empire. During the sixth century, depictions of Christ on the Cross were used on pilgrims' *ampullae*, in church décor, liturgical objects, sculpture, even clothing accessories and jewellery. In 586, for example, a 'realistic' depiction of the Crucifixion was produced in the so-called Rabbula Gospels, which were made in the Zagba Monastery in Syria and brought to the West shortly afterwards (they are now in Florence). Notably, Christ is depicted here as clothed in a full-length, dark-coloured sleeveless tunic. A similar clothed depiction of Christ appears on the painted reliquary box, probably produced in Palestine around the same time, and which is now part of the Cappella Sancta Sanctorum treasure in the Vatican Museum. By the late sixth century onwards, therefore, depictions of the Crucifixion had achieved popularity in both Eastern and Western art forms.[32]

In the Visigothic territories, where the Arian heresy had formed the official belief of the Visigothic monarchy until the end of the sixth century, religious art had underplayed the humanity of Christ, for obvious reasons. Thus, the adoption of the Cross and its associated themes of pain, rejection and misery at the end of the sixth century and beginning of the seventh century have sometimes been seen as artistic representations of the deliberate rejection of Arianism in the Visigothic kingdom. This is very plausible, but it should not obscure other possibilities. For example, the vitality of the pre-587 Church in Mérida suggests that Arianism may not always have been relevant to the debate within religious art. The building of churches in or around the villa complexes of the wealthy might also point to the same suggestion. It is not out of the question, moreover, that the art and architecture often said to reflect Eastern influences in the Visigothic and Frankish kingdoms (including depictions of Christ on the Cross), was produced not for Visigothic or Frankish patrons, but for Easterners living in the West. As in Lyon, we may be wise to entertain the possibility that churches may have been built for and/or used by the 'Eastern' community.[33]

The same might also apply to areas of south-west Gaul, which were part of the Visigothic kingdom of Toulouse until 507, and where Arian ideas, if not core beliefs, lingered for the rest of the sixth century. Gregory of Tours draws attention to a church at Narbonne where a 'realistic' depiction of Christ on the Cross scandalised the local population to the extent that the bishop was called in to cover the painting with a veil. On the basis that there are textually attested 'Syrian' concerns in Narbonne, and given that in general the material culture of south-west Gaul shows little sign of contacts with the Eastern Mediterranean, it is possible that this was a 'Syrian' church, rather than a Frankish one. The intervention of the bishop need not negate this, for we know that in Paris one of the sixth-century bishops was himself a 'Syrian', suggesting that at least one part of the 'Syrian' population was active in the

Frankish Church. Another bishop, Eufronius, consecrated Bishop of Autun in 456, may also have been from the East. In this context, perhaps more attention should be given to the late antique churches of 'Clos-de-la-Lombarde' at Narbonne and St Cecilia at Loupian, with their internal apses and lateral chambers, and to St Bertrand-de-Comminges (south-west of Toulouse), which had a distinctive trapezoid apse, seen more often in the East than in the West.[34]

The ecclesiastical architecture of the Iberian peninsula

When it comes to the ecclesiastical architecture of the Iberian peninsula there has also been an understandable tendency to interpret any evidence of architectural links between it and the Byzantine Empire in terms of the conversion of the Visigothic King to catholic Christianity in 587. Doubtless, the evangelisation of the Visigothic population was achieved, in part, by Byzantine clergy accompanying the political and military officials who administered Byzantine territories in the south-east of the peninsula.[35]

Yet, to assign 'Byzantine' patterns in ecclesiastical architecture wholly to the conversion of the Visigothic monarchy would be to assume that Arian architects and patrons were cut off from the broader Mediterranean context of late antique architecture. After all, the Ostrogothic Arian élite in Ravenna looked to the East for architectural principles, as we have seen in chapter 4, and given Theodoric's political and military interests in the Iberian peninsula, it is possible that similar architectural tastes were expressed there.

The assumption that only the Arian élite was wealthy or powerful enough to build monumental architecture has also been undermined, usually in the light of archaeological evidence. The partial survival of elements of the villa system in the Iberian peninsula suggests that it may have been possible for some parts of the sixth-century sub-Roman population to build churches and 'private' monasteries. Indeed, the villa site at Pla de Nadal shows evidence of occupation into the seventh century and at Pedraza and Fraga, central parts of two large Late Roman villas were converted into churches in the fifth and sixth centuries. Excavation at the villa site at San Miguel de Escalada yielded a church of sixth- to ninth-century date, suggesting that it, too, may have been converted into a form of ecclesiastical use in the fourth or fifth century. Unfortunately, with the exception of some extra-mural cemetery churches, other fifth- and sixth-century ecclesiastical monuments have left very little trace archaeologically, not least due to continued settlement into the medieval period and their presumed replacement by newer structures. However, where there is evidence – as at Tarragona and Barcelona – the church plans indicate that pre-Conversion Iberia was linked into the wider late antique world. For example, the early sixth-century church at Ségobriga has a transept, as well as a crypt and the distinctive 'horseshoe-shaped' apse that features in later

Visigothic ecclesiastical monuments and has parallels in the East. It may or may not be significant, in this context, that Ségobriga lies near the bank of the River Guadiana not far east of Mérida, where the presence of Byzantine merchants is attested in the sixth century. Ease of access may, therefore, have facilitated any putative links with the East.[36]

Pre-Justinianic links with the East might also be seen in the church at Marialba de la Ribera in northern Spain. This has a rectangular nave and 'horseshoe-shaped' apse, dated to the fourth century. Pilasters and a narthex with semicircular ends were added about a century later. Horseshoe-shaped apses in ecclesiastical contexts, some with polygonal exteriors, are generally agreed to have their antecedents in fifth-century central Anatolia, and so, if this really is a fourth-century feature of the church at Marialba, it is probably unique. Apses of this shape are unusual in the West outside the Iberian peninsula – rare examples include that of the church at Draguignan (Provence), the church at Riom, slightly north of Clermont, and the seventh-century phase of the church of St Martin at Angers.[37]

With its apparently fifth-century additions, the Marialba church bears an architectural similarity to the late antique churches in the Byzantine Empire, such as the church of the Forty Martyrs of Sebaste, recently excavated at Saranda in Albania. Here, the side openings are seen as an intrinsic part of the church's role as a centre of pilgrimage, partly on the grounds that the crypt is divided into about 10 cells – part of the original design – presumably intended for the display of relics and tombs. Parallels have been drawn between the Albanian church and the churches of San Apollinare in Classe, Ravenna and St Catherine's, Sinai. Although there appears to have been no crypt at Marialba, it is possible that this church, too, was intended, after its fifth- or sixth-century alterations, to serve as a pilgrimage centre. The unusual presence in the apse of 13 burials of fifth- or sixth-century date might confirm the continuing importance of the church as a martyrium into the Visigothic period. These could be burials *ad sanctos*. It is possible that Phase Two alternations at Marialba were made in response to the increasing popularity of the cult of relics in northern Spain in this period. Whatever the case, the evidence seems to suggest that architects in the Iberian peninsula were part of a wider network facilitating the spread of architectural and artistic ideals across the Mediterranean world well before the Reconquest and the conversion of the Visigothic monarchy.[38]

Those 'Visigothic' churches that remain standing have been the subject of much debate. Very few of these monuments can be assigned even a relatively secure date and some may be later than the Visigothic period. Two have been dated by epigraphy to the 660s: San Juan de Baños (Cerrato, Palencia), which has an inscription dating its construction to 661, and the mausoleum of São Frutuoso (Montelios, Portugal), which is seemingly dated to 665. Both monuments fall just outside the period under consideration here but, in the absence of securely dated buildings before 650, a brief comment on one of them is in order.[39]

The cruciform-plan mausoleum of São Frutuoso might reflect, as Jerrilynn Dodds has suggested, 'a preoccupation with Eastern or perhaps Justinianic forms seen by Fructuosus at the Visigothic royal court [at Toledo]'. Of course, we should bear in mind that there may already have been cruciform-plan mausolea in the Iberian peninsula in the Roman period, and it would be unwise 'automatically' to attribute the design of equal-armed cross-plan buildings to contemporary contact with Ravenna or the Byzantine East. Indeed, the so-called mausoleum of Galla Placidia at Ravenna, which does bear a distinct resemblance to the São Frutuoso mausoleum, was built around 424. It was, therefore, already 200 years old when its Iberian counterpart was constructed, and even the buildings erected by Justinian at Ravenna were by then over a century old. At most, it might be suggested that, in the context of other evidence for Byzantine links with the Iberian peninsula, the revival of cruciform mausolea in the seventh century could reflect a new-found desire to adopt architectural forms that spoke of links with other Christian populations. It is even possible that these were chosen to echo Justinian's own choice of mausoleum: a cruciform structure to the north-west of the Church of the Holy Apostles in Constantinople (**33**).[40]

These buildings are part of a group of ecclesiastical monuments with some shared architectural features. Most of the group have few, if any, features enabling them to be dated to anything more specific than the Visigothic period. It is unlikely, although not impossible, that their origins lie after the Islamic invasion of 711. In view of the lack of precise dating, these buildings are perhaps best taken as a group, notwithstanding the possibility that some may in fact post-date 650 and exceed the chronological limits of this book. Nevertheless, dated examples show that construction of the group as a whole began before the end of the seventh century. Moreover, the similarity in architecture and decoration between the buildings within the group implies that any such later structures reflect architectural and decorative styles that had already entered the local repertoire before 661 – for example, the use of stylised floral and geometric motifs. Consequently, parallels may be sought between the architecture and decoration of these buildings and other structures in the late antique Mediterranean.

In fact, the ecclesiastical architecture of Syria has been suggested as a model for some of these churches. Whereas church builders in Constantinople and the rest of the north-east Mediterranean favoured the use of mortared stone masonry with bands of thin bricks, those in Syria and its environs utilised large ashlar blocks of sandstone. In southern Anatolia and Armenia these were used as facing for a fill that was principally rubble, but in Syria they formed the entire wall. A similar style of construction was favoured in the Iberian peninsula. For example, the churches of San Pedro de la Nave (Zamora) and Santa María de Quintanilla de las Viñas (Burgos) have walls of similarly well-cut ashlar blocks, also made out of hard sandstone, as in the case of the Syrian churches (**colour plate 14**). Like some of their postulated Syrian counterparts, these churches

33 *The mausoleum of Galla Placidia, Ravenna. Fifth century.*
Reproduced with the kind permission of Zoë Harris

sometimes have high small windows cut out of the stone, occasionally framed by a horseshoe arch, as at Santa Lucía del Trampal, just north of Mérida. Here, the rectangular triple apse has Eastern precedents, and so it is perhaps notable that the building has been interpreted as a 'communal hermitage', where several monks might live as anchorites in close physical proximity. This was not dissimilar to the type of monasticism being developed in Egypt and elsewhere in the East in the fifth and sixth centuries, and so might also point to a link with Byzantium. A monastic function has been suggested for the church of Santa María de Melque, south of Toledo, although here the extent to which coenobitic or eremitical monasticism was favoured is not clear (**34**).[41]

Without implying that the architects of these churches simply mimicked contemporary churches in Syria — there are too many differences to suggest that — it may be helpful to note other architectural features that could have originated in the Near Eastern Byzantine world. These include tri-windowed apses, latticework window frames (sometimes divided by a small column), horseshoe-shaped arches above the lintels, tripartite apses and decorative friezes around the exterior walls. In some cases, as in the sixth-century phase at the Vega del Mar church near Málaga or at São Gião de Nazaré (Lamego, Portugal), the chancel is separated from the nave by an actual wall with only a small door to allow access. This is more akin to the church plans of southern Anatolia and Syria, and contrasts with the plans of the earliest Iberian churches

– as at Marialba, for example – where the congregation could easily see and approach the altar from the nave. Of course, the compartmentalisation of liturgical space was taking place to differing extents all over the former Roman world, and this may be an independent innovation. However, it would be wrong to assume it was an 'automatic' development or one dictated merely by fashion, rather than a deliberate and thoughtful response to then-current theological and doctrinal discussion, which itself might indicate a steady flow of ideas between East and West.[42]

Some scholars have linked other developments in Iberian ecclesiastical architecture specifically to elements of the Syrian liturgy, but this cannot be proven. The most commonly cited example of this is the practice of constructing lateral chambers either side of the chancel or apse, sometimes preceded by a transept. This plan was developed in the fifth and sixth centuries, possibly in North Africa. However, early non-African examples are known, such as St Thecla at Meryemlik, on the southern coast of Asia Minor, which was probably financed by the Emperor Zeno in the late fifth century. There were analogous churches at Yeniyurt Kale (Isauria) and at Petra.[43]

In sixth-century Syria, the arrangement took on a new feature as doorways were opened so that the chambers communicated with the apse and/or the chancel and the aisles. It is this feature that can be seen, by the seventh century, throughout the Continental West. Churches with these plans

34 *Santa Lucía del Trampal, near Mérida. The triple apse has parallels in Syria and the church is thought to have been an eremitical monastery of the type more common in the Byzantine Empire.* Reproduced with the kind permission of Roger Collins

are found in southern Gaul, as at Lyon, as well as in the Iberian peninsula, as at San Pedro de la Mata, Santa Comba de Bande and possibly San Juan de Baños and San Pedro de la Nave, the latter both extensively reconstructed in the nineteenth and twentieth centuries respectively. However, whether their use in the Iberian peninsula and elsewhere in the West evolved as a response to the liturgical customs of the East is unclear. In Syrian churches, the chamber on the north side of the apse served as the *diaconicon,* the room where the Eucharist was prepared, while the southern room sometimes served as a martyr's chapel. Without further research and excavation it seems impossible to tell the extent to which the construction of correlate rooms in Western churches was a reflex of this. It is perhaps more likely that the development was simply a response to the increasing complexity of liturgical demands.

Yet, in the context of architectural parallels, it is worth noting that the sculptural ornamentation at some of these churches also hints at links with the East. At the church of San Pedro de la Nave, the capitals in the highly ornamented chancel depict the sacrifice of Isaac, Daniel in the lion's den, and a man praying in the *orans* style, all motifs of Eastern Mediterranean origin. It must be noted that these are found elsewhere in the West earlier than these churches, and the 'Daniel' motif is found on other categories of Visigothic material, such as belt buckles. Nonetheless, in the context of other architectural evidence in the Iberian peninsula, they cannot be discarded as possible hints of East-West contacts. Indeed, the use of animal depictions on column capitals derived from the fifth-century Byzantine Empire, possibly Constantinople itself (**colour plate 13**).[44]

Close parallels are found at Santa María de Quintanilla de las Viñas, where the low relief sculptural frieze around the exterior of the church also has Byzantine antecedents. The motifs employed here include chi-rhos hung with the alpha and omega and enclosed in an ornate roundel, birds and petalled floral motifs, all of which have Eastern counterparts also arranged as exterior friezes on churches, as at Deir Si'man, for instance (**colour plates 14 & 16**). Ignacio Peña has observed a further similarity, drawing attention to the position of the motifs in relation to the plan of the church: '[the] crosses are engraved almost exclusively on the east wall (side of the apse) and on the south wall (side of the Chapel of Martyrs), positions identical to those in Syrian churches' (**35**).[45]

The workmanship of the stone-carving required is so regular that the blocks must almost certainly have been carved in a workshop on a horizontal surface, rather than *in situ* after the church's construction. Yet, the artisans who produced the frieze at Santa María clearly knew the exact dimensions of the church, since the blocks fit precisely together in the middle of the pattern's sequence. It is possible that elements of this monument were 'prefabricated', in the sense that they were manufactured away from the construction site, to precise specifications, and then brought together for assembly. However, such a practice cannot be demonstrated at this stage, although it is well attested by the Marzamemi shipwreck.[46]

THE ROLE OF THE CHURCH

If these motifs and depictions are modelled on Syrian prototypes, as seems possible, the question remains as to their mode of transmission. The presence of itinerant missionaries and other clergy from the Byzantine Empire may partially account for this, but the precision with which they are reproduced suggests a material, rather than an ideational, model. In archaeological terms, this might be represented by portable items such belt buckles or jewellery. For example, the distinctive 'lyre-shaped' belt buckles that are sometimes found in late sixth- and early seventh-century Visigothic burials are thought to be 'copies' of Byzantine prototypes, and these often bear motifs similar to those seen in ecclesiastical ornamentation. While not a lyre-form buckle, a Byzantine belt tab said to have been found at Málaga bears the familiar eight-petalled floral motif (**36** & **37**).[47]

Of course, we may simply be seeing the product of the craftsmanship of Syrian artisans who found refuge and work in Spain after the Arab invasion. A seventh-century exodus to Spain is textually attested. Yet, the exodus itself raises the question of why Syrian refugees should have focused on the Iberian peninsula. After all, the easiest passage to the West would have delivered them to Italy, where there was already a substantial Syrian population in the late fifth and early sixth centuries. It seems possible that they were attracted to the peninsula for the same reason that some other refugees were attracted to Italy: because there was already an Eastern community there and Eastern patterns of life were well-established.[48]

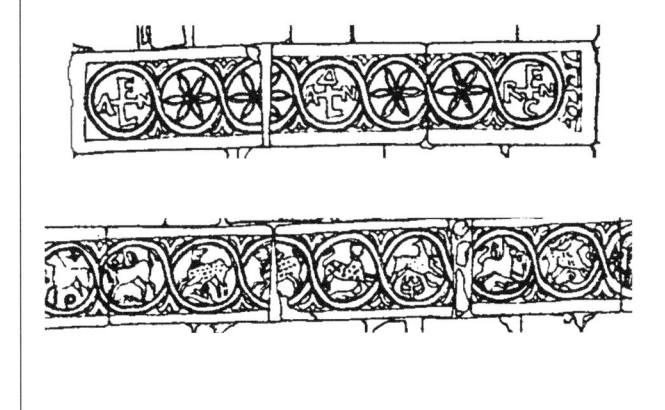

35 *Comparison of sculptured exterior friezes from churches in Spain and Syria.* After Arbeiter (1990) and Fernández (2000)

Above: section of external relief decoration at Santa María de Quintanilla de las Viñas, Spain. Right: section of external relief decoration at Deir Sambil, Syria

127

Ascribing far-flung prototypes to buildings can be problematic, and one must, of course, always search first for a nearer source of inspiration. However, in this case, as in the other cases touched upon in this chapter, there seems good reason to look further afield than Western Europe. At the latest, the relevant Iberian churches have been dated to about 711, some 200 years after their first postulated counterparts in the East were built. This would render it unlikely that they were the product of direct contacts with the East but there may be a case for dating some of the Iberian churches to the sixth century, in which case the time lag would be shorter.

This has some support in textual evidence. E.A. Thompson long ago argued that 'the second half of the sixth century saw the beginning of a profound Byzantine influence on objects of daily use among the Visigoths'. This is particularly evident in the culture of local ecclesiastical élites. At Mérida, for example, the clergy wore vestments fashioned of Byzantine silk and used Byzantine liturgical vessels and other ornaments, while the town's most important relic – the tunic of the patron saint, Eulalia – is thought to have been modelled on an Eastern design. Two of the city's bishops, Paul and Fidelis, also hailed from the Eastern Mediterranean. Both men were Byzantines who had arrived in Spain in the 540s on a merchant ship from the East. Paul was a physician and is recorded as having performed a successful caesarean section on the wife of a local dignitary, an allusion to the high regard in which Byzantine medicine was held in the West. Intriguingly, at Dumio in the same period, a monastery founded by an Eastern monk from Braga in the north-west of the peninsula, the monks were forbidden to drink wine

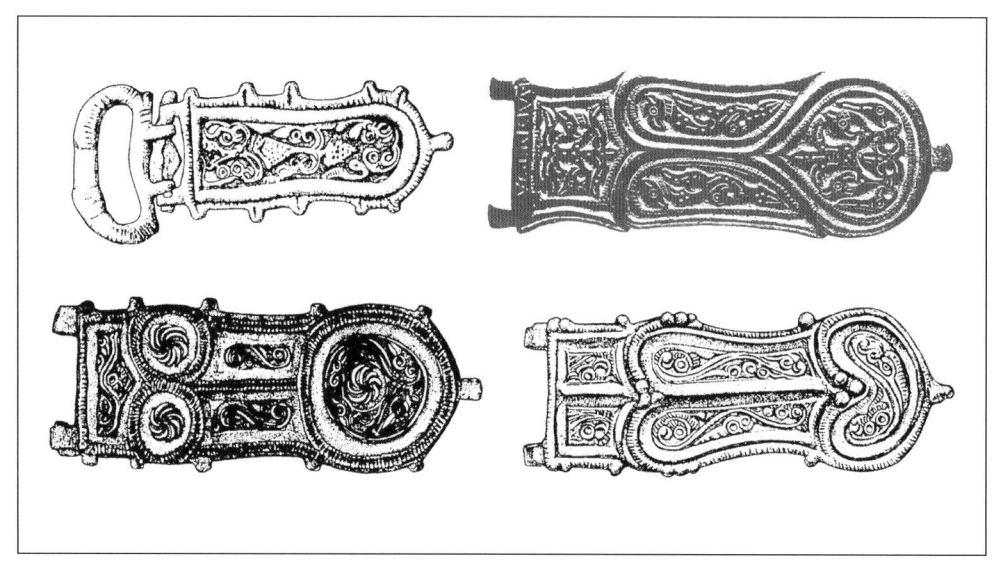

36 *Byzantine-style buckles from Spain.*
After Ebel-Zepezauer (2000)/O'Neill and Howard *et al.* (1993)

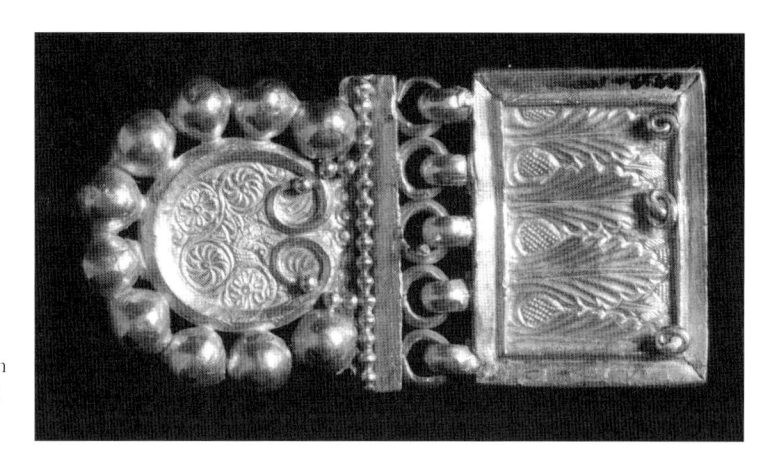

37 *Fifth- or sixth-century Byzantine gold belt tab, found near Malaga, Spain.* Reproduced with the kind permission of the Victoria and Albert Museum

imported from the Eastern Mediterranean. Evidently these wines were available in Spain and may, until the ban, have been directly imported by the monastery itself, although why they should be banned is a mystery – perhaps the order was meant to imply that they should abstain from all wines.[49]

If some of the churches discussed above were built during these years of intense Byzantine contact with Spain, this would permit the Syrian architects to have come to the peninsula at the very time when Syrian architectural schools were flourishing. Moreover, this was a time when an analogous cultural context existed in Syria and the Iberian peninsula: a late antique Christian society (among the sub-Roman population and the Byzantine south) with both regions, albeit to differing degrees, in contact with the imperial authorities in Constantinople. Finally, and perhaps most importantly, there was an obvious means of transmission in the form of the Syrians – merchants and others – who are documented in the Iberian peninsula during this period. On this basis, there could well be a relationship between Iberian and Syrian architecture with its origins in sixth-century, as well as seventh-century, contacts between the two regions. Indeed, it is hard to believe that the similarities are wholly independent of the other evidence for possible connections with Syria that we have seen in chapter 3.

Finally, we might mention an anomalous group of ecclesiastical 'buildings' found in the Valley of the Ebro. These are 'rock-cut' structures, one of which may be epigraphically dated to 587 and which bears a Greek graffito. Many are multi-roomed structures, some resembling churches and some have Christian graffiti, including crosses. While not all these structures are necessarily churches, nor are of the same date, some appear to have had an ecclesiastical function and their chronology demonstrably spans the period discussed here. Even those structures that more plausibly date from the medieval period are sometimes thought to have antecedents in Late Antiquity, such as where a naturally-formed cave forms the nucleus of a later carved rock-cut church. This may be seen at San Millán (or Emilian) de la Cogolla, where the hermit is said to have died in his cave hermitage in the region around Berceo in 574.[50]

The rock-cut churches include structures that superficially resemble examples from Eastern monastic sites, such as Kellia in Egypt (in layout) and the Middle Byzantine-period Cappadocian rock-cut churches of Anatolia. Although published as 'hermitages' they need not have been the cells of solitaries so much as 'hermitage monasteries' of the type better known in Late Antiquity in the Eastern Mediterranean. Obviously, this prompts one to wonder whether hermitages, too, may have Byzantine prototypes, a point given new prominence by the buildings discussed so far.[51]

Western eremiticism and the East

The whole issue of hermits in the West following Byzantine prototypes has often been at the centre of debates over East-West links in Late Antiquity. However, the evidence that any Western hermits copied Byzantine models is surprisingly slim and the problems involved can be well illustrated by evidence from Gaul.

Here, eremiticism had become widely-known through the fourth-century career of St Martin of Tours, who spent part of his life living as a hermit, first in Milan and then on the island of Gallinaria, off the Genoan coast, yet apparently without known contact with the East. Thereafter, many were drawn to the eremitical life as an expression of their allegiance to St Martin, although after his death in 397 some of his followers did travel to the East to visit anchorites there, and so even Martinian monasticism was influenced by Eastern models of behaviour by the early fifth century. Yet, although fifth-century Martinian monasticism cannot be seen as wholly separate from developments in the East, there was another strand of asceticism that was influential in the West before c.400. This was favoured by the sub-Roman aristocracy and also had links with the East by the late fourth century, when John Cassian travelled from Marseille to Syria in 381 to experience the eremitic life at first hand. Around the same time, the letters of Jerome, who had spent time as a hermit in the Syrian desert in 375 and had written of his experiences in letters to Christians in Rome, were widely circulated. Other Western clerics also spent time as hermits in the East in the late fourth century, although more probably lived as anchorites in a wholly Western context.[52]

Our main textual sources for eremiticism in fifth- and sixth-century Gaul are the writings of Gregory of Tours and the *Lives* of the 'Jura Fathers', a group of hagiographical writings concerning the lives of solitaries living in the Jura region in the east of Gaul. Both make it clear that those who chose to become hermits were inspired as much by Western ascetics, most often St Martin, as by the famous Eastern monks of the day in Syria or the Holy Land. Moreover, an examination of where Gregory locates hermits indicates no special correlation with places known to have had links with the East in the fifth and sixth centuries. It is unsurprising that most of Gregory's hermits come from the Tours area, given that this was where he was based. Nevertheless, there are Byzantine ceramics attested at Tours and textual sources also indicate links between the town and the East. For example, news of events in the Antioch region was brought to Tours by Simon, a visiting bishop from Syria. So it is possible that the popularity of eremiticism there was partially a consequence of Eastern contacts.[53]

Despite this, the legacy of St Martin in Tours is sufficient to outweigh any suggestion that these hermits were indubitably in contact with the East. Most other solitaries mentioned by Gregory are from the Auvergne, an area which, as we have seen in the church architecture at Clermont, may also have had links with Byzantium. Indeed, one Eastern monk, Abraham, from the Euphrates region, is described as founding a 'communal hermitage' there, so it is not out of the question that local eremiticism thereafter was inspired by his example. However, in the context of late fourth-century asceticism in Gaul, as well as the strong memory of St Martin, it seems likely that the hermits of the Auvergne were responding to more than one monastic reflex.[54]

However, some indication of a genuinely Byzantine contribution to Gallic monasticism may be gained from textual evidence. It is salient that when Gregory mentions 'foreign' hermits, or advocates of the eremitical lifestyle, they are often from the East, rather than from Italy or the Iberian peninsula. In addition to Abraham, who had originally been on his way 'to go into the wilderness of Egypt to visit the hermits' before he came to Gaul, Gregory mentions Quintianus, an African who walked around the city walls of Clermont praying and singing psalms 'in the Eastern manner', when it was under siege in around 525. We hear, too, of Vulfoliac, who lived on a pillar near Trier, specifically in imitation of the Syrian monk, Symeon Stylites. Another ascetic, Amandus, was installed by his bishop in one of the towers along the city walls of Bourges, while a monk named Hospitius wrapped himself in chains, dressed only in a hair shirt, and dwelt in a tower near Nice. Both of these men may have been emulating Syrian tower-hermits. In fact, Hospitius is described by Gregory as living off herbs imported from Egypt, in the manner of hermits back in the East – perhaps an oblique reference to trade with Egypt and to a broader understanding of eremitical lifestyles in the East.[55]

The archaeology of eremiticism

Despite some hints at the material circumstances of their lives – cells, huts, towers, chains – and despite the emphasis that has been placed on southern Gaul in relation to this question, the archaeological evidence for eremiticism remains weak. Whether this need concern us is less clear cut because even St

Martin has very little supporting archaeological evidence. The only object that may directly be connected with the saint's own life is an inscribed stone from Gaul that apparently refers to a miracle mentioned in Sulpicius Severus' biography of the saint (*Vita Martini*).[56]

It may simply be that hermits leave few distinctive archaeological traces. Identifying eremitical activity is extremely difficult, principally because a true hermit might be expected to leave very little in the way of material remains. He or she may not even have lived in a shelter built especially for that purpose, but rather in some pre-existing structure. Tower hermitages demonstrate at the outset that eremiticism might be archaeologically recognised, but that recognition might also be very difficult unless we are able to define specifically eremitical features such as these towers. How many archaeologists working on the West would interpret a tower as a hermitage, or at least entertain the possibility that it might, at some stage, have been employed in an eremitical context? The features of an Eastern hermit's cell: a stone couch for sleeping, small recesses for oil lamps, prayer niches and stone benches, are not distinctive enough to be immediately recognisable, if unexpected. The use of simple, perhaps just one-roomed, buildings or caves, or the reuse of 'old' structures (for example the *cellae* of pagan temples), would render eremitical occupation especially hard to recognise. Hermits may have used few artefacts that were specifically religious or 'eremitical' in character: broken pottery and food debris might be all that remained after the death or removal of the hermit. Moreover, although hermits sought out a *desertum* for themselves, it was possible for this to be a mental *desertum*, rather than a physical one. As noted above, hermits could live in close proximity to, if not within, local communities, even towns. Thus, hermits elude the archaeologist in most cases and we must probably assume that all but a tiny minority of eremitical sites cannot now be detected archaeologically.[57]

Few sites in Gaul have yielded any 'archaeology of early eremiticism'. Those investigated include Marseille and the Île St Honorat, the smallest of the Îles de Lérins, just off the coast of present-day Cannes. A late 1970s survey of the Île St Honorat found various archaeological features, but none dating unquestionably from the fifth to seventh century. Nevertheless, Lérins is known to have already been important in the early fifth century, when its regime is mentioned as being particularly strict. Its founder, Honoratus (d. 430), had 'trained' as a hermit in Egypt, before returning to Gaul to found this retreat for fellow anchorites, which then produced several members of the ecclesiastical establishment. For example, in 429 Germanus of Auxerre travelled to Britain in the company of a former monk from Lérins, Lupus of Troyes.[58]

Most of the other Gallic archaeological evidence is from Brittany, but this is also ambiguous. Pierre-Roland Giot has suggested that the Île Saint Maudez, Castel Cos and Castel Meur might be early eremitical sites, but these have not been excavated. Lavret on the Isles de Bréhat, a cluster of small islets just off the coast near Paimpol in northern Brittany, may be the only excavated site in the

Armorican peninsula (Brittany) that has produced convincing evidence of what may be a Breton monastery of pre-*c*.600 date (**colour plate 21**). The site was originally used for a Gallo-Roman villa and this seems to have been occupied into the early fifth century. The walls still partially stand, and around and within them excavation by Giot has discovered traces of occupation associated with Byzantine ceramic imports (LR1) and E-ware pottery. Radiocarbon dates extend to the eighth century. The date range of the occupation may, then, extend from the fifth to eighth century, although it is uncertain if this was in an unbroken sequence. The villa-site was later used for a small Viking Age and Carolingian burial ground and medieval chapel, the latter associated with what may be hermits' cells dated by *céramique onctueuse*. Lavret is arguably analogous to Lérins in topographical terms and could represent a similar 'communal eremitical' monastic foundation off the Breton coast.[59]

The small enclosed settlement on Enez Guennoc ('the white island') off the north-western coast of Finistère may also have been a focus of eremiticism, but again the evidence is inconclusive. The site has been well-excavated and one phase of activity is radiocarbon dated to the sixth century, but there is nothing specifically ecclesiastical about the excavated features. However, the island is very harsh and can only have supported the poorest of farms, so it is possible that this was an eremitical settlement instead. It is nevertheless more likely that the site represents much more widespread forms of enclosure – analogous to Cornish 'rounds' – better preserved here because of the atypical location. In less inhospitable settings, similar sites may have been destroyed or obscured by later farms or farming. There are no diagnostic finds capable of positing an Eastern link with this site, although the LR1 amphora sherd from Lavret and 'chance finds' of Byzantine coins elsewhere in Brittany do not rule this out.[60]

Another island with possible eremitical evidence is the Île Agois, off the coast of Jersey, classified here as part of Armorica on geographical grounds. The remains of some 25 small curvilinear huts have been compared with small, remote eremitical sites in Ireland and northern Britain. A Carolingian coin was found on the island, and is unlikely to be a casual loss, but there is no definitive date for the series of small huts that occupy this remote, inhospitable island. Notwithstanding this disappointing lack of diagnostic evidence, the physical location of the buildings, and shared characteristics with later sites interpreted as hermitages in coastal regions of Ireland and northern Britain, suggest a possible eremitical use.[61]

Place-name evidence also suggests that the Channel Islands were attractive to would-be anchorites during Late Antiquity: St Helier is associated with Hélier, a monk from Tongeren (Belgium) who journeyed there to become a hermit. Hermitage Rock is said to have been the location for Hélier's cell, and there is a small medieval chapel on the site, although no direct evidence for activity during the fifth to seventh centuries. It is hardly surprising that a group of islands with so many smaller islands, islets and rocky headlands should attract people desiring the ascetic life, but remarkably there is little archaeological evidence to make a convincing case for early eremitical activity here. Other sites have associations with Insular saints, but, once again, no definitive evidence.[62]

Pilgrimage to the Eastern Mediterranean

Although there is little evidence for Western eremiticism having Byzantine origins, many Westerners could well have travelled to the East as pilgrims. A rapid rise in the popularity of Christian pilgrimage had begun in the fourth century. Christians travelled across the length of the Roman world, including from the West, to visit places associated with the life of Christ or the saints, especially where new churches were being constructed under imperial patronage. The fourth-century phase of this movement focused on Jerusalem and the Holy Land, but soon Rome and other great episcopal centres attracted pilgrims.

The 'diary' of Egeria – an aristocratic woman probably from north-west Spain – provides a clear picture of late fourth-century pilgrimage from the West, and highlights the emergence of new devotional patterns. Whereas earlier pilgrims seem to have relied upon the Roman public facilities to ease their journeys, Egeria received hospitality almost exclusively from bishops and monks. She and pilgrims like her were anxious to avoid being exposed to the more 'secular' aspects of life in the places through which they had to travel, and made sure they lodged in monastic dwellings wherever possible. Around the same time, a Church Council meeting in the southern Gallic city of Nîmes, in 396, issued a canon against those who abused the goodwill of local congregations 'on the pretext of pilgrimage'. It would seem that by the beginning of the fifth century, pilgrimage was reaching new levels of popularity and new modes of hospitality were emerging to accommodate pilgrims.[63]

Jerusalem remained a popular and potent symbol throughout the fifth- to seventh-century period, uniting Christians across the Mediterranean world and beyond. This was remarkable, given that it could take up to a year to make the journey from Western Europe to Jerusalem. Jerusalem itself was, as we have seen, monumentalised through buildings connected with pilgrimage and the wealth this generated, and remained the foremost pilgrimage centre in the Christian world long after its capture by the Arabs in 638. As the principal site associated with the life of Christ, it was a focal point for people across both the Byzantine East and the former Roman West, providing them with an outlet for expressing shared religious and cultural affinities.[64]

Images of Jerusalem in the time of Christ were reproduced on items of both religious and secular significance, such as the ivory belt buckle from Arles, showing Roman soldiers asleep outside the tomb at Gethsemane (**colour plate 18**). According to Paul the Deacon, the Frankish king, Guntram, built a 'golden canopy', and 'wished to send it, adorned with many precious gems, to Jerusalem to the sepulchre of our Lord'. However, 'when he could not at all do this he caused it to be placed over the body of St Marcellus the martyr who was buried in the city of Cabillonum', the 'capital' of the Burgundian kingdom (modern Chalon-sur-Saône). Presumably, the logistics of transporting the canopy from Frankia to Jerusalem prevented Guntram from achieving his ambition, and he was forced to express his affinity with Jerusalem in a more localised fashion, in the funerary church that he had established for his own burial.[65]

From the beginning of the fifth century, new foci of pilgrimage became increasingly popular. Many Western pilgrims travelled to Rome to visit the sites associated with St Peter and St Paul. For those who went as far as the Eastern Mediterranean, Syria and Egypt were now particularly popular destinations, as was Constantinople. In these places, the shrines of holy men and women were the focus of attention, and if the holy person in question was still living, so much the better. Symeon Stylites, the Syrian monk who lived for over 30 years on top of a column in an act of self-denial, received visitors from as far afield as Britain. Another Eastern stylite, Daniel, was visited by a man from Gaul by the name of Titus, who had been sent by the Emperor Leo. Symeon obtained such popularity amongst the ordinary people of Rome that, according to his biographer, shopkeepers pinned pictures of him on the doorposts of their shops. This may well be true, for other forms of evidence also suggest that Symeon's memory was part of popular religious culture outside the Eastern Empire, and that this remained the case until at least the beginning of the eighth century. A depiction of the saint decorated the hypogeum of Mellebaude at Poitiers, dating from around 700, and a relief, also from Gaul, carries the name of both Symeon and his disciple, Abramios. The erection of the imposing church at Qal'at Si'man, some 30 years after his death, testifies to Symeon's enduring popularity in the East (**29, 38** & **colour plate 3**).[66]

In archaeological terms, the increased popularity of pilgrimage is indicated by the presence in the West of portable objects that could have been obtained at pilgrim shrines and easily transported home. After this long and arduous journey, which the vast majority of pilgrims would only make once in a lifetime, something was needed to remind them of their experience and, perhaps, to provide a conduit through which they might relive it. Such artefacts are represented archaeologically through *ampullae,* small pottery flasks that were probably originally filled with sanctified oil or water. The memoir of a sixth-century Italian traveller to the Holy Land provides a vivid picture of the context in which these might be used: '. . . they offer oil to be blessed in little flasks. When the mouth of one of the little flasks touches the Wood of the Cross, the oil instantly bubbles over, and unless it is closed very quickly it all spills out'.[67]

By far the largest group of these receptacles derives from the shrine of St Menas, which was approximately 40 miles from Alexandria and marked by the impressive Abu Mîna church. The flasks were mass-produced and have been

38 *Qal'at Si'man, Syria, built c.490 to enclose the column of St Symeon Stylites.* Reproduced with the kind permission of Stuart Whatling

found throughout Western Europe, as far from Egypt as the Wirral peninsula on Merseyside (**colour plates 5** & **19**). Their distribution and manufacture from inexpensive materials mean that they can be seen as a response to new developments in pilgrimage in the early fifth century. Insofar as their fifth- to seventh-century Western distribution can be ascertained with any accuracy, they cluster around northern Italy, the coastal regions of southern Gaul and the Rhône/Rhine corridor to the north. As we saw in chapter 3, this has a correlation with contemporary trade routes, and may suggest that not all St Menas flasks arrived at their destination in a purely pilgrimage context. That said, and as noted above, it is likely that pilgrims and merchants shared modes of transportation, so that the distributional correlation of 'pilgrimage artefacts' and objects associated with commercial exchange need not cause any difficulties of interpretation. Pilgrims, such as Egeria, are attested as travelling on ships bound for Eastern Mediterranean ports, and vessels are known to have provided places for persons travelling on business other than trade.[68]

The mass production of St Menas flasks may reflect pilgrimage amongst less wealthy Westerners, perhaps facilitated by increased contacts between the Eastern Mediterranean in other contexts. It is possible that more monks were now enabled to make the journey, although it should not be assumed that monks were always poor. For the more affluent, there were reliquary boxes, such as that in the Cappella Sancta Sanctorum treasure, often decorated with scenes of the life of Christ or of the places associated with Him. Pilgrims may also have taken books home with them, for the production of religious books in the Holy Land increased in the fifth and sixth centuries. Carlo Bertelli has noted that the production of copies of Genesis and the Gospels rose comparatively steeply in sixth- and seventh-century Palestine, and suggests that this was a response to demand from wealthy pilgrims for 'souvenirs' of their pilgrimages. Of course, the élite was not excluded from an interest in *ampullae*, and these were not necessarily obtained only in a pilgrimage context. For example, Pope Gregory the Great sent a diplomatic gift of many silver Byzantine *ampullae* to the Lombard queen, Theodelinda, which she placed in her richly-decorated church at Monza, along with other gifts, including a Byzantine gold cross.[69]

Given the popularity of St Menas, it is intriguing that there was an ecclesiastical guild of St Menas – consisting of merchants from Egypt – in fifth-century Rome, and it is possible that Eastern guilds (with ecclesiastical links) were represented in other parts of the late antique West. This may, for example, be the most likely explanation behind Gregory of Tours' account of Eastern traders parading through the streets of sixth-century Orléans singing hymns and carrying standards. The importance attached to resident guilds in the West might also explain why Eastern Mediterranean religious practices were sometimes assimilated into Western behaviour. For example, in Sarragosa, the inhabitants fasted and marched around the city walls in a manner reminiscent of the inhabitants of Constantinople. But whereas Constantinopolitans carried the tunic of the Virgin in their procession, the people of Saragossa carried the tunic of St Vincent. Similar practices are attested at Mérida in attitudes towards the relics of St Eulalia and, as seen above, at Nantes, when the security of the town was threatened.[70]

Pilgrimage and other forms of 'religious' travel may help to explain the circulation of Byzantine books and Byzantine copies of the sacred texts in the late antique West. Books would be unlikely objects of long-distance trade in their own right, although those who carried them may have travelled on merchants' ships. The Rabbula Gospels may have come to the West in this way. As Averil Cameron has demonstrated, Gregory of Tours had access to at least one Byzantine chronicle and probably other Byzantine written sources.[71]

It may be that one of these sources was the late fifth-century *Life* of Daniel the Stylite. This describes how a 'barbarian' from Gaul who aspired to become a hermit was renamed by the holy man Daniel as 'Anatolius'. There are parallels here with the story in Gregory's *Historia Francorum* where another Gallic individual named Anatolius, a 12-year-old boy in the service of a merchant in Bordeaux, is described as seeking permission from his master to become a hermit. The similarities between the two stories make it possible that Gregory was able to use the *Life* of Daniel the Stylite when composing his own work. Conversely, it is also possible that the name Anatolius carried special associations with the solitary life in Gaul and that the boy at Bordeaux had been given the name as confirmation of his eremitical calling. If so, it is interesting that this pattern of behaviour has a specific link with the Syrian community and its entourage.[72]

It is clear, then, that Western pilgrims and other ecclesiastical travellers were instrumental in facilitating Mediterranean-wide religious identities in this period, enabled to do so, perhaps, by trading networks and other pathways of interaction. They might have returned home (if they were fortunate) with a range of incidental Eastern ecclesiastical exports, including St Menas flasks and other *ampullae*, books and reliquaries. Pilgrims returning from the East had also been exposed to the heart of the Christian eremitical monastic world and potentially to new ideas about monastic forms. In this sense it is perhaps surprising that the archaeological evidence for pre-seventh-century eremiticism is so thin.

Conclusion

Thus, although early eremiticism cannot be seen as forming the critical connection between Eastern and Western Churches that is often supposed, there is enough evidence to show that contacts structured by 'religious' contexts were important in the development of the fifth- and sixth-century West. Despite the proliferation of church types in the fifth century, Westerners built churches 'copying' those of the Byzantine world. At least, such churches were built in the West – it is possible that Easterners themselves had a hand in their construction. These and other churches were sometimes also dedicated in an Eastern manner. There seems, too, to be some evidence that church structures and dedications could be related, as in the case of Gallic dedications of cruciform churches to the Holy Apostles.

Likewise, the popularity of Eastern pilgrimage and other forms of 'religious' travel from the late fourth and early fifth century onwards not only formed an *oikoumenê*-wide ecclesiastical network, but was instrumental in shaping the literary and material culture of the fifth- and sixth-century West. It is interesting to note where these links seem to correlate with other evidence for East-West contacts in this period, such as those implied by ceramics and metalwork, and it is reasonable to suggest that, at least in part, these contacts were mutually supportive. The question remains, therefore, of how far Britain was part of this series of relationships and whether they were equally instrumental in shaping the cultural life of the island in this period. This is the subject of the next chapter.

6

BRITAIN & BYZANTIUM

Introduction: the seventh-century transformation of the late antique world

Many scholars have argued that post-Roman Britain only became reconnected to Continental Europe after the arrival of the Papal mission led by Augustine in Kent in 597. However, while the subsequent conversion of the Anglo-Saxons to Christianity may have re-established a direct institutional link between the south-east of Britain and Rome, this was the outcome of a pattern of longer-term developments in the east of the island, starting perhaps as early as the mid-sixth century. This, in turn, was characterised by intensified commercial and probably political relations between Kent and Frankia, and may have borne some relationship to the emergence of larger political units in eastern Britain in the late sixth century.

The acceptance of an ecclesiastical structure based in Rome facilitated a range of contacts between seventh-century eastern Britain and Byzantine Italy, perhaps as much with Ravenna as with Rome. In both cities, the importance of the Byzantine Empire meant that there was no lack of opportunity to obtain materials from the Eastern Mediterranean. It may have been on a visit to Italy by an ecclesiastical traveller, for example, that the late sixth- or early seventh-century Byzantine silk was acquired that was later used in the tomb of St Cuthbert. The Church envoy and later founder of the Monkwearmouth and Jarrow monasteries, Benedict Biscop, brought at least two silk cloaks back from Rome in 685 or 686, and later exchanged them for land in Britain.[1]

The role of early seventh-century Frankia as a conduit for contacts with Byzantium should also not be underestimated. It is all too easy with hindsight to see the growing power of Frankia in political and cultural terms as part of a process of 'throwing off' Byzantine hegemony. However, for the seventh-century Anglo-Saxons, the relative economic stability of the Franks and their confident expressions of kingship and authority may have appeared proof of imperial favour and confirmation that the court in Constantinople remained the ultimate source of political authority. After all, had not Constantine the Great come from the lands of the Franks, according to Byzantine (and possibly Frankish) mistaken belief? Seen, too, in the context of the Anglo-Saxons' newly-found Christian faith, the religious beliefs of the Franks may have made them appear linked to a Christian world that was still, to some extent, focused on the Eastern Mediterranean.[2]

Those Anglo-Saxon clerics who travelled to Italy on ecclesiastical business during the first half of the seventh century may well have had these and other ideas emphasised to them as they made their way through Frankia. In this way, a sense of a shared cultural world, of which they were now full members, may have become more meaningful to the Anglo-Saxons in the first decades of the seventh century, consolidating the cultural contacts of the late sixth century and concomitant expressions of identity.

In other words, cultural change in Anglo-Saxon England in the first half of the seventh century may have been driven by a desire for affiliation with a still-existing Roman Empire which was at the centre of the Christian world. The mission to the Anglo-Saxons had, after all, been initiated by Gregory the Great, who had spent time as a diplomat (papal legate) in Constantinople from 579 to 585. Gregory was thoroughly imbued with the Byzantine idea that the Pope was the equal, rather than the superior, of the Patriarch of Constantinople, and that he was also the secular representative of the Emperor in the Byzantine duchy of Rome. It is possible that Gregory also shared the Byzantine perception of Britain as representing the farthest reaches of the *oikoumenê*, the world that was both 'Roman' and 'Christian'. Several decades after Augustine's mission, in writing to Edwin of Northumbria, Pope Boniface V still referred to Britain as one of 'the most distant nations of the world', and this sentiment may have also influenced Gregory's desire to incorporate it more fully into the 'Christian Empire'. In this sense, then, the origins of the famous Papal mission to the Anglo-Saxons may have been linked to currents of thought in the Byzantine world.[3]

However, once Augustine reached eastern Britain and settled down to nurture the Church there, his links with Rome and the Papacy took precedence over any lingering Byzantine ideals. Emerging Anglo-Saxon ecclesiastical and monastic life took on what was in essence a 'Western' form, strongly influenced by contacts with Rome, and these were consolidated after the Synod of Whitby in 664. Most seventh-century monastic establishments were coenobitic (communal) and often housed large numbers of monks, as Bede's (admittedly eighth-century) comments show. In 716, when Abbot Ceolfrid left the Jarrow-Monkwearmouth foundation with 80 people, he left 600 behind.[4]

In Anglo-Saxon ecclesiastical architecture, too, there are only the merest hints at contact with the Byzantine world until after the mid-seventh century. Thereafter, a great flowering of art and architecture made Britain a focus for new cultural syntheses, some of them drawn from the Eastern Mediterranean. However, these are irrelevant here. At Augustine's church of Sts Peter and Paul, Canterbury, built in the early seventh century, the plan includes two lateral chambers, one on the north side of the church and the other on the south side. As a funerary church, these chambers were intended as burial places for the ecclesiastical and secular élite: seventh- and eighth-century bishops and archbishops were buried in the north chamber and members of the Kentish secular élite (King Æthelberht and Queen Bertha) in the south chamber. It might be thought that this reflects some of the church plans seen in the East and discussed in the previous chapter, but by the seventh century it is not possible to attribute this design specifically to Byzantine church-building practices, for similar plans had been adopted in several Iberian, Frankish and Italian churches by the sixth and seventh centuries. Moreover, we know little or nothing about the decoration of the church at Canterbury (**39** & **40**).[5]

Augustine and those who followed him to Britain had travelled through Frankia, where they had spent time and enjoyed hospitality in important late antique urban centres such as Arles, Vienne, Lyon, Autun and Tours. The architecture they saw there, as well as that of Italy, may well have provided them with models for the construction of their own churches. It is perhaps more appropriate, therefore, to interpret the churches that were built in seventh-century Anglo-Saxon England both as a mélange of various Frankish styles and as part of the general 'renaissance' of Italo-Byzantine styles that took place in the second part of the seventh century.

Ironically, Rome itself drew heavily on Byzantine artistic and architectural models throughout this period. The famous St Augustine Gospels, which a plausible tradition holds that Augustine brought with him to Britain in 597, are plainly 'Byzantine' in their artistic derivation, although the manuscript itself (now in the library of Corpus Christi College, Cambridge) was probably produced in a Western context, almost certainly Italy. Neither should the 'Byzantinised' nature of the late antique Papacy be underestimated. For most of the period, the Byzantine authorities were able to harness the political strength of the Papacy to their own cause, particularly after Byzantine rule in Rome was re-enforced from 536 onward (it lasted until 756). Papal legates were welcomed to Constantinople and given a privileged position at court, as well as the use of their own palace. From the early sixth century until the early eighth century, representatives from the Roman Church were key participants in ecumenical Church Councils.[6]

Many of the papal diplomats serving in Constantinople in the sixth and seventh centuries went on to become Bishops of Rome, including Pope Gregory the Great. In Rome itself, the Emperor continued to be revered in the life of the Church despite the political upheaval going on around it. Regular prayers were said for him and the rest of the imperial family until the beginning of the Iconoclast crisis in 731. Roman diptychs were marked with the names of both the Emperor and the Patriarch of Constantinople, and coins minted in Rome continued to carry the image of the Emperor. In many ways, these 'Byzantine' aspects of ecclesiastical behaviour appear to have been so naturalised into the life of the Roman Church that for much of the seventh century they escaped negative comment. This was not the case elsewhere in Italy: in 598, for instance, Gregory the Great had to placate the bishops in Sicily, who complained of inappropriate 'Greek' (that is, 'Byzantine') influence in the Church there.[7]

39 *Seventh-century foundations of Sts Peter and Paul, the funerary church for St Augustine and the first Anglo-Saxon monarchs.* Photograph by Anthea Harris

40 *Seventh-century foundations of the Chapel of St Pancras, Canterbury.* Photograph by Anthea Harris

So the Papal Rome that was the key model for the Anglo-Saxon Church was itself a conduit of Byzantine cultural influences on eastern Britain. Yet, the Western European world around it was, by the seventh century, rapidly developing new patterns of social, economic and political behaviour. So those aspects of Byzantine culture that reached the Anglo-Saxons did so as part of a changing cultural world, one that could now be termed 'early medieval', rather than 'late antique'. Nonetheless, if we look at the fifth and sixth centuries a very different pattern becomes apparent.

Fifth- and sixth-century Britain

In order to understand Byzantine relations with Britain before the 590s, we must start by looking once more at the evidence from the Continent. We have previously seen that two different networks of maritime commercial contact may have connected Byzantium and the West. One brought luxury goods up the Rhine, probably via either northern Italy or the Rhône, and other European rivers. A case was made for Egypt as the possible point of origin of this network. The objects, which acquired high-status associations in some contexts, may have been transferred either through trade or through diplomatic exchange. The other network appears to have had a more explicitly diplomatic purpose and might have involved the utilisation of official supply systems, bringing, amongst other items, LR1 (Bii) and LR2 (Bi) amphorae. This network may have originated in Syria. There is some evidence to suggest that each of these networks terminated in Britain but in separate zones: one system fed into eastern Britain, while the other led to the west of the country, and perhaps also to Ireland.

These two zones have another association. In the fifth and sixth centuries the Anglo-Saxons, barbarian migrants from outside the Roman Empire, settled in the eastern areas of Britain, gradually spreading west and north. As we shall see, the Rhineland network may have supplied luxuries to Anglo-Saxon communities, whereas the 'British West' retained a population of indigenous Britons, living in 'sub-Roman' communities well into the period, before they were finally incorporated into 'Anglo-Saxon England' in the seventh and eighth centuries. In the fifth and sixth centuries, however, these western areas were home to people descended from Romano-British citizens (the 'Britons'), who dwelt outside of barbarian rule, living under their own rulers as the only entirely independent sub-Roman kingdoms in the West.

Western Britain

These two zones may be used to organise not merely our thoughts about Britain during the fifth to seventh centuries, but also this chapter. We may begin in the West, with the independent British kingdoms, where the evidence for direct Byzantine contacts is more plentiful and where links with the Eastern Mediterranean appear to have been forged during the fifth century, at a notably earlier point than in the rest of Britain.

The ceramic evidence and the British West

In the British West, the descendants of the citizens of Roman Britain organised their own political, social and economic life for much longer than elsewhere in the former provinces of the diocese of *Britanniae*, although the details of these polities are much debated and the evidence subject to different interpretations. The most widespread, and most discussed, evidence for direct contacts with the Byzantine Empire comprises sherds of imported ceramic vessels from Cornwall, Devon, Somerset, Wales and western Scotland.[8]

The ceramic material from Cornwall and Devon far exceeds the quantity of Byzantine imports found in other areas of Britain, although it comprises only fragmentary material and at any specific site only a handful of sherds of imported pottery may occur. Larger assemblages of Byzantine ceramics are known from Tintagel, Cadbury Congresbury, South Cadbury and Bantham, as well as at other sites. Obviously, this small quantity of material is merely the archaeological representation of the presence of Byzantine ceramics on these sites and in this area. The usual caveats of archaeological interpretation concerning sampling, survival and the recognition of exotic material all need to be borne in mind in relation to the question of how many imports may in fact be evidenced by such finds.[9]

The Byzantine pottery in Britain comprises both finewares and coarsewares. The fineware (dishes, plates and bowls) is mostly Phocaean Red Slip Ware (PRSW) with smaller quantities of African Red Slip Ware (ARSW). The coarseware is largely comprised of amphorae, mostly LR1 (Bii) and LR2 (Bi), but with most of the major classes of Byzantine amphora represented in smaller quantities. Amphora stoppers have been found at some British sites with imports, and markings comprising red painted *dipinti*, characteristic of LR1, have been discovered at Tintagel, along with North African coarseware vessels.[10]

Very little non-ceramic material of Byzantine origin has been found along with the pottery, so cargoes of amphorae or of a perishable commodity (such as cloth, papyrus or wooden objects) were probably the main cargoes carried. The few non-ceramic finds include Eastern beads, Eastern (possibly Egyptian) glass vessels, an intaglio of probable Byzantine origin found on Anglesey, a St Menas flask from the Wirral, a coin weight from Somerset and a few Byzantine coins (**colour plate 19**). A Byzantine censer (liturgical incense burner) was found at Glastonbury during the digging of a drain in the early 1980s. The latter may or may not be a contemporary import, although a similar one is known from a seventh-century context in Spain (**41**, **42** & **43**).[11]

BRITAIN & BYZANTIUM

Although Byzantine pottery is found on sites elsewhere in Western Europe, as we have seen, by far the largest assemblage of Byzantine ceramics north of the Mediterranean comes from Tintagel (**colour plates 15** & **20**). This immediately attracts attention to the British material in any discussion of Byzantine contacts with the West. Here, almost all of the ceramics at the site are imports from the Eastern Mediterranean, although a small amount of superficially late Romano-British pottery was also found. The assemblage in total comprises thousands of sherds, although only a small part of the eroded coastal headland has been excavated. Wherever new excavation takes place at Tintagel more Byzantine imports are discovered.

The composition of the assemblage found at this site may provide detailed information about its origin and character. Its most striking feature is that it is comprised of very few classes of pottery overall and that approximately 75 per cent of the identifiable imports are Eastern Mediterranean, the remaining 25

41 *A leaded bronze censer from the Byzantine Empire, found at Glastonbury.* Reproduced with the kind permission of The British Museum

42 *A sixth-century Byzantine coin-weight possibly from Constantinople, found in Somerset.* Reproduced with the kind permission of The British Museum

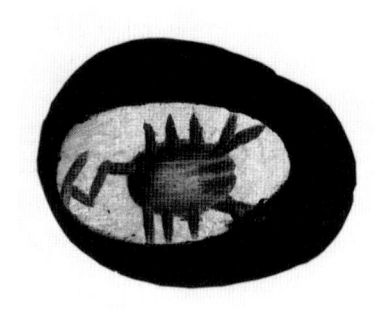

43 *Byzantine intaglio from Cefn Cwmwd, Anglesey (approximately 1cm high).* Reproduced with the kind permission of Birmingham University Field Archaeology Unit

per cent originating in North Africa. Michael Fulford has suggested that the combination of PRSW, ARSW and amphora types indicate a specifically Constantinopolitan origin for the Tintagel assemblage. The presence of 'water jars' similar to those from a Byzantine shipwreck indicates that this could have involved direct exchange with Byzantine vessels. As we saw in chapter 3, such vessels are unlikely to have had cargoes primarily composed of finewares such as PRSW or ARSW. Instead, the bulk of their main cargo was probably contained within amphorae, hence the many sherds that have been found.[12]

In fact, the relative quantities of Byzantine amphora class from Tintagel are similar to those at the Danubian sites that Karagiorgou has posited as recipients of the *annona*. That is to say, not only do LR1 and LR2 predominate in the assemblage but – perhaps uniquely on Western sites – LR2 is the predominant amphora type overall. In this context, and in the context of the Byzantine-Western patterns of exchange discussed in chapter 3 (including the Portuguese evidence), the presence of these amphorae at Tintagel might suggest that south-west Britain was connected to the East-West (possibly 'Syrian') exchange system.[13]

There is no suggestion that the majority of the pottery was in transit to other sites and Tintagel may have been a royal centre of this period. Much of the imported pottery may, therefore, have been brought to the site specifically for use there and what might be storage facilities associated with this pottery have been excavated. Consequently, this may have been a site occupied by local rulers, but supplied through the same Byzantine official system that we have traced elsewhere. There is no evidence that this was a specifically Byzantine outpost, such as might be provided by Greek inscriptions, and the site is, of course, very far from the Mediterranean. Possibly the most likely interpretation of this evidence is to see it in terms of direct contact between the East-West exchange system and the authorities controlling part (perhaps a large part) of south-west Britain.

Given the length of time that Eastern sailors would have had to stay at Tintagel until weather conditions permitted them to make the return voyage, it is possible that we may be seeing the British equivalent of the mercantile communities attested at Mérida, Paris and elsewhere. Again, a sustained (perhaps even semi-permanent) presence at this political centre would explain the directionality evidenced in the distribution of the ceramic material. As such, Britain might have been much more closely connected to Byzantine diplomacy than is generally considered possible.

Although the site with the most Byzantine ceramics, Tintagel is not the only British site with such assemblages. Indeed, several dozen sites across western Britain and Ireland have Byzantine ceramic imports. A similar range of imports has been found at all of these sites and, together, British finds can, according to Ewan Campbell, be dated to between *c.*475 and *c.*550. This suggests a discrete phase of importation, lasting no more than 75 years and possibly far less. Although sixth-century Eastern Mediterranean pottery also occurs in seventh-century deposits at Tintagel, this may, of course, represent the deposition of 'old' material rather than the continuation of contacts into the seventh century. The relative homogeneity of the assemblages and the restrictive date-range suggest a single explanation might be applied to all this material. Our interpretation of the Tintagel finds seems, therefore, to offer a convincing explanation for the British imports as a whole and, if so, this suggests that it may be extrapolated across the whole of western Britain, especially the area around the Severn Sea. Élites across this wide zone – particularly at Tintagel and the hill-fort site at Dinas Powys – may have been in direct contact with the same exchange system that connected their Continental Western European counterparts to the Byzantine court.[14]

This is not to say that all Byzantine pottery in Britain occurs at high-status sites. Indeed, some redistribution of imported goods might be expected within kingdoms, for domestic political purposes or through networks of social relationships. It is possible, in other words, that British élites used Byzantine imports (and other 'luxury' items) to create social and economic obligation in their societies. This might be archaeologically visible in Cornwall, where Mediterranean pottery seems to have been especially common. Here, imported ceramics occur on site-types usually seen as lower- or middle-status in Romano-British terms, notably 'rounds', such as Trethurgy and Grambla. Redistribution may have also taken place in an ecclesiastical context, for although the exchange seems to have been directed at secular settlements in the first instance, sherds of Byzantine amphorae and fineware are found at several possible ecclesiastical sites in the south-west, such as Glastonbury Tor. Imported Mediterranean pottery has also been found at ecclesiastical and élite settlements in Ireland (such as Reask and Clogher) but it is unclear whether this represents direct imports from Byzantine ships or secondary distribution via western Britain (**44**).[15]

Recent research on Byzantine ceramic imports in Britain has also drawn attention to so-called 'sand-dune sites', most famously Bantham in south Devon (**colour plates 23** & **24**). These appear to have been key coastal exchange centres in fifth- to seventh-century Britain. It is from such a site at

Meols (Wirral) that the flask from the shrine of St Menas in Egypt was found and, more recently, three Byzantine coins. Studies of geomorphological evidence suggest that the Wirral peninsula extended much further into the Liverpool Bay during Late Antiquity than it does today. The Meols vicinity would, therefore, have been a prime stopping-off point for ships making their way around the coast of western Britain. It may also have provided a departure point for ships taking cargoes to Ireland, although no evidence for the direction of trade has been identified. However, the distribution of sand-dune sites suggests a trading network (or at least 'exchange') centred on the Irish Sea and not primarily focused on the Mediterranean or Continental Europe. This is likely to have been separate from the network supplying Tintagel.[16]

Frankish imports suggest that, in addition to Byzantine and Insular contacts, western Britons traded with their Continental neighbours. In the past, the presence of Frankish pottery prompted scholars to suggest that the

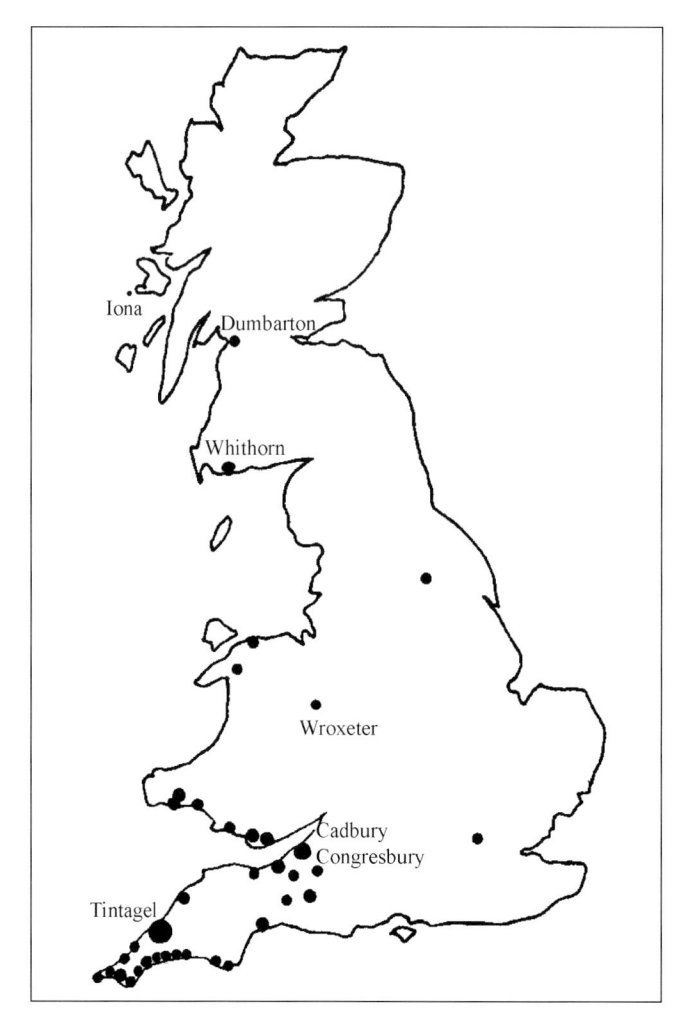

44 *Distribution of Byzantine imported pottery in Britain.* After Dark (2000)

Byzantine material arrived by transhipment as part of cargoes of mixed origin. However, PRSW found in Britain dates to several decades before the arrival of the first Frankish pottery. At Whithorn, for example, LR2 amphora sherds are found in layers earlier than those containing the first Gallic ceramic imports. The most common Frankish ceramic known from the west of Britain, E-ware, may be largely seventh-century in date, although some (along with another Frankish import, D-ware) could belong to the sixth century. Given that Byzantine ceramics are rare on sites in northern France, this would seem an unlikely route for the passage of Byzantine ceramics to Britain.[17]

Recent discoveries in maritime archaeology indicate that direct contacts between Byzantium and Western Britain were technically possible in the fifth to seventh century. Rather than having to adopt a 'land-hugging' approach to long-distance navigation, the technology of late antique seafaring was such that ships' captains were probably able to take their vessels out of sight of the coast. Thus, it may have been possible, after traversing the Mediterranean and the Straits of Gibraltar, for ships to sail north to Britain without having to make more than a few stops in Spain and Gaul for taking aboard fresh water. Seán McGrail's work on tidal patterns and maritime activity appears to confirm this, suggesting that the tides around far south-west Britain and north-west Armorica would have made sites such as Tintagel dangerous for ships arriving from northern Gaul, but a logical disembarking point for ships arriving from further out in the Atlantic. The ceramic evidence from the western coast of Gaul points to the same conclusion, for almost no Byzantine imports have yet been identified here. This cannot be attributed to misidentification, as Jonathan Wooding has pointed out: 'Centres such as Bordeaux, Orléans and Tours have all seen extensive exploration and related late-Roman wares are known from these sites. We would not now expect PRS or class 43 [LR2 or Bi] amphorae to exist unrecognised in those centres' (**45**).[18]

If the products had been traded via southern Gaul, Visigothic Spain or Italy, the assemblage would probably have been more varied or contained vessels of different origin. As Fulford has put it, in relation to Tintagel: 'There is no other way that the integrity of the assemblage which reached Britain could have been maintained unless the ships concerned put together their cargoes in the general area of origin of the pottery which they carried'. Campbell has confirmed this, writing: 'If the distribution of these wares was the product of some form of 'tramping' trade one would expect a variety of mixed wares to be carried, with local products picked up en route gradually replacing the Aegean wares at increasing distance from the production-area'. As he points out, this is not the case. Byzantine imports from Spanish and British sites are approximate to each other in relative quantities, despite Britain's greater remove from the Eastern Mediterranean.[19]

This suggests direct contact between Britain and the Byzantine East and probably a connection via the same 'Syrian' system previously discussed.

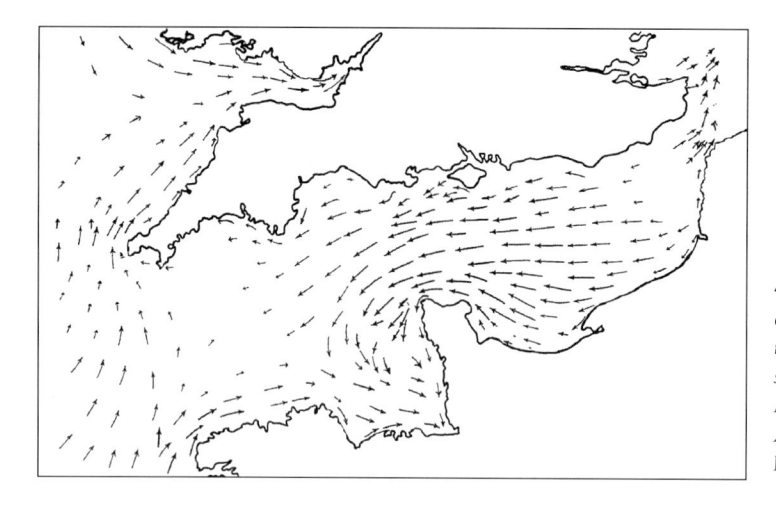

45 *Map showing direction of tides in northern France and southern England. After* Tidal Stream Atlas *(1973) in McGrail (1997)*

However, it is possible that there may have been a few stops en route. A sixth- or seventh-century glass vessel found at Tintagel appears to have close parallels with vessels from sixth- or seventh-century Málaga and Cadiz. This need mean no more than Byzantine ships stopping off in Byzantine-controlled Spain for supplies or shore leave. The presence of ARSW (which is mainly confined to Tintagel) in some assemblages might be most plausibly explained by stopovers in North Africa, while the small quantities of D-ware (also known as *dérivées paléochrétienne grise*) at Cadbury Congresbury might be explained by a stopover in western Frankia. This last material is only very occasionally found in sixth- and seventh-century contexts in Britain and is thought to originate in the Loire Valley or Bordeaux area. Thus, a long-distance sea-route around the Iberian peninsula, with a few coastal stops for provisioning, remains more likely than sequential transhipment.[20]

The precise period over which this direct contact took place is uncertain. The quantity and (especially) distribution of these ceramics now almost certainly rules out a 'one-off' shipment, as once supposed. A posited Byzantine desire for mineral resources, particularly Cornish tin, has become the standard explanation for the 'trade' on the basis of Egyptian textual references and, as tin was mined in Britain in Late Antiquity, it cannot be ruled out as a component of the exchange.[21]

However, it is unlikely that tin was the principal reason for the voyages, for tin was already mined within the Byzantine Empire. For example, there were tin mines in Cappadocia and, as McCormick has recently pointed out, in the fifth and sixth centuries at least one Cilician town collected tolls from caravans transporting lead and tin to the sea. So it is nothing but a scholarly myth that Constantinople's nearest supplies of tin were in Spain, Brittany and Britain. Although a rare mineral in the Byzantine world, it was far from unknown.[22]

The Byzantine pottery found in Britain probably comes from Syria or western Anatolia, if not Constantinople itself, and there is no evidence of

Egyptian Red Slip Ware being exported to British shores. The only western British evidence for Egyptian contacts, apart from the St Menas flask, comprises a few sherds of glass and possibly some of the beads. Given the quantity of other ceramics and the ubiquity of Egyptian pottery on Egyptian sites of this date, it seems inconceivable that there is so little diagnostically Egyptian from the British West if this is really where the ships originated. Moreover, there is no evidence from papyri to suggest that Egypt even processed foods for export.[23]

Nevertheless, contact with Egypt need not necessitate the presence of ceramics. The seventh-century *Life* of St John the Almsgiver (on whose evidence most claims for the tin trade rely) suggests that the Patriarch of the Alexandrian Church sent a ship carrying grain to Britain in a time of famine. However it was intended, the shipment was not received as a gift, for the British paid one *nomisma* (*solidus*) per bushel for half the cargo, and a quantity of tin ingots for the other half. This seems to be a clear account of a trading venture (or what turned into a trading venture) to Britain but it is difficult to determine the reliability of the source.[24]

Sailing from Alexandria to Britain would have taken several months – perhaps about four. Thus, it is unlikely that grain would have been the principal cargo, as this would have deteriorated during the voyage unless specially treated. Perhaps, instead, the source for this part of the *Life* was confused. It is possible that an Egyptian quayside observer, familiar with wheat shipments from Alexandria to elsewhere in the Mediterranean, merely assumed that the Britain-bound ship contained grain. Or perhaps he or she remembered only that the ship's ultimate destination was Britain, forgetting that it was due to stop en route at another port in the Eastern Mediterranean, possibly Antioch, where it would exchange its grain for amphorae. After all, we are told that on the return leg of its voyage, the ship stopped off in Cyrenaica for the sale of some of its cargo, and so it is plausible to suggest that its outward journey also took part in stages. Given that grain was regularly transported to Constantinople as official shipments, the confusion could also have arisen because a similar ship was involved. This might bring us back to networks of official supply and a Constantinopolitan connection, albeit now with a possible Egyptian component.[25]

In fact, there might even be a hint that the ship was operated by a Syrian. Although sailing from Egypt (in a ship belonging to the Alexandrian Church), the captain is described as 'foreign'. However, his words to the Patriarch suggest that he was a Christian and so this narrows the range of possibilities for his identity: 'Have mercy on me as God had mercy upon the world'. If the account is to be believed, the captain may have come from Syria, for the same hagiographer also observes that, previously, Syrians 'came in great numbers' by sea to Egypt as refugees from the Persian invasion of their homeland. The silence of the British written sources on this subject should not concern us unduly; it may simply reflect their scarcity.[26]

Similarly, Anne Bowman's work on seasonal sailing times has shown that trade for a purely commercial motive between Britain and Byzantium was probably impractical and more recent discussions of the evidence have suggested that a diplomatic purpose lay behind the initiative. Byzantine-British diplomacy is hinted at in Byzantine textual sources of the period, but has usually been dismissed as unlikely and at most rhetorical. For example, in the *Anekdota* ('Secret History'), Procopius claimed that Justinian I made diplomatic payments to the inhabitants of Britain. There is no evidence that this was unambiguously the case, although the subject of a diplomatic relationship with Britain is raised elsewhere in Procopius's work. In Book II of his *History of the Wars* he claims that Belisarius, the military master-mind of the Reconquest, offered Britain to the Ostrogoths in return for Sicily. If the account is true, it would suggest that Belisarius, and probably others at the Constantinopolitan court, viewed Britain as at least in the theoretical possession of the Emperor.[27]

There is, as one would expect, no reference to this in British sources. Yet, it may be significant that Gildas, writing in the mid-sixth century, was familiar with both the terminology and concept of the *annona*. As he uses the term to describe the 'supplying' of barbarians employed by fifth-century British rulers, it is unlikely to derive in his text from a Roman-period source. It is, therefore, possible that this is another hint at a diplomatically-motivated directional trade aimed at the élites ruling western Britain.[28]

We have seen in chapter 3 that this British evidence might fit into a larger picture of Byzantine contacts with the West, and pan-Mediterranean routes of 'exchange' in particular. Britain might now be seen as the ultimate destination of the exchange network that traversed the Mediterranean and the Straits of Gibraltar, and sailed up the Atlantic littoral of modern-day Portugal. The network may, therefore, have represented an extension of imperial diplomacy to the very limit of the former Roman world, with internal secondary distribution to smaller centres in the British West. Secondary distribution also seems the most plausible explanation for the imports in Ireland, where pottery may have arrived through trade or as gifts from British secular élites and the British Church. If they were used as diplomatic gifts, however, it is fascinating that the Britons chose to use Byzantine artefacts for their own 'international diplomacy'.

Byzantine coins in western Britain

It might be thought that numismatic evidence would illuminate motives for Byzantine-British contacts, but unfortunately this is not the case. There are relatively few Byzantine coin finds in either western or eastern Britain. Most are without a stratified archaeological context and cannot, therefore, be interpreted as representing activities of the fifth to seventh centuries. Where Byzantine coins do occur on archaeological sites, they are usually found in contexts that imply their use as jewellery (often as pendants) or other items of cultural significance, rather than as units of monetary exchange. The largest group is from the area around Exeter, where a series of 'chance finds' include sixth-century Byzantine coins found on Dartmoor and on the beach at Exmouth. These, along with most other Byzantine coin finds in Britain, such as at Caerwent and London, have been dismissed as much later imports, although it has been noted that some of the find spots do seem improbable for modern losses.[29]

It is interesting that since the setting up of the Portable Antiquities Scheme in the UK in 1996, a trickle of additional Byzantine and 'pseudo-imperial' coins have come to light, mainly as metal-detector finds. The more recent of these include a *solidus* from Gloucestershire minted in the name of Maurice Tiberius, and another *solidus* in the name of Anastasius I from Hampshire (**colour plate 25**). Both coins have 'CONOB' inscriptions on their reverse sides, although they have been identified as 'pseudo-imperial'. These, and most other 'Byzantine' gold coins found in Britain show evidence of having been used as pendants, although of course this need only represent a final stage of their use in Britain and does not, in itself, indicate that they were never used in economic transactions.[30]

The poverty of the coin record need not be a cause for concern. Byzantine coin finds from Frankia, for example, are small in relation to the vast numbers that are textually attested (**colour plate 8**). The coins that Clovis scattered on the streets of Tours, or the 50,000 *solidi* received by Childebert II from the Byzantine Emperor have little or no representation in the archaeological record. Probably, they were melted down at some later stage and made into jewellery or, more likely, used in the production of Merovingian and Carolingian coins. If Byzantine coins made their way into Britain in any number, it is likely that these, too, were melted down and put to another use, especially if, as some suggest, post-Roman Britain was a non-monetary society.[31]

However, as Robert Philpott has recently pointed out, the three coin finds from the Meols area, while chance finds, do meet two of George Boon's key criteria for acceptance as genuine losses. In addition to having been identified as of authentic provenance, they were discovered at an area of coastline whose 'several thousand metal finds' over many decades have demonstrated that the area was occupied from the early Roman period to the fourteenth century. Artefacts dating to between the fifth and seventh centuries include penannular brooches, two buckle plates and zoomorphic buckles, as well as the St Menas flask already mentioned. This might indicate that there was a contemporary settlement there, although this cannot be demonstrated at present.[32]

The coins from the Meols area comprise a small bronze *decanummium* of Justinian I with a Carthage mint mark, and two bronzes with Constantinopolitan mint marks (both *folles),* one of Justin I and the other of

Maurice Tiberius. The latter two coins were found together and the coin of Maurice Tiberius gives this find a *terminus post quem* of 601. An early seventh-century date appears rather late for the coins to have been deposited in the context of the direct Byzantine-British links indicated by the ceramic evidence. They might, of course, hint at later Byzantine-British contact with western Britain but it is more likely that the coin made its may to Meols by means of intermediaries, perhaps the Frankish merchants delivering E-ware to western British coastal sites in the seventh century. Another suggestion might be that the coins came to Meols via the Anglo-Saxon east of Britain, perhaps arriving on Merseyside by river from the kingdom of Mercia sometime in the seventh century. The existence of a route from the Midlands to the coast might also explain the presence of the St Menas flask at Meols, which is otherwise anomalous in western Britain. A chance find of two Byzantine coins and one Ostrogothic coin from the Roman-period fort site at Manchester could support this hypothesis, given that this site, too, has other evidence of occupation in the fifth to seventh centuries (**46, 47 & 48**).[33]

The British Church and the Byzantine East

The British Church has long been the subject of scholarly attention, and it might be expected, given the direct contacts between Britain and the Eastern Mediterranean, that there would be evidence of links between it and the Byzantine Empire. Whether or not this is the case, the beliefs and liturgy of the British Church lay within the mainstream of Eastern Mediterranean orthodoxy

46 *Bronze coin of Justinian I (527-565), found near Meols, Wirral (reverse only)*. Copyright The Board and Trustees of the National Museums and Galleries on Merseyside

47 *Bronze coin of Justin I (518-527), found near Meols, Wirral (reverse only)*. Copyright The Board and Trustees of the National Museums and Galleries on Merseyside

48 *Bronze coin of Maurice (582-602), found near Meols, Wirral (reverse only).* Copyright The Board and Trustees of the National Museums and Galleries on Merseyside

in the fifth and sixth centuries. Historians have shown that the fifth- to seventh-century British Church can no longer be conceptualised in terms of a well-defined but idiosyncratic 'Celtic Church'. Most of what was different in British ecclesiastical life derived from a remarkable theological and liturgical conservatism, expressed in terms of such features as monastic tonsure, the calculation of the date of Easter, a refusal to regard the views of their fellow Briton, Pelagius, as heretical and probably Church organisation. These conservative propensities have been shown to derive, not from isolation and exclusion from Continental Church life, but from deliberate choices made by British clerics to reject Continental innovations from the fifth century onwards.[34]

This rendered the British Church in *c*.600 far more like that of Italy in *c*.400 than that of Pope Gregory the Great's Rome, its actual contemporary. The tendency towards conservatism may have derived from the Romano-British past and could well explain some apparent anomalies in the 'Church archaeology', such as it is, of Roman Britain. There is no reason, then, why Byzantine Christians could not have interacted on equal terms with their British counterparts if they were able to do so. The British pilgrim who apparently visited St Symeon Stylites in Syria in the fifth century would have found many shared beliefs and practices between himself and his hosts.[35]

The most plentiful source of archaeological evidence for the Church in western Britain comprises inscribed stone monuments bearing Christian memorial formulae or symbols (Class-1 stones) and cross-marked stones without inscriptions (Class-2 stones) (**49** & **50**). It is usually agreed that the former date from the fifth to seventh centuries, with some later examples of uncertain significance. Class-2 stones may begin in the sixth century (as an excavated stone from Tintagel churchyard suggests), but remained in use in the seventh century and later. It is interesting that both classes occur almost entirely in those areas of Britain that had been least fully integrated into the Roman Empire before *c*.400. They therefore attest active post-Roman contact,

155

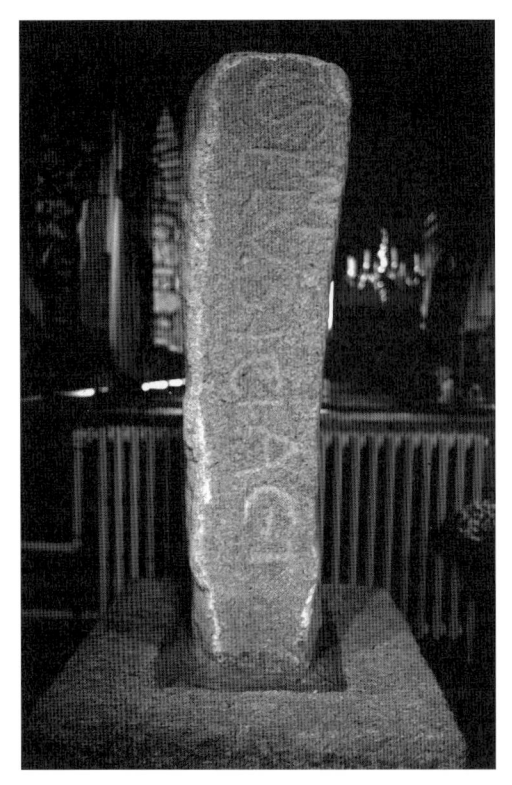

49 *Class-1 Latin-inscribed ('Selnius') stone from St Just, Cornwall. Inscriptions such as this show that Continental memorial formulae were used in Britain in Late Antiquity.* Reproduced with the kind permission of Ken Dark

50 *Class-2 cross-marked stone from St Non's Chapel, near St David's, Wales.* Reproduced with the kind permission of Ken Dark

reflecting contemporary, not archaic, Latin formulae known from fifth-century contexts elsewhere in the West. Clearly, these inscriptions do not represent residual *romanitas* from the Late Roman past.[36]

Another, purely Insular, phenomenon is the production of *ogom* (also called 'ogham' and 'ogam') stones, inscriptions with texts in the *ogom* script. This script was used to place brief Irish language inscriptions on stone monuments, some of which were definitely tombstones. Such inscriptions are found largely in south-west Ireland and south-west Wales, with outlying examples in Cornwall, south-west Scotland and elsewhere. Although belonging to the fifth to seventh centuries, *ogom* inscriptions are without parallel outside an Insular context and so not relevant in this context (**51**).[37]

The plain crosses found on cross-marked stones seldom permit meaningful parallels to be drawn. Both Latin and equal armed crosses were principally post-Roman innovations in Western Christian symbolism and these symbols were certainly known in Britain by the sixth century, as imported pottery (such as a sherd of ARSW from Cadbury Congresbury) attests. But this affords little more help than assisting a post-Roman dating for Class-2 (**52**).[38]

More important for our purposes, is the long-standing observation that Class-1 stones are related to contemporary stones from the Continent. Recent work has shown that there is a range of possible origins for the formulae found in Britain, concentrating in central-southern and western Gaul. The Continental stones often bear internal absolute dates and Knight has suggested that, on the basis of their coastal distribution, the earliest Gallic-derived British Latin memorial stones may yield a *terminus post quem* of 450 to 480 for the British series.[39]

Unlike the Gallic stones, Class-1 inscriptions do not usually include dates. However, the 'Penmachno' stone from Gwynedd shows an example of the consular dating system of the Late Roman period, a practice that continued in Gaul until the seventh century. It has been interpreted as reading 'IN TEMPORE IUSTINI CONSULIS', and as referring to the consulship of Flavius Justinius, eastern consul in 540. If accurate, this could suggest that someone in north Wales was in a position to know the correct identity of the Western consul for that year, although of course, the stone provides, at most, only a *terminus post quem* for its dating.[40]

Neither the Penmachno stone nor the other Class-1 inscriptions need show any direct link with the Eastern Mediterranean. Their key importance here is that they confirm the British Church's links to the wider Western European ecclesiastical world in the fifth and sixth centuries. More specifically, they show that some people in western Britain were familiar with the detail of Christian memorial formulae used in Gaul and elsewhere. That this involved Continental memorial formulae successively introduced in Gaul during the course of the fifth century suggests that this familiarity extended through that century and possibly beyond.

51 Ogom *stone. This example is from County Kerry, but* ogom *stones are also found in western Britain.* Photograph by Anthea Harris

52 *A sherd of African Red-Slipped Ware showing Chi-Rho impressed decoration.* Reproduced with the kind permission of The British Musem

The first parallels between western British and Gallic Latin inscribed stones were recognised at Lyon in central Gaul by V.E. Nash-Williams. Despite the evidence for Byzantine mercantile activity at both Lyon and western Britain, Lyon would not seem an obvious place to look for links with Britain. Indeed, Lyon is no longer thought to be the only derivation of the formulae used on Class-1 stones, for Knight has noted that the British stones also show affinities with inscriptions from western Gaul, as at Camiac (Gironde), Gaillardon (Vendée) and Protet (Haute Garonne). Nevertheless, it is worth noting that the links between the inscriptions of the area around Lyon and Vienne and the western British stones are among the closest yet identified and that there may be hints at other contacts between the two areas. For example, a more exact parallel can be drawn between the British stones in general and those of the Lyon/Vienne area because they sometimes share the mis-spelling 'HIC IACIT' for 'HIC IACET' ('here lies').[41]

Another hint at such a link might be seen in Cornish place-name evidence. Nothing is known of the 'St Just' venerated in medieval Cornwall. However, at Lyon, where the veneration of 'St Just' was also well-established, the identity of the man is textually accredited. The 'St Just' venerated at Lyon was a fourth-century bishop (Justus) of that city, who had retired to the Eastern Mediterranean as a hermit. One of the principal churches of late antique and medieval Lyon was later dedicated to him, and this is actually one of the churches whose cemetery contains early fifth-century Christian memorial stones similar to those found in Britain. Given that St Just's, Cornwall, is in the same area as the majority of Byzantine imports in the British West, then a possible link between them seems worthy of consideration.[42]

Unfortunately, like most other western British ecclesiastical sites of this date, St Just, Cornwall, has no known late antique architecture. However, there is a Class-1 stone with an inscription containing the formula 'SELNIUS IC IACIT' ('Selnius lies here') known from St Just, implying that the locality was linked into a wider network of contacts (**49**). Charles Thomas has dated this to the mid-sixth century. The HIC IACET/IACIT formula was used more widely in the West than in Gaul, but its presence at St Just at least allows the possibility of contact between this site and Lyon, in the fifth or sixth century. Nor would a Byzantine dedication be unique in western Britain, for Ken Dark has already suggested that other churches in western Britain may have Byzantine-derived dedications of this period. These include St Ia and St Madron in Cornwall, and the intriguing St Stinian ('St Justinian') in Wales. If so, this might be seen to strengthen the case for this as a possible Lyonnaise link with western Britain. In this context, it is possible that the western Gallic stones with parallels in the British West, to which Knight has drawn attention, might be seen (along with D-ware imports) as a reflection of the Loire route that would probably have been taken by travellers from Lyon to the west of Britain. At least potentially then, an indirect connection between the Eastern Mediterranean and western Britain via Lyon can be established.[43]

Although there are no Byzantine ceramics from St Just, as noted above, Byzantine ceramic imports are found at ecclesiastical, as well as high-status secular, sites. Whithorn, an important focus of the British Church throughout the fifth to seventh centuries, has yielded Eastern Mediterranean imports comprised principally of LR1 and LR2 amphorae, with some representation of other amphora classes, as well as ARSW. Of course, this does not necessarily provide evidence of direct contact between the British and Byzantine Churches, and the relevance of this material must not be overstated. The imports could be a result of secondary distribution from another British political or ecclesiastical centre.[44]

Perhaps more interestingly, for our purposes, Byzantine imports are found at sites sometimes thought to be associated with early monasticism. In addition to Whithorn itself, these include Llandough, Glastonbury Tor and Caldey Island. Again, this was probably a result of redistribution rather than primary importation, but it raises the possibility that early monasticism in western Britain developed in a partially 'Eastern' context, perhaps facilitated by the activities and organisation of the sub-Roman British Church in areas such as the West Country. We have seen that it may be unwise to underestimate the attraction of Byzantine culture in the fifth- to seventh-century West, both here and on the Continent.[45]

Imported amphorae sherds from Glastonbury Tor might, like the LR1 amphora sherd from Lavret (Bréhat, Brittany, seen in the previous chapter), also point to a link between Insular eremiticism and Byzantium. This would contrast with the usual view that early eremiticism developed in Britain as a reflex of Martinian monasticism in Frankia. It is interesting that none of these monastic sites have Frankish imports, although this, of course, does not indicate that there was no contact with Frankia or Frankish monasticism. Yet, it is quite possible that ships bringing imports to Britain may also have provided a passage for would-be hermits, anxious to reach what was perceived by Byzantines as the furthest reaches of the *oikoumenê*. At the start of the period covered by this book, Jerome implied as much when he wrote: 'The cross is in Britain, in India, in the whole world . . . . Happy is he who carries in his own heart the cross, the Resurrection, the place of the Nativity of Christ and his Ascension.' Elsewhere, again implying that Britain was somehow 'at the edge of the world' he wrote: 'Access to the courts of heaven is as easy from Britain as it is from Jerusalem'. Britain might, therefore, have appeared to represent the most extreme version of the *desertum* that adherents of the eremitical life avidly sought. To passengers on ships sailing to Tintagel from the Mediterranean, Britain (especially western Britain) might have seemed an ideal location for a hermitage.[46]

Imported pottery, inscriptions and – to an unsurprisingly limited extent – textual sources, suggest that western Britain was in contact with the Byzantine Empire, and that this contact may have been mediated through the East-West

('Syrian') network of exchange detectable in the Continental evidence. The lack of written sources denies us the possibility of the detailed historical information provided by Gregory of Tours for Gaul, but the distribution of PRSW and LR1/LR2 amphorae firmly connect western British evidence with the broader pattern pointed out in previous chapters. But if western Britain was part of the Eastern Mediterranean network facilitated by the 'Syrians', the evidence from eastern Britain suggests a contrasting picture (**53**).

Byzantium and the Anglo-Saxon east of Britain

The distinguishing characteristics of eastern Britain ('Early Anglo-Saxon England') in the fifth and sixth centuries, compared to western Britain, are twofold. First, a non-British (today called 'Anglo-Saxon') élite ruled much of

53 *Map of Britain showing selected sites mentioned in the text*

the area and this had – to a greater or lesser extent – a culture derived from that of 'Germanic' north-west Europe and Scandinavia. Second, this Anglo-Saxon élite wholly or largely followed one or more pagan religions. Although pockets of Christianity may have survived from Roman Britain, the institutions of an organised Church are not visible in the Anglo-Saxon east of Britain at this date. The question of how much of the population in fact derived from migrants from across the North Sea is, at present, hotly debated.[47]

However, clearly this area contained many people who followed cultural and social practices far removed from those of the Eastern Mediterranean Byzantine world and, it increasingly seems, from their British neighbours. Among the key differences resulting from these distinguishing characteristics was that the Anglo-Saxons may have been organised into much smaller political units than the Britons. They may have had less bureaucratic or administrative infrastructure than is implied, for example, in Book One of Gildas's *De Excidio Britanniae,* where the Britons are depicted as living in kingdoms based on *civitates,* with kings who may have been Christians (if only superficially).[48]

These cultural, religious and political differences profoundly affected the ways in which the 'Early Anglo-Saxons' (the Anglo-Saxons of the fifth to seventh centuries) were able to interact with the Byzantine world. With this in mind, it would obviously be folly to look for much indication of Byzantine ecclesiastical contacts in the Anglo-Saxon areas of eastern Britain. Moreover, whether Byzantine diplomacy would have targeted local-level Anglo-Saxon rulers in the same ways that it might have focused on British kings ruling large ('*civitas*-sized') kingdoms is debatable. So, if we are to look for Byzantine connections in this area we have to recognise that possible connections will be structured by the character of Early Anglo-Saxon society and culture.

The Anglo-Saxon area was also constrained by geography. It was much less easily reached directly by sea from the Mediterranean than western Britain or Frankia, so it is probable that any Byzantine contacts would have been mediated through one of those other areas. Moreover, we have to allow for the possibility that Byzantine objects and styles might have entered the Anglo-Saxon world with their cultural connotations already transformed by such mediation, so that 'Byzantine' objects from our point of view might have appeared 'Frankish', or even 'British', to an Anglo-Saxon recipient. In a pagan context, too, the meaning of religious symbolism may have been partially understood or misinterpreted, so that objects with what would normally be considered religious associations may have been differently interpreted or simply not exported to communities known to be pagan. Needless to say, after the Augustinian mission of 597 and the creation of an ecclesiastical context in this region, objects might more easily be accorded a religious and, specifically, Christian significance.

Another problem derives from the extent to which the Anglo-Saxon élite, notably the élite in Kent, participated in the culture of the Merovingian aristocracy. As we saw in chapter 2, Frankia's interest in Kent may have been more than merely cultural. As a result, Byzantine symbolism may have carried a principally 'high status' meaning (rather than any other significance) in those areas where sixth-century Anglo-Saxons sought to emulate Merovingian rulers or nobles. Consequently, one must handle the material from Anglo-Saxon contexts with especial caution.[49]

Byzantine objects in Anglo-Saxon graves

Nevertheless, despite these caveats, there are several points that deserve consideration, and these include the presence of Byzantine objects in Anglo-Saxon graves. By far the most evidence for Anglo-Saxon links with the Byzantine Empire is found in the mass of burial evidence from the Anglo-Saxon world – hardly a surprise given the traditional focus on burial analysis in Anglo-Saxon archaeology. This takes the form either of Byzantine artefacts buried as grave-goods, or of objects that while not actually Byzantine themselves may have come to Britain via the Eastern Mediterranean. Finally, as recent research has suggested, evidence for links with the Byzantine Empire might be seen in Mediterranean and more specifically Byzantine dress-styles.[50]

In contrast to western Britain, there is very little imported Eastern Mediterranean pottery in this area. Very few sherds have been found in eastern Britain, and these may be explicable in terms of sub-Roman British occupation at London and *Verulamium* (St Albans). There is a St Menas flask from Canterbury, and possibly others from elsewhere, but none of these are from indisputable fifth- to seventh-century contexts. Even compared to western Britain, where a site might have only a few Eastern Mediterranean sherds, this does not constitute a great deal of unambiguous Byzantine ceramic material at all.[51]

Byzantine coins from the east of Britain

Byzantine coin finds from the east of Britain, as a whole, are no more reliable as evidence for Byzantine contacts than those from the west of the island. All the same problems of interpretation, at present, appertain to these also and only a few can be incontrovertibly described as genuine imports of the fifth, sixth or seventh century. This does not mean to say there are no Byzantine coins, but most of those that can be assigned to known contexts are from burials, and often incorporated into jewellery. Even when they are not found as part of jewellery items, they are still usually found in funerary contexts, where their cultural significance is ambiguous at best.

Most of the relevant coins come from Kentish contexts, such as the necklace from Sarre with 'pseudo-imperial'(Frankish-minted) *solidi* of Maurice

Tiberius or the Byzantine *tremissis* (from an Italian mint) in the so-called 'St Martin's hoard' at Canterbury, which may have come from an Anglo-Saxon grave. Imitation 'Byzantine' *tremisses* have been found at other cemetery sites, such as Eastry and Gilton. The cemetery at Gilton also yielded two Byzantine coin weights. These all come from graves, but it is interesting that gold coins from apparently non-funerary contexts also usually show signs of having been used as jewellery. More recently, these include two imitation 'Byzantine' coins – a *tremissis* and a *solidus* – from Oxborough (Norfolk). Sixth-century burials have been excavated at Oxborough, although the coins themselves were metal-detector finds. Another 'chance find', a gold *solidus* minted in the name of Maurice Tiberius at Ravenna, comes from Robertsbridge (East Sussex). This coin, which was not associated with any funerary contexts, showed signs of having been removed from a mount.[52]

Copper-alloy vessels from the Eastern Mediterranean

In contrast to western Britain, the majority of Byzantine artefacts found in eastern Britain are copper-alloy vessels, over 30 of which are known. East Anglia and Kent provide the richest repositories of them. The most common of these vessels are often described as 'Coptic'. As we saw in a previous chapter, this is a misnomer, for they were not necessarily produced in Egypt, although they are certainly Byzantine in origin. The most common types found in Britain are Werner's class B1: roughly hemispherical vessels, often with openwork foot-rings, 'omega-shaped' drop-handles, occasionally decorated with scenes or even inscriptions, but more often plain (**54**).[53]

Like other Byzantine imports, 'Coptic' vessels most frequently come from burial contexts, although they were not always used in the same way in the grave. The vessel found at Wickham Market (Suffolk) (B1) contained the remains of a copper-alloy comb; one of possibly four examples from Faversham (Kent) (B1) contained hazelnuts, as did one of the two from Sarre (Kent) (B1). At Westwell (Kent) (B1) the 'Coptic' vessel held two amber cups. At Wingham (Kent) (B1) an inhumation with a Byzantine copper-alloy bowl was placed perpendicular to a particularly richly-furnished burial. The grave-goods of the latter included an amethyst and bead necklace, a cowrie shell, two gold brooches, several pieces of silver jewellery, a composite gold and garnet brooch and a copper-alloy pin ornamented with a gold and garnet panel.

Other 'Coptic' vessels from Britain include those from Caistor-by-Norwich (Norfolk) (B1), Needham Market (Suffolk) (B1), Sudbury (Suffolk) (B1), Wickhambreux (Kent) (B1), Gilton (Kent) (B1), Teynham (Kent) (B1) and Wheathampstead (Hertfordshire) (B4), where nothing remained in the grave except the imported copper-alloy vessel itself. This is a rare type which parallels the B4 vessel from the Ávilla area in Spain and which most resembles

54 *Class B1 'Coptic' bowl. This example is from Sutton Hoo mound 1.* Reproduced with the kind permission of The British Museum

a ewer. Most recently, three 'Coptic' bowls (all B1) have been excavated at an Anglo-Saxon cemetery at Saltwood (Kent) and two fragments of a 'Coptic' bowl footing have been found at Wymondham (Norfolk). The Saltwood vessels were all found in the graves of high-status males (graves 5, 7 & 200), along with weapons and other grave-goods, including wooden buckets held together with iron bands, gaming pieces, buckles and a section of a horse harness. There was a horse burial adjacent to grave 5, perhaps permitting a parallel with some of the aristocratic Germanic graves from the Continent. Interestingly, a buckle from the same site, although not associated with these particular burials, has been identified as being of Byzantine origin. This would render this a unique find in Britain from a secure archaeological context and may, in time, come to shed more light on the means by which the 'Coptic' vessels arrived at the same cemetery.[54]

The Byzantine copper-alloy vessel found furthest west in Britain has no burial associations, and is from the seashore at Boscombe Chine (Dorset) (B1). It has been suggested that this could have been eroded from a cliff-top grave, but it is also possible that it derives from a shipwreck or, perhaps more plausibly, fifth- to seventh-century beach activity analogous to that thought to have taken place at Bantham Bay (Devon).[55]

The famous richly-furnished chamber grave at Taplow (Buckinghamshire) also contained a Byzantine copper-alloy bowl, in this case a particularly unusual type (Richards' class B5), with a tall pedestal. In fact there seems a particular association between very elaborate chamber burials and the use of these bowls, often more elaborate examples than usually found. Sutton Hoo Mound 1 (Suffolk) yielded a class C vessel of Eastern Mediterranean origin, while at Asthall Barrow (Oxon) the cremation of a man and a horse was deposited in the context of grave-goods that included a silver cup, imported Merovingian pottery, belt fittings, gaming pieces, horn or wooden vessels, as well as a Byzantine copper-alloy bowl (B1). The burial here may have taken place in a wooden chamber, as at Sutton Hoo and Taplow. Yet another Byzantine elaborate copper-alloy vessel (class C, and sometimes described as a 'bucket') was found at Cuddesdon (Oxon). This is another élite barrow burial, where the grave also contained two swords, two blue glass bowls of a Kentish type, and a fragment of what was presumably a garnet-inlaid piece of jewellery, possibly a brooch (**55**).[56]

This association with elaborate late sixth- and early seventh-century chamber burials shows that, whatever the social range that used these objects, 'Coptic' vessels were acceptable even to the most status-conscious members of Anglo-Saxon society. Although they were also used in less grand burials, these objects may have held special status either as exotic imports or for more specific associations. The recent example from grave 7 at Saltwood had been repaired before its deposition in the grave, but the repair was of such high quality that it was only detected under X-ray. This perhaps suggests that the vessel was both a prized object and one that had been well used before it came to be deposited in the grave.[57]

It is interesting, too, that the vessels from Britain are distinct in their homogeneity. Most of the British vessels are class B1 – the B5 vessel from Taplow and the B4 vessel from Wheathampstead are exceptions, as is the

55 *Class C (or B5) 'Coptic' bowl from the chamber grave at Taplow, Buckinghamshire.* Reproduced with the kind permission of the British Museum

anomalous class C. However, it is still more interesting that, amongst all the classes of 'Coptic' bowls found in the West, only B1 and B5 vessels have distinct parallels in Egypt. It is not clear how this might relate to the exchange network that brought these vessels to Britain, attested, as we have seen in chapter 3, in the Rhineland region of Germany and the Upper Danube. A more varied range of copper-alloy vessels was carried along this part of the 'trade route', if this is an accurate term for it.

Of course, the explanation might be as prosaic as the fact that these vessels would have been easier to stack and may, therefore, have been the most 'cost-effective' to bring to Britain. Conversely, the predominance of B1 vessels in Britain might suggest that the Rhineland network was fragmented and that only those traders transporting this particular type of vessel made the journey across the Channel. It might also provide some hint of a genuinely Egyptian role in the exchange network that brought at least some of these vessels to Britain although, as we have seen, there is little additional evidence for this at present.[58]

A related type of Byzantine artefact – the *situla* – is found in eastern Britain. Most of these belong to a specific group of *situlae* and seem to have been perceived as high-status objects even in the Eastern Mediterranean, or at least not objects of everyday use. They are often described as 'buckets', but were probably a form of drinking vessel, with a flat base and straight sides. *Situlae* belonging to this group are much less common, both in Britain and elsewehere, than 'Coptic' copper-alloy vessels. They, too, are made of a copper alloy, but are brass rather than bronze, perhaps suggesting production at a different metalworking centre from their 'Coptic' counterparts in Britain.

Only three examples have been found in Britain to date: from Chessell Down (Isle of Wight), from Bromeswell (Suffolk) and, most recently, from Breamore (Hampshire) (**colour plate 26**). The Chessell Down and Breamore 'buckets' were found in high-status burial contexts. The latter has not yet been extensively studied, but the example from Chessell Down, the result of a nine-teenth-century excavation, was found in a richly-furnished grave (grave 45) and in close proximity to a plainer Byzantine copper-alloy 'bucket' (grave 26) (Werner's Class C). The vessel in grave 45 was part of an inhumation burial, and lay at the feet of a female skeleton in a grave that also contained a garnet-inlaid silver disc brooch, a crystal ball in a silver sling, a perforated spoon, weaving batten, silver rims from wooden cups, three square-headed brooches, and an equal-armed brooch. The skeleton had gold braid – possibly Byzantine, but more likely to have originated in Frankia – around its forehead. The Bromeswell example was a surface find, although its proximity to the Sutton Hoo site (less than 1km away) suggests that it may also have been associated with burial (**56**).[59]

If these finds sound rather few in number, then it is worth noting that they form a group of which only nine examples are known in total (including throughout the Byzantine Empire). That is, a third of the known examples –

56 Detail of Byzantine copper-alloy 'bucket' from Breamore, Hampshire. Reproduced with the kind permission of Hampshire Portable Antiquities Scheme

and all but one of the provenanced Western examples (one from Rome must be seen in a Byzantine context) – are from Britain. The only other provenanced 'bucket' of this type in the West outside Britain comes from Bueña in Spain and, at present, seems rather anomalous. The Britain-centred distribution is remarkable, therefore, especially if, as seems possible, the vessels were all made in the same workshop.[60]

However, two previously unrecognised references to similar vessels might be found in the list of the so-called 'Treasure' of Bishop Desiderus of Auxerre. The list, preserved in a ninth-century text, describes 'two gilded cans of like form weighing five pounds, encircled with images of men and wild beasts'. These, from their description, seem to resemble the *situlae* from Anglo-Saxon contexts, although of course this cannot now be verified. The 'Treasure' was given to the cathedral at Auxerre by Bishop Desiderus (603-21/3), who was a relative of the politically powerful Merovingian queen, Brunhild, and we know that he received at least one object as a result of his royal connections. This was a 'deep dish of medium size . . . weighing three and a half pounds, with four stamps below and little berries around the rim'. With possible control stamps and a rim decoration that appears to have resembled Byzantine metalwork, this, too, may have been of Byzantine origin. In this context, and given the attested connection with the Merovingian royal family, it is quite possible that the 'two gilded cans' in the 'Treasure' were *situlae* from the Eastern Mediterranean similar to those in the group discussed here.[61]

Dated to the sixth century and possibly provenanced to the Antioch region of Syria, several of the vessels identified as part of this group are, as mentioned, decorated with punched outlines of hunting scenes. Some have Greek inscriptions. The inscription on the Bromeswell example reads (allowing for mis-spelling and poor grammar), 'Use this in good health, Master Count, for many happy years', while the Breamore inscription reads, 'Use this, Lady, for many happy years'. These rejoinders would imply personal use and perhaps that they were intended as gifts, but the reasons for their manufacture are still unclear. Production in a state workshop has been suggested, as well as a military association, although it is unlikely that they can be associated with the burials of warriors, as Heinrich Härke's work on the meaning of 'weapon graves' has shown. Härke has argued that weapons were probably placed in graves to signify status and perhaps even ethnicity, not the role of the individual whose body was accompanied in this way. This point is extremely relevant here because these objects, too, can be seen as status symbols and an indication of affiliations beyond the immediate community in which they were deposited.[62]

Again, then, there seems a close association between Byzantine copper-alloy vessels and secular élites in eastern Britain, although by no means all were found in graves thought to represent the highest stratum of Anglo-Saxon society. The Breamore 'bucket' was found in the context of several non-Byzantine buckets of decreasing size, and it is possible that they stacked neatly into each other for storage or transportation. If transportation, this might indicate their possession by a local chief and his entourage, perhaps travelling on horseback. It might suggest, too, a possible way in which Byzantine copper-alloy vessels were used in Britain. This also raises the question of whether it was primarily the 'luxury' associations of such objects (combined with their practicality) that gave them special status in Britain.

Other Byzantine objects with high-status associations

To address this question we can turn to silver. This is the only other Byzantine metalwork found in Britain, and is much rarer than copper-alloy. The key example is that from Sutton Hoo mound 1, which represents one of the largest finds of Byzantine silver anywhere, and certainly in the former Roman West. In this sense, too, the evidence from Britain appears to be unique. Mound 1, dating perhaps to 624/5, is likely to be the grave of an élite individual, probably a King judging from the accompanying regalia. The conventional interpretation is still that the burial is that of an East Anglian king, Raedwald, which would concur with the *terminus post quem* (*c*.613) given by the gold Merovingian *tremisses* in the purse that was placed in the burial chamber. As far as the 16 pieces of silver are concerned, the most important is a large silver dish with control-stamps inside the foot-ring that date it to the reign of Anastasius I (491-518). There was also a fluted silver bowl bearing the design of a woman's head, a set of ten smaller silver bowls with cruciform motifs, a plain silver bowl, a ladle, and a pair of spoons, marked 'Paulos' and 'Saulos'. The latter has sometimes been interpreted as an allusion to the conversion of St Paul and it has been suggested that the spoons were a conversion gift to Raedwald. More recent work confirms, however, that the 'Saulos' inscription is probably a bad copy of 'Paulos', perhaps inscribed in a barbarian workshop. This is an exceptional group and may require a special explanation, but it clearly belongs to the category of objects used as status symbols in eastern Britain and yet were also high-status objects in their Byzantine context (**57**, **58**, **63** & **cover photograph**).[63]

On its own, this material might represent the use of Byzantine valuables in Anglo-Saxon England simply because their value was equally appreciated there. Alternatively, it might allude to a deeper political meaning if the material represented a relationship with the imperial court. But these items are far from alone in eastern Britain, even if they are the most visually impressive. Various other objects found in Anglo-Saxon burial contexts may also derive from the Byzantine Empire, even if they were not manufactured in Byzantium itself. The amethysts, garnets, ivory rings and other exotica occasionally found in Anglo-Saxon graves of this period were almost certainly traded through Byzantine ports (possibly Alexandria or Constantinople) on their way from the Far East or Africa. Again, whether their arrival in Britain was via trading networks or the exchange of diplomatic gifts, or by some other means altogether, is not known.[64]

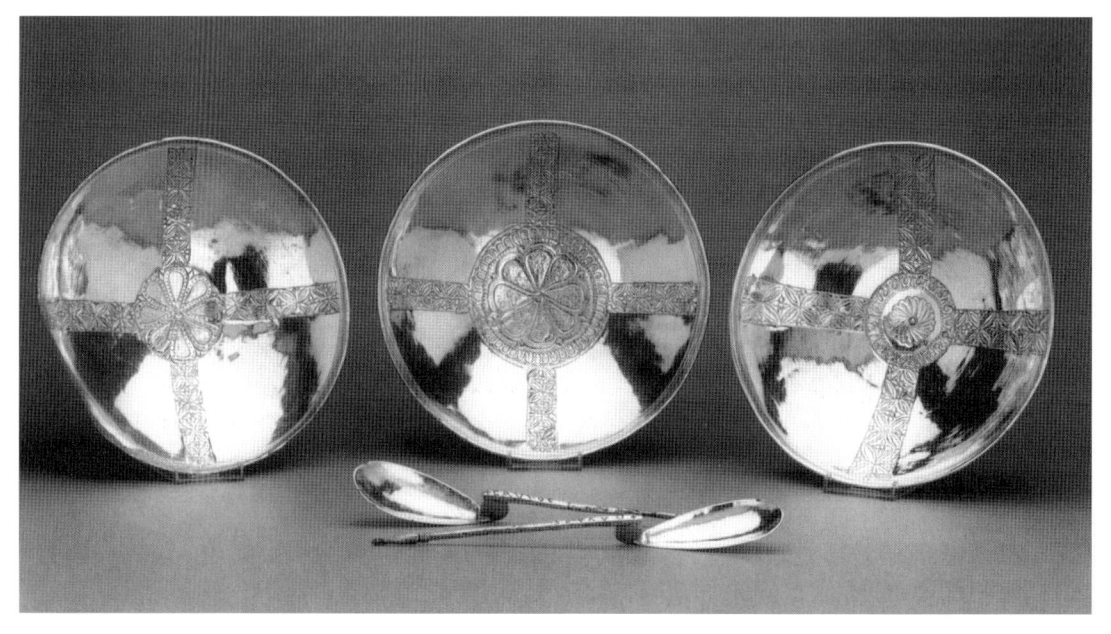

57 *Byzantine silver bowls and pair of spoons from the Sutton Hoo mound 1 burial*. Reproduced with the kind permission of The British Museum

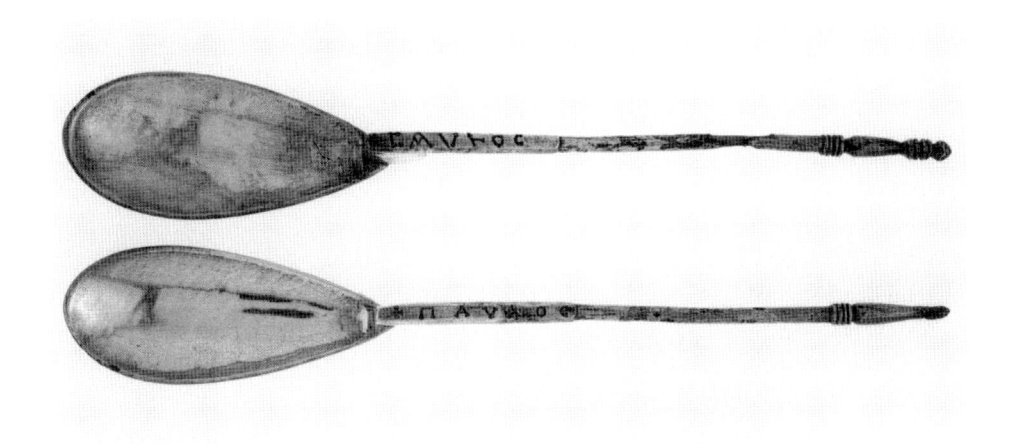

58 *Silver Byzantine spoons from Sutton Hoo Mound 1, inscribed 'Saulos' and 'Paulos'.* Reproduced with the kind permission of The British Museum

Garnets, the most common of the semi-precious stones found in Anglo-Saxon graves, appear to have been available throughout the period. They are found in contexts from the fifth to seventh centuries, perhaps most notably composite disc brooches, plated disc brooches and keystone garnet brooches, all thought to be of Kentish origin. As on the Continent, they were the premier stone for use in objects appearing to symbolise status. Garnets are essential components of the very high-status burials, such as Sutton Hoo and Taplow, where they were used in cloisonné work on sword hilts, purses, belt buckles and the like (**colour plate 27**). Some of the Sutton Hoo garnets are even thought to have been cut in a specialist workshop in Constantinople. While this was not the case with most other British examples, they often appear in contexts that indicate the high regard in which garnets were held. For example, the large cabochon garnet mounted on a pendant from grave 172/2 at Lechlade (Gloucestershire) appears to have been deposited in a completely unworn condition. The central position of garnets in other jewellery at the same late sixth- and seventh-century cemetery also shows a continuing high regard, although it is not clear what other 'meanings' should be attached to them by this date (**colour plate 28**). As noted in chapter 4, gold and garnet jewellery was widely available by the mid-sixth century, and cannot be seen to represent the presence of solely the social and political élite.[65]

Yet, garnets may have symbolised wealth and status in their own right, rather than simply as components of jewellery. For example, the young man in mound 17 at Sutton Hoo was buried with a purse containing not coins, but garnets – suggesting perhaps that in the highest social and political circles garnets were an alternative unit of exchange, one that represented an absolute value in late antique society. The same interpretation might be applied to the over 200 uncut polished garnets (along with a cowrie shell) associated with an iron 'purse mount' from grave 71 at Lechlade.[66]

Analogous distributions are attested for amethyst beads, cowrie shells and ivory rings. Amethysts, like garnets, are found in Romano-British as well as Anglo-Saxon contexts, and were a relatively common component of Late Roman jewellery, although the suggestion that their circulation in the sixth and seventh centuries was a result of the raiding of Romano-British graves has long ago been abandoned. They were probably mostly contemporary imports. It is possible, therefore, that they carried both 'Roman' and contemporary 'Byzantine' connotations in the fifth- to seventh-century period. Amethysts are found principally in Kent, as at Faversham, Sibertswold and Buckland, but also scattered lightly throughout the east of Britain, with small concentrations in Cambridgeshire, Yorkshire and the Upper Thames Valley area. The rather anomalous cowrie shells and ivory rings reflect this distribution to a degree, but they are found in smaller quantities. The cowrie shells were used as jewellery

59 *Distribution of cowrie shells in Anglo-Saxon graves.* Reproduced with the kind permission of Jeremy Huggett

items and possibly as talismen, while the ivory rings may have been attached to the neck of a looped bag or small sack. There is a small concentration of the latter in Kent, but the largest groups come from cemeteries in East Anglia, especially Lackford (Suffolk) and Illington (Norfolk). They are usually thought to have been made with the tusks of African elephants, which points to an Egyptian or North African role in their distribution, although the tusks of other animals – such as walruses – cannot be ruled out in some cases (**59, 60** & **61**).[67]

Occasionally, an item of jewellery or some other object is found that can more reliably be associated with the Byzantine Empire. Examples include the cornelian intaglio with a scorpion design from Ozingell (Kent) or the garnet intaglio, also with a scorpion design, from Alfriston (Sussex). Both of these artefacts have parallels with the probable Byzantine intaglio found at Anglesey, which is of sixth- or seventh-century date, and also provide evidence for the use of Byzantine status symbols in the Anglo-Saxon east. There is a possible Byzantine garnet intaglio from Sibertswold, but this could date from the

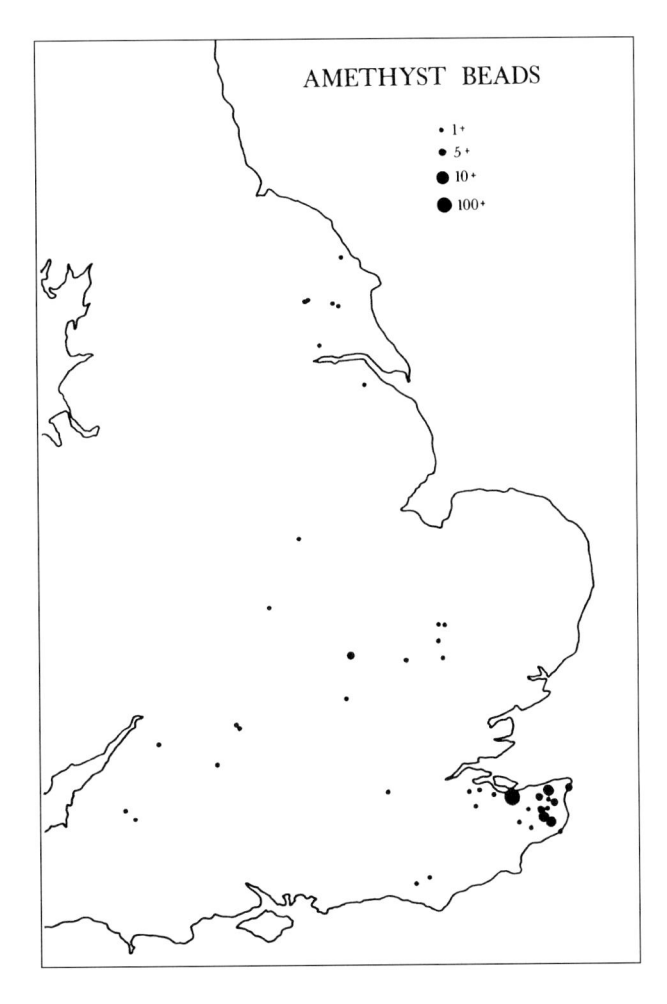

60 *Distribution of amethysts in Anglo-Saxon graves.*
Reproduced with the kind permission of Jeremy Huggett

second half of the seventh century, in which case it would be outside our chronological remit. Another finger-ring from Sibertswold has been identified as a Byzantine import, although this is without an intaglio. The ring has a solid silver bezel flanked on each side by three silver balls.[68]

For an example of a non-jewellery artefact of possible Byzantine origin, we might point to the copper-alloy reliquary cross from Haddenham (Cambridgeshire). This was a 'chance find' without a formal archaeological context, but has often been accepted as a genuinely sixth- or seventh-century import. It has parallels with a Byzantine reliquary cross from a sub-Roman site at Montcaret (Dordogne) and is interesting, too, insofar as it bears some trace of a Greek inscription and depicts Christ on the Cross fully-clothed, in a style similar to that used in the Rabbula Gospels. It may, therefore, be of Syrian or Palestinian origin, although this does not mean that it was brought to Britain directly from that region.[69]

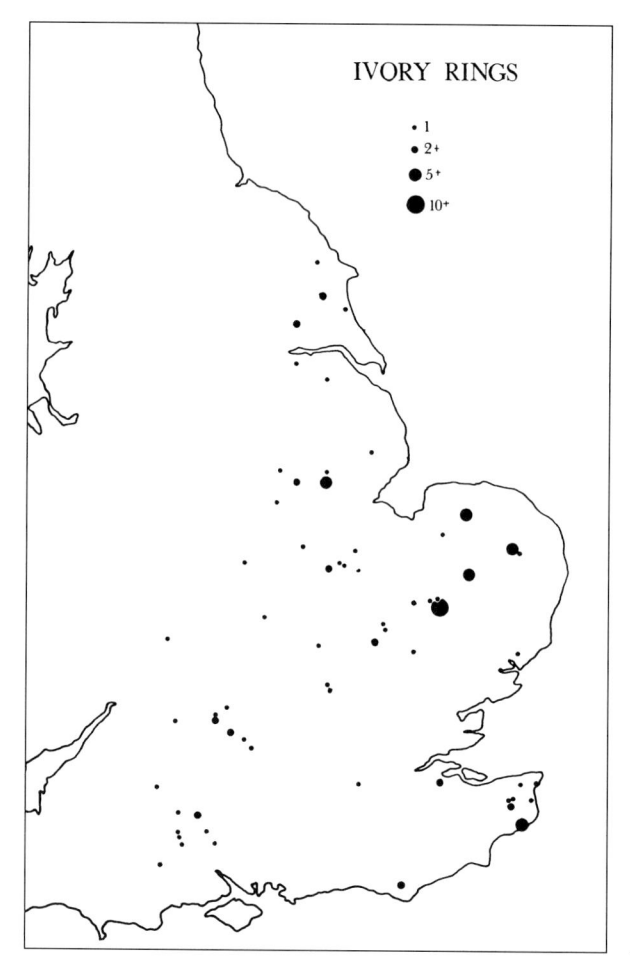

61 *Distribution of ivory rings in Anglo-Saxon graves.* Reproduced with the kind permission of Jeremy Huggett

How did Byzantine objects reach Anglo-Saxon England?

It is immediately clear that these items contrast with the many ceramic and glass finds in the British West. Metalwork forms the most important component of the Byzantine finds from eastern Britain, supporting the view that different networks of supply or exchange brought Byzantine objects to the British and Anglo-Saxon areas of sixth- to seventh-century Britain. It is interesting, in this context, that no 'Coptic' bowls have been found north of Caistor-by-Norwich. Possibly, the trade network that brought them to Britain was confined to the south and south-east of the country, where they are found, or perhaps whatever 'meaning' was attached to them did not extend further north. Whatever the case, the distribution suggests that 'Coptic' vessels were not part of either the funerary furniture or everyday life in the kingdoms of Bernicia and Deira, just as in the British kingdoms further to the south and west.[70]

The range of exotic objects found in Anglo-Saxon contexts is so similar to that found along the Rhine route in Frankia that it seems logical to suggest that the distribution represents a continuation, in fact the termination, of that long riverine route. The copper-alloy vessels, garnets, cowrie shells and other non-European exotica found in the Anglo-Saxon region of Britain arrived there, we should presumably imagine, through the hands of the same traders who were active along this route in Frankia, or at least by the same network of exchange.

The existence of a cross-Channel route to the south-east of Britain is, in fact, evidenced in the Byzantine world also. Procopius had among his sources people with first-hand knowledge of sailor's lore about Britain. The latter seems to hint at the 'Egyptian' route to the West, because this lore derives from confusion over the meaning of 'Thanet', then an island off the Kent coast, misconstrued as *thanatos* ('the isle of death' perhaps) by the writer. Procopius describes ships that sail from Frankia to Thanet. Judging from the distribution of the objects concerned – it is, indeed, in Kent that we find the greatest concentration of Byzantine imports in the Anglo-Saxon region – and the importance of Richborough near Thanet as a Romano-British port, this would have been close to the point of entry of the 'Coptic' vessels. So it may be that Procopius was aware, albeit imprecisely, of both networks archaeologically evidenced in Britain.[71]

This implies that the pattern associated with the Rhine trade route on the Continent may also be extrapolated to the Anglo-Saxon areas of Britain. Long-distance merchants from the Byzantine Empire, possibly Egypt, brought luxury goods, primarily for commercial gain, up through Frankia, either via northern Italy or by the Rhône. From there, they (or other traders) transported the objects into eastern Britain, where they were redistributed principally by means of the Thames and its tributaries. By contrast, 'Syrian' mercantile communities, which may have been established for a combination of commercial and diplomatic purposes, brought their goods to the British West, where they were probably also redistributed (in part) by a river system: the Severn and its associated rivers.

It is interesting, in this context, that Gildas described Britain as having 'two splendid rivers, the Thames and the Severn, arms of the sea along which luxuries from overseas used to be brought by ship'. Although Gildas does not refer to the Byzantine Empire as the source for these luxuries, nevertheless, it could be construed from this remark that he was living just after the period in which Eastern imports were brought into western Britain. If this is true, it might strengthen the case for Gildas writing around the middle of the sixth century, rather than at an earlier date, as some have argued.[72]

We have seen, too, that the same group of 'merchants' who supplied the Western Mediterranean with, *inter alia*, LR1 and LR2 amphorae, may have brought Byzantine ceramics and, perhaps, glass to Britain. In contrast, a separate group of 'merchants' (not necessarily Byzantines) bought metalwork, exotic natural objects and other luxury items. The absence of Byzantine pottery from most Anglo-Saxon contexts may also suggest that, if any Byzantines were present in eastern Britain, they were not from the same group that supplied western Britain with goods. This conforms well with the expectation that Byzantine diplomacy might have disregarded the petty chiefs of the Anglo-Saxon east in the fifth and sixth centuries, and is also consistent with the geography of the two Byzantine networks: the possible 'Egyptian' network focused on the Rhine route, and the East-West, 'Syrian', route focused on the Straits of Gibraltar and the Atlantic Ocean.

But were there any Byzantine traders in eastern Britain at all? The discovery of a (possibly sixth-century) Byzantine lead seal at the London foreshore at Putney and Procopius' reference to Thanet could suggest that Byzantine merchants reached eastern Britain, but it is unclear whether this was only in areas remaining under British control. There is also a Byzantine bread stamp from Upper Layham (Suffolk), but this is anomalous and was not found in an archaeological context. Nevertheless, Upper Layham's geographical location (beside the River Brett, which runs into the Stour estuary and enters the North Sea at Harwich) may render it worthy of consideration in this context. The entrance to the Stour estuary is less than seven kilometres from the entrance to the River Deben, the route by which the Bromeswell *situla* and some of the objects in the Sutton Hoo cemetery may have travelled, and so an association might be possible (**62**).[73]

Several scholars have suggested that London and the area around it and present-day St Albans remained under British rule in the fifth and sixth centuries and, if so, the Putney seal might derive from short-lived Byzantine contacts with this former trading centre. Interestingly, both London and St Albans do have sherds of imported Byzantine pottery – that at the Lower Thames Street bath

62 *Byzantine lead seal from Putney. After Collingwood and Wright (1990)*

house in London and that from the Forum at *Verulamium*. It may be, therefore, that these apparent contradictions to the Anglo-Saxon pattern in fact suggest a separate eastern 'British' area, with different overseas relationships. That this is only thinly represented in terms of archaeological material might be no more than an index of its constrained and short-lived character. Elsewhere in the Anglo-Saxon zone of Britain, there is no direct evidence for Byzantine traders. Moreover, the lack of references to Eastern traders in northern Gaul in the fifth to seventh century reduces the likelihood that there were communities of Byzantines living on the southern side of the Channel who would have been prepared to make short-term visits to eastern Britain for trading purposes. It does not rule out the possibility, of course, that Byzantine traders made their way into eastern Britain via the West Country.[74]

However, the over-riding problem with using any of this as evidence for direct Byzantine contact has long seemed to be the point that there were undoubtedly contacts between Britain and Frankia throughout this period. Byzantine imports in Kent, for example, are found alongside the greatest concentration of Frankish imports, the latter, of course, suggesting a cross-Channel trade with Frankia. The role of Byzantine merchants in this trade is usually assumed to have been non-existent. But even in Frankia the possible 'Egyptian' network is relatively unevidenced in texts in comparison to the 'Syrian' network, so in Britain – where the east of the island was virtually 'prehistoric' in these centuries – we would not expect to find it mentioned in texts, even if it had existed. Therefore, it must remain extremely uncertain whether any Byzantine traders, let alone diplomats, were active in the Anglo-Saxon areas during the fifth and sixth centuries.[75]

Nevertheless, in the absence of other evidence, the question comes to the fore of what the Byzantines might have hoped to achieve, either in economic or political terms, in initiating any contact with the Anglo-Saxons. In a non-monetary society that did not exploit its mineral resources to any significant degree, and whose manufactured goods are not reflected in the contemporary archaeological record of the East, it is difficult to see what the Byzantine merchants could have taken away with them. It is difficult, too, to suggest a diplomatic motive, since this was a non-urban society and, at least in the fifth and sixth centuries, one without established political centres. An ecclesiastical diplomatic motive also seems unlikely, given that the region did not have an episcopal structure, if it had many Christians at all. If a missionary explanation lay behind the interaction, we would expect Gregory the Great to have taken this into account when commissioning Augustine's mission of 597, given that he had spent time at the Byzantine court in Constantinople before acceding to the Papacy. Without further evidence, the likelihood is that Anglo-Saxon England was outside the Byzantine-directed trade networks identified as extending across Western Europe, and excluded from Byzantine interest, although why this should have been the case is an interesting question.

The same pattern highlights the one group of Byzantine silver vessels known from Britain as a true anomaly. These are, as we have seen, the silver

63 *The sixth-century 'Anastasius' bowl from Sutton Hoo mound 1. Four control stamps date this to the reign of the Emperor Anastasius I (491-518).* Reproduced with the kind permission of The British Museum

vessels from Sutton Hoo mound 1, including the famous 'Anastasius dish' with stamp marks indicating that it was made between 491 and 518. A silver plate bearing an imperial stamp might be seen as a possible diplomatic gift. Indeed, recent work suggests that it was 'made as a largesse dish for the Emperor in Constantinople' and likely to 'belong to that class of objects which the Emperor gave on special occasions to the holders of high imperial rank or to barbarian kings'. If so, this may mean that the dish is more likely to have arrived via the East-West route through the Mediterranean and up the Atlantic coast, rather than the possible 'Egyptian' network so far identified. It may well be, then, as Jonathan Harris has suggested, that the 'Anastasius dish' found its way to Sutton Hoo via western Britain. Analysis of its ornamentation showed that it had not been made with 'barbarian' tastes in mind, as some analogous Byzantine silver dishes seem to have been, and this might support the suggestion that it was originally intended for a recipient in the British West. Two of the four small medallions on the inner ornamental frieze are thought to represent Rome and Constantinople, while the other two are thought to be possible personifications of provinces. One of these is holding what appears to be a boat. Was this intended as an oblique reference to those lands that lay at the very edge of the *oikoumenē*? If the dish was brought to Sutton Hoo via western Britain this explanation may account for some of the other pre-seventh-century silver vessels in that burial – perhaps the set of ten bowls – and presumably suggests that these were derived, by gift, tribute, trade or booty, from a court in the British territories. They would have been in circulation for over a century, if imported shortly after their manufacture, before being deposited in mound 1 (**63**).[76]

Other kings of the seventh century may have had analogous goods, perhaps melted down at a later date or disposed of in other ways, sometimes even in the same period. King Oswald of Northumbria, according to Bede, was able to command that a silver dish be taken from his table, broken up and the pieces distributed to the poor. As William Filmer-Sankey and Barbara Yorke have both recently commented, the dish sounds as if it was similar to the 'Anastasius dish' from Sutton Hoo.[77]

Interestingly, Oswald reigned over a kingdom with close links to the northern British kingdoms. If the British kingdoms really were in contact with the Byzantine Empire in the fifth and sixth centuries, it might not be surprising to see Byzantine objects being used in diplomatic exchange with neighbouring kingdoms during the course of the next 100 years. There is a glimmer of evidence to suggest that silver objects destined for diplomatic exchange might have been manufactured en masse: Susan Youngs has shown that the ornamentation of the 'Anastasius dish' was probably carried out relatively quickly, with the emphasis on 'showmanship', although the dish itself was plainly a high-quality object. It may or may not be of relevance to this point that the ornamentation of the Breamore 'bucket' or *situla* also shows signs of having been carried out with some speed, and the mis-spelling of the inscription on the Bromeswell 'bucket' may demonstrate the same phenomenon. These objects, although both produced in a copper-alloy fabric, were 'tinned' on their exterior surface so that they would have superficially resembled silver. This, too, might suggest use in diplomatic gift-exchange.[78]

It has been proposed that the Byzantine 'bucket' from grave 45 at Chessell Down might also represent Byzantine metalwork reaching eastern Britain via the Britain West. Otherwise, its deposition in a sixth-century context would make it a very early reflection of the Rhine riverine system, for elsewhere in Britain Byzantine copper-alloy imports are generally deposited in late sixth- or seventh-century contexts. A similar point might be made in relation to the Byzantine coin-weight from a sixth-century grave at Watchfield (Oxfordshire). If the dating evidence for these graves is accepted, it may be most plausible to see both objects as having reached their place of deposition by means of trade or diplomatic exchange with élites in the west of Britain.[79]

If the Chessell Down 'bucket' did reach Britain via the Atlantic seaboard and the west, this raises the possibility that some of the others – perhaps all of them – also came this way. One might even speculate as to whether the inscriptions on the Bromeswell and Breamore examples refer to their original Byzantine owners. Perhaps these were merchants or their relatives who were given them as tokens of governmental acknowledgement for their long-distance voyages to the West, and who later exchanged them in Britain for goods or services. It is even possible, although unlikely (given that they are in Greek), that at least one of the inscriptions refers to a British recipient of the 'bucket'. The *comes* or 'Count' mentioned on the Bromeswell 'bucket' could refer to one of the British kings (who after all used Roman-period titles). Such a hypothesis would be consistent with the suggestion that this series of *situlae* could have been produced in workshops that were under state control, analogous to those which produced silk and military equipment. It is not out of the question, therefore, that the examples from Britain may have been used in Byzantine diplomacy with British kingdoms, although more work is necessary before this hypothesis can be advanced.[80]

Sutton Hoo and its Byzantine associations

Some scholars have seen the rulers of eastern Britain as emulating Roman models of political behaviour by the seventh century. According to this interpretation, those who organised the Sutton Hoo mound 1 ship burial deliberately chose Roman symbols of power to place in the grave of their leader. The belt buckle, helmet and sceptre may draw upon Roman concepts of rank and authority, while Filmer-Sankey has argued that the gold cloisonné shoulder-clasps may be the only surviving part of a Roman-style leather breastplate. Hodges has suggested this was the impulse behind 'exotic' objects in the graves of aristocrats more generally: 'The Anglo-Saxon cemeteries after c.550 were affluent with imported Byzantine, Frankish and Scandinavian gifts to the gods.... Anglo-Saxon society was almost certainly responding to the strains of a demand for primitive valuables, as individuals sought to identify themselves as Late Roman aristocrats had, and as south Scandinavians were doing.'[81]

It is not clear, however, that an antiquarian association was attached to objects made or deposited in emulation of the 'Roman' style. Although scholars have pointed out that Byzantine models were used as inspiration for the 'Roman-style' artefacts in mound 1, the actual contemporary of the objects in Byzantium is seldom fully appreciated. Most of the objects often argued to carry Late Roman associations would have carried the same associations in the Byzantine Empire during Late Antiquity. Sceptres were still carried in procession by the Emperor and large gold belt buckles have parallels in both seventh-century Byzantium and the Western Roman Empire.[82]

There is little reason to assume that 'Roman' and 'Byzantine' were disassociated in the minds of fifth- to seventh-century Westerners, or that what we would understand as the 'end of the Western Roman Empire' had terminated the sense of the Roman Empire having any living presence in the West at all. The coins in the grave should ensure this point, including as they do depictions (albeit Frankish copies) of Justin II (565-578) and Maurice Tiberius (582-602), even if we assume that the other Byzantine objects deposited were not understood as 'Byzantine'. Even the most famous of all Anglo-Saxon burials has, then, several identifiable Byzantine elements and it is no more than an assumption that the significance of these was lost on the intended 'audience'.[83]

Of course, we would not expect the rulers of small-scale Anglo-Saxon kingdoms to symbolise their 'Roman' or 'Byzantine' identity exactly as an Eastern ruler might have done. In the probable absence of direct links between the east of Britain and the Byzantine Empire, ideas and information about Byzantine regalia, dress and ceremony would have been mediated through the Frankish and possibly Lombard kingdoms. It is not surprising then that there were distortions in the way Anglo-Saxon élites symbolised their affinity with the Eastern Roman ('Byzantine') Empire. Indeed, it is surprising that there are not more distortions, for as early as 508 when Clovis received the title of consul from Anastasius, his behaviour was curiously more that of an Emperor than a new consul. Yet even Gregory of Tours, who was linked into sub-Roman networks in Gaul and might have been expected to know about such things, did not see this as unusual or inappropriate.[84]

Nor was mound 1 the first or only burial at Sutton Hoo to have Byzantine associations. Mound 3 yielded Byzantine objects in the context of the remains of a cremated male and a horse, probably placed in a bronze container. A bone box with a *chi-rho* inscription, part of a copper-alloy ewer from – effectively 'Byzantine' – Nubia and a limestone plaque with a winged

Victory or angel from Alexandria were found amongst other, more functional, grave-goods. So, despite the use of cremation for the body, several of the grave-goods may carry Byzantine, not 'Germanic', associations. In other words, if burial at Sutton Hoo was about showing identity and affinities, as Martin Carver has argued, then the latter were sometimes with the Byzantine world, as well as (or even perhaps instead of) 'the Germanic North'. Moreover, some of the Byzantine objects used as status symbols at Sutton Hoo were often those which would have indicated high status even in the Byzantine world itself: most Byzantines did not have limestone sculpted plaques in their homes or their graves – let alone silver dishes with imperial stamps![85]

Byzantine fashions, the role of Frankia and the Anglo-Saxon evidence

Byzantine vessels and other objects were, then, circulating in the highest social groups in eastern Britain by (and before) the seventh century. Access to them may have had great significance in local circles. In other high-status, but not necessarily 'royal', graves, there are both Frankish and Byzantine artefacts and the emulation of Frankish dress styles. Although the latter might seem irrelevant to a discussion of Byzantine contacts, Frankish styles were sometimes ultimately derived from the court dresses of the Byzantine East, as noted in chapter 4. This might not only apply to the styles, but the fabrics as well. For instance, the fine diamond twill textile (SH1) from Sutton Hoo mound 1 may derive from a Syrian context, and there is a hint of evidence for other Byzantine textiles in Anglo-Saxon graves (such as at Banstead Down), although most are extremely badly preserved and so cannot be provenanced with any certainty. Gold braid has been found in burial contexts, as at Taplow, which, although it probably was imported from Frankia, may also reflect contemporary Byzantine fashions. That the Byzantine court should possibly be emulated in this way – consciously or unconsciously – is intriguing in a context where the local élite used Byzantine objects as symbols of rank.[86]

Helen Geake's important study of seventh-century grave-goods is of special note here. She has argued that many of the grave-goods of 'Conversion-period' England (seventh to ninth century) point to a cultural affinity with the Byzantine Empire. A detailed study of the way in which jewellery and other objects were used in Anglo-Saxon burials has led Geake to the conclusion that explicitly 'Germanic' frames of reference were abandoned in the late sixth and early seventh century as Anglo-Saxon communities emerged in new forms. Seventh-century Anglo-Saxon culture was, according to this view, based much more on 'Roman' and 'Byzantine' models than had hitherto been the case.[87]

It is difficult to cite one clear source for the inspiration behind the contents of seventh-century Anglo-Saxon graves because several of these categories of evidence have pre-fifth-century Roman antecedents, particularly as far as the jewellery in female graves is concerned. So, for example, the garnet cabochon and bulla pendants found in seventh-century graves have parallels with jewellery from the Roman period, as does the use of amethysts, pins for fastening garments, and 'flat-section' annular and penannular brooches. Yet these objects were also contemporary in the Byzantine Empire and knowledge of this may have lain behind the decision to employ them as grave-goods or to wear them in life. In the same way, the Roman intaglio set in a seventh-century gold ring from the boat burial near the Alde estuary at Snape (Suffolk) may have been intended as a statement of identification with the contemporary 'Roman' (that is, 'Byzantine'), rather than with the Late Roman, world. A similar interpretation might be applied to the barrow burial at Bloodmoor Hill, at Pakefield by the Suffolk coast, which contained Roman coins in gold settings, a garnet necklace and a crystal engraved with a cross. The presence of the engraved cross might be of especial significance in assigning this burial a 'Byzantine', rather than merely Late Roman, association.[88]

The absence of some of this material in Frankish graves of the seventh century might lead one to suppose that the Anglo-Saxons were looking beyond Frankia – both in geographical and chronological terms – to the pre-fifth-century Romano-British past. After all, they may well have been able to utilise buildings and objects left over from the fifth century, and perhaps later, if one accepts that a Romano-British way of life survived (to some extent) into the sixth century in some areas. The difficulty then remains that much of the material that symbolises this apparent 'Roman renaissance' is concentrated in Kentish graves, the very area of Britain that we know to have had strong links with Frankia both in the seventh century and preceding this.

Caution must, therefore, be exercised in dismissing Frankia as a source for cultural change in Early Anglo-Saxon England. This is not merely because of its proximity and attested links, but because we would actively expect any form of identity to be qualitatively different when expressed through the 'Anglo-Saxon', as opposed to the 'Frankish', idiom. The decision of Franks not to express this postulated 'Roman' identity in the same way as Anglo-Saxons when burying their dead, does not in itself permit us to dismiss Frankia as a vehicle for new types of material culture. Indeed, the presence of 'Coptic' bowls in both Frankish and Anglo-Saxon graves of this period (including outside of Kent) confirms the successful passage of ideas across the Channel from the direction of the Rhine.

It must be remembered, too, that by the seventh century a considerable amount of cultural interchange between western Britain and the Anglo-Saxon areas could have taken place. In such circumstances, it would not be surprising to find that elements of seventh-century Anglo-Saxon *romanitas* were a composite of Romano-British and contemporary Byzantine styles, perhaps even with a more 'Romano-British' than 'Byzantine' flavour. To take the example of amethyst bead necklaces, we might note that these were used as jewellery in both the fifth- to seventh-century Byzantine world and the pre-fifth-century Roman Empire. Their presence in Anglo-Saxon graves of the early seventh century might point, therefore, to a cultural similarity with either the Late Roman or Byzantine world.

The question then remains of how the distinctly 'Byzantine' aspects of this Conversion-period material culture arrived in Britain. That Anglo-Saxons were not simply drawing on residual Romano-British culture is clear, as Geake has pointed out. For example, the short necklaces of the seventh century (which replace the long strings of polychrome glass and amber beads common to 'Germanic-style' graves of the sixth century) have several parallels in the Byzantine world. Most notably, they are seen on the sixth-century mosaic from the church of San Vitale in Ravenna, depicting the Empress Theodora and her attendants. Here, Theodora is wearing a short bead necklace with a deep collar and large pendants below. Next to her, two attendants are wearing short necklaces of pendants, and they are followed by a woman with a necklace of large pendants, and finally two women with beaded necklaces. All the necklaces shown on the mosaic have parallels – in their individual elements – in seventh-century necklaces from Anglo-Saxon cemeteries. One might even point to Anglo-Saxon finger-rings that are more likely to have been selected under 'Byzantine', rather than pre-fifth-century 'Romano-British', influences: for example, the rings with ball-mouldings, such as those from Finglesham (Kent), have many more prototypes from the Byzantine Empire than from Romano-British contexts.[89]

Such evidence would seem to suggest that the trading network bringing amethysts, 'Coptic' bowls and other exotica to the emerging Anglo-Saxon kingdoms also brought ideas and news of contemporary Byzantine fashions. These did not dissipate immediately, but were carried through in manufacturing processes and everyday expressions of material culture. Rather than seeing the popularity of Byzantine styles simply in Kent, or wherever they first entered Britain, we may see them many kilometres away at Chamberlain's Barn (Bedfordshire) or Desborough (Northamptonshire). Michael Pinder's analysis of garnet cloisonné composite disc brooches and his suggestion that they were manufactured by only a small number of Anglo-Saxon jewellery workshops, would appear to support this view, suggesting as it does that there were itinerant craftsmen or merchants operating during this period. The fewer people there were in the transmission process, the more homogeneous we might anticipate expressions of this material culture to be.[90]

We have already seen that Frankia cannot be discounted as a source for the explicitly 'Byzantine' prototypes in Anglo-Saxon jewellery of the seventh century. Yet it is possible that western Britain, too, was instrumental in the transmission of these styles. The apparent lack of evidence for material culture in fifth- to seventh-century western Britain has often puzzled archaeologists, yet it cannot be allowed to exclude this area from explanations of how aspects of Eastern Mediterranean material culture arrived in Early Anglo-Saxon England. If Frankish burial practices cannot necessarily be used as evidence that Byzantine-style jewellery did not reach Britain via Frankia, western British burial practices – that is, unfurnished west-east orientated inhumation – cannot necessarily be used to suggest that western Britons did not have access to similar categories of material culture and analogous fashions. The attested links with the Byzantine Empire in the fifth and probably sixth centuries may well have brought more than pottery to the shores of western Britain. It has already been suggested that Byzantine silver and copper-alloy objects may have made their way to the Anglo-Saxons via the British West, and so it is a logical step to suggest, tentatively, that jewellery styles could have arrived via the same route, even if this cannot be demonstrated at present.

How this cultural change was interpreted in Anglo-Saxon society is unclear. Geake argues for the possibility that Anglo-Saxon élites – whether kings or landowners – sought to stabilise and consolidate the emergent socio-political order by drawing upon a 'new *romanitas*'. One of the more noticeable features of Final Phase or Conversion-period burial is the sudden decrease in the amount of wealth deposited in graves, thereby making élites more difficult to identify. Various explanations for this have been put forward, but they are not relevant to the discussion here.[91]

However, if it is assumed, in the most general of terms, that the 'richer' the grave deposits, the higher the status of the person who was buried there, then one is permitted to recognise a putative élite stratum of society. It is interesting, therefore, that the graves of this stratum are those in which objects are found that derive from Byzantine prototypes. For example, as Geake has pointed out, the short necklace found in a seventh-century inhumation grave at Desborough has parallels with a contemporary Byzantine gold necklace from Sardinia. Its drop-shaped garnet cabochon pendants and cross-shaped pendant are similar to those on a late sixth-century example from Constantinople. The necklaces from cemetery sites at Galley Low (Derbyshire) and Roundway Down (Wiltshire) also have distinct parallels in the Byzantine Empire. Again, their manufacturers were not drawing on Romano-British prototypes that simply 'happened' to be current in the East at the same time, for the cross-shaped pendants with semi-precious stone insets are absent from the Romano-British archaeological record, although common in the sixth- and seventh-century Byzantine East.[92]

By contrast, non-jewellery items in graves – such as buckles, toilet items and spoons – do not usually show such strong cultural associations, either with the Roman past or with contemporary Byzantium. This may support the view that it was primarily high-status members of society who adopted the styles associated with the Byzantine Empire, because most of the non-jewellery items (with the exception of some weapons) are not usually interpreted as high-status artefacts. As non-jewellery objects, the 'Coptic' bowls are, of course, an exception to this, but it is possible that by the time these arrived in eastern Britain they were no longer associated with the Eastern Mediterranean. Instead, they may have been seen as part of the cultural fabric of Frankia or Italy, whence they travelled to Britain. In any case, they are not found exclusively in the richest Anglo-Saxon graves, as we saw in the example of the B4 vessel from the otherwise unfurnished grave at Wheathampstead. Nevertheless, they were undoubtedly indicators of some wealth, as their presence in Sutton Hoo mound 1 and the Taplow burial indicates.

Whether seventh-century Anglo-Saxons, and élite Anglo-Saxons in particular, saw themselves as identifying with a pre-fifth-century Roman Empire or with the contemporary Byzantine Empire is perhaps a moot point. By the end of the seventh century, and beyond the end of the period under investigation here, aspects of the Roman past were brought into play to validate kingly rule. But in the first half of the seventh century this may have been a secondary issue. The knowledge that the Roman Empire continued to exist in the East and that the authority of the Emperor was acknowledged, even if only tacitly, in parts of Italy, Frankia and, possibly, western Britain, may have prompted a desire on the part of the Anglo-Saxons to become part of this cultural world.

There is no evidence, in the first part of the seventh century, that Anglo-Saxon élites deferred to the authority of the Byzantine Emperor, but we would not necessarily expect this. As we have seen elsewhere in the West, arguably, the Emperor's ultimate authority was often taken for granted, glimpsed only in the occasional diplomatic missive or encoded in the acceptance of a gift. That it was merely a formality is by no means certain: even by the mid-seventh century it was only a matter of decades since Byzantine administration had been withdrawn from Spain and North Africa. It still operated in parts of Italy and Rome may have appeared a very 'imperial' city. To a Frank or an Anglo-Saxon, or even a Briton, the authority of the Emperor in Constantinople may have been perceived as real, even if it was not exercised. Rome, after all, was in the hands of the Empire for much of the period, at least in principle.

Conversely, there is no evidence that the Anglo-Saxons explicitly rejected the authority of the Byzantine Emperor. Although a compelling case has been made for Sutton Hoo mound 1 as the grave of a person buried with trappings analogous to those of the imperial office, it neither follows that that person regarded themselves as an Emperor, nor that other people regarded them in this way. The grave-goods could have been intended to symbolise another rank or perhaps the dead person wished to emulate the Emperor, rather than compete with him. As we have seen, even Gregory of Tours seems to have misunderstood the type of behaviour that it would have been appropriate for a consul to display, and so we cannot expect statements of identity to be encoded this clearly.

On this point, it is important to note that objects and modes of expression that were not strictly speaking 'Byzantine' may have acquired 'Byzantine' associations that were only visible to Anglo-Saxon eyes. For example, objects such as cowrie shells may have been rendered 'Byzantine' by their exotic nature, whether or not they were collected in or merely mediated through the Empire. In Britain, far from the Mediterranean coastlands, such associations might, ironically, have been stronger than in southern Gaul or Italy where the true origins of such objects could, perhaps, have been known. On this basis, the fourth-century Egyptian flask with a Greek inscription found in an Anglo-Saxon grave at Ferring (West Sussex) may have been placed in the grave because of its perceived associations with the Byzantine world, although of course it probably reached Britain in a Late Roman context (**colour plate 17**). So we should not dismiss too lightly the possibility that some objects were assigned 'Byzantine' connotations in a British context.[93]

It is, then, possible to suggest that by the seventh century, some Anglo-Saxons were ready to 'buy into' a long-lived, stable, cultural world inhabited – as they saw it – by élites throughout the West. These élites may have included those residing in Frankia or in western Britain. To have been exposed to analogous ideas and (to a lesser extent) material culture from two different directions may explain why the cultural change was so radical and long-lasting. In this context, small differences between the material cultures of these neighbouring regions need not overly concern us, for the Anglo-Saxons would have 'bought into' this late antique cultural world using a medley of Roman and contemporary Byzantine items, focusing, reasonably enough, on what was most readily available to them. While some Romano-British objects may have signified Anglo-Saxon identities, this need not necessarily have been the case. In the mind of an Anglo-Saxon leader, to reiterate, there may have been no difference between 'Roman' and 'Byzantine' as concepts, and if this was the case, we would except to see Romano-British objects 'standing in' for Byzantine objects in high-status graves of this period.[94]

Conclusion

In summary, therefore, it is clear that Britain was an integral part of the late antique world that developed after the collapse of Western Roman authority in the fifth century. The ceramic evidence, while retaining many puzzles and uncertainties, suggests that the Byzantine Empire maintained an active interest in Britain, especially the south-west peninsula. This interest might, for a 'window' of up to 75 years, have been characterised by the shipment of official supplies from the Eastern Mediterranean, possibly with only provisioning stopovers en route. Looked at in conjunction with the evidence from Frankia and elsewhere in the West, it seems possible that these shipments were organised from Syria and sanctioned by the imperial authorities at Constantinople. Given the evidence for the possible integration of Egyptian and Syrian shipping routes in the Mediterranean, an Egyptian component cannot be ruled out at this stage, although there is very little evidence for its existence. The silver from the Sutton Hoo mound 1 burial and possibly one or more of the copper-alloy (brass) 'buckets', may provide us with another glimpse of diplomatic relations between British and Byzantine élites.

By contrast, the eastern part of Britain appears to have remained relatively insulated from Byzantine activities until the second half of the sixth century, although it may have received Byzantine objects via the British West before that date. When it did come into contact with Byzantium, it probably did so indirectly, through a trading network that extended through the Rhineland and into Kent and East Anglia. This network, or perhaps series of networks, brought copper-alloy vessels, cowrie shells, ivory rings, amethysts and probably other, now archaeologically invisible, objects. Many of these were used as indicators of status and wealth in burial, and probably also in life. In a sense, the Sutton Hoo burials of the early seventh century represent the final moments of this late antique world, including as they do Byzantine 'exotic' imports – garnets cut in Constantinople, a winged Victory plaque and copper-alloy vessels – and possible allusions not simply to 'Roman', but to 'Byzantine', authority. Set apart from the activities of Augustine and his entourage in Canterbury, yet showing contacts with both the British West and the Rhineland trading networks, Sutton Hoo demonstrates that Britain remained linked into the broader world of Late Antiquity until as late as the early seventh century. As we saw at the beginning of this chapter, by the time the Roman Church was established in Anglo-Saxon England the relationship between Britain and the Byzantine Empire was beginning to take on a completely new form.

7

CONCLUSION
A BYZANTINE COMMONWEALTH IN LATE ANTIQUITY?

The relationship between the Byzantine Empire and the Western kingdoms during the fifth to seventh centuries was a more integral and complex affair than most studies have allowed. Although they developed out of the vestiges of the Late Roman Western Empire, the new kingdoms depended, to a great extent, on contemporary contacts with the Byzantine Empire in order to function as stable entities. Sometimes these links were mediated through Byzantine possessions in the West, such as Ravenna, but this was by no means always the case, particularly in relation to Gaul (Frankia) and Britain, and there is plentiful evidence for direct contacts between the West and the Eastern Mediterranean.

There was, of course, a solid foundation for fifth- to seventh-century East-West contacts in the form of the Late Roman Empire. This had, to some extent, united East and West in a common culture whose constituent parts included literacy, urbanism, an Empire-wide monetary system and, in its final century, Christianity. It is not surprising that rulers in the Western successor kingdoms adopted many of these cultural components. It was an expedient and politically astute move to make. Moreover, it would have been a 'natural' development insofar as the barbarian kings of the Continental West, and the Franks in particular, had already been exposed to the *romanitas* that permeated everyday life in the Late Roman Empire. They knew through their interactions with high-level Late Roman officials, as *foederati,* as enemies and as traders, much of the ideology that lay behind the functioning of the upper echelons of the Roman state. It comes as no great surprise, therefore, to observe late fifth-century barbarian élites styling themselves as high-level Roman officials, seen most vividly in the evidence from the tomb of Childeric at Tournai. With substantial sub-Roman populations and a discrete stratum of sub-Roman administrators present in their kingdoms, it made political sense to legitimise themselves with reference to the Roman Empire. In portraying their own authority as linked to Roman authority they might seek to convey that there had been a seamless transfer of power during the course of the traumatic fifth century.

These kings were remarkably successful in their initiative. Their kingdoms were more stable and long-lived than might have been expected, given the dramatic circumstances in which they often emerged. The Ostrogothic kingdom founded by Theodoric was able to withstand the onslaught of the Byzantine military machine for years before it capitulated in the mid-sixth century, while Childeric and his son Clovis laid foundations for a Frankish state that to a large extent withstood the civil wars of the sixth and seventh centuries. The foundation of their kingdoms in notions of Roman authority and legitimacy can be seen, in part, as a reason for their success.

However, this book has demonstrated that references to Late Roman culture were made in the context of a contemporary and continuing relationship with the Eastern Roman Empire: Byzantium. New Western élites were in contact with a still existing Roman authority, now based in the Eastern Mediterranean, and this may be the reason why *romanitas* remained an important symbol of stability and authority in the West until the seventh century. Had their *romanitas* been based solely on an early fifth-century memory of the Western Roman Empire, its potency might have been expected to decline rapidly after *c*.500 and new frames of reference emerge as the underpinnings of the barbarian kingdoms. This, for the most part, was not the case. Instead, the Byzantine Empire played a key role in the development of Western kingdoms. In extensively interacting with them by a variety of means – political, religious and economic – Byzantium provided the basis for their subsequent development.

So far as Britain is concerned, we have seen that the western side of the island was linked into fifth- and sixth-century Eastern Mediterranean dynamics to a far greater extent than usually allowed. Ceramic evidence points to a direct and sustained link between Britain and the Byzantine Empire in the late fifth and early sixth centuries. The deliberate directionality of these imports means that this evidence cannot be explained in purely commercial terms. Seen in the context of the Western Mediterranean ceramic evidence, and its possible associations with official Byzantine intervention in that region, the British material, too, might be seen as evidence of official imperial interests. In particular, given that the relative quantities of LR1 and LR2 amphorae at Tintagel are similar to those at Eastern sites thought to have received official Byzantine supplies in the same period, the case for an official interest in western Britain is strengthened. We have seen that this may have been the ultimate destination of a network that could have had its origins in Syria. It is likely that the British élites in receipt of Eastern Mediterranean commodities appeared to acknowledge the over-arching authority of the Byzantine Emperor who had sent them, even if this was more a matter of political expediency than true devotion. One can hardly suppose that the

Byzantine court would have continued to supply British kings who they knew flaunted imperial authority.

Ironically, this evidence might suggest that western Britain, at the farthest reach of the former Roman Empire, was more linked into Eastern Mediterranean governmental dynamics than were some areas of Continental Western Europe. The quantities of imported Byzantine ceramics from northwest Gaul, for example, are negligible compared to the quantities from western Britain in the same period. Conversely, quantities of Gallic pottery found in western Britain are negligible compared to quantities of Byzantine pottery, at least until the second half of the sixth century. That western Britain was one of the least 'romanized' areas of Roman Britain before $c.400$ makes this first phenomenon all the more remarkable. It is even more interesting that this should be the case, given what has often been seen as a lack of material evidence for everyday life in fifth- to seventh-century western Britain. It raises the point that expressions of political identity might not be straightforwardly detectable in the material evidence and that the same political identities might be expressed in different ways across the same region, materially or otherwise.

The links between the Anglo-Saxon east of Britain and the Byzantine Empire took a more indirect form and operated later in the fifth- to seventh-century period than those between Byzantium and western Britain. There is no evidence that these contacts were facilitated by the imperial court and it is more likely that they were commercial in nature. It is possible that they originated in Byzantine Egypt, whence a range of products chosen with Western tastes and preferences in mind was transported across the Mediterranean, before being transported over the Alps and shipped along the Rhine to the English Channel. It is probable that these goods were not in the hands of actual Byzantines for most of this journey.

Like their Continental contemporaries, late sixth- and seventh-century élites in eastern Britain may have drawn upon the material culture of the Late Roman past to set themselves apart from their social inferiors: for example, in the use of Romano-British-style jewellery. However, they did not employ this material culture in a vacuum, but in the knowledge that the Roman Empire still existed in the Eastern Mediterranean. This knowledge affected the way they chose to express *romanitas*, although in other ways Anglo-Saxon culture was mostly Germanic in origin. That this was the case may be seen in the adoption of fashions in early seventh-century Anglo-Saxon England that are not evidenced in the Romano-British period.[1]

The extent to which over-arching Byzantine political authority can be detected in the archaeology of eastern Britain is less certain. The inherent difficulties in the interpretation of burial evidence mean that the 'message' intended by the deposition of a particular object in the grave is obscure. In contrast with some of the Continental cases, especially in those areas where we also have textual evidence, it is merely possible to suggest that some objects were more associated with wealth and status than others. After all, Anglo-Saxons may not even have realised the Byzantine origin of the objects they employed as status symbols: they may have been seen as 'Frankish' or simply 'foreign'.

Yet, the case of the man buried in Sutton Hoo mound 1 suggests that the idea of Roman political authority was still alive in Anglo-Saxon England in the 620s. As we have seen, his grave-goods and their composition drew heavily upon notions of imperial military power.[2] However, they also drew upon aspects of imperial power that were still current in the Byzantine Empire, raising the possibility that those who buried the occupant of the mound 1 tomb were making reference to the Byzantine Emperor in Constantinople. They were not necessarily alluding to some long-dead Roman Empire. The presence of imported objects – some from the Eastern Mediterranean itself – indicates that the East Anglian kingdom was linked into wider networks of exchange and supply. It might reasonably be expected, therefore, to have received information about the East alongside the goods that it acquired, even if this information was heavily distorted. If so, the 'Roman' aspects of Sutton Hoo should not be seen as a seventh-century 'revival' of *romanitas* based principally on the memory of the Western Roman Empire, but an evocation of contemporary Byzantium. In any case, by the early decades of the seventh century very few 'memories' of the Western Roman Empire may have been at all meaningful.[3]

In setting the British evidence in its contemporary European context this study has demonstrated that Britain can (and should) be integrated into the broader study of Late Antiquity. It should not be thought that the West, and the Continent in particular, adopted Eastern Roman (Byzantine) culture without question or that it deferred to the authority of the Emperor in every case. The torturous events of the Reconquest alone ensure this point. Rather, Western indigenous political authority grew out of a relationship with the East in which the Emperor in Constantinople was seen as legitimising the rule of Western élites. For example, the first phase of barbarian gold coinage (the 'pseudo-imperial' *solidi*) sought simply to pass itself off as 'Byzantine' but, by the last decades of the sixth century, Western gold coin issues bore both the image of the Emperor and the monogram of the barbarian king. In other words, the authority of Continental barbarian kings had now been established, but this was still legitimised by the Byzantine Emperor in Constantinople. It will be recalled that there were no external commercial reasons for a Byzantine model to be so closely followed in the development of the fifth- to seventh-century Western monetary system and so coin design was principally a matter of political choices.

Cultural identity is a multi-faceted phenomenon and the contacts between the Byzantine Empire and the West discussed in this book did not result, of course, in a homogeneous late antique Western culture. Neither was Western culture in the fifth to seventh centuries entirely derivative of

Byzantine culture. Other cultures, derivative of both barbarian and provincial Roman cultures, existed and were elaborated throughout the fifth- to seventh-century West. It must be recognised that by far the majority of archaeological sites in Western Europe do not show evidence either of contacts with the Byzantine world or of the adoption of Eastern culture. Moreover, those aspects of Byzantine culture that were accepted in the West were interpreted in new social contexts and changed according to the needs and cultural perspectives of those who employed them.

However, it is important to realise that the exceptional cases, where contacts with Byzantium are in evidence, might represent only a proportion of other, unrecognised or undiscovered, sites showing cultural activities that were derived from the Byzantine world. By discussing a range of evidence in relation to the question of East-West contacts during Late Antiquity, this point has been emphasised, whilst showing that Byzantine contacts with the West were not confined to one sphere of activity or another.

It might come as a surprise to some that the Church did not, apparently, play a more important role in facilitating East-West links. Where the Church did facilitate contacts these usually took place in an informal context, such as pilgrimage, rather than in the realm of ecclesiastical politics. This is not to say that shared religious beliefs were unimportant, but that interactions facilitated by them may have been directed along pathways intended principally for political and economic exchange. To a greater extent than might otherwise be imagined, the Byzantine state and traders of luxury objects and foodstuffs were responsible for bringing about, and sustaining, relations between the two regions. These were not always mutually exclusive categories: Byzantine court business and trading activities sometimes took place alongside each other. Thus, pathways of economic interaction often facilitated networks of political exchange, and vice versa, whilst the two together provided a context for other forms of contact.

It is hardly necessary to say that this has not been a comprehensive discussion of evidence for Byzantine-Western relations during Late Antiquity. Instead, it has been an examination of the various forms taken by these contacts and, in so doing, has illuminated areas where future work on the subject might usefully be directed. Nevertheless, this study has demonstrated that the links between the Eastern Mediterranean and Western kingdoms, especially élites within those kingdoms, were more wide-ranging and long-lasting than often supposed. In particular, it has shown that the political involvement of the Byzantine Empire in the West outlived the fall of the Western Roman Empire. In this light, the Reconquest may be seen as just one – politically unsophisticated – stage of these contacts, which probably hastened the end of the *oikoumenê* and associated ideas about the role of imperial authority in Constantinople.

Finally, it might be suggested that the network of East-West relations explored in this book constituted a chronologically discrete 'international order'. This could be likened to what the late Dimitri Obolensky, in a seminal work, described as a 'Byzantine commonwealth': that is, an 'international order' comprised of cultural contacts between Byzantium and the region that was then its closest partner in international affairs, Eastern Europe. The conceptual similarities between the 'Byzantine commonwealth' and the relationships discussed in this book are striking, so much so that the term 'Late Antique Byzantine commonwealth' might be a valid way of describing them. Just as in Obolensky's 'commonwealth', shared beliefs and identities shaped relations between the two regions in question, promoting coherent forms of political, economic and social identity, some of which were to last for several centuries, and which, taken together, laid foundations for both the medieval and modern state-systems.[4]

It is important to recognise that the place of Britain in the study of this 'Late Antique Byzantine commonwealth' is ensured, for the British evidence illuminates not only Byzantine-British relations in their own right, but provides an important background for the analysis of Byzantine-Western relations more generally. Without a consideration of the British evidence the role of the Byzantine Empire in the fifth- to seventh-century West would only be partially understood.

BYZANTINE EMPERORS FROM THEODOSIUS I TO CONSTANS II

378–395	Theodosius I
396–408	Arcadius
408–450	Theodosius II
450–457	Marcian
457–474	Leo I
474	Leo II
474–475	Zeno (first term)
475–476	Basiliscus
476–491	Zeno (second term)
491–518	Anastasius I
518–527	Justin I
527–565	Justinian I
565–578	Justin II
578–582	Tiberius I
582–602	Maurice Tiberius
602–610	Phocas
610–641	Heraclius
641	Constantine III & Heraclonas
641–668	Constans II

NOTES & BIBLIOGRAPHY

Chapter 1
1. J. Haldon (1990), *Byzantium and the seventh century, the transformation of a culture*, Cambridge.
2. P. Brown (1971), *The World of Late Antiquity*, London. A. Cameron (1993), *The Mediterranean World in Late Antiquity*, London.
3. H. Pirenne (1939), *Mohammed and Charlemagne*, London.
4. R. Hodges & D. Whitehouse (1983), *Mohammed, Charlemagne and the origins of Europe*, London. R. Van Dam (1992), 'The Pirenne thesis and fifth-century Gaul', in J. Drinkwater & H. Elton (eds), *Fifth-century Gaul: a crisis of identity?* Cambridge, pp.321-33. S.T. Loseby (1998), 'Marseille and the Pirenne Thesis, I: Gregory of Tours, the Merovingian Kings and "Un Grand Port"', in R. Hodges & W. Bowden (eds), *The Sixth Century: Production, Distribution and Demand*, Leiden, pp.203-29.
5. K. Randsborg (1991), *The First Millennium AD in Europe and the Mediterranean: An Archaeological Essay*, Cambridge.
6. Shipwrecks: G.F. Bass & F.H. van Doornick (1982), *Yassı Ada. Vol.1. A seventh-century Byzantine shipwreck*, College Station, Texas. A.J. Parker (1992), *Ancient Shipwrecks of the Mediterranean and the Roman Provinces*, British Archaeological Reports, International Series 580. S. Kingsley (2002), *A Sixth-Century AD Shipwreck off the Carmel Coast, Israel: Dor D and Holy Land Wine Trade*, Oxford, British Archaeological Reports, International Series 1065.
7. K.R. Dark (1995), *Theoretical Archaeology*, London.
8. P. Barker (1977), *Techniques of Archaeological Excavation*, London. P. Barker (1986), *Understanding Archaeological Excavation*, London.
9. C. Mango (1980), *Byzantium: Empire of the New Rome*, London. P. Sarris (2002), 'The Eastern Roman Empire from Constantine to Heraclius (306-41)', in C. Mango (ed.), *The Oxford History of Byzantium*, Oxford, pp.19-59.
10. A.H.M. Jones (1964), *The Later Roman Empire, 284-602*, (3 volumes) London. A. Cameron (1993), *The Later Roman Empire (284-439)*, London.
11. P. Horden & N. Purcell (2000), *The Corrupting Sea: a study of Mediterranean history*, Oxford.
12. J. Herrin (1987), *The Formation of Christendom*, London.
13. M. McCormick (2001), *Origins of the European Economy: Communications and Commerce, A.D. 300-900*, Cambridge, pp.80-81.
14. P. Horden & N. Purcell (2000), *The Corrupting Sea: a study of Mediterranean history*, Oxford.
15. Verulamium: Bede, *Historia Ecclesiastica*, 1. 7. Ed. & trans. L. Sherley-Price (1968), *History of the English Church and People*, Harmondsworth. R. Niblett (2001), *Verulamium: The Roman city of St Albans*, Stroud. E. A. Thompson (1984), *St Germanus of Auxerre and the end of Roman Britain*, London. Urbanism: T. W. Potter (1995), *Towns in Late Antiquity: Iol Caesarea and its context*, Sheffield. J. Drinkwater & H. Elton (1992) (eds), *Fifth-century Gaul: a crisis of identity?* Cambridge. R. Hodges & R. Hobley (1988) (eds), *The Rebirth of Towns in the West AD 700-1050*, London. R.F.J. Jones et al. (1988), *First Millennium Papers. Western Europe in the first Millennium AD*, Oxford, pp.159-73.
16. C. Wickham (1994), *Land and Power: Studies in Italian and European Social History, 400–1200*, London. R. Hodges (1997), *Light in the Dark Ages: The rise and fall of San Vincenzo al Volturno*, London.
17. D. Obolensky (1971), *The Byzantine Commonwealth: Eastern Europe 550 – 1500*, London.

18 For discussion of main East-West routes during Late Antiquity: A. Avramea (2001), 'Land and Sea Communications, Fourth-Fifteenth Centuries', in A. Laiou (ed.), *The economic history of Byzantium: From the Seventh through the Fifteenth Century*, Washington D.C., pp.57-90 (= Dumbarton Oaks Studies 39). M. McCormick (2001), *Origins of the European Economy: Communications and Commerce, AD 300-900*, chapter 3, pp.64ff.

19 M. Millett (1990), *The Romanization of Britain*, Cambridge. D.J. Mattingly (1997) (ed.), *Dialogues in Roman Imperialism: power, discourse and discrepant experience in the Roman Empire*, Portsmouth, Rhode Island (= Journal of Roman Archaeology supplementary series 23).

20 I. Wood (1987), 'The fall of the western Empire and the end of Roman Britain', *Britannia*, 18, pp.251-62.

Chapter 2

1 *The Christian Topography of Cosmas Indicopleustes*, II. 16. Ed. & trans. J. McCrindle (1887), New York. John Malalas, *Chronographia*, XVIII. esp. 56, 73, 106. Eds & trans. E. Jeffreys, M. Jeffreys, R. Scott (1986), Melbourne. C.R. Whittaker (1994), *Frontiers of the Roman Empire*, Baltimore. A. Kazhdan (1991), 'Oikoumene', in A. Kazhdan, A.-M. Talbot et al (eds), *Oxford Dictionary of Byzantium*, Oxford, p.1518.

2 Cassiodorus, *Variae Epistolae*. V.1. Ed. & trans. T. Hodgkin (1886), London. Also: ed. & trans. S.J.B. Barnish (1992), Liverpool. The modern-day usage of the adjective, 'byzantine', refers to this aspect of diplomatic practice. E. Chrysos (1992), 'Byzantine diplomacy, AD 300-800: means and ends', in J. Shepard & S. Franklin (eds), *Byzantine Diplomacy: Papers from the Twenty-Fourth Spring Symposium of Byzantine Studies*, Aldershot, pp.25-39.

3 For an examination of the constitutional relationship of the Empire to other geographical zones: E. Chrysos (1978), 'The Title Βασιλευς in Early Byzantine International Relations', *Dumbarton Oaks Papers*, 32, pp.29-75. R.A. Markus (1990), *The End of Ancient Christianity*, Cambridge, p.218.

4 C. Mango (1980), *Byzantium: Empire of the New Rome*, London.

5 E. James (1977), *The Merovingian Archaeology of South-West Gaul*, Oxford, British Archaeological Reports, International Series 25 (2 volumes), p.79.

6 Sidonius Apollinaris, *Epistolae*, IV. 17. 1. Ed. & trans. O.M. Dalton (1915), Oxford.

7 J. Harries (1994), *Sidonius Apollinaris and the Fall of Rome*, Oxford. P. Heather (1999), 'The barbarian in late antiquity: image, reality and transformation', in R. Miles (ed.), *Constructing Identities in Late Antiquity*, London, pp.234-58, 245-7.

8 A.D. Lee (1993), *Information and Frontiers: Roman Foreign Relations in Late Antiquity*, Cambridge, chapter 1.

9 R.W. Mathisen (1986), 'Patricians as Diplomats in Late Antiquity', *Byzantinische Zeitschrift*, 79, pp.36-49. E. Chrysos (1992), 'Byzantine diplomacy, AD 300-800: means and ends', in J. Shepard & S. Franklin (eds), *Byzantine Diplomacy: Papers from the Twenty-Fourth Spring Symposium of Byzantine Studies*, Aldershot, pp.25-39. M. Whitby (1992), 'From frontier to palace: the personal role of the emperor in diplomacy', in J. Shepard & S. Franklin (eds), *Byzantine Diplomacy. Papers from the Twenty-fourth Spring Symposium of Byzantine Studies*, Aldershot, pp.295-303, 301. B. Brennan (1995), 'Venantius Fortunatus: Byzantine Agent?' *Byzantion*, 65, pp.7-16, *passim*.

10 E. Chrysos (1992), 'Byzantine diplomacy, AD 300-800: means and ends', in J. Shepard & S. Franklin (eds), *Byzantine Diplomacy: Papers from the Twenty-Fourth Spring Symposium of Byzantine Studies*, Aldershot, pp.25-39, 32. P. Barnwell (1997), 'War and Peace: historiography and seventh-century embassies', *Early Medieval Europe*, 6, pp.127-139.

11 Gregory of Tours, *Historia Francorum*, VI. 2. Ed. & trans. L. Thorpe (1974), *The History of the Franks*, Harmondsworth.

12 E. Chrysos (1978), 'The Title Βασιλευς in Early Byzantine International Relations', *Dumbarton Oaks Papers*, 32, pp.29-75.

13 J. Moorhead (1992), *Theodoric in Italy*, Oxford, pp.6-7.

14 J. Moorhead (1992), *Theodoric in Italy*, Oxford, p.8.

15 The following section on Ostrogothic rule and Byzantine-Ostrogothic diplomacy is based on: J. Moorhead (1992), *Theodoric in Italy*, Oxford and P. Heather (1998), *The Goths*, Oxford. Other sources are cited where relevant.

16 Theodoric may have been born shortly after the defeat of Attila and his Ostrogothic allies in 451. If so, one wonders whether his name was chosen in order to signal a change of political affiliation. The principal allies of Aetius, the Roman *magister militum* responsible for the defeat of Attila were the Visigoths, whose leader was also named Theodoric. It would have been fortuitous for Theodemer to be politically expedient whilst still giving his son a Gothic name.

17 The daughter in question was Anicia Juliana, who later built the church of St Polyeuktos in Constantinople. She married another barbarian, Areobindus Dagalaifus Areobindus, who, incidentally, was acclaimed Emperor in 512 in Constantinople, although he was never crowned. J. Moorhead (1992), *Theodoric in Italy*, Oxford, p.84.

18 John Malalas, *Chronographia*, XV. 9. Eds & trans. E. Jeffreys, M. Jeffreys & R. Scott (1986), Melbourne. J. Moorhead (1992) *Theodoric in Italy*, Oxford, pp.60, 88. B. Kiilerich (1996), 'Continuity and Change in Ruler Imagery: The Eternal Victor, *c.*400 to 800 AD', in P. Åström (ed.), *Rome and the North,* Göteborg, pp.95-110, 99. A sister of Theodoric is recorded as having been present at the imperial court in 487.

19 Procopius, *History of the Wars*. Book V, 5. 1; Book IX, 6. 16. Trans. H.B. Dewing (1919), *Procopius*, Vol. III & Vol. VI, London.

20 Cassiodorus, *Variae Epistolae*, I. 1, 2. Ed. & trans. T. Hodgkin (1886), London. Also: ed. & trans. S.J.B. Barnish (1992), Liverpool.

21 Fredegar, *Chronicle,* III. 2. Reproduced in A.C. Murray (2000) (ed.), *From Roman to Merovingian Gaul*, Ontario, p.612-3. Procopius, *History of the Wars,* Book VII, xxiii, 4; Book VIII, xx. 7-9. Ed. & trans. H.B. Dewing (1919), *Procopius*, Vol. VII & Vol. VIII, London. J. Moorhead (1992), *Theodoric in Italy*, Oxford, p.186.

22 Gregory of Tours, *Historia Francorum*, I. 39; II. 38. Ed. & trans. L. Thorpe (1974), *The History of the Franks,* Harmondsworth. Note that Ian Wood suggests Voulon, near Poitiers as the site of the battle: I. Wood (1994), *The Merovingian Kingdoms, 450-751,* London, p.46. It is generally accepted that Clovis was not made 'Augustus', since he never used that title. It is much more likely that he was made an honorary *ex consule*.

23 Gregory of Tours, *Historia Francorum*, II. 38. Ed. & trans. L. Thorpe (1974), *The History of the Franks,* Harmondsworth. I. Wood (1994) *The Merovingian Kingdoms, 450-751,* London, p.51. J. Moorhead (1992), *Theodoric in Italy*, Oxford, p.185. M. Mundell Mango (2002), 'Status and its symbols', in C. Mango (ed.), *The Oxford History of Byzantium*, Oxford, pp.60-3.

24 Sigismund is quoted in E. Chrysos (1997), 'The empire in east and west', in L. Webster & M. Brown (eds), *The Transformation of the Roman World, AD 400 – 900,* London, pp.9-19, 10. Fredegar, *Fourth Book of the Chronicle of Fredegar, with its continuations.* 62, 65. Ed. & trans. J.M. Wallace-Hadrill (1960), London.

25 John Malalas, *Chronographia*, XVII. 9. Eds. & trans. E. Jeffreys, M. Jeffreys & R. Scott (1986), Melbourne. E. Chrysos (1978), 'The Title Βασιλευς in Early Byzantine International Relations', *Dumbarton Oaks Papers,* 32, pp.29-75, 39. E. Chrysos (1992), 'Byzantine diplomacy, AD 300-800: means and ends', in J. Shepard & S. Franklin (eds), *Byzantine Diplomacy: Papers from the Twenty-Fourth Spring Symposium of Byzantine Studies,* Aldershot, pp.25-39, 34.

26 J. Moorhead (1992), *Theodoric in Italy*, Oxford, p.191. P. Heather (1998), *The Goths*, Oxford, pp.249, 277.

27 J. Moorhead (1992), *Theodoric in Italy*, Oxford, p.201.

28 R. Macrides (1992), 'Dynastic marriages and political kinship', in J. Shepard & S. Franklin (eds), *Byzantine Diplomacy. Papers from the Twenty-fourth Spring Symposium of Byzantine Studies,* Aldershot, pp.263-79, pp.274-5, 277.

29 Theophanes, *Chronographia*, 6.21.11; 16.9.8.3.27. Ed. & trans. H. Turtledove (1982), Philadelphia. D. Obolensky (1971), *Byzantium and the Slavs,* London, II, 485ff. For the limited cultural exchanges that took place as a result of this marriage, and that of Constantine V, see M. Whittow (1996), *The Making of Orthodox Byzantium, 600 - 1025,* Basingstoke, pp.225-6.

30 King Sigibert of Austrasia married the Visigothic princess, Brunhild, in 566. I. Wood (1994), *The Merovingian Kingdoms, 450-751,* London, p.126-36.

31 Gregory of Tours, *Historia Francorum*, IV. 3. Ed. & trans. L. Thorpe (1974), *The History of the Franks,* Harmondsworth. Paul the Deacon, *History of the Lombards,* IV. 30. Ed. W.D. Foulke, trans. E. Peters (1974), Philadelphia. N. Christie (1995), *The Lombards: The Ancient Longobards,* Oxford, p.57.

32 Wood (1994), *The Merovingian Kingdoms, 450-751,* London, p.121.

33 Procopius, *History of the Wars*, Book VIII, xx. 7-9. Trans. H. B. Dewing (1919), *Procopius*, Vol. V, London.

34 Gregory of Tours, *Historia Francorum*, IV. 26; IX. 26. Ed. & trans. L. Thorpe (1974), *The History of the Franks*, Harmondsworth. Bede, *Historia Ecclesiastica,* II, 1, 5. Ed. & trans. L. Sherley-Price (1968), *History of the English Church and People,* Harmondsworth. I. Wood (1983), *The Merovingian North Sea,* Alingsås. I. Wood (1994), *The Merovingian Kingdoms, 450-751,* London, pp.176-80.

35 M.V. Girvés (1996), 'The treaties between Justinian and Athanagild and the legality of the Byzantine possessions on the Iberian peninsula', *Byzantion,* 66, pp.208-18. L. A. García Moreno (1996), 'The creation of Byzantium's Spanish Province', *Byzantion,* 66, pp.101-19.

36 Gregory of Tours, *Historia Francorum*, VI. 18. Ed. & trans. L. Thorpe (1974), *The History of the Franks,* Harmondsworth. R. Macrides (1992), 'Dynastic marriages and political kinship', in J. Shepard & S. Franklin (eds), *Byzantine Diplomacy. Papers from the Twenty-fourth Spring Symposium of Byzantine Studies,* Aldershot, pp.263-79.

37 Gregory of Tours, *Historia Francorum*, VI. 2, 42. Ed. & trans. L. Thorpe (1974), *The History of the Franks,* Harmondsworth.

38 Fredegar, *Fourth Book of the Chronicle of Fredegar, with its continuations.* 6. Ed. & trans. J.M. Wallace-Hadrill (1960), London.

39 Gregory of Tours, *Historia Francorum*, VI. 24; VII. 32. Ed. & trans. L. Thorpe (1974), *The History of the Franks,* Harmondsworth.

40 Gregory of Tours, *Historia Francorum*, VI. 23, 34; VII. 10-39. Ed. & trans. L. Thorpe (1974), *The History of the Franks,* Harmondsworth. Venantius Fortunatus, *The Life of the Holy Radegund*. In J. Holbory, J.A. McNamara & G. Whatley (1992), *Sainted Women of the Dark Ages,* London. E. James (1988) *The Franks,* Oxford, pp.175-82.

Chapter 3

1 Gregory of Tours, *Historia Francorum*, IV. 29, 42. Ed. & trans. L. Thorpe (1974), *The History of the Franks,* Harmondsworth. For papyrus and spices: M. McCormick (2001), *Origins of the European Economy: Communications and Commerce, AD 300-900,* Cambridge, pp.704ff. Alaric: B. Lançon (2000), *Rome in Late Antiquity*, Edinburgh, p.37.

2 G. Kapitän (1969), 'The Church Wreck off Marzamemi', *Archaeology*, 22, pp.122-133C. J.-P. Sodini (1989), 'Le commerce des marbres à l'époche protobyzantine', *Hommes et richesses, Tôme 1: IV-VII siècle,* Paris, pp.163-86. A.J. Parker (1992), *Ancient Shipwrecks of the Mediterranean and the Roman Provinces,* Oxford, British Archaeological Reports, International Series, 580, pp.121, 267. Barsanti (1995), 'Alcune riflessioni sulla diffusione dei materiali di marmo proconnesio in Italia e in Tunisia', *Acta XII Congressus Internationalis Archaeologiae Christianae,* Vatican City, pp.515-23, pl.63-4.

3 M.G. Fulford (1989), 'Byzantium and Britain: a Mediterranean perspective on Post-Roman Mediterranean Imports in Western Britain and Ireland', *Medieval Archaeology,* 33, pp.1-6.

4 F.K. Yegül (1986), *The Bath-Gymnasium Complex at Sardis,* (Sardis Monograph 3), Cambridge, Mass, pp.14-15. M. McCormick (2001), *Origins of the European Economy: Communications and Commerce, AD 300-900,* Cambridge, pp.42-53.

5 F.H. van Doorninck (1989), 'The Cargo Amphoras of the Seventh-Century Yassı Ada and Eleventh-Century Serçe Limany Shipwrecks: two examples of a reuse of Byzantine amphoras as transport jars', in V. Déroche & J.-M. Spieser (eds), *Recherches sur la céramique,* pp.247-57 (= Bulletin de Correspondance Hellénique, Supplement 18).

6 K.R. Dark (2001), *Byzantine Pottery,* Stroud, pp.31-42.

7 *Ibid.*, pp.23-5.

8 The best introduction to these ceramics remains: J.W. Hayes (1972), *Late Roman Pottery,* London. J.W. Hayes (1980), *A Supplement to Late Roman Pottery,* London. Also: J.W. Hayes (1998), 'Pottery of the Sixth and Seventh Centuries', in N. Cambi & E. Marin (eds), *Acta XIII Congressus Internationalis Archaeologiae Christianae. II,* Vatican City & Split, pp.541-49.

9 D.P.S. Peacock & D.F. Williams (1986), *Amphorae and the Roman Economy: an introductory guide,* London. M. Sciallano & P. Sibella (1994), *Amphores: Comment les identifier?,* (2nd ed.) Aix-en-Provence. P. Arthur (1998), 'Eastern Mediterranean Amphorae between 500 and 700: a view from Italy', in L. Saguì (ed.), *Ceramica in Italia: VI-VII secolo. Atti del convegno in onore di John W. Hayes,* Florence, pp.157-83. K.R. Dark (2001), *Byzantine Pottery,* Stroud. S. Kingsley (2002), *A Sixth-Century AD Shipwreck off the Carmel Coast, Israel: Dor D and Holy Land Wine Trade,* Oxford, British Archaeological Reports, International Series 1065.

10 J.-Y. Empereur & M. Picon (1989), 'Les regions de production d'amphores imperials en Méditerranée orientale', in *Actes du colloque de Sienne (22-24 mai 1986): Amphores romaines et histoire économique: dix ans de recherché,* Rome, pp.223-48.

11 S.J. Keay (1984), *Late Roman Amphorae in the Western Mediterranean,* Oxford, British Archaeological Reports, International Series 196, p.428. P. Reynolds (1995), *Trade in the Western Mediterranean, AD 400-700: the ceramic evidence,* Oxford, British Archaeological Reports, International Series 604. These are used throughout the following account that follows. Other sources are referenced as relevant.

12 Carthage: M.G. Fulford & D.P.S. Peacock (1984), *Excavations at Carthage. The British Mission*, Sheffield. J. Timby (1994), 'The Red-Slipped Wares', in M. Fulford & R. Tomber (eds), *Excavations at Sabratha, 1948-51. The Finds, Part 2: The Fineware and Lamps*, Vol. 2, London, pp.67-117, 84-117. Italy: P. Arthur (1985), 'Naples: notes on the economy of a Dark Age city', in C. Malone & S. Stoddart (eds), *Papers in Italian Archaeology*, Vol. 4, Oxford, British Archaeological Reports, pp.247-59. S.J.B. Barnish (1987), 'Pigs, plebians and potentes: Rome's economic hinterland, *c*.350 - 600 AD', *Papers of the British School at Rome*, 55, pp.157-82. D. Whitehouse (1988), 'Rome and Naples: Survival and revival in central and southern Italy', in R. Hodges & B. Hobley (eds), *The rebirth of towns in the west, AD 700 – 1050*, London, pp.28-31. M.M. Lovecchio (1989), 'Commercio e ceramica bizantina in Italia', in V. Déroche & J.-M. Spieser (eds), *Recherches sur la céramique*, Paris, pp.95-107 (= Bulletin de Correspondence Hellénique, supplement 18). R. Hodges (1993), *San Vincenzo al Volturno: The 1980-86 Excavations Part I*, Vol. 1, London. T.W. Potter & A.C. King (1997), *Excavations at the Mola di Monte Gelato: A Roman and Medieval Settlement in South Etruria*, London. P. Arthur (1998), 'Eastern Mediterranean Amphorae between 500 and 700: a view from Italy', in L. Saguì (ed.), *Ceramica in Italia: VI-VII secolo. Atti del convegno in onore di John W. Hayes*, Florence, pp.157-83. S. Keay (1998), 'African Amphorae', in L. Saguì (ed.), *Ceramica in Italia: VI-VII secolo. Atti del convegno in onore di John W. Hayes*, Florence, pp.141-55. Also: K. Randsborg (1991), *The First Millennium AD in Europe and the Mediterranean: An Archaeological Essay*, Cambridge, pp.4-5.

13 R. Hodges & D. Whitehouse (1983), *Mohammed, Charlemagne and the origins of Europe*, London, pp.28-30. C. Wickham (1984), 'From the Ancient World to Feudalism', *Past and Present*, 103, pp.3-36. Spain: S. J. Keay (1984), *Late Roman Amphorae in the Western Mediterranean*, Oxford, British Archaeological Reports, International Series 196, pp.428-30. S.J. Keay (1996), 'Tarraco in Late Antiquity', in N. Christie & S.T. Loseby (eds), *Towns in Transition: Urban evolution in Late Antiquity and the Early Middle Ages*, Aldershot, pp.18-44, 38. S.G. Lloret (1998), 'Eastern Spain in the sixth century in the light of archaeology', in R. Hodges & W. Bowden (eds), *The Sixth Century: Production, Distribution and Demand*, Leiden, pp.161-84, 182-31.

14 M. Bonifay, M.-B. Carre & Y. Rigoir (1998) (eds), *Fouilles à Marseille. Les mobiliers (I*ᵉʳ*-VII*ᵉ *siècles ap. J.-C.)*, Paris. S.T. Loseby (1992), 'Marseille: A Late Antique Success Story?' *Journal of Roman Studies*, 82, pp.165-85, 172, 184-5. M. Bonifay & D. Piéri (1995), 'Amphores du Ve au VIIe s. à Marseille: nouvelles données sur la typologie and le contenu', *Journal of Roman Archaeology*, 8, pp.94-120. S.T. Loseby (1998), 'Marseille and the Pirenne Thesis, I: Gregory of Tours, the Merovingian Kings and 'Un Grand Port'', in R. Hodges & W. Bowden, *The Sixth Century: Production, Distribution and Demand*, pp.203-29.

15 G. Démians d'Archimbaud (1994), *L'oppidum de Saint-Blaise du Ve au VIIe siècles*, Paris.

16 R.B. Hitchner (1992), 'Meridional Gaul, trade and the Mediterranean economy in late antiquity', in J. Drinkwater & H. Elton (eds), *Fifth-century Gaul: a crisis of identity?* Cambridge, pp.122-31, 128-9. B. Lançon (2000), *Rome in Late Antiquity*, Edinburgh, p.107.

17 Gregory of Tours, *Historia Francorum*, III. 34. Ed. & trans. L. Thorpe (1974), *The History of the Franks*, Harmondsworth.

18 Gregory of Tours, *Historia Francorum*, V. 5. Ed. & trans. L. Thorpe (1974), *The History of the Franks*, Harmondsworth. Cassiodorus, *Variae Epistolae*, III. 7. Ed. & trans. T. Hodgkin (1886), London; also: Ed. & trans. S.J.B. Barnish (1992), Liverpool. *Life of St John the Almsgiver*, 10. In E. Dawes & N. Baynes (1996), *Three Byzantine Saints*, Crestwood, New York.

19 S. Bruni (2000) (ed.), *Le navi antiche di Pisa: ad un anno dall'inizio delle ricerche*, Pisa.

20 D. Whitehouse, G. Barker, R. Reece & D. Reese (1982), 'The Schola Praeconum I: the coins, pottery, lamps and fauna', *Papers of the British School at Rome*, 50, pp.53-9. M.G. Fulford & D.P.S. Peacock (1984), *Excavations at Carthage. The British Mission*, Sheffield. S.J. Keay (1984), *Late Roman Amphorae in the Western Mediterranean*, Oxford, British Archaeological Reports, International Series 196, p.429. K. Randsborg (1991), *The First Millennium AD in Europe and the Mediterranean: An Archaeological Essay*, Cambridge, p.129. P. Arthur (1998), 'Eastern Mediterranean Amphorae between 500 and 700: a view from Italy', in L. Saguì (ed.), *Ceramica in Italia: VI-VII secolo. Atti del convegno in onore di John W. Hayes*, Florence, pp.157-83. Gaul/Frankia: M. Bonifay & F. Villedieu (1989), 'Importations d'amphores orientales en Gaule (Ve-VIIe siècles)', in V. Déroche & J.-M. Spieser (eds), *Recherches sur la céramique*, Strasbourg, pp.17-46, 41 (= Bulletin de Correspondence Hellénique, Supplement 18). See also sources given for Marseille, above.

21 S.T. Loseby (1998), 'Marseille and the Pirenne Thesis, I: Gregory of Tours, the Merovingian Kings and 'Un Grand Port'', in R. Hodges & W. Bowden (eds), *The Sixth Century: Production, Distribution and Demand*, Leiden, pp.203-29. The Saint-Gervais II cargo also consisted of a layer of wheat, a layer of pitch, a wooden barrel, oriental finewares, Beltan 60 amphorae, *spatheia*, and D-Ware.

22 P. Reynolds (1995), *Trade in the Western Mediterranean, AD 400-700: the ceramic evidence*, Oxford, British Archaeological Reports, International Series 604, especially chapter 5.
23 M. McCormick (2001), *Origins of the European Economy: Communications and Commerce, AD 300-900*.
24 For discussion of this question in relation to a later period of Byzantine history: N. Oikonomedes (2001), 'The role of the Byzantine state in the economy', in Laiou (ed.), *The economic history of Byzantium: From the Seventh through the Fifteenth Century*, Washington D.C., pp.966-1050 (= Dumbarton Oaks Studies 39).
25 B. Brennan (1995), 'Venantius Fortunatus: Byzantine Agent?', *Byzantion*, 65, pp.7-16.
26 P. Reynolds (1995), *Trade in the Western Mediterranean, AD 400-700: the ceramic evidence*, Oxford, British Archaeological Reports, International Series 604, p.104.
27 J.W. Hayes (1972), *Late Roman Pottery*, London, p.404. Tin is sometimes said to have been called the 'British metal' in the Byzantine Empire. On this, see: J. M. Wooding (1996), *Communication and commerce along the western sealanes AD 400-800*, Oxford, British Archaeological Reports, International Series 654, p.46: 'whether this is informed by Classical or more recent knowledge is not clear'.
28 P. Reynolds (1995), *Trade in the Western Mediterranean, AD 400-700: the ceramic evidence*, Oxford, British Archaeological Reports, International Series 604, pp.126-7.
29 F.H. van Doorninck (1989), 'The Cargo Amphoras of the Seventh-Century Yassı Ada and Eleventh-Century Serçe Limanı Shipwrecks: two examples of a reuse of Byzantine amphoras as transport jars', in V. Déroche & J.-M. Spieser (eds), *Recherches sur la céramique*, Strasbourg, pp.247-57 (= Bulletin de Correspondance Hellénique, Supplement 18). S. Kingsley (1994-5), 'Bag-shaped Amphorae and Byzantine Trade: Expanding Horizons', *Bulletin of the Anglo-Israel Archaeological Society*, 14, pp.39-56.
30 M. Mundell Mango (2001), 'Beyond the Amphora: Non-Ceramic Evidence for Late Antique Industry and Trade', in S. Kingsley & M. Decker (eds), *Economy and Exchange in the East Mediterranean during Late Antiquity*, Oxford, pp.87-106, 98.
31 S. Keay (1984), *Late Roman Amphorae in the Western Mediterranean*, Oxford, British Archaeological Reports, International Series 196, pp.270-1. P.G. Van Alfen (1996), 'New Light on the Seventh-Century Yassı Ada Shipwreck: Capacities and Standard Sizes of LR1 amphoras', *Journal of Roman Archaeology*, 9, pp.189-213. O. Karagiorgou (2001), 'LR2: A Container for the Military *annona* on the Danubian Border?' in S. Kingsley & M. Decker (2001), *Economy and Exchange in the East Mediterranean during Late Antiquity*, Oxford, pp.129-66, 149. For a discussion of state-subsidised shipping in Late Antiquity see: M. McCormick (2001), *Origins of the European Economy: Communications and Commerce, AD 300-900,* Cambridge, pp.87ff.
32 S.J. Keay (1984), *Late Roman Amphorae in the Western Mediterranean*, Oxford, British Archaeological Reports, International Series 196, pp.414, 424. O. Karagiorgou (2001), 'LR2: A Container for the Military *annona* on the Danubian Border?' in S. Kingsley & M. Decker (2001), *Economy and Exchange in the East Mediterranean during Late Antiquity*, Oxford, pp.129-66, 155.
33 P. Reynolds (1995), *Trade in the Western Mediterranean, AD 400-700: the ceramic evidence*, Oxford, British Archaeological Reports, International Series 604, p.304. Lyon: M. Bonifay & F. Villedieu (1989), 'Importations d'amphores orientales en Gaule (Ve-VIIe siècles)', in V. Déroche & J.-M. Spieser (eds), *Recherches sur la céramique*, Strasbourg, pp.17-46, 21 (= Bulletin de Correspondance Hellénique, Supplement 18).
34 For Syrian merchants see: K.R. Dark (forthcoming), 'Early Byzantine Mercantile Communities in the West', in C. Entwistle (ed.), *Through a Glass Brightly: Studies presented to David Buckton*, London. I am most grateful to Ken Dark for allowing me to see this paper in advance of publication and for discussing the subject with me at length.
35 C. Mango (1985), *Le developpement urbain de Constantinople,* Paris, p.38. R. Bagnall (1993), *Egypt in Late Antiquity*, Princeton, pp.88-9. M. McCormick (2001), *Origins of the European Economy: Communications and Commerce, AD 300-900,* Cambridge, pp.108-9. S. Kingsley & M. Decker (2001), 'New Rome, new theories on inter-regional exchange. An introduction to the East Mediterranean during Late Antiquity', in S. Kingsley & M. Decker (eds), *Economy and Exchange in the East Mediterranean during Late Antiquity*, Oxford, pp.1-27, 2.
36 Forts: P. Reynolds (1995), *Trade in the Western Mediterranean, AD 400-700: the ceramic evidence*, Oxford, British Archaeological Reports, International Series 604, chapter 5. O. Karagiorgou (2001), 'LR2: A Container for the Military *annona* on the Danubian Border?' in S. Kingsley & M. Decker (2001), *Economy and Exchange in the East Mediterranean during Late Antiquity*, Oxford, pp.129-66.
37 Salvian, *The Governance of God*, Book IV. 14. Trans. J.F. O'Sullivan (1947), *The writings of Salvian the Presbyter*, New York. Procopius, *History of the Wars*, Book III, XX. 1-7. Trans. H. B. Dewing (1919), *Procopius*, Vol. II, London. D. Noy (2000), *Foreigners at Rome: Citizens and Strangers*, London. See also note 100 in M. McCormick (2001), *Origins of the European Economy: Communications and Commerce, AD 300-900,* Cambridge, p.107.

38 Gregory of Tours, *Gloria Martyrum,* 77. Ed. & trans. R. Van Dam (1988), *Glory of the Martyrs,* Liverpool. Gregory of Tours, *Historia Francorum,* III. 34; VIII. 1. Ed. & trans. L. Thorpe (1974), *The History of the Franks,* Harmondsworth. Cassiodorus, *Variae Epistolae,* II. 38. Ed. & tr. T. Hodgkin (1886), London; also: Ed. & trans. S.J.B. Barnish (1992), Liverpool. Salvian, *The Governance of God,* Book IV. 14. Trans. J.F. O'Sullivan (1947), *The writings of Salvian the Presbyter,* New York. L. Bréhier (1903), 'Les Colonies d'Orientaux en Occident au commencement du moyen-âge', *Byzantinische Zeitschrift,* 12, pp.1-39. E. A. Thompson (1969), *The Goths in Spain,* pp.21-2. L.A. García (1972), 'Colonias de commerciantes orientales en la Península Ibérica, s. V-VII', *Habis,* 3. pp.127-54: discussed in N.F. Retamero (1999), 'As coins go home: towns, merchants, bishops and kings in Visigothic Hispania', in P. Heather (ed.), *The Visigoths from the Migration Period to the Seventh Century: an ethnographic approach,* Woodbridge, pp.271-304, 274-5. B. Lançon (1995), *Rome in Late Antiquity,* Edinburgh, p.81. J.M. Wooding (1996), *Communication and commerce along the western sealanes AD 400-800,* Oxford, British Archaeological Reports, International Series 654, p.47. I. Peña (1997), *The Christian art of Byzantine Syria,* London, p.229-30. K.R. Dark (forthcoming), 'Early Byzantine Mercantile Communities in the West', in C. Entwistle (ed.), *Through a Glass Brightly: Studies presented to David Buckton,* London. See note 34 above.

39 Gregory of Tours, *Historia Francorum,* VII. 31. Ed. & trans. L. Thorpe (1974), *The History of the Franks,* Harmondsworth.

40 M. Bonifay & F. Villedieu (1989), 'Importations d'amphores orientales en Gaule (Ve-VIIe siècles)', in V. Déroche & J.-M. Spieser (eds), *Recherches sur la céramique,* Strasbourg, pp.17-46 (= Bulletin de Correspondence Hellénique, Supplement 18).

41 K.R. Dark (forthcoming), 'Early Byzantine Mercantile Communities in the West' in C. Entwistle (ed.), *Through a Glass Brightly: Studies presented to David Buckton,* London.

42 Gregory of Tours, *Historia Francorum,* IV. 40. Ed. & trans. L. Thorpe (1974), *The History of the Franks,* Harmondsworth. Gregory of Tours, *Vitae Patrum,* 3. 1; 4. 2. Ed. & trans. E. James (1988) (2nd ed.), *The Lives of the Fathers,* Liverpool. D. Noy (2000), 'Immigrants in Late Imperial Rome', in S. Mitchell & G. Greatrex (eds), *Ethnicity and culture in late antiquity,* London & Swansea, pp.15-30, 28. D. Noy (2000), *Foreigners at Rome: Citizens and Strangers,* London. This said, Gregory of Tours mistakenly describes Antioch as being in Egypt when he comes to describe the Persian invasions. However, this confusion is likely to reflect his use of other sources for an event so far away.

43 Jerome, *Commentary on Ezekiel,* 8. 225. Jerome, *Epistolae,* 130. 7. Both quoted in I. Peña (1997), *The Christian Art of Byzantine Syria,* London, p.228.

44 The population of Syria grew during late antiquity, peaking in about 550 and then declined from about 600. J.H.W.G. Liebeschuetz (1972), *Antioch: City and Imperial Administration in the Later Roman Empire,* Oxford, pp.60-100. A. Walmsley (1996), 'Byzantine Palestine and Arabia: Urban Prosperity in Late Antiquity', in N. Christie & S.T. Loseby (eds), *Towns in Transition: Urban Evolution in Late Antiquity and the Early Middle Ages,* Aldershot, pp.126-58. M. Decker (2000), 'Food for an Empire: Wine and Oil Production in North Syria', in S. Kingley & M. Decker (eds), *Economy and Exchange in the East Mediterranean during Late Antiquity,* Oxford, pp.87-106, 69-86. M. McCormick (2001), *Origins of the European Economy: Communications and Commerce, AD 300-900,* Cambridge, p.33. Note, however, Procopius' exaggerations about the refurbishment of sixth-century Antioch: L.M. Whitby (1989), 'Procopius and Antioch', in D.H. French & C.S. Lightfoot (eds), *The Eastern Frontier of the Roman Empire, Part II,* Oxford, British Archaeological Reports, International Series 553(ii), pp.537-53 (= British Institute of Archaeology at Ankara Monograph 11). Chinese texts: F. Hirth (1885), *China and the Roman Orient,* Chicago, pp.207-14.

45 C. Foss (1997), 'Syria in Transition: AD 550-750: an archaeological approach', *Dumbarton Oaks Papers,* 51, pp.189-270. Indication stamps and roof tiles: R. Thorpe (1998), 'Which way is up? Context formation and transformation: the life and deaths of a hot bath in Beirut', *Assemblage,* 4 (University of Sheffield internet publication; no page numbers) and Philip Mills, pers. comm. November 2002.

46 E. Campbell (1997), 'The Dark Age ceramics', in P. Hill *et al, Whithorn and St Ninian: The excavations of a monastic town 1984-91,* Stroud, pp.315-22, 315.

47 This account is based on: J. Werner (1961), 'Fernhandel und Naturalwirtschaft im östlichen Merowingerreich nach archäologischen und numismatischen Zeugnissen', *Bericht der Römisch-Germanischeen Kommission,* 42, pp.307-46, p.311. P. Richards (1980), *Byzantine bronze vessels in England and Europe: the origins of Anglo-Saxon trade,* University of Cambridge, unpublished PhD thesis. P. Périn (1992), 'A propos des vases de bronzes 'coptes' du VIIe siècle en Europe de l'Ouest: le pichet de Bardouville (Seine-Maritime)', *Cahiers Archéologiques,* 40, pp.35-50.

48 H. Bentson & V. Milojèiæ *et al* (1978), *Grosser Historischer Weltatlas,* Munich, p.54. P. Richards (1980), *Byzantine bronze vessels in England and Europe: the origins of Anglo-Saxon trade*, University of Cambridge, unpublished PhD thesis, pp.167. S. Ladstätter (2000), *Die materielle Kultur der Spätantike in den Ostalpen*, Wien.

49 There are five examples of B3 vessels in the Rhineland area, grouped closely together to the north of the Italian alps. These were interpreted by Joachim Werner as possible diplomatic gifts between the Franks and the Lombards in 591. For a discussion of the B3 vessels in the West: P. Périn (1992), 'A propos des vases de bronzes 'coptes' du VIIe siècle en Europe de l'Ouest: le pichet de Bardouville (Seine-Maritime)', *Cahiers Archéologiques*, 40, pp.35-50, 47.

50 P. Richards (1980), *Byzantine bronze vessels in England and Europe: the origins of Anglo-Saxon trade*, University of Cambridge, unpublished PhD thesis, pp.96-7, Appendix 2. A.J. Parker (1992), *Ancient Shipwrecks of the Mediterranean and the Roman Provinces*, Oxford, British Archaeological Reports, International Series 580, p.176. Imitation vessels: G. Ripoll López (1993), 'The Formation of Visigothic Spain', in J.P. O'Neill, K. Howard *et al* (eds), *The art of medieval Spain, AD 500-1200*, New York, pp.41-71, 51-3.

51 For the debate on their origin: P. Périn (1992), 'A propos des vases de bronzes 'coptes' du VIIe siècle en Europe de l'Ouest: le pichet de Bardouville (Seine-Maritime)', *Cahiers Archéologiques*, 40, pp.35-50, 40-6. J.M. Carrié (1990), 'Économie et societé de l'Egypte romano-byzantine (IVe-VIIe siècles). À propos de quelques publications récentes', *Antiquité Tardive*, 7, pp.331-352.

52 Gregory of Tours, *Gloria Confessorum*, 79, 95. Ed & trans. R. Van Dam (1988), *Glory of the Confessors*, Liverpool. R. Bagnall (1993), *Egypt in Late Antiquity*, Princeton, p.84. C. Morrisson (1995), 'La diffusion de la monnaie de Constantinople: routes commerciales ou routes politiques?', in C. Mango, G. Dagron & G. Greatrex (eds), *Constantinople and its Hinterland,* Aldershot, pp.77-89, 87. E. Rodziewicz (1998), 'Archaeological evidence of bone and ivory carvings in Alexandria', in J.-Y. Empereur (ed.), *Commerce et artisanat dans l'Alexandrie héllenistique et romaine*, Paris, pp.136-58 (= Bulletin de Correspondance Héllénique, supplement 33). M. Mundell Mango (2001), 'Beyond the Amphora: Non-Ceramic Evidence for Late Antique Industry and Trade', in S. Kingsley & M. Decker (eds), *Economy and Exchange in the East Mediterranean during Late Antiquity*, Oxford, pp.87-106, 87.

53 P. Sarris, paper read to the 'Reconstructing Byzantine Constantinople' conference, University of Reading, 26 October 2002.

54 J. Werner (1961), 'Fernhandel und Naturalwirtschaft im östlichen Merowingerreich nach archäologischen und numismatischen Zeugnissen', *Bericht der Römisch-Germanischeen Kommission*, 42, pp.307-46. C. Lambert & P. Pedemonte Demeglio (1994), 'Ampolle Devozionali ed Itinerari di Pellegrinaggio tra IV e VII secolo', *Antiqué Tardive*, 2, pp.205-31. M. Mundell Mango (2001), 'Beyond the Amphora: Non-Ceramic Evidence for Late Antique Industry and Trade', in S. Kingsley & M. Decker (eds), *Economy and Exchange in the East Mediterranean during Late Antiquity*, Oxford, pp.87-106, 89-90. Egyptian ceramics: M. Bonifay & F. Villedieu (1989), 'Importations d'amphores orientales en Gaule (Ve-VIIe siècles)', in V. Déroche & J.-M. Spieser (eds), *Recherches sur la céramique,* Strasbourg, pp.17-46, 31-2 (= Bulletin de Correspondance Hellénique, Supplement 18). P. Reynolds (1995), *Trade in the Western Mediterranean, AD 400-700: the ceramic evidence*, Oxford, British Archaeological Reports, International Series 604, p.173. R. Tomber & D. Williams (2000), 'Egyptian amphorae in Britain and the western provinces', *Britannia*, 31, pp.41-54. K.R. Dark (2001), *Byzantine Pottery*, Stroud, pp.118-9.

55 Theodoret of Cyrrhus, *Religiosa historia*, xxvi. 11. Trans. R. M. Price (1985), *History of the Monks of Syria*, Kalamazoo, p.165. E. D. Hunt (1982), *Holy Land Pilgrimage in the Later Roman Empire AD 312-460*, Oxford, pp.53, 72.

56 E.M. Stern (1999), 'Roman Glassblowing in a Cultural Context', *American Journal of Archaeology*, 103, pp.441-84.

57 J. Lafaurie & C. Morrisson (1987), 'La pénétration des monnaies Byzantines en Gaul mérovingienne et visigotique du VIe au VIIIe siècle', *Revue Numismatique,* (6th series) 29, pp.38-98. C. Morrisson (1995), 'La diffusion de la monnaie de Constantinople: routes commerciales ou routes politiques?', in C. Mango, G. Dagron & G. Greatrex (eds), *Constantinople and its Hinterland,* Aldershot, pp.77-89. The Gruisson coins are discussed in D.M. Metcalf (1995), 'Byzantine Coins from Exeter', in S. Efthymiadis *et al* (eds), *Bosphorus: essays in honour of Cyril Mango*, Amsterdam, pp.253-61. M. Mundell Mango (2001), 'Beyond the Amphora: Non-Ceramic Evidence for Late Antique Industry and Trade', in S. Kingsley & M. Decker (eds), *Economy and Exchange in the East Mediterranean during Late Antiquity*, Oxford, pp.87-106, 100-101.

58 M. Mundell Mango (1998), 'The Archaeological Context of Finds of Silver in and beyond the Eastern Empire', in N. Cambi & E. Marin (eds), *Acta XIII Congressus Internationalis Archaeologiae Christianae.* II, Vatican City and Split, pp.207-52. M. Mundell Mango (2001), 'Beyond the Amphora: Non-Ceramic Evidence for Late Antique Industry and Trade', in S. Kingsley & M. Decker (eds), *Economy and Exchange in the East Mediterranean during Late Antiquity*, Oxford, pp.87-106, 93.

59 E. Chrysos (1992), 'Byzantine Diplomacy, AD 300 - 800: means and ends', in J. Shepard & S. Franklin (eds), *Byzantine Diplomacy. Papers from the Twenty-fourth Spring Symposium of Byzantine Studies,* Aldershot, pp.25-39. For the *annona* in Rome: B. Lançon (2000), *Rome in Late Antiquity*, Edinburgh, pp.119-20.

60 Plague: C. Morrisson & J.-P. Sodini (2001), 'The Sixth-Century Economy', in A. Laiou (ed.), *The economic history of Byzantium: From the Seventh through the Fifteenth Century*, Washington D.C., pp.171-220, 193-5 (= Dumbarton Oaks Studies 39).

61 A. Hermanry, A. Hesnard & H. Tréziny (1999), *Marseille Gréque: La cité phocéenne*, Paris. Agathias: L. Bréhier (1903), 'Les Colonies d'Orientaux en Occident au commencement du moyen-âge', *Byzantinische Zeitschrift,* 12, pp.1-39, 11.

Chapter 4

1 G. Halsall (1995), *Settlement and social organisation: the Merovingian region of Metz*, Cambridge. G. Halsall (1996), 'Towns, Societies and Ideas: The Not-so-strange Case of Late Roman and Early Merovingian Metz', in N. Christie & S.T. Loseby (eds), *Towns in Transition: Urban evolution in Late Antiquity and the Early Middle Ages,* Aldershot, pp.235-61. Theodoric: R. Reece (2000), *The Later Roman Empire: an archaeology AD 150-600*, Stroud, pp.102-4. Agnellus, *Liber Pontificalis*, 29 (Petrus III), 15. Reproduced in C. Davis-Weyer (1986) (ed.), *Early Medieval Art 300-1150*, Toronto, pp.49-50.

2 M. Mauss (1966), *The Gift: forms and functions of exchange in archaic societies,* London. I. Johansen (1994), *Gift Exchange in Late Antiquity,* University of Oxford, unpublished DPhil thesis.

3 I.M. Ploumis (1997), 'Gifts in the Late Roman Iconography', in S. Isager & B. Poulsen (eds), *Patron and Pavement in Late Antiquity*, Odense, pp.125-41, 125 (= Halicarnassian Studies II).

4 A. Cutler (2001), 'Gifts and Gift Exchange as Aspects of the Byzantine, Arab and Related Economies', *Dumbarton Oaks Papers*, 55, pp.247-78, 261-4.

5 Hungarian crowns: D. Obolensky (1971) *The Byzantine Commonwealth: Eastern Europe 550 – 1500,* London. F. Fülep (1978) (ed.), *The Hungarian National Museum*, Budapest. R. Cormack (1992), 'But is it art?' in J. Shepard and S. Franklin (eds), *Byzantine Diplomacy. Papers from the Twenty-fourth Spring Symposium of Byzantine Studies*, Aldershot, pp.219-35, 231-5. Spanish crowns: G. Ripoll López (1993), 'The Formation of Visigothic Spain', in J.P. O'Neill, K. Howard *et al.* (eds), *The art of medieval Spain, AD 500-1200*, New York, pp.53-9.

6 *Ibid*.

7 K. Brown (1984), *The gold breast chain from the early Byzantine period in the Römisch-Germanisches Zentralmuseum,* Mainz, pp.11-13. Saint-Dénis: Les Musées de la Ville de Paris (ed.), *Les Francs: précurseurs de l'Europe*, Paris, p.89. G. Ripoll López (1993), 'The Formation of Visigothic Spain', in J.P. O'Neill, K. Howard *et al.* (eds), *The art of medieval Spain, AD 500-1200*, New York, pp.53-9.

8 The pilgrim's account is from *Travels of the Piacenza Pilgrim*, and is quoted in: S. Coleman & J. Elsner (1995), *Pilgrimage: past and present in the world's religions*, London, p.87.

9 For some of the problems inherent in the interpretation of graves and grave-goods: P. Rahtz, T.M. Dickinson and L. Watts (1980), *Anglo-Saxon Cemeteries,* Oxford. R. Chapman, I. Kinnes & K. Randsborg (1981) (eds), *The Archaeology of Death,* Cambridge. E. James (1989), 'Burial and Status in the Early Medieval West', *Transactions of the Royal Historical Society,* 39 (5th series), pp.23-40. G. Halsall (1995), *Early Medieval Cemeteries: an introduction to burial archaeology in the post-Roman West*, Glasgow.

10 G. Halsall (1995), *Early Medieval Cemeteries: an introduction to burial archaeology in the post-Roman West*, Glasgow. E. James & S. Burnell (1999), 'The Archaeology of Conversion on the Continent in the Sixth and Seventh Centuries: Some Observations and Comparisons with Anglo-Saxon England', in R. Gameson (ed.), *St Augustine and the Conversion of England*, Stroud, pp.83-106, 84.

11 E. James (1982), *The Origins of France: From Clovis to the Capetians, 500-1000*, London, pp.130-33. G. Halsall (1992), 'The origins of the *Reihengräberzivilisation*: forty years on', in J. Drinkwater & H. Elton (eds), *Fifth-century Gaul: a crisis of identity?* Cambridge, pp.196-207. Lavoye and aristocratic tombs: M. Kazanski (1997), 'La naissance du royaume mérovingien', in Les Musées de la Ville de Paris (ed.), *Les Francs: précurseurs de l'Europe*, Paris, pp.64-9, including bibliography. Jug: F. Vallet (1990), *Les Mérovingiens d'après l'archéologie*, Paris, pp.20-1. Ivory comb: Les Musées de la Ville de Paris (ed.), *Les Francs: précurseurs de l'Europe*, Paris, p.124.

12 Jewelled swords and other weapons fittings: B. Arrhenius (1985), *Merovingian Garnet Jewellery: Emergence and Social Implications*, Stockholm, p.100-101, 124-6, 197. D. Kidd (1990), 'Gilt-silver and garnet-inlaid sheath fittings from Hungary: early medieval recent acquisitions in the British Museum (I)', *Archäologisches Korrespondenzblatt*, 20, pp.125-7. Regalia: D. Janes (2002), *Romans and Christians*, Stroud, p.138.
13 M. Kazanski (1997), 'La naissance du royaume mérovingien', in Les Musées de la Ville de Paris (ed.), *Les Francs: précurseurs de l'Europe*, Paris, pp.64-9.
14 The following account is based on: F. Dumas (1982), *La tombe de Childéric, père de Clovis*, Paris. E. James (1988), *The Franks*, Oxford, pp.58-64. E. James (1992), 'Royal Burials among the Franks', in M. Carver (ed.), *The Age of Sutton Hoo*, Woodbridge, pp.243-54. M. Todd (1992), *The Early Germans*, Oxford, pp.198-9. P. Périn & F. Vallet (1997), 'Sépultures royals et princières des Francs', in Les Musées de la Ville de Paris (ed.), *Les Francs: précurseurs de l'Europe*, Paris, pp.84-91, including bibliography. E. Swift (2000), *The End of the Western Roman Empire: An Archaeological Investigation*, Stroud, pp.122-8. M. Todd (2001), *Migrants and Invaders: The Movement of Peoples in the Ancient World*, Stroud, pp.79-80.
15 M. Mundell Mango (1994), 'Gold opus interrasile bracelet', in D. Buckton (ed.), *Byzantium: Treasures of Byzantine Art and Culture*, London, pp.52-3. B. Arrhenius (1985), *Merovingian Garnet Jewellery: Emergence and Social Implications*, Stockholm, pp.84-5, 100-113. M. Kazanski (1997), 'La naissance du royaume mérovingien', in Les Musées de la Ville de Paris (ed.), *Les Francs: précurseurs de l'Europe*, Paris, pp.64-9.
16 R. Brulet *et al.* (1990), *Les Fouilles du Quartier Saint-Brice à Tournai: l'environment funéraire de la sépulture de Childeric, I*, Louvain-la-Neuve. R. Brulet *et al.* (1991), *Les Fouilles du Quartier Saint-Brice à Tournai: l'environment funéraire de la sépulture de Childeric, II*, Louvain-la-Neuve.
17 M. Todd (2001), *Migrants and Invaders: The Movement of Peoples in the Ancient World*, Stroud, p.80.
18 E. James (1988), *The Franks*, London, pp.158-9. P. Périn (1992), 'The Undiscovered Grave of Clovis I', in M. Carver (ed.), *The Age of Sutton Hoo: the seventh century in north-western Europe*, Woodbridge, pp.255-64.
19 B. Ward-Perkins (1984), *From Classical Antiquity to the Middle Ages: Urban Public Building in Northern and Central Italy, AD 300-850*, Oxford, pp.215-7. R. Krautheimer (1986), *Early Christian and Byzantine Architecture*, (4th ed.) Harmondsworth, pp.271-3. B. Kiilerich (1996), 'Continuity and Change in Ruler Imagery: The Eternal Victor, c.400 to 800 AD', in P. Åström (ed.), *Rome and the North*, Göteborg, pp.95-110.
20 This account is based on: D.M. Wilson (1964), 'A Ring of Queen Arnegunde', *Germania*, 42, pp.265-8. (1979), *Dossiers de l'archéologie*, 32, *passim* (Special issue). E. James (1988), *The Franks*, London, pp.156-7. N. Duval, J. Fontaine, P.-A. Février *et al.* (1991), *Naissance des Arts Chrétiens: Atlas des Monuments Paléochrétiens de la France*, Paris, pp.110-1. E. James (1992), 'Royal Burials among the Franks', in M. Carver (ed.), *The Age of Sutton Hoo*, Woodbridge, pp.243-54. P. Périn (1997), 'La Basilique de Saint-Dénis, nécropole royale mérovingienne', *L'Archéologie*, 29, pp.23-6.
21 Attila: *Priscus of Panium*, 22. Reproduced in A.C. Murray (2000) (ed.), *From Roman to Merovingian Gaul*, Ontario, p.150.
22 E. Swift (2000), *The End of the Western Roman Empire: An Archaeological Investigation*, Stroud, p.17.
23 A. Muthesius (1997), *Byzantine Silk Weaving, AD 400-1200*, Vienna.
24 This account is based on: J. Werner (1964), 'Frankish Royal Tombs in the Cathedrals of Cologne and St-Denis', *Antiquity*, 38, pp.201-16. E. James (1992), 'Royal Burials among the Franks', in M. Carver (ed.), *The Age of Sutton Hoo*, Woodbridge, pp.243-54. P. Périn and F. Vallet (1997), 'Sépultures royals et princières des Francs', in Les Musées de la Ville de Paris (ed.), *Les Francs*, Paris, pp.84-91, including bibliography.
25 L. Bender Jørgensen (1988), 'A Coptic Fabric from the Frankish Boy's Grave of Cologne Cathedral', in *Archaeological Textiles: Report from the 2nd NESAT symposium, Copenhagen*, pp.126-132. There may be a similar piece of textile from the cemetery at Rhenen, The Netherlands, but this is obviously outside the geographical remit of this book: L. Bender Jørgensen (1992), *North European Textiles until AD 1000*, Aarhus, p.47-8. The helmet is not the only Byzantine helmet known from Frankia: another sixth-century example was found at Vézeronce, near Grenoble. J. Durand *et al.* (1992), *Byzance: L'art byzantin dans les collections publiques françaises*, Paris, no. 74.
26 Procopius, *History of the Wars*, Book VIII. xvii. 1-8. Trans. H.B. Dewing (1919), *Procopius*, Vol.V, London. Compare Procopius, *Anekdota*, XXV. 12. Trans. G.A. Williamson (1966), *Secret History*, Harmondsworth: 'the manufacture of silken garments had for many generations been a staple industry of Beirut and Tyre'.

27 Invasion of the Syrian provinces: I. Peña (1997), *The Christian Art of Byzantine Syria*, London, p.229. F. Hirth (1885), *China and the Roman Orient*, Chicago. A. Muthesius (1989), 'From Seed to Samite: Aspects of Byzantine Silk Production', *Textile History*, 20, pp.135-49, 137. Muthesius discusses the other sources mentioned here.
28 A. Muthesius (1997), *Byzantine Silk Weaving, AD 400-1200*, Vienna, p.27.
29 R.S. Lopez (1946), 'Silk Industry in the Byzantine Empire', *Speculum*, 20, pp.1-42. N. Oikonomedes (1986), 'Silk Trade and Production in Byzantium from the sixth to the ninth century: The Seals of Kommerkiarioi', *Dumbarton Oaks Papers*, 40, pp.33-53.
30 Berenice: A. Wilson (2001), 'Urban Economies of Late Antique Cyrenaica', in S. Kingsley & M. Decker (eds), *Economy and Exchange in the East Mediterranean during Late Antiquity*, Oxford, pp.44-68. Sardis: J. Stephens Crawford (1990), *The Byzantine Shops at Sardis* (Sardis Monograph 9), Cambridge, Mass. A. Harris (in press), 'Shops, retailing and local economy in the Early Byzantine Empire: the evidence from Sardis re-examined', in K. R. Dark (ed.), *Secular Buildings and the Archaeology of Everyday Life in the Byzantine Empire*, Oxford. Aperlae: R.L. Hohlfelder, paper read to the Roman Archaeology Conference, University of Glasgow, April 2001. R.L. Hohlfelder and R.L. Vann (2000), 'Cabotage at Aperlae in ancient Lycia', *International Journal of Nautical Archaeology*, 29, pp.126-35. Diospolis and Dor: S. Kingsley (in press), 'Late Antique Trade and Field Methodologies', in L. Lavan (ed.), *Late Antique Archaeology: Method and Theory*, Oxford. I am grateful to Sean Kingsley for permitting me to see a pre-publication copy of his paper.
31 See photograph in E. James (1988), *The Franks*, Oxford, p.155.
32 Sidonius Apollinaris, *Epistolae*, II. 6. Ed. & trans. O.M. Dalton (1915), Oxford. Gregory of Tours, *Historia Francorum*, VI. 6, 10; VII. 22; X. 16. Ed. & trans. L. Thorpe (1974), *The History of the Franks*, Harmondsworth. The church at Tours had a silken altar covering, according to Gregory. R.J. Collins (1980), 'Mérida and Toledo: 550-585', in E. James (ed.), *Visigothic Spain: New Approaches*, Oxford, pp.189-219.
33 J. Herrin (1987), *The Formation of Christendom*, London, pp.263-5.
34 'Purple' silks have been identified amongst Byzantine silks in the West, but these are too late for our purposes here. A. Muthesius (1997), *Byzantine Silk Weaving, AD 400-1200*, Vienna, p.29. L. Bender Jørgensen (1992), *North European Textiles until AD 1000*, Aarhus, p.77. Contamination: P.W. Rogers (2001), note in W. Filmer-Sankey & T. Pestell, *Snape Anglo-Saxon Cemetery: Excavations and Surveys 1824-1992*, Ipswich, pp.212-3 (= East Anglian Archaeology Report 95).
35 R. Boyer et al. (1987), *Vie et mort à Marseille à la fin de l'Antiquité*, Marseille, pp.45-93. S. Desosiers & A. Lorquin (1998), 'Gallo-Roman period archaeological textiles found in France', in L. Bender Jørgensen & C. Rinaldo (eds), *Textiles in European Archaeology*, Götenborg, pp.53-72.
36 A. Muthesius (1997), *Byzantine Silk Weaving, AD 400-1200*, Vienna.
37 A. Muthesius (1997), *Byzantine Silk Weaving, AD 400-1200*, Vienna, pp.80-2, 165-72. E. Vogt (1958), 'Frühmittelalterliche Stoffe aus der Abtei St-Maurice', *Zeitschrift fur Schweizerische Archaeologie und Kunstsechicht*, 18, pp.110-40. Chur: B. Schmedding (1978), *Mittelalterliche Textilien in Kirchen und Klöstern der Schweiz: Katalog*, Bern. M. McCormick (2001), *Origins of the European Economy: Communications and Commerce, A.D. 300-900*, Cambridge, pp.77-8: 'One could follow the upper Rhine toward its source in the Alps, and in the vicinity of Chur choose between the mule road over the Splügen pass or the cart roads toward Italy'.
38 L. Bender Jørgensen (1992), *North European Textiles until AD 1000*, Aarhus, pp.69, 76-7, 143-4. Chelles: H. Vierck (1978), 'La Chemise de Saint-Bathilde à Chelles et l'influence byzantine sur le cour mérovingien au VIIe siècle', *Actes du Colloque International d'Archéologie, Rouen, 1975*, 3, pp.521-64, pl., I-VI.
39 A. Cutler (2001), paper read to the XXe Congrès Byzantin, Paris, September 2002. See also A. Cutler (2001), 'Gifts and Gift Exchange as Aspects of the Byzantine, Arab and Related Economies', *Dumbarton Oaks Papers*, 55, pp.247-78, 261-4.
40 A. Muthesius (1997), *Byzantine Silk Weaving, AD 400-1200*, Vienna, chapter 14.
41 R. Reece (2002), *The Coinage of Roman Britain*, Stroud. J. Werner (1980) 'Der goldene Armring des Frankenkönigs Childerich und die germanischen Handgelenkringe der jungen Kaiserzeit', *Frühmittelaltliche Studien*, 14, pp.1-49. Discussed in E. Swift (2000), *The End of the Western Roman Empire: An Archaeological Investigation*, Stroud, pp.126-32.
42 P. Grierson & M. Blackburn (1986), *Medieval European Coinage*, Cambridge p.9. One hundred years later, the Lombards also used the tribute they received from the Byzantine Emperor as an indicator of élite wealth and rank. N. Christie (1995), *The Lombards: The Ancient Longobards*, Oxford, p.111.

43 P. Grierson & M. Blackburn (1986), *Medieval European Coinage,* Cambridge p.50.
44 J. Herrin (1987), *The Formation of Christendom,* London, p.454.
45 *The Christian Topography of Cosmas Indicopleustes.* Ed. & trans. J. McCrindle (1887), New York, p.116. This paragraph and the section that follows are based on: P. Grierson (1979), *Dark Age Numismatics: Selected Studies,* London. P. Grierson (1990), *Byzantine coinage in its international setting,* Cambridge. P. Grierson (1991), *The Coins of Medieval Europe,* London. P. Grierson & M. Blackburn (1986), *Medieval European Coinage,* Cambridge. W. Hahn and W.E. Metcalf (1988) (eds), *Studies in Early Byzantine Gold Coinage,* New York (= The American Numismatic Society, Studies no. 17). C.E. King (1992), 'Roman, local, and barbarian coinages in fifth-century Gaul', in J. Drinkwater & H. Elton (eds), *Fifth-century Gaul: a crisis of identity?* Cambridge, pp.184-95. A.M. Stahl (1994), *Mérovingiens et Royaumes barbares,* Paris. C. Brenot (1996), 'Du monnayage imperial au monnayage mérovingien: l'exemple d'Arles et de Marseille', in C. Lepelley (ed.), *La fin de la cité antique et le début de la cité médiévale,* Bari, pp.147-60. P. Grierson (1999), *Byzantine Coinage,* Washington D.C.. C. Morrisson & J.-P. Sodini (2001), 'The Sixth-Century Economy', in A. Laiou (ed.), *The economic history of Byzantium: From the Seventh through the Fifteenth Century,* Washington D.C. pp.171-220 (Dumbarton Oaks Studies 39).
46 Gregory of Tours, *Historia Francorum,* IV. 43; V.18. Ed. & trans. L. Thorpe (1974), *The History of the Franks,* Harmondsworth.
47 Gregory of Tours, *Historia Francorum,* II. 37-8; IV.1. Ed. & trans. L. Thorpe (1974), *The History of the Franks,* Harmondsworth. Merovingian silver coinage: P. Grierson & M. Blackburn (1986), *Medieval European Coinage,* Cambridge, pp.90-97. Edict of 452: I.M. Ploumis (1997), 'Gifts in the Late Roman Iconography', in S. Isager & B. Poulsen (eds), *Patron and Pavement in Late Antiquity,* Odense, pp.125-41, 125 (= Halicarnassian Studies II).
48 Difficulties in interpretation: C.E. King (1992), 'Roman, local and barbarian coinages in fifth-century Gaul', in J. Drinkwater & H. Elton (eds), *Fifth-century Gaul: a crisis of identity?* Cambridge, pp.184-95.
49 For discussion of the terminology in relation to Gaul: S. Fanning (1992), 'Emperors and Empires in fifth-century Gaul', in J. Drinkwater & H. Elton (eds), *Fifth-century Gaul: a crisis of identity?* Cambridge, pp.288-97. E. James (1989), 'The origins of barbarian kingdoms: the continental evidence', in S. Bassett (ed.), *The Origins of Anglo-Saxon Kingdoms,* Leicester, pp.40-52.
50 P. Grierson (1991), *The Coins of Medieval Europe,* London, pp.4-5. P. Grierson & M. Blackburn (1986), *Medieval European Coinage,* Cambridge, p.10.
51 Oxborough: A. Popescu (2001), 'Coin finds from Norfolk', *Norfolk Archaeology,* XLIII, p.692. Norfolk Sites and Monuments Record 34131-NF38227.
52 P. Grierson & M. Blackburn (1986), *Medieval European Coinage,* Cambridge, p.13. Professor Grierson confirms that this is also the case to his knowledge (pers. comm. November 2002).
53 Antioch: S.H. Weber (1934), 'The Coins', in G.W. Elderkin (ed.), *Antioch-on-the-Orantes I,* Princeton, pp.76-82. D.B. Waage (1952), *Antioch-on-the-Orantes IV.2: Greek, Roman, Byzantine and Crusaders' Coins,* Princeton. Athens: M. Thompson (1954), *The Athenian Agora, Vol. II: the Coins,* Princeton. Here, 11 Vandal and Ostrogothic coins were found (pp.64-71), most bearing both the bust of the Emperor and the monogram of the barbarian king. As elsewhere, no actual 'pseudo-imperial' coins have been identified. Beirut: K. Butcher (1999), 'Coinage in Sixth-Century Beirut: preliminary observations', *Berytus,* 43 (1997-98), pp.173-80. Carthage: W.M. Metcalf (1982), 'The Coins', in J.H. Humphrey (ed.), *Excavations at Carthage 1978: Conducted by the University of Michigan. Vol. 7,* Ann Arbor, pp.63-168S. R. Reece (1984), 'Coins', in H.R. Hurst & S.P. Roskams et al., *Excavations at Carthage: The British Mission. Vol I.1,* Sheffield, pp.171-81. Constantinople: M. Hendy (1986), 'The Coins', in M. Harrison et al., *Excavations at Saraçhane in Istanbul I,* Princeton, pp.278-372. Corinth: A.F. Bellinger (1930), *Catalogue of the coins found at Corinth,* New Haven. K. Edwards (1933), *Coins, 1896-1929. Corinth VI,* Cambridge, Mass. Déhès: C. Morrisson (1980), 'Les Monnaies', *Syria,* 57, pp.267-87. Idalion: I. Nicolaou (1989), 'VI. Numismatics Catalogue', in L.E. Stager & A.M. Walker (eds), *American Expedition to Idalion, Cyprus, 1973-1980,* Chicago. Pergamon: A. Conze et al. (1912), *Pergamon I: Stadt und Landschaft,* Berlin, p.359. H. Voegtli (1984), 'Münzan', in G. De Luca et al., *Das Asklepieion. 4. Teil via Tecta und Hallenstrasse die Funde. (Altertümer von Pergamon, Band XI 4),* Berlin, pp.60-77. Sardis: G.E. Bates (1971), *The Byzantine Coins (Archaeological Exploration of Sardis I),* Cambridge, Mass. A. Kindler (1999), 'Summary of twelve years of numismatic finds in the excavations of Sumaqa (1983-1995)', in S. Dar (ed.), *Sumaqa: A Roman and Byzantine Jewish Village on Mount Carmel, Israel,* Oxford, British Archaeological Reports, International Series 815, pp.347-61. More generally, see also: M. Hendy (1985), *Studies in the Byzantine Monetary Economy, c.300 – 1450,* Cambridge. D. Parrish (2001) (ed.),

Urbanism in Western Asia Minor: new studies on Aphrodisias, Ephesos, Hierapolis, Pergamon, Perge and Xanthos, Portsmouth, Rhode Island (= Journal of Roman Archaeology Supplementary Series 45). *Solidi* in the collection of the Israel Antiquities Authority: pers. comm. Gabriela Bijovsky, Coin Department, Israeli Antiquities Authority, November 2002. I am grateful to Dr Bijovsky for providing me with information on Israel.

54 P. Grierson & M. Blackburn (1986), *Medieval European Coinage*, Cambridge, p.13.
55 *Ibid.*, p.116.
56 P. Grierson (1991), *The Coins of Medieval Europe*, London, p.16. See also: R.J. Collins (1983), 'Theodebert I, 'Rex Magnus Francorum'', in P. Wormald (ed.), *Ideal and Reality in Frankish and Anglo-Saxon History*, Oxford, pp.7-33. I. Wood (1996), 'Roman Law in the Barbarian Kingdoms', in P. Åström (ed.), *Rome and the North*, Göteborg, pp.5-14.
57 Fredegar, *Fourth Book of the Chronicle of Fredegar, with its continuations*, IV.73. Reproduced in A.C. Murray (2000) (ed.), *From Roman to Merovingian Gaul*, Ontario, p.481.
58 P. Grierson & M. Blackburn (1986), *Medieval European Coinage*, Cambridge, pp.129-30.
59 M. Brown & L. Webster (1995), *The Transformation of the Roman World*, London, p.192, no.42.
60 P. Grierson & M. Blackburn (1986), *Medieval European Coinage*, Cambridge, p.5.
61 E.A. Thompson (1982), *Romans and Barbarians: The Decline of the Western Empire*, Madison, Wisconsin, p.170. C. Wickham (1981), *Early Medieval Italy: Central Power and Local Society 400-1000*, Basingstoke, p.34: 'Agilulf, clearly, was concerned to establish, through a fairly eclectic set of images, a late Roman aura of kingship'. J. Herrin (1987), *The Formation of Christendom*, p.226. Leovigild also founded a city, and named it after his son, Recceswinth, in the Byzantine style: Reccopolis.

Chapter 5

1 C. Thomas (1981), *Christianity in Roman Britain to AD 500*, London. C. Thomas (1986), 'Recognising Christian origins: an archaeological and historical dilemma', in L.A.S. Butler & R.K. Morris (eds), *The Anglo-Saxon Church*, London, pp.121-5. R. Krautheimer (1986), *Early Christian and Byzantine Architecture*, (4th ed.) Harmondsworth.
2 J. Guyon (2000), *Les Premiers Baptistères des Gaules (IVe – VIIIe siècles)*, Rome.
3 R. Krautheimer (1986), *Early Christian and Byzantine Architecture*, (4th ed.) Harmondsworth. C. Mango (1986), *Byzantine Architecture*, London. R. Reece (1999), *The Later Roman Empire: an archaeology*, AD 150-600, Stroud, chapter 5.
4 R. Krautheimer (1971), 'On Constantine's Church of the Apostles', reproduced in his *Studies in Early Christian Medieval and Renaissance Art*, London, pp.27-34. C. Mango (1993), 'Constantine's Mausoleum and the translation of relics', reproduced in his *Studies on Constantinople*, Aldershot, V. K.R. Dark & F. Özgümüş (2002), 'New evidence for the Byzantine Church of the Holy Apostles from Fatih Camii, Istanbul', *Oxford Journal of Archaeology*, 21, pp.393-413.
5 R. Krautheimer (1971), 'Postscript to 'The beginning of Early Christian Architecture'', reproduced in his *Studies in Early Christian Medieval and Renaissance Art*, London, pp.1-20, 20. R. Krautheimer (1971), 'Introduction to an 'Iconography of Medieval Architecture'', reproduced in his *Studies in Early Christian Medieval and Renaissance Art*, London, pp.115-150, 123.
6 P. Grossman (1998), 'The Pilgrimage Centre of Abû Mînâ', in D. Frankfurter (ed.), *Pilgrimage and Holy Space in Late Antique Egypt*, Leiden, pp.281-302.
7 J.M. Huskinson (1982), *'Concordia Apostolorum': Christian Propaganda at Rome in the Fourth and Fifth Centuries. A Study in Early Christian Iconography and Iconology*, Oxford, British Archaeological Reports, International Series 148. Note that Krautheimer has drawn a parallel between the martyrial church of St Gereon at Cologne (*c.*380) with its mausoleum off the eastern apse of the church and Constantine's mausoleum at Constantinople: R. Krautheimer (1986), *Early Christian and Byzantine Architecture*, (4th ed.) Harmondsworth, pp.86-7.
8 R. Krautheimer (1986), *Early Christian and Byzantine Architecture*, (4th ed.) Harmondsworth, pp.82. G.C. Menis (1992), *I Longobardi*, Milan, pp.235-98.
9 L. Bréhier (1903), 'Les Colonies d'Orientaux en Occident au commencement du moyen-âge', *Byzantinische Zeitschrift*, 12, pp.1-39, 22.
10 J.K. Knight (1999), *The End of Antiquity: Archaeology, Society and Religion, AD 235-700*, Stroud.
11 N. Duval, J. Fontaine, P.-A. Février, et al. (1991), *Naissance des Arts Chrétiens: Atlas des Monuments Paléochrétiens de la France*. Paris, pp.194-7. G. Barruol (1996), 'Riez: Groupe episcopal, Cathedrale et baptistère', in N. Duval (ed.), *Les premiers monuments chrétiens de la France*, Vol.1, Paris, pp.85-93. R.

Broecker and P.-A. Février (1996), 'La Cadière-d'Azur: Église Saint-Damien', in N. Duval (ed.), *Les premiers monuments chrétiens de la France*, Vol.1, Paris, pp.165-6. J.K. Knight (1999), *The End of Antiquity: Archaeology, Society and Religion, AD 235-700*, Stroud, p.94. Corsica: see the churches at Pianottoli-Caldarello, Vico and Linguizetta, all discussed in N. Duval (1996) (ed.), *Les premiers monuments chrétiens de la France*, Vol.1, Paris, pp.316-21, 324-9, 336-42. G. Moracchini-Mazel (1994), 'Les architectures Paléochrétiennes de Corse, typologie, decoration, datation', *III Reunió d'Arqueologia Cristiana Hispànica, Maó, 12-17 de setembre de 1988*, Barcelona, pp.213-20.

12 J.-F. Reynaud (1998), *Lugdunum christianum: Lyon de IVe au VIIIe*, Paris, pp.134, 244-8 (= Documents d'Archéologie Française 69).

13 R. Krautheimer (1986), *Early Christian and Byzantine Architecture,* (4th ed.) Harmondsworth, p.110. In a tripartite church the arms of the transept are separated from the central bay of the nave, usually by colonnades.

14 P. Guigon (1997), *Les eglises du haut moyen âge en Bretagne*, St. Malo, pp.38-51. J.K. Knight (1999), *The End of Antiquity: Archaeology, Society and Religion, AD 235-700*, Stroud, p.99.

15 Gregory of Tours, *Gloria Martyrum*, 59. Ed. & trans. R. Van Dam (1988), *The Glory of the Martyrs*, Liverpool.

16 J.K. Knight (1999), *The End of Antiquity: Archaeology, Society and Religion, AD 235-700*, Stroud.

17 L. Bréhier (1903), 'Les Colonies d'Orientaux en Occident au commencement du moyen-âge', *Byzantinische Zeitschrift*, 12, pp.1-39. M. Jannet-Vallat, R. Lauxerois and J.-F. Reynaud (1986), *Vienne aux Premiers Temps Chrétiens*, Paris, pp.41ff. M. Jannet-Vallat (1996), 'Vienne: basilique Saint-Pierre, Église Saint-Georges', in N. Duval (ed.), *Les premiers monuments chrétiens de la France*, Vol.1, Paris, pp.254-66. J.K. Knight (1999), *The end of Antiquity: Archaeology, Society and Religion, AD 235-700*, Stroud, p.90.

18 R. Krautheimer (1986), *Early Christian and Byzantine Architecture,* (4th ed.) Harmondsworth, p.73.

19 C. Mango (1993), 'Constantine's Porphyry Column and the Chapel of Constantine', reproduced in his *Studies on Constantinople*, Aldershot, IV. J.K. Knight (1999), *The End of Antiquity: Archaeology, Society and Religion, AD 235-700*, Stroud, p.69.

20 Gregory of Tours, *Historia Francorum*, II. 39. Ed. & trans. L. Thorpe (1974), *The History of the Franks*, Harmondsworth. I. Peña (1997), *The Christian Art of Byzantine Syria*, London, p.231.

21 Gregory of Tours, *Historia Francorum*, X. 31. Ed. & trans. L. Thorpe (1974), *The History of the Franks*, Harmondsworth. I. Peña (1997) *The Christian art of Byzantine Syria*, London, p.233. J.K. Knight (1999), *The End of Antiquity: Archaeology, Society and Religion, AD 235-700*, Stroud, p 80.

22 Gregory of Tours, *Historia Francorum*, VII. 31. Ed. & trans. L. Thorpe (1974), *The History of the Franks*, Harmondsworth.

23 Gregory of Tours, *Historia Francorum*, I. 31. Ed. & trans. L. Thorpe (1974), *The History of the Franks*, Harmondsworth.

24 R. Krautheimer (1971), 'Santo Stefano Rotondo and the Holy Sepulchre Rotunda', reproduced in his *Studies in Early Christian Medieval and Renaissance Art*, London, pp.69-106. J.K. Knight (1999), *The End of Antiquity: Archaeology, Society and Religion, AD 235-700*, Stroud, pp.69, 82.

25 Gregory of Tours, *Historia Francorum*, II. 6, 17; VI. 11. Ed. & trans. L. Thorpe (1974), *The History of the Franks,* Harmondsworth. *The Anonymous History of the Franks,* 50. Reproduced in A.C. Murray (2000), *From Rome to Merovingian Gaul*, Ontario. J.-F. Reynaud (1998), *Lugdunum christianum: Lyon de IVe au VIIIe,* Paris, p.190 (= Documents d'Archéologie Française 69). J.K. Knight (1999), *The End of Antiquity: Archaeology, Society and Religion, AD 235-700*, Stroud, pp.74-7, 96.

26 R. Janin (1969), *La géographie ecclesiastique de l'empire byzantin. I,* Paris, pp.511-2. K.G. Holum and G. Vikan (1979), 'The Trier Ivory, Adventus Ceremonial and the Relics of St Stephen', *Dumbarton Oaks Papers*, 33, pp.113-34. J.M. Huskinson (1982), *'Concordia Apostolorum': Christian Propaganda at Rome in the Fourth and Fifth Centuries. A Study in Early Christian Iconography and Iconology*, Oxford, British Archaeological Reports, International Series 148, pp.96-7.

27 Gregory of Tours, *Gloria Martyrum*, 64. Ed. & trans. R. Van Dam (1988), *The Glory of the Martyrs*, Liverpool. Gregory of Tours, *Historia Francorum*, II. 16, VII. 9-10. Ed. & trans. L. Thorpe (1974), *The History of the Franks,* Harmondsworth. E. James (1977), *The Merovingian Archaeology of South-West Gaul*, Oxford, British Archaeological Reports, International Series 25 (2 vols), p.271. E. James (1988), *The Franks*, Oxford, p.150.

28 *Monasticon Benedictinum*, Paris, Bibliothèque Nationale, Ms. Lat. 12680, fols. 231-35. Reproduced in C. Davis-Weyer (1986) (ed.), *Early Medieval Art 300-1150,* Toronto, p.59-66. E. James (1988), *The Franks*, Oxford, p.151. N. Duval, J. Fontaine, P.-A. Février, *et al.* (1991), *Naissance des Arts Chrétiens: Atlas des Monuments Paléochrétiens de la France,* Paris, pp.238-48.

29 See however: P. Pensabene (1986), 'La decorazione architettonica, l'impiego del marmo e l'importazione di manufatti orientali a Roma, in Italia e in Africa (II-VI d. C.)', in A. Giardina (ed.), *Società romana e Impero tardoantico*, III, Rome, pp.285-429, 397-98. J.-P. Sodini (1989), 'Le commerce des marbres à l'époche protobyzantine', *Hommes et richesses, Tome 1: IV-VII siècle*, Paris, pp.163-86. M.-P. Flèche Mourgues (1998), 'La Morphologie des Tombes dans le Nord de l'Europe (VIe-VIIe siècles)', in N. Cambi & E. Marin (eds), *Acta XIII Congressus Internationalis Archaeologiae Christianae. II*, Vatican City and Split, pp.423-38. A.-B. Mérel-Brandenburg (1998), 'La Sculpture en Septimanie en Haut Moyen-Âge (VIe-VIIIe s.)', in N. Cambi & E. Marin (eds), *Acta XIII Congressus Internationalis Archaeologiae Christianae. II*, Vatican City and Split, pp.637-52.

30 Sidonius Apollinaris, *Epistolae*, II. 2. Ed. & trans. O.M. Dalton (1915), Oxford. G. Kapitän (1969), 'The Church Wreck off Marzamemi', *Archaeology*, 22, pp.122-133. R.B. Hitchner (1992), 'Meridional Gaul, trade and the Mediterranean economy in late antiquity', in J. Drinkwater & H. Elton (eds), *Fifth-century Gaul: a crisis of identity?* Cambridge, pp.122-131, 127. C. Sintès and M. Moutashar (1996) (eds), *Musée de l'Arles antique*, Arles, p.164. F. van Doorninck (2001), 'Byzantine Shipwrecks', in A. Laiou (ed.), *The economic history of Byzantium: From the Seventh through the Fifteenth Century*, Washington D.C., pp.891-97, 891 (= Dumbarton Oaks Studies 39).

31 Bede, *Historia Ecclesiastica*, II. 25. Ed. & trans. L. Sherley-Price (1968), *History of the English Church and People*, Harmondsworth. E. Kitzinger (1954), 'The cult of icons in the age before Iconoclasm', *Dumbarton Oaks Papers*, 8, pp.83-150, 132. R.A. Markus (1978), 'The Cult of Icons in Sixth-Century Gaul', *The Journal of Theological Studies*, 29, pp.151-57. Reproduced in his (1983), *From Augustine to Gregory the Great: History and Christianity in Late Antiquity*, London.

32 Rabbula Gospels: L. Rodley (1994), *Byzantine Art and Architecture*, Cambridge, pp.104-8. Sancta Sanctorum: G. Vikan (1997), 'Sancta Sanctorum', in A. Kahzdan *et al.* (eds) *Oxford Dictionary of Byzantium*, Oxford, p.1838.

33 R.J. Collins (1980), 'Mérida and Toledo: 550–585', in E. James (ed.), *Visigothic Spain: New Approaches*, Oxford, pp.189-219.

34 Gregory of Tours, *Gloria Martyrum*, 22. Ed. & trans. R. Van Dam (1988), *The Glory of the Martyrs*, Liverpool. Gregory of Tours, *Historia Francorum*, II. 15. Ed. & trans. L. Thorpe (1974), *The History of the Franks*, Harmondsworth. Y. Solier (1996), 'Narbonne: la basilique funéraire du Clos-de-la-Lombarde', in N. Duval (ed.), *Les premiers monuments chrétiens de la France*, Vol.1, Paris, pp.32-8. C. Pellecuer (1996), 'Loupian: Église Sainte-Cécile', in N. Duval (ed.), *Les premiers monuments chrétiens de la France*, Vol.1, Paris, pp.47-50. J. Guyon & J.-L. Paillet (1996), 'Saint-Bertrand-de-Comminges', in N. Duval (ed.), *Les premiers monuments chrétiens de la France*, Vol.2, Paris, pp.177-89. South-west Gaul: E. James (1977), *The Merovingian Archaeology of South-West Gaul*, Oxford, British Archaeological Reports, International Series 25 (2 vols), chapter 2.

35 N.F. Retamero (1999), 'As coins go home: towns, merchants, bishops and kings in Visigothic Hispania', in P. Heather (ed.), *The Visigoths from the Migration Period to the Seventh Century: an ethnographic approach*, Woodbridge, pp.271-304.

36 P. Banks (1984), 'The Roman Inheritance and Topographical Transitions in Early Medieval Barcelona', in T.F.C. Blagg, R.F.J. Jones and S.J. Keay (eds), *Papers in Iberian Archaeology*, Oxford, British Archaeological Reports, International Series 193, pp.600-34. J.D. Dodds (1989), *Architecture and Ideology in Early Medieval Spain*, University Park, Pennsylvania, p.15. Taller Escola d'Arquologia (1994), 'Noves aportacions a l'estudi de la Basílica Cristiana de l'Amfiteatre de Tàrraco', *III Reunió d'Arqueologia Cristiana Hispànica*, Barcelona, pp.167-84.

37 G. Ripoll & I. Velázquez (1999), 'Origen y desarrollo des las *parrachiae* en la Hispania de la antigüedad tardía', in P. Pergola (ed.), *Alle origini della parrocchia rurale (IV-VIII sec.)*, Vatican City, pp.101-65. Outside the Iberian peninsula: J.-F. Reynaud (1998), *Lugdunum christianum: Lyon de IVe au VIIIe*, Paris, p.236 (= Documents d'Archéologie Française 69). Y. Codou (1996), 'Draguignan: Église Saint-Hermentaire', in N. Duval (ed.), *Les premiers monuments chrétiens de la France*, Vol.1, Paris, pp.151-4. J. Mallet *et al.* (1996), 'Angers: Église Saint-Martin', in N. Duval (ed.) *Les premiers monuments chrétiens de la France*, Vol.2, Paris, pp.232-37. B. Fizellier-Sauget & J.-M. Sauget (1996), 'Riom, lieu-dit la Chapelle de Pessat, Église Saint-Martin-de-Pessat', in N. Duval (ed.), *Les premiers monuments chrétiens de la France*, Vol.2, Paris, pp.75-7.

38 W. Bowden & J. Mitchell (2001), 'The Church of the Forty Martyrs', *Minerva*, 13, pp.31-33.

39 This paragraph and the following account are based on: J.D. Dodds (1989), *Architecture and Ideology in Early Medieval Spain*, University Park, Pennsylvania. R.J. Collins (1989), 'Doubts and Certainties on the

Churches of Early Medieval Spain', in D.W. Lomax and D. Mackenzie (eds), *God and Man in Medieval Spain*, Warminster, pp.1-18. A. Arbeiter (1990), 'Die Westgotenzeitliche Kirche Von Quintanilla de las Viñas: Kommentar zur Architektonischen Gestalt', *Madrider Mitteilungen*, 31, pp.393-427. G. Ripoll López (1993), 'The Formation of Visigothic Spain', in J.P. O'Neill, K. Howard et al. (eds), *The art of medieval Spain, AD 500-1200*, New York, pp.41-71. R.J. Collins (2000), *Spain: an Oxford archaeological guide*, Oxford. J.M. Maciel (1998), 'Trois églises de plan cruciforme au Portugal et les Trajets Méditerranéens', in N. Cambi & E. Marin (eds), *Acta XIII Congressus Internationalis Archaeologiae Christianae. II*, Vatican City and Split, pp.745-56.

40 J.D. Dodds (1989), *Architecture and Ideology in Early Medieval Spain*, University Park, Pennsylvania, p.12.

41 R. Krautheimer (1986), *Early Christian and Byzantine, Architecture*, (4th ed.) Harmondsworth, p.135. J.D. Dodds (1989), *Architecture and Ideology in Early Medieval Spain*, University Park, Pennsylvania, p.15. E.R. Ruprechtsberger (1993), *Syrien: Von den Aposteln zu den Kalifen*, Linz.

42 I. Peña (1997), *The Christian art of Byzantine Syria*, London, pp.235-9.

43 R. Krautheimer (1986), *Early Christian and Byzantine Architecture*, (4th ed.) Harmondsworth, p.109. H. Hellenkemper (1994), 'Early Church Architecture in Southern Asia Minor', in K. Painter (ed.), *Churches Built in Ancient Times: Recent Studies in Early Christian Archaeology*, London, pp.213-38, 225. N. Duval (1994), 'L'architecture chrétienne et les pratiques liturgiques en Jordanie en rapport avec la Palestine: Recherches Nouvelles', in K. Painter (ed.), *Churches Built in Ancient Times: Recent Studies in Early Christian Archaeology*, London, pp.149-212, 167-9. S. Hill (1996), *The early Byzantine churches of Cilicia and Isauria*, Aldershot. R.W. Daniel & M. Lehtinen (1999), 'Petra Church Project, Petra papyri', *American Journal of Archaeology*, 103, p.511.

44 The Daniel in the lions' den motif may be represented on fourth-century mosaics elsewhere in Spain (for example, the mausoleum at the villa site of Centcelles), but this does not necessitate their use as a model for artists working at San Pedro some 300 years later. 'Daniel' belt buckles: G. Ripoll López (1999), 'Symbolic Life and Signs of Identity in Visigothic Times', in P. Heather (ed.), *The Visigoths from the Migration Period to the Seventh Century: an ethnographic approach*, Woodbridge pp.403-31. Animal depictions: S. Alpaslan (2001), 'Architectural sculpture in Constantinople and the influence of the capital in Anatolia', in N. Necipoglu (ed.), *Byzantine Constantinople: Monuments, Topography and Everyday Life*, Leiden, pp.187-201, 193.

45 A. Arbeiter (1990), 'Die Westgotenzeitliche Kirche Von Quintanilla de las Viñas: Kommentar zur Architektonischen Gestalt', *Madrider Mitteilungen*, 31, pp.393-427. I. Peña (1997), *The Christian art of Byzantine Syria*, London, p.236.

46 G. Kapitän (1969), 'The Church Wreck off Marzamemi', *Archaeology*, 22, pp.122-133.

47 Belt-tab: C. Entwistle (1994), 'Gold belt-tab', in D. Buckton (ed.), *Byzantium: Treasures of Byzantine Art and Culture*, London, p.69. 'Lyre-shaped' buckles: G. Ripoll (1985), *La necropolis visigoda de El Carpio de Tajo (Toldeo)*, Madrid, pp.60-2. G. Ripoll López (1993), 'The Formation of Visigothic Spain', in J.P. O'Neill, K. Howard et al. (eds), *The art of medieval Spain, AD 500-1200*, New York, pp.41-71, 66-7. W. Ebel-Zepezauer (2000), *Studien zue Archäologie der Westgoten vom 5.-7. Jh. N. Chr.*, mainz am Rhein, pp.38-41, 66-75 (= *Iberia Archaeologica*, Band 2, Deutsches Archäologisches Institut, Madrid). B. Sasse (2000), *'Westgotische' Gräberfelder auf der Iberischen Halbinsel: aus Beispiel der Funde aus El Carpio de Tajo (Torrijos, Toledo)*, Mainz am Rhein.

48 I. Peña (1997), *The Christian Art of Byzantine Syria*, London, p.232.

49 E.A. Thompson (1969), *The Goths in Spain*, Oxford, pp.21-2, 43. R.J. Collins (1980), *Early Medieval Spain*, London, pp.203-4. R.J. Collins (1980), 'Mérida and Toledo: 550 - 585', in E. James (ed.), *Visigothic Spain: New Approaches*, Oxford, pp.189-219. J. Herrin (1987), *The Formation of Christendom*, London, pp.222-3.

50 L.A.M. Jimeno (1989), *Eremitorios Rupestres Altomedievales (El alto valle del Ebro)*, Bilbao. R. Grande del Brío (1997), *Eremitorios Altomedievales en las Provincias de Salamanca y Zamora*, Salamanca.

51 N. Aravecchia (2001), 'Hermitages and Spatial Analysis: Use of Space at the Kellia', in S. McNally (ed.), *Shaping Community: The Art and Archaeology of Monasticism*, Oxford, British Archaeological Reports, International Series 941, pp.29-40. M. Thompson (2001), *Cloister, Abbot and Precinct*, Stroud, pp.19-30.

52 Sulpicius Severus, *The Life of St Martin*. In F.R. Hoare (1954), *The Western Fathers*, London. C. Stancliffe (1983), *St. Martin and his hagiographer: history and miracle in Sulpicius Severus*, Oxford, especially chapter 7.

53 Gregory of Tours, *Historia Francorum*, X, 24. Ed. & trans. L. Thorpe (1974), *The History of the Franks*, Harmondsworth. *Vita Patrum Iurensium*, Ed. & trans. F. Martine (1968), *Vies des Pères du Jura*, Sources Chrétiennes 142, Paris. I. Wood (1981), 'A prelude to Columbanus: the monastic achievement in the Burgundian territories', in H.B. Clarke and M. Brennan (eds), *Columbanus and Merovingian Monasticism*, Oxford, British Archaeological Reports, International Series 113, pp.4-8.

54 Gregory of Tours, *Vitae Patrum*, 3. 1. Ed. & trans. E. James (1988) (2nd ed.), *The Lives of the Fathers*, Liverpool.
55 Gregory of Tours, *Vitae Patrum*, 4. 2. Ed. & trans. E. James (1988) (2nd ed.), *The Lives of the Fathers* Liverpool. Gregory of Tours, *Historia Francorum,* VI. 6. Ed. & trans. L. Thorpe (1974), *The History of the Franks,* Harmondsworth. Gregory of Tours, *Gloria Confessorum*, 79, 95. Ed. & trans. R. Van Dam (1988), *The Glory of the Confessors*, Liverpool. Sidonius Apollinaris, *Epistolae*, VII 17. Ed. & trans. O.M. Dalton (1915), Oxford.
56 E. Le Blant (1865), *Inscriptions Chrétiennes de la Gaule antérieures au VIIIe siècle*, (2 vols) Paris. E. James (1981), 'Archaeology and Merovingian monasticism', in H.B. Clarke & H. Brennan (eds), *Columbanus and Merovingian Monasticism*, Oxford, British Archaeological Reports, International Series 113, pp.33-58.
57 Y. Hirschfeld (1992), *The Judean Desert Monasteries in the Byzantine Period*, New Haven, p.180. I. Peña (1997), *The Christian art of Byzantine Syria*, London, p.105: 107 of these towers have been identified in Syria, which, if their interpretation is reliable, attests archaeologically the popularity of eremiticism in this period and in this part of the Empire in particular.
58 E. Fletcher (1980), 'The monastery of Lérins', *Journal of the British Archaeological Association*, 133, pp.17-29. P.-A. Février (1996), 'Cannes: Lérins', in N. Duval (ed.), *Les premiers monuments chrétiens de la France*, Vol.2, Paris, pp.98-9. J.K. Knight (1999), *The End of Antiquity: Archaeology, Society and Religion, AD 235-700*, Stroud, p.61.
59 L. Fleuriot & P.-R. Giot (1977), 'Early Brittany', *Antiquity*, LI, pp.106-116. P.-R. Giot & G. Querré (1985), 'Le tesson d'amphore B2 de l'Île Lavret (Bréhat, Côtes du Nord)', *Revue Archéologique Ouest*, 2, pp.95-100.
60 P.-R. Giot et al. (1982), *Les Premiers Bretons*, Chateaulin, pp.24-5. P.-R. Giot et al. (1982), 'Enez Guennoc ou Geignog, un ancien microcosme celtique', *Melanges M. de Boûard*, Rennes, pp.179-87. T.A. Bastide (2000), *Les structures de l'habitat rural protohistorique dans le sud-ouest de l'Angleterre et le nord-ouest de la France*, Oxford, British Archaeological Reports, International Series 847. Coins: A.-H. Dizerbo, M. Le Goffic & P. Galliou (1993), 'Notices d'Archéologie Finistérienne', *Bulletin de la Société archéologique du finistère*, 138, p.59. P. Galliou (1977), 'Monnaies de Bronze des VIe–VIIe siècles découvertes ou conserves en Bretagne', *Archéologie en Bretagne*, 14, pp.17-24.
61 M. Finlaison & P. Holdsworth (1979), 'Excavation on the Île Agois, Jersey', *Société Jersiaise Annual Bulletin*, 22, pp.332-46.
62 W. Rodwell (1994), 'The Archaeology of the Early Church in the Channel Islands', in K. Painter (ed.), *Churches Built in Ancient Times: Recent Studies in Early Christian Archaeology,* London, pp.295-312, 301.
63 Pilgrimage was further popularised by Helena, the mother of Constantine I, and continued by later Byzantine Empresses, such as Eudocia, the wife of Theodosius I. John Malalas, *Chronographia,* XIII. 5, XIV. 8. Eds. and trans. E. Jeffreys, M. Jeffreys & R. Scott (1986), Melbourne. *Egeria's Travels*. Ed. & trans. J. Wilkinson (1971), London. E.D. Hunt (1982), *Holy Land Pilgrimage in the Later Roman Empire, A.D. 312-460,* Oxford. E.D. Hunt (1999), 'Were there Christian Pilgrims before Constantine?', in J. Stopford (ed.), *Pilgrimage Explored,* Woodbridge, pp.25-40.
64 E.D. Hunt (1992), 'Gaul and the Holy Land in the early fifth century', in J. Drinkwater & H. Elton (eds), *Fifth-century Gaul: a crisis of identity?* Cambridge, pp.264-74. Journey time: M. Aldhouse-Green (1999), *Pilgrims in Stone: Stone images from the Gallo-Roman sanctuary of Fontes Sequanae*, Oxford, British Archaeological Reports, International Series 754, p.104.
65 Paul the Deacon, *History of the Lombards,* III. 34. Ed. W.D. Foulke, trans. E. Peters (1974), Philadelphia. But on the 'apocryphal' nature of this story see: R. Van Dam (1993), *Saints and Their Miracles in Late Antique Gaul,* Princeton, p.139, n.108. H. Richardson (1995), 'The Jewelled Cross and its Canopy', in C. Bourke (ed.), *From the Isles of the North: Early Medieval Art in Ireland and Britain,* Belfast, pp.177-86. C. Sintès & M. Moutashar (1996) (eds), *Musée de l'Arles antique,* Arles, p.166.
66 Theodoret of Cyrrhus, *Religiosa historia*, xxvi. 11. Trans. R. M. Price (1985), *History of the Monks of Syria*, Kalamazoo, p.165. *Life of St Daniel the Stylite,* 60. In E. Dawes & N. Baynes (1996), *Three Byzantine Saints*, Crestwood, New York. E.D. Hunt (1992), 'Gaul and the Holy Land in the early fifth century', in J. Drinkwater & H. Elton (eds), *Fifth-century Gaul: a crisis of identity?* Cambridge, pp.264-74.
67 *Travels of the Piacenza Pilgrim,* 20. Quoted in S. Coleman & J. Elsner (1995), *Pilgrimage: Past and Present in the World's Religions,* London, p.85.
68 C. Lambert & P. Pedemonte Demeglio (1994), 'Ampolle Devozionali ed Itinerari di Pellegrinaggio tra IV e VII secolo', *Antiquité Tardive*, 2, pp.205-31. The distribution map does not indicate the provenance of these artefacts. These form the subject of a major research project being undertaken by Susanne Bangert and I am grateful for having had the opportunity to discuss St Menas flasks with her.

69 C. Bertelli (1998), 'The Production and Distribution of Books in Late Antiquity', in R. Hodges & W. Bowden (eds), *The Sixth Century: Production, Distribution and Demand*, Leiden, pp.41-60, 57.

70 Guild of St. Menas: L. Bréhier (1903), 'Les Colonies d'Orientaux en Occident au commencement du moyen-âge', *Byzantinische Zeitschrift,* 12, pp.1-39, 4. K.R. Dark (forthcoming), 'Early Byzantine Mercantile Communities in the West', in C. Entwistle (ed.), *Through a Glass Brightly: Studies presented to David Buckton*, London. Towns: Gregory of Tours, *Historia Francorum*, III. 29; VIII. 1. Ed. & trans. L. Thorpe (1974), *The History of the Franks*, Harmondsworth. R.J. Collins (1980), 'Mérida and Toledo: 550 – 585', in E. James (ed.), *Visigothic Spain: New Approaches,* Oxford, pp.189-219.

71 A. Cameron (1975), 'The Byzantine sources of Gregory of Tours', *Journal of Theological Studies*, 26, pp.421-6.

72 *Life of St Daniel the Stylite*, 64. In E. Dawes & N. Baynes (1996), *Three Byzantine Saints*, Crestwood, New York. Gregory of Tours, *Historia Francorum*, VIII. 34. Ed. & trans. L. Thorpe (1974), *The History of the Franks,* Harmondsworth.

Chapter 6

1 T.E.C. Blagg (1981), 'Some Roman Architectural Traditions in the Early Saxon Churches of Kent', in A. Detsicas (ed.), *Collectanea Historica: Essays in Honour of Stuart Rigold,* Maidstone, pp.51-3. A. Thacker (1999), 'In Gregory's Shadow: The Pre-Conquest Cult of St Augustine', in R. Gameson (ed.), *St Augustine and the Conversion of England*, Sutton, pp.374-90, 386.

2 Constantine VII Porphyrogenitus, *De Administrando Imperio,* 13 (71-3). Ed. & trans. R. J. H. Jenkins (1967), Washington D.C. On this passage see: P. Magdalino (1991), *Tradition and Transformation in Medieval Byzantium,* Aldershot, XIV, p.5.

3 Bede, *Historia Ecclesiastica*, II.10. Ed. & trans. L. Sherley-Price (1968), *History of the English Church and People*, Harmondsworth.

4 *Anglo-Saxon Chronicle*, E, *sub anno*, 794. In D. Whitelock (1955), *English Historical Documents, c. 500-1042*, London. Quoted in R. Cramp (1981), 'Monastic Sites', in D. Wilson (ed.), *The Archaeology of Anglo-Saxon England*, Cambridge, pp.201-52, 212-215, 230. R. Cramp (1994), 'Monkwearmouth and Jarrow in their continental context', in K. Painter (ed.), *Churches built in Ancient Times: Recent Studies in Early Christian Archaeology,* London, pp.279-94. R.A. Markus (1999), 'Augustine and Gregory the Great', in R. Gameson (ed.), *St Augustine and the Conversion of England*, Sutton, pp.41-9.

5 B. Cherry (1981), 'Ecclesiastical architecture', in D. Wilson (ed.), *The Archaeology of Anglo-Saxon England*, Cambridge, pp.151-200. S. Kelly (1997), 'The Anglo-Saxon Abbey', in R. Gem (ed.), *St Augustine's Abbey, Canterbury*, London, pp.33-49. E. Cambridge (1999), The Architecture of the Augustinian Mission', in R. Gameson (ed.), *St Augustine and the Conversion of England*, Sutton, pp.202-36.

6 D.M. Dumville (1995), 'The importation of Mediterranean manuscripts in Theodore's England', in M. Lapidge (ed.), *Archbishop Theodore: Commemorative studies on his life and influence*, Cambridge, pp.96-119.

7 J. Richards (1979), *The Popes and the Papacy in the Early Middle Ages 476 – 752,* London, pp.293-5. 'Byzantine' Rome: J. Herrin (1973), 'Aspects of the Process of Hellenization in the Early Middle Ages', *Annual of the British School of Archaeology at Athens,* 68, pp.113-26. J. Herrin (1987), *The Formation of Christendom,* London, pp.157-61. H. Mayr-Harting (1991), *The Coming of Christianity to Anglo-Saxon England,* (3rd ed.) London, pp.170-1. J. Herrin (1992), 'Constantinople, Rome and the Franks in the seventh and eighth centuries', in J. Shepard & S. Franklin (eds), *Byzantine Diplomacy. Papers from the Twenty-fourth Spring Symposium of Byzantine Studies,* Aldershot, pp.91-107. T.F.X. Noble (1995), 'Rome in the seventh century', in M. Lapidge (ed.), *Archbishop Theodore: Commemorative studies on his life and influence,* Cambridge, pp.68-87.

8 A.S. Esmonde Cleary (1989), *The Ending of Roman Britain*, London. K.R. Dark (2000), *Britain and the end of the Roman Empire*, Stroud.

9 C. Orton (2000), *Sampling in Archaeology*, Cambridge.

10 The following discussion of the ceramic evidence is based on: A.C. Thomas (1981), *A provisional list of imported pottery in post-Roman Britain and Ireland*, Redruth. E. Campbell (1988), 'The post-Roman pottery', in N. Edwards & A. Lane (1988), *Early Medieval settlements in Wales AD 400-1100*, Cardiff, pp.124-136. M.G. Fulford (1989), 'Byzantium and Britain: a Mediterranean perspective on Post-Roman Mediterranean Imports in Western Britain and Ireland', *Medieval Archaeology,* 33, pp.1-6. A.C. Thomas (1990), "Gallici Nautae de Galliarum Provinciis'–A sixth/seventh century trade with Gaul, reconsidered', *Medieval Archaeology,* 34, pp.1-26. C.D. Morris, J. Nowakowski and A.C. Thomas (1990),

Tintagel, Cornwall: the 1990 excavations', *Antiquity*, 64, pp.843-9. E. Campbell & A. Lane (1993) (eds), 'Excavations at Longbury Bank, Dyfed, an early medieval settlement in South Wales', *Medieval Archaeology*, 37, pp.15-77. K.R. Dark (1994), *Discovery by Design: the identification of secular élite settlements in western Britain AD 400-700*, Oxford, British Archaeological Reports, British Series 237. C.D. Morris (1994) (ed.), *Tintagel Castle Excavations 1993,* Glasgow. E. Campbell (1995), 'Early medieval pottery and glass', in P.F. Wilkinson, 'Excavations at Hen Gastell, Britton Ferry, West Glamorgan 1991-2', *Medieval Archaeology,* 39, pp.18-23. D. Williams & C. Carreras (1995), 'North African amphorae in Roman Britain: a re-appraisal', *Britannia*, 26, pp.231-52. E. Campbell (1996), 'The Archaeological Evidence for External Contacts: Imports, Trade and Economy in Celtic Britain AD 400-800', in K.R. Dark (ed.), *External Contacts and the Economy of Late Roman and Post-Roman Britain,* Woodbridge, pp.83-96. E. Campbell (1996), 'Trade in the Dark Age West: a peripheral activity?' in B.E. Crawford (ed.), *Scotland in Dark Age Britain*, St Andrews, pp.79-91. J. M. Wooding (1996), 'Cargoes in Trade along the Western Seaboard', in K.R. Dark (ed.), *External Contacts and the Economy of Late Roman and Post-Roman Britain*, Woodbridge, pp.67-82. J.M. Wooding (1996), *Communication and Commerce along the Western Sealanes AD 400–800,* Oxford, British Archaeological Reports, International Series 654. E. Campbell (1997), 'The Dark Age Ceramics', in P. Hill *et al.*, *Whithorn and St Ninian: The Excavation of a Monastic Town, 1984-91,* Stroud, pp.315-22. C.D. Morris & R. Harry (1997), 'Excavations on the Lower Terrace, Site C, Tintagel Island, 1990-94', *The Antiquaries Journal,* 77, pp.1-143. C.D. Morris, C.E. Batey *et al.* (1999), 'Recent work at Tintagel', *Medieval Archaeology*, 43, pp.206-15. P. Rahtz *et al.* (2000), *Cannington*, London, especially pp.293-5.

11 Gemstone: S. Denison (2000), 'Gemstone evidence for late Roman survival', *British Archaeology,* 52, p.4. Beads: L. Alcock (1987), *Economy, Society and warfare among the Britons and Saxons*, Cardiff, pp.148-9. St Menas flask: D. Griffith (2001), 'Meols', *British Archaeology*, 62, pp.19-25. Glass: for example, P. Rahtz, A. Woodward *et al.* (1992), *Cadbury Congresbury 1968-73. A late/post-Roman hilltop settlement in Somerset*, Oxford, British Archaeological Reports, British Series 223, pp.134, 139-40. Censer: P. Rahtz (1993), *Glastonbury*, London, pp.99-100. G. Ripoll López (1993), 'The Formation of Visigothic Spain', in J.P. O'Neill, K. Howard *et al.* (eds), *The art of medieval Spain, AD 500-1200*, New York, pp.52-3. Coin weight: C. Entwistle (1994), 'Coin-weight from Somerset', in D. Buckton (ed.), *Byzantium: Treasures of Byzantine Art and Culture*, London, p.86. For coins, see note 29 below.

12 L. Alcock (1987), *Economy, society, and warfare among the Britons and Saxons.* Cardiff, pp.187-91. C.D. Morris & R. Harry (1997), 'Excavations on the Lower Terrace, Site C, Tintagel Island, 1990-94', *The Antiquaries Journal,* 77, pp.1-143, esp.74-82. M.G. Fulford (1989), 'Byzantium and Britain: a Mediterranean perspective on Post-Roman Mediterranean Imports in Western Britain and Ireland', *Medieval Archaeology,* 33, pp.1-6, 4. F.H. van Doorninck (1989), 'The Cargo Amphoras of the 7th Century Yassι Ada and 11th Century Serçe Limany Shipwrecks: two examples of a reuse of Byzantine amphoras as transport jars', in V. Déroche & J.-M. Spieser (eds), *Recherches sur la céramique,* pp.247-57 (= Bulletin de Correspondence Hellénique, Supplement 18).

13 P. Reynolds (1995), *Trade in the Western Mediterranean, AD 400-700: the ceramic evidence*, Oxford, British Archaeological Reports, International Series 604, p.274. O. Karagiorgou (2001), 'LR2: A Container for the Military *annona* on the Danubian Border?' in S. Kingsley & M. Decker (eds), *Economy and Exchange in the East Mediterranean during Late Antiquity*, Oxford, pp.129-66, 146.

14 E. Campbell (1996), 'The Archaeological Evidence for External Contacts: Imports, Trade and Economy in Celtic Britain AD 400-800', in K.R. Dark (ed.), *External Contacts and the Economy of Late Roman and Post-Roman Britain,* Woodbridge, pp.83-96, 85.

15 M. Comber (2001), 'Trade and Communication Networks in Early Historic Ireland', *Journal of Irish Archaeology*, 10, pp.73-91.

16 R.J. Silvester (1981), 'An Excavation on the Post-Roman Site at Bantham, South Devon', *Proceedings of the Devon Archaeological Society*, 39, pp.89-118. F.M. Griffith (1986), 'Salvage observations at the Dark Age Site at Bantham Ham, Thurlestone, in 1982', *Proceedings of the Devon Archaeological Society*, 44, pp.39-57, 47. J. May & P. Weddell (2002), 'Bantham: a Dark Age puzzle', *Current Archaeology*, 178, pp.420-2. There is a sherd of Byzantine pottery from Iona, but this may reflect independent travel, perhaps pilgrimage. D. Griffith (2001), 'Meols', *British Archaeology*, 62, pp.19-25.

17 P. Hill (1997), 'The Early Medieval imports: distribution and chronology', in P. Hill *et al.*, *Whithorn and St Ninian: The Excavation of a Monastic Town, 1984-91*, Stroud, pp.322-26, 324.

18 S. McGrail (1997), 'Cross Channel Seamanship and Navigation in the late First Millennium BC', in his *Studies in Maritime Archaeology*, Oxford, British Archaeological Reports, British Series 256, pp.265-88.

J.M. Wooding (1996), *Communication and Commerce along the Western Sealanes AD 400 – 800,* Oxford, British Archaeological Reports, International Series 654, pp.42.

19 M.G. Fulford (1989), 'Byzantium and Britain: a Mediterranean perspective on Post-Roman Mediterranean Imports in Western Britain and Ireland', *Medieval Archaeology,* 33, pp.1-6, 4. E. Campbell (1996), 'The Archaeological Evidence for External Contacts: Imports, Trade and Economy in Celtic Britain AD 400-800', in K.R. Dark (ed.), *External Contacts and the Economy of Late Roman and Post-Roman Britain,* Woodbridge, pp.83-96, 86.

20 C.D. Morris, C.E. Batey *et al.* (1999), 'Recent work at Tintagel', *Medieval Archaeology,* 43, pp.206-15, 213.

21 R.D. Penhallurick (1986), *Tin in antiquity: its mining and trade throughout the ancient world with particular reference to Cornwall,* London, pp.212, 234.

22 M. McCormick (2001), *Origins of the European Economy: Communications and Commerce, AD 300-900,* Cambridge, p.47.

23 For St Menas flask, Egyptian glass and beads, see note 11 above. The distinctive Egyptian 'Ankh' cross appears on a bone cross from Winchester, probably of fifth- to seventh-century date, although this was not found in an archaeological context (Winchester Museum). K.R. Dark (2000), *Britain and the End of the Roman Empire,* Stroud, p.101. Processed foods and papyri: R. Bagnall (1993), *Egypt in Late Antiquity,* Princeton, p.80. A single sherd of Egyptian Red Slip Ware has been found at London: R. Tomber & D. Williams (2000), 'Egyptian amphorae in Britain and the western provinces', *Britannia,* 31, pp.41-54, 48-9.

24 *Life of St John the Almsgiver,* 10. In E. Dawes & N. Baynes (1996), *Three Byzantine Saints,* Crestwood, New York.

25 Although note that Paul Reynolds suggests grain as the principal cargo on ships sailing from the Eastern Mediterranean to western Portugal: *Trade in the Western Mediterranean, AD 400-700: the ceramic evidence,* Oxford, British Archaeological Reports, International Series, 604, p.129. M. Mundell Mango (2001), 'Beyond the Amphora: Non-Ceramic Evidence for Late Antique Industry and Trade', in S. Kingsley & M. Decker (eds), *Economy and Exchange in the East Mediterranean during Late Antiquity,* Oxford, pp.87-106, 96. A. Bowman (1996), 'Post-Roman Imports in Britain and Ireland: A Maritime Perspective', in K.R. Dark (ed.), *External Contacts and the Economy of Late Roman and Post-Roman Britain,* Woodbridge, pp.97-107. She notes (p.101) that a return voyage from Turkey to south-west Britain would take at least half the sailing season (which ran from mid-April to mid-October).

26 *Life of St John the Almsgiver,* 6, 10. In E. Dawes & N. Baynes (1996), *Three Byzantine Saints,* Crestwood, New York.

27 Procopius, *Secret History,* XIX. 13. Trans. G.A. Williamson (1966), *The Secret History,* Harmondsworth. Procopius, *History of the Wars,* Book II, vi. 28. Trans. H.B. Dewing (1919), *Procopius,* Vol. III, London. For discussion of and reservations about the value of these textual references as evidence for British-Byzantine contacts: J.M. Wooding (1996), *Communication and Commerce along the Western Sealanes AD 400–800,* Oxford, British Archaeological Reports, International Series 654, pp.46-7. Procopius's references to Britain are also discussed in J.O. Ward (1968), 'Procopius, 'Bellum Gothicum' II.6.28: the problem of contacts between Justinian I and Britain', *Byzantion,* 38, pp.460-71. E.A. Thompson (1980), 'Procopius on Brittia and Britannia', *The Classical Quarterly,* 30, pp.498-507. A. Bowman (1996), 'Post-Roman Imports in Britain and Ireland: A Maritime Perspective', in K.R. Dark (ed.), *External Contacts and the Economy of Late Roman and Post-Roman Britain,* Woodbridge, pp.97-107.

28 Gildas, *De Excidio Britanniae,* Book One, 23.5. Ed. & trans. M. Winterbottom (1978), *The Ruin of Britain and other works,* London and Chichester. S. Chadwick Hawkes (1989), 'The south-east after the Romans: the Saxon settlement', in V.A. Maxfield (ed.), *The Saxon Shore: a handbook,* Exeter, pp.78-95 (= Exeter Studies in History 25). On the sources: D.M. Dumville (1977), 'Sub-Roman Britain: History and Legend', *History,* 62, pp.173-92. P. Bartholomew (1982), 'Fifth-Century Facts', *Britannia,* 13, pp.261-70.

29 G.C. Boon (1991), 'Byzantine and other ancient bronze coins from Exeter', in N. Holbrook & P.T. Bidwell (eds), *Roman Finds from Exeter,* Exeter, pp.38-45 (= Exeter Archaeological Reports Volume 4). D.M. Metcalf (1995), 'Byzantine Coins from Exeter', in S. Efthymiadis *et al.,* (eds), *Bosphorus: essays in honour of Cyril Mango,* Amsterdam, pp.253-61. K.D. Dark (2000), *Britain and the End of the Roman Empire,* Stroud, p.162.

30 Portable Antiquities Scheme finds database: www.finds.org.uk. B. Ager (2001), 'Winchester area (1), Hampshire: Gold imitation coin pendant', *Treasure Annual Report 1998-1999,* London, p.30.

31 Gregory of Tours, *Historia Francorum,* II. 38. Ed. & trans. L. Thorpe (1974), *The History of the Franks,* Harmondsworth. J. Lafaurie (1972), 'Trouvailles de monnaies des VIe-VIIe siècles de l'Empire d'Orient en Gaul mérovingienne', *Bulletin pour la Societé Française de Numismatique,* 27, pp.206-7.

32 R.A. Philpott (1999), 'Three Byzantine Coins found near the North Wirral Coast in Merseyside', in *Transactions of the Historic Society of Lancashire and Cheshire 1998*, 148, pp.197-202. A major research project on Meols is underway, directed by David Griffith and Robert Philpott, and will doubtless shed more light on these objects.

33 *Ibid.*

34 N. Edwards & A. Lane (1992) (eds), *The Early Church in Wales and the West*, Oxford.

35 Theodoret of Cyrrhus, *Religiosa historia*, xxvi. 11. Trans. R.M. Price (1985), *History of the Monks of Syria*, Kalamazoo, p.165.

36 This paragraph and the following account is based on: J.K. Knight (1981), '*In Tempore Iustini Consulis*: Contacts between the British and Gaulish Churches before Augustine', in A. Detsicas (ed.), *Collectanea Historica: Essays in memory of Stuart Rigold,* Maidstone, pp.54-62. W. Davies (1982), *Wales in the Early Middle Ages,* Leicester. N. Edwards and A. Lane (1992) (eds), *The Early Church in Wales and the West*, Oxford. K.R. Dark (1994), *Discovery by Design: the identification of secular élite settlements in western Britain AD 400-700,* Oxford, British Archaeological Reports, British Series 237. K.R. Dark (1994), *Civitas to Kingdom: British political continuity 300-800,* Leicester. J.K. Knight (1996), 'Seasoned with Salt: Insular-Gallic contacts in the Early Memorial Stones and Cross Slabs', in K.R. Dark (ed.), *External Contacts and the Economy of Late Roman and Post-Roman Britain,* Woodbridge, pp.109-120. J.K. Knight (1999), *The End of Antiquity: Archaeology, Society and Religion, AD 235 – 700,* Stroud. N. Edwards (2000), 'Early Medieval Inscribed Stones and Stone Sculpture in Wales: Context and Function', *Medieval Archaeology*, XLV, pp.15-39.

37 For *ogom* (also sometimes spelled *ogam* and *ogham*), the first Irish script: N. Edwards (1996), *The Archaeology of Early Medieval Ireland,* London, pp.103-4. There is an *ogom* stone from Silchester (Hampshire), but the context of this has been much disputed. Most recently: M. Fulford *et al.* (2000), 'An early date for Ogham: The Silchester Ogham Stone Rehabilitated', *Medieval Archaeology*, XLIV, pp.1-23.

38 P. Rahtz, A. Woodward *et al.* (1992), *Cadbury Congresbury 1968-73. A late/post-Roman hilltop settlement in Somerset,* Oxford, British Archaeological Reports, British Series 223, p.165. The direct emulation of Byzantine art is not, however, without possible evidence. Parallels have been drawn between Ulster cross-slabs and Eastern (particularly Armenian) stone sculpture. The motif in question has no known intermediary outside these two locations, and might provide further evidence that the British Isles were linked into a cultural world with its origin in the East. H. Richardson (1987), 'Observations on Christian Art in Early Ireland, Georgia and Armenia', in M. Ryan (ed.), *Ireland and Insular Art, AD 500-1200,* Dublin, pp.129-37.

39 J.K. Knight (1996), 'Seasoned with Salt: Insular-Gallic contacts in the Early Memorial Stones and Cross Slabs', in K.R. Dark (ed.), *External Contacts and the Economy of Late Roman and Post-Roman Britain,* Woodbridge, pp.109-120, 112.

40 J.K. Knight (1981), '*In Tempore Iustini Consulis*: Contacts between the British and Gaulish Churches before Augustine', in A. Detsicas (ed.), *Collectanea Historica: Essays in memory of Stuart Rigold,* Maidstone, pp.54-62, 62. J.K. Knight (1996), 'Seasoned with Salt: Insular-Gallic contacts in the Early Memorial Stones and Cross Slabs', in K.R. Dark (ed.), *External Contacts and the Economy of Late Roman and Post-Roman Britain,* Woodbridge, pp.109-120, 112-15.

41 V.E. Nash-Williams (1950), *The Early Christian Monuments of Wales*, Cardiff, pp.55, 93. J.K. Knight (1999), *The End of Antiquity: Archaeology, Society and Religion, AD 235–700,* Stroud, p.109.

42 J.-C. Decourt & G. Lucas (1993), *Lyon dans les texts Grecs et Latins,* Lyon, pp.142-3. J.-F. Reynaud (1998), *Lugdunum christianum: Lyon de IVe au VIIIe,* Paris (= Documents d'Archéologie Française 69).

43 O. Padel (1985), *Cornish Place-name Elements,* Nottingham: 'St Just' is not derived from any Cornish word. S. Pearce (1978), *The Kingdom of Dumnonia: studies in history and tradition in south western Britain AD 350-1150,* Padstow. E. Okasha (1993), *Corpus of Early Christian Inscribed Stones of South-West Britain,* Leicester, pp.243-6. C. Thomas (1994), *And shall these mute stones speak? post-Roman inscriptions in western Britain,* Cardiff, pp.286-7. E. Okasha (1996), 'The Early Christian Carved and Inscribed Stones of south-west Britain', in B. E. Crawford (ed.), *Scotland in Dark Age Britain*, pp.21-35, 25-6. University College London 'Celtic Inscribed Stones Project' number: SJUST. Although note Olson's argument that the memorial stones of south-west Britain have less Continental content than those from elsewhere in the country. L. Olson (1989), *Early Monasteries in Cornwall,* Oxford, p.40. Other place names: K.R. Dark (2000), *Britain and the End of the Roman Empire,* Stroud, pp.155, 163.

44 C. Thomas (1982), 'East and West: Tintagel, Mediterranean imports and the early Insular Church', in S.M. Pearce (ed.), *The early Church in Western Britain and Ireland,* Oxford, British Archaeological Reports, British Series 102, pp.17-34.

45 Llandough: A. Thomas & N. Holbrook (1996), 'Llandough', *Current Archaeology*, 146, pp.73-7. Glastonbury: P. Rahtz (1993), *Glastonbury*, London, pp.54-5. Caldey Island: E. Campbell (1988), 'Imported pottery from St David's, Caldey', *Archaeology in Wales* 28, p.75.

46 Jerome, *Epistolae,* 58.2. Ed. & trans. P. Schaff & H. Wace (1988-91), *A Select library of Nicene and post-Nicene Fathers of the Christian Church. Second series, Vol. 6. St. Jerome: Letters and Select Works,* Grand Rapids.

47 K.R. Dark (2000), *Britain and the End of the Roman Empire*, Stroud, chapter 2.

48 Gildas, *De Excidio Britanniae*. Ed. & trans. M. Winterbottom (1978), *The Ruin of Britain and other works*, London and Chichester.

49 I. Wood (1990), 'The Channel from the 4th to the 7th centuries AD', in S. McGrail (ed.), *Maritime Celts, Frisians and Saxons,* London, pp.93-7 (= Council for British Archaeology Research Report 71). I. Wood (1992), 'Frankish hegemony in England', in M. Carver (ed.), *The Age of Sutton Hoo*, Woodbridge, pp.235-41.

50 H. Geake (1997), *The Use of Grave-Goods in Conversion-Period England, c.600-c.850,* Oxford, British Archaeological Reports, British Series 261. S. Lucy (2000), *The Anglo-Saxon Way of Death,* London.

51 M. Biddle, D. Hudson & C. Heighway (1973), *The Future of London's Past*, Worcester. C. Thomas (1981), *Christianity in Roman Britain to AD 500*, London, pp.260-1. P. Arthur (1986), 'Roman Amphorae from Canterbury', *Britannia*, 17, pp.239-58. A. Selkirk (1990), 'Verulamium', *Current Archaeology*, 120, pp.410-17. K.R. Dark (1994), *Civitas to Kingdom: British political continuity 300-800,* Leicester, pp.86-9. There is a published St. Menas flask from Derby Museum, but it is of uncertain provenance (it was uncovered on a building site): R.S.M. O'Farrall (1951), 'A Pilgrim's Flask found at Derby', *Journal of the Derbyshire Archaeological and Natural History Society*, 24, pp.78-9. There may be a handful of other St. Menas flasks from Britain, but the archaeological evidence is highly tenuous: Susanne Bangert, pers. comm. May and December 2002. I am most grateful to Ms Bangert for the opportunity to discuss these with her.

52 S. Heslop & J. Mitchell (1997), 'The Arts and Learning', in R. Gem (ed.), *St Augustine's Abbey Canterbury,* London, pp.67-89, 68. C. Entwistle (1994), 'Coin-weight from Somerset', in D. Buckton (ed.), *Byzantium: Treasures of Art and Culture*, London, p.86. A. Popescu (2001), 'Coin finds from Norfolk', *Norfolk Archaeology*, XLIII, p.692. Norfolk Sites and Monuments Record 34131-NF38227. K. Penn (1998), *An Anglo-Saxon Cemetery at Oxborough, West Norfolk. Excavations 1990*, Ipswich (= East Anglian Archaeology Occasional Papers No. 5). Katie Hind, Norfolk County Council, pers. comm. August 2002. Andrew Richardson, Kent County Council, pers. comm. August 2002.

53 The following account is based on: J. Werner (1961), 'Fernhandel und Naturalwirtschaft im östlichen Merowingerreich nach archäologischen und numismatischen Zeugnissen', *Bericht der Römisch-Germanischeen Kommission*, 42, pp.307-46. A. Meaney (1964), *A Gazetteer of Early Anglo-Saxon Burial Sites,* London. R.W. Higginbottom (1975), *Anglo-Saxon contact with the Eastern Mediterranean, AD 400-700*, unpublished University of Manchester MA dissertation. P. Richards (1980), *Byzantine bronze vessels in England and Europe: the origins of Anglo-Saxon trade*, University of Cambridge, unpublished PhD thesis. S. Chadwick Hawkes (1982), 'Anglo-Saxon Kent, c. 425-725', in P.E. Leach (ed.), *Archaeology in Kent to AD 1500,* London, pp.64-78. Fig. 33 (= Council for British Archaeology Research Report 48.) M. Mundell Mango, C. Mango, A. Care Evans & M. Hughes (1989), 'A 6th-Century Mediterranean Bucket from Bromeswell Parish, Suffolk', *Antiquity*, 63, pp.295-311. E. O'Brien (1999), *Post-Roman Britain to Anglo-Saxon England: Burial Practices Reviewed*, Oxford, British Archaeological Reports, British Series 289.

54 D. Gurney (2001), 'Archaeological finds in Norfolk in 2000', *Norfolk Archaeology*, XLIII, p.702. Ian Riddler, pers. comm. September 2002.

55 E. O'Brien (1999), *Post-Roman Britain to Anglo-Saxon England: Burial Practices Reviewed*, Oxford, British Archaeological Reports, British Series 289, p.173.

56 T. Dickinson (1974), *Cuddesdon and Dorchester-on-Thames, Oxfordshire: two early Saxon 'princely' sites in Wessex*, Oxford, British Archaeological Reports, British Series 1. R. Bruce-Mitford (1983), 'The Coptic Bowl', in R. Bruce-Mitford *et al.*, *The Sutton Hoo Ship-Burial, Volume 3,* London, pp.732-52. T. Dickinson & G. Speake (1992), 'The seventh-century cremation burial in Asthall Barrow, Oxfordshire: a reassessment', in M. Carver (ed.), *Age of Sutton Hoo,* Woodbridge, pp.95-130, 101. J. Blair (1994),

Anglo-Saxon Oxfordshire, Stroud, pp.46-8. E. O'Brien (1999), *Post-Roman Britain to Anglo-Saxon England: Burial Practices Reviewed*, Oxford, British Archaeological Reports, British Series 289, p.163.

57 Ian Riddler, pers. comm. September 2002.

58 P. Richards (1980), *Byzantine bronze vessels in England and Europe: the origins of Anglo-Saxon trade*, University of Cambridge, unpublished PhD thesis, p.85.

59 C.J. Arnold (1982), *Anglo-Saxon Cemeteries of the Isle of Wight*, London, pp.24, 27. M. Mundell Mango, C. Mango, A. Care Evans & M. Hughes (1989), 'A 6th-Century Mediterranean Bucket from Bromeswell Parish, Suffolk', *Antiquity*, 63, pp.295-311. E. O'Brien (1999), *Post-Roman Britain to Anglo-Saxon England: Burial Practices Reviewed*, Oxford: British Archaeological Reports, British Series 289. D. Allen (2002), 'Editorial', *Hampshire Field Club and Archaeology Society Newsletter*, 37, p.3.

60 J. Arce (1982), 'La Sítula tardorromana de Bueña (Teruel)', *Estudios de iconografía I: Museo Arqueologico Nacional, Catalogos y monografias*, pp.113-62.

61 *Gesta Pontificum Autissiodorensium*. Reproduced in C. Davis-Weyer (1986), *Early Medieval Art 300-1150*, Toronto, pp.66-9.

62 M. Mundell Mango, C. Mango, A. Care Evans & M. Hughes (1989), 'A 6th-Century Mediterranean Bucket from Bromeswell Parish, Suffolk', *Antiquity*, 63, pp.295-311. H. Härke (1992), 'Changing symbols in a changing society: the Anglo-Saxon weapon burial rite in the seventh century', in M. Carver (ed.), *The Age of Sutton Hoo*, Woodbridge, pp.149-65. D. Allen (2002), 'Editorial', *Hampshire Field Club and Archaeology Society Newsletter*, 37, p.3.

63 R. Bruce-Mitford et al. (1983), *The Sutton Hoo Ship-Burial, Volume 3*, London, pp.136-46, 125-46. J. Werner (1992), 'A Review of the Sutton Hoo Ship Burial Volume 3: Some remarks, thoughts and proposals', *Anglo-Saxon Studies in Archaeology and History*, 5, pp.1-24.

64 J. Huggett (1988), 'Imported grave goods and the early Anglo-Saxon economy', *Medieval Archaeology*, 32, pp.63-96.

65 R. Avent (1975), *Anglo-Saxon Garnet Inlaid Disc and Composite Brooches*, Oxford, British Archaeological Reports, British Series 11. B. Arrhenius (1985), *Merovingian Garnet Jewellery: Emergence and Social Implications*, Stockholm, p.196. A. Boyle, D. Jennings, D. Miles & S. Palmer (1998), *The Anglo-Saxon Cemetery at Butler's Field, Lechlade, Gloucestershire*, Oxford, pp.84-5, 127, 196-7 (= Thames Valley Landscapes Monograph 10).

66 M. Carver (1998), *Sutton Hoo: Burial Ground of Kings?* London, p.89: the Sutton Hoo purse contained 'seven rough-cut garnets, a single garnet in the form of a bird's beak and a fragment of red and blue millefiori glass'. A. Boyle, D. Jennings, D. Miles & S. Palmer (1998), *The Anglo-Saxon Cemetery at Butler's Field, Lechlade, Gloucestershire*, Oxford, pp.84-5 (= Thames Valley Landscapes Monograph 10).

67 V.I. Evison (1987), *Dover: The Buckland Anglo-Saxon Cemetery*, London. J. Huggett (1988), 'Imported grave goods and the early Anglo-Saxon economy', *Medieval Archaeology*, 32, pp.63-96, 66, 68. J. Hines (1999), 'The Anglo-Saxon archaeology of the Cambridgeshire region and the middle Anglian kingdom', *Anglo-Saxon Studies in Archaeology and History*, 10, pp.135-50.

68 M. Henig (1974), *A Corpus of Roman Engraved Gemstones from British Sites*, Oxford, British Archaeological Reports, British Series 102, II, 85 no. 634; II, 94, no. 718. R.H. White (1988), *Roman and Celtic Objects from Anglo-Saxon Graves: a catalogue and an interpretation of their use*, Oxford, British Archaeological Reports, British Series 191, pp.104-105.

69 E. James (1977), *The Merovingian Archaeology of South-West Gaul*, Oxford, British Archaeological Reports, International Series 25 (2 vols), pp.247, 258 and Pl. 64. P. Richards (1980), *Byzantine bronze vessels in England and Europe: the origins of Anglo-Saxon trade*, University of Cambridge, unpublished PhD thesis, p.204. Cambridge, Fitzwilliam Museum, accession number M.11-1978.

70 E. O'Brien (1999), *Post-Roman Britain to Anglo-Saxon England: Burial Practices Reviewed*, Oxford, British Archaeological Reports, British Series 289.

71 Procopius, *History of the Wars*, Book I, iv. 20; Book VIII, xx. 1-6, 48-58. Trans. H.B. Dewing (1919), *Procopius*, Vols. I & V, London.

72 Gildas, *De Excidio Britanniae*, Book I, III. 1. Ed. & trans. M. Winterbottom (1978), *The Ruin of Britain and other works*, London & Chichester.

73 R.G. Collingwood & R.P. Wright (1990), *The Roman Inscriptions of Britain, Volume II: Instrumentum Domesticum*, Stroud, pp.81, 124.

74 See note 51 above.

75 S. Chadwick Hawkes (1982), 'Anglo-Saxon Kent, c.425-725', in P.E. Leach (ed.), *Archaeology in Kent to AD 1500*, London, pp.64-78. Fig. 33 (= Council for British Archaeology Research Report 48). B.

Brugmann (1999), 'The role of Continental artefact-types in sixth-century Kentish chronology', in J. Hines et al., *The Pace of Change: Studies in Early-Medieval Chronology*, Oxford, pp.37-64.

76 Quotation: J. Werner (1992), 'A Review of the Sutton Hoo Ship Burial Volume 3: Some remarks, thoughts and proposals', *Anglo-Saxon Studies in Archaeology and History*, 5, pp.1-24, 2, 21. R. Bruce-Mitford et al. (1983), *The Sutton Hoo Ship-Burial, Volume 3*, London, p.164. I.M. Ploumis (1997), 'Gifts in the Late Roman Iconography', in S. Isager & B. Poulsen (eds), *Patron and Pavement in Late Antiquity*, Odense, pp.125-41, 133. J. Harris (1999), 'Wars and Rumours of Wars: England and the Byzantine World in the Eighth and Ninth Centuries', *Mediterranean Historical Review*, 14, pp.29-46.

77 W. Filmer-Sankey (1996), 'The 'Roman Emperor' in the Sutton Hoo Ship Burial', *Journal of the British Archaeological Association*, CXLIX, pp.1-9. B. Yorke (1999), 'The Reception of Christianity at the Anglo-Saxon Courts', in R. Gameson (ed.), *St Augustine and the Conversion of England*, Sutton, pp.152-73, 57.

78 S. Youngs (1983), 'The manufacture of the Sutton Hoo Silver', in R. Bruce-Mitford et al., *The Sutton Hoo Ship-Burial, Volume 3*, London, pp.166-201, 176. M. Mundell Mango, C. Mango, A. Care Evans & M. Hughes (1989), 'A 6th-Century Mediterranean Bucket from Bromeswell Parish, Suffolk', *Antiquity*, 63, pp.295-311. I am grateful to Sally Worrell for the observation on the 'hurried' decoration on the Breamore 'bucket' (pers. comm. November 2002).

79 C. Scull (1986), 'A sixth-century grave containing a balance and weights from Watchfield, Oxfordshire, England', *Germania*, 64, p.115, no. 21, fig. 18. M. Mundell Mango, C. Mango, A. Care Evans & M. Hughes (1989), 'A 6th-Century Mediterranean Bucket from Bromeswell Parish, Suffolk', *Antiquity*, 63, pp.295-311.

80 Roman-period titles: D. Petts (1999), 'Christianity and the end of Roman Britain', in P. Baker et al. (eds), *Theoretical Roman Archaeology Conference Proceedings 98*, Oxford, pp.86-95, 89-90. State workshops: M. Mundell Mango, C. Mango, A. Care Evans & M. Hughes (1989), 'A 6th-Century Mediterranean Bucket from Bromeswell Parish, Suffolk', *Antiquity*, 63, pp.295-311.

81 W. Filmer-Sankey (1996), 'The 'Roman Emperor' in the Sutton Hoo Ship Burial', *Journal of the British Archaeological Association*, CXLIX, pp.1-9. R. Hodges (1998), 'Henri Pirenne and the question of demand in the sixth century', in R. Hodges & W. Bowden (eds), *The Sixth Century: Production, Distribution and Demand*, Leiden, pp.3-14, 13.

82 M. McCormick (1986), *Eternal Victory: triumphal rulership in Late Antiquity, Byzantium and the Early Medieval West*, Cambridge.

83 J. Werner (1984), *Der Grabfund von Malaja Peresceptina und Kuvrat, Kagan der Bulgaren*, Bayerische Akademie der Wissenschaft. A. M. Stahl (1992), 'The nature of the Sutton Hoo coin parcel', in C.B. Kendall & P.S. Wells (eds), *Voyage to the Other World: The Legacy of Sutton Hoo*, Minneapolis, pp.3-14.

84 J. Moorhead (1992), *Theodoric in Italy*, Oxford, p.185.

85 M. Carver (1998), *Sutton Hoo: Burial Ground of Kings?* London.

86 H. Vierck (1978), 'La Chemise de Saint-Bathilde à Chelles et l'influence byzantine sur le cour mérovingien au VIIe siècle', *Actes du Colloque International d'Archéologie, Rouen, 1975*, 3, pp.521-64, pl., I-VI. E. Crowfoot (1983), 'The Textiles', in R. Bruce-Mitford et al., *The Sutton Hoo Ship-Burial, Volume 3*, London, pp.409-62, especially 424, 455-7. L. Bender Jørgensen (1992), *North European Textiles until AD 1000*, Aarhus.

87 H. Geake (1997), *The Use of Grave-Goods in Conversion-Period England, c.600-c.850*, Oxford, British Archaeological Reports, British Series 261. H. Geake (1999), 'Invisible kingdoms: the use of grave-goods in seventh-century England', *Anglo-Saxon Studies in Archaeology and History*, 10, pp.203-15. These works are referred to throughout the following account.

88 S. Carnegie & W. Filmer-Sankey (1993), 'A Saxon Cremation Pyre from the Snape Anglo-Saxon Cemetery, Suffolk', *Anglo-Saxon Studies in Archaeology and History*, 6, pp.107-11. W. Filmer-Sankey & T. Pestell (2001), *Snape Anglo-Saxon Cemetery: Excavations and Surveys 1824-1992*, Ipswich, pp.195-8 (=East Anglian Archaeology Report 95).

89 H. Geake (1997), *The Use of Grave-Goods in Conversion-Period England, c.600-c.850*, Oxford, British Archaeological Reports, British Series 261, pp.107-22. J. Huggett (1988), 'Imported grave goods and the early Anglo-Saxon economy', *Medieval Archaeology*, 32, pp.63-96.

90 B. Arrhenius (1985), *Merovingian Garnet Jewellery: Emergence and Social Implications*, Stockholm, pp.157-8. M. Pinder (1995), 'Anglo-Saxon garnet cloisonné composite brooches: some aspects of their construction', *Journal of the British Archaeological Association*, 148, pp.6-28. H. Geake (1997), *The Use of Grave-Goods in Conversion-Period England, c.600-c.850*, Oxford, British Archaeological Reports, British Series 261, Section 4.16, Figs 4.11 and 4.12.

91 H. Geake (1999), 'Invisible kingdoms: the use of grave-goods in seventh-century England', *Anglo-Saxon Studies in Archaeology and History*, 10, pp.203-15.
92 H. Geake (1997), *The Use of Grave-Goods in Conversion-Period England, c.600-c.850*, Oxford, British Archaeological Reports, British Series 261, p.109, Figs. 4.12, 5.4, 5.7, 5.10.
93 M.G. Welch (1983), *Early Anglo-Saxon Sussex*, Oxford, British Archaeological Reports, British Series 112, Part ii, p.472, fig.103c. D. Buckton (1994), 'Glass flask from an Anglo-Saxon burial', in D. Buckton (ed.), *Byzantium: Treasures of Byzantine Art and Culture,* no.21, p.42.
94 R.H. White (1988), *Roman and Celtic Objects from Anglo-Saxon Graves: a catalogue and an interpretation of their use*, Oxford, British Archaeological Reports, British Series 191.

Chapter 7
1 H. Geake (1997), *The Use of Grave-Goods in Conversion-Period England, c.600-c.850,* Oxford, British Archaeological Reports, British Series 261.
2 W. Filmer-Sankey (1996), 'The 'Roman Emperor' in the Sutton Hoo Ship Burial', *Journal of the British Archaeological Association*, CXLIX, pp.1-9.
3 K.R. Dark (2000), *Britain and the End of the Roman Empire*, Stroud, chapter 6.
4 D. Obolensky (1971), *The Byzantine Commonwealth: Eastern Europe 550-1500*, London.

INDEX

Abraham, 131
Abu Mîna, 107, 136
Adaloald, 37
Adriatic, 12, 52, 106
Aegean, 12, 45, 57, 64, 149
Æthelberht, 37, 141
Aetius, 27
Agathias, 72
Alaric I, 11, 27, 35, 42, 95
Alaric II, 32
Alboin, 36
Alexandria, 12, 56, 68-69, 72, 81, 95, 98, 136, 151, 171, 182
Alfriston, 173
Alicante, 57
Alps, 13, 14, 42, 65, 70, 91, 110, 191
Amalafrida, 35
Amalaric, 34
Amalasuintha, 34, 35, 103-104
Amandus, 131
Ambrose, 109
amethysts, 65, 170, 173, 183, 184, 188
amphorae, *see* Byzantine pottery
Ampurias, 52, 61
Anatolia, 44, 45, 111, 122, 123, 124, 130, 150
Anatolius, 137-138
Anekdota, 152
Anglesey, 144, 146, 173
annona, 53, 57, 59-60, 72, 146, 152
Antioch, 12, 47, 63, 64, 68, 69, 98, 99, 108, 131, 151, 169
Aperlae, 88

Apulia, 31, 109
Arabs, 9, 13, 76, 93, 127, 134
Arbogast, 23
Arculf, 107
'Aregundis' burial, 83-85, 88, 90
Arianism, 30, 68, 120, 121
Arles, 31, 42, 61, 98, 118, 119, 134, 141, **colour plates 4, 5, 18**
Arlon, 80
ARSW, *see* Byzantine pottery
Asia, 21, 87, 125
Asthall, 161, 166
Astorga, 115
Athalaric, 34, 97, 104
Athens, 12, 54, 99
Atlantic, 13, 52, 59, 149, 152, 160, 176, 179, 180
Attila, 27, 28, 84, 87
Augustine of Canterbury, 37, 74, 119, 139, 140, 141, 178, 188
Augustine of Hippo, 115
Autun, 61, 118, 121, 141

Balkans, 13, 16, 17, 38, 98
Banstead Down, 182
Bantham, 144, 147, 161, 165, **colour plates 23, 24**
Barcelona, 52, 98, 121
Bari, 17
Bedburg-Morken-Harff, 90
Bede, 140, 179

Beirut, *see* Berytus
Belisarius, 12, 37, 152
belt buckles, 15, 78, 80, 84, 85, 126, 127, 134, 171, 180, 181, **colour plate 18**
Benalúa, 57
Benedict Biscop, 139
Berenice, 88
Bertha, 37, 141
Berytus, 64, 99
Black Sea, 33
Bloodmoor Hill, 183
Bordeaux, 51, 61, 96, 116, 117, 137-138, 149, 150
Boscombe Chine, 165
Bourges, 116, 117, 131
Breamore, 167, 168, 169, 179-180, **colour plate 26**
Bréhat, 15, 133, 160, **colour plate 21**
Bromeswell, 167, 169, 176, 180
Buckland, 172
Burgundy, 26, 31, 34, 100, 135
'Byzantine Commonwealth', 194
Byzantine pottery, 41, 43-60, 62-64, 69, 72, 133, 143-152, 158, 160-161, 176, 190-191

Cabillonum, 135
Cadbury Congresbury, 144, 148, 150, 157, 161
Cadiz, 38, 150
Caerwent, 153
Caistor-by-Norwich,

161, 164, 175
Caldey Island, 160
Calonge, 66
Camiac, 159
Canterbury, 74, 140, 141, 142, 161, 163, 164, 188
Carcassonne, 31
Cartagena, 38, 49, 52, 57, 61
Carthage, 12, 44, 49, 51, 52, 53, 57, 61, 98, 153
Cassiodorus, 16, 21, 30, 50
Castel Cos, 132
Castel Meur, 132
Chamberlain's Barn, 184
Channel Islands, 15, 133
Charibert, 37
Charlemagne, 36
Chelles, 92
Chessell Down, 161, 167, 180
Childebert I, 111
Childebert II, 37, 39, 153
Childebert III, 117
Childeric, 31, 32, 80-82, 85, 94, 189, 190
Chilperic I, 26, 39, 40, 74, 84, 94
China, 21, 63, 87
Chlodoswintha, 36, 37
Chlothar I, 36, 39, 84
Chlothar II, 39, 102
Choisy-au-Bac, 117
Christian Topography of Cosmas Indicopleustes, 21, 95
Chronicle of Fredegar, 33, 39, 101
Chur, 91

221

churches and cathedrals, *see also* Holy Apostles, churches; St Stephen, dedications to
Church of the Forty Martyrs, Saranda, 122
'Clos-de-la-Lombard', Narbonne, 121
Hagia Sophia, Constantinople, 77, **colour plate 12**
Holy Apostles, Constantinople, 82, 106-110, 112, 113, 123
Holy Apostles, Paris, 82-83, 110-111, 112
Holy Sepulchre, Jerusalem, 77, 107, 117
Qal'at Si'man, Syria, 108, 135, 136, **colour plates 3, 16**
Saint-Dénis, Paris, 77, 83, 84, 86, 90, 104
San Apollinare in Classe, 109, 122
San Apollinare Nuovo, Ravenna, 73, 83, 109
San Juan de Baños, Cerrato, 122, 126
San Nazaro (Holy Apostles), Milan, 108-112, **colour plate 10**
San Pedro de la Mata, Toledo, 126
San Pedro de la Nave, Zamora, 123, 126, **colour plate 13**
San Pietro in Vincoli, Rome, 108
San Simpliciano, Milan, 108, 109, **colour plate 11**
San Stefano Rotondo, Rome, 116
San Stefano, Verona, 109
San Vitale, Ravenna, 77, 109, 110, 184
Santa Comba de Bande, Orense, 126
Santa Croce, Ravenna, 109
Santa Euphemia, Como, 109

Santa Lucía del Trampal, Mérida, 124, 125
Santa María de Melque, Toledo, 124
Santa María de Quintanilla de la Viñas, Burgos, 123, 126, 127, **colour plate 14**
Santa Sabina, Rome, 120
São Frutuoso, Montelios, 122-123
São Gião de Nazaré, Lamego, 124
St Babylas, Antioch, 108
St Catherine's, Sinai, 122
St Cecilia, Loupian, 121
St John the Evangelist, Castelseprio, 109
St John, Ephesus, 107
St Just, Lyon, 111, 159
St Laurent, Aosta, 110
St Laurent-de-Choulans, Lyon, 111, 112
St Martin, Angers, 122
St Martin, Autun, 118
St Martin, Tours, 32, 95
St Peter, Rome, 107, 108, 113, 135
St Tecla, Milan, 106, 107
St Thecla, Meryemlik, 125
St Vincent, Paris (St Germain-des-Prés), 111
Sts Peter and Paul, Canterbury, 140, 142
Sts Sergius and Bacchus, Constantinople, 110
Cimiez, 110
Classe, 41, 49, 109, 122
Class-1 stones, 155, 156, 157, 159
Class-2 stones, 155, 156, 157
Clermont, 110, 117, 118, 119, 122, 131
Clogher, 147

Clovis, 32-33, 35, 40, 61, 80, 82-83, 95-96, 110, 112, 113, 115, 153, 181, 190
Codex Argenteus, 30, **colour plate 2**
coinage, 15, 18, 27, 29, 32, 50, 68, 70, 73, 74, 81-82, 86, 93-104, 116, 133, 141, 144, 148, 152-155, 163-164, 171, 181, 183, 192, **colour plates 8, 25**
Cologne, 14, 15, 83, 85, 86, 90, 92, 104, 108
Columbanus, 13
Como, 61, 109
Conimbriga, 59
'Coptic' vessels, 65-68, 86, 164-167, 175, 183, 184, 186
Córdoba, 38, 61
Corinth, 17, 54, 99
Corsica, 110
Council of Nicaea, 11
cowrie shells, 65, 68, 172, 173, 175, 187, 188
Cuddesdon, 166
Cyrenaica, 88, 151

Dagobert I, 84, 101
Danube, 16, 27, 57, 167
De Excidio Britanniae, 162
Desborough, 161, 184, 185
Diaspolis, 88
Dinas Powys, 147, 161
Dor, 88
Draguignan, 122
Dumio, 128
Durazzo, 17
D-ware, 149, 150, 159

Eastry, 164
Edwin of Northumbria, 140
Egeria, 134, 136
Egypt, 8, 13, 25, 42, 44, 45, 47, 52, 56, 63, 65, 68, 69, 71, 86, 107, 124, 130, 131, 132, 135, 136, 137, 143, 148, 151, 164, 167, 175, 191

Emperors
Anastasius I, 30, 31, 32, 34, 86, 95, 117, 153, 170, 178, 181, **colour plate 25**
Basiliscus, 28
Constans II, 38, 43, 88
Constantine I, 11, 28, 77, 83, 95, 105, 106, 108, 113, 115, 139
Diocletian, 11, **colour plate 1**
Heraclius, 33, 95
Julius Nepos, 12, 27, 98
Justin I, 33-34, 85, 86, 100, 153, 154
Justin II, 40, 87, 181
Justinian I, 22, 30, 32, 37, 38, 72, 77, 87, 88, 96, 97, 100, 107, 110, 113, 123, 152, 153, 154
Justinian II, 35
Leo I, 28, 135
Maurice, 39, 74, 153-154, 155, 164, 181
Romulus Augustulus, 12, 26, 27
Theodosius I, 11, 12, 28
Theodosius II, 87, 94
Tiberius, 26, 38, 39
Valentinian III, 98
Zeno, 27, 28, 29, 34, 81, 108, 109, 125
Enez Guennoc, 133
Ephesus, 12, 99, 107
eremiticism, 130-134, 138
Eudocia, Byzantine Empress, 117
Eufronius (of Bordeaux), 61, 116
Eufronius (Bishop of Autun), 121
Eutharic, 34, 35
Exeter, 153
extra-mural cemeteries, 16, 49, 113, 117, 121
E-ware, 133, 149, 154

Faversham, 164, 172
Ferring, 161, 187, **colour plate 17**
Finglesham, 184

INDEX

Flonheim, 80
Fos-sur-Mer, 13, 51, 60
Fraga, 121

Gaillardon, 159
Gaza, 41, 45, 51, 56, 61
Geneva, 13, 106
gift-exchange, 28, 29, 31, 35, 39, 40, 55, 70, 72, 73, 74-77, 81, 87, 88, 93, 137, 152, 169, 171, 180
Gildas, 152, 162, 176
Gilton, 164
glass, 15, 69, 77, 85, 86, 144, 150, 151, 166, 176, 184, 187
Glastonbury, 144, 145, 147, 160
gold-and-garnet jewellery, 70, 77, 79, 80-81, 85-86, 164, 170-171, 175, 188, **colour plates 9**, **27, 28**
Grambla, 147
grave-goods, 10, 42, 78-82, 84-86, 92-93, 163-167, 182-183, 185-188, 191-192
Gregory of Tours, 16, 26, 32, 38, 40, 50, 61, 63, 94, 96, 112, 116, 117, 119, 120, 130, 137, 161, 181, 186
Grenoble, 110
Griesheim, 79
Guadiana River, 13, 122
Guarrazar Treasure, 76-77, **colour plates 6, 7**
Gundomar II, 100
Gundovald, 39, 40, 116
Guntram, 39, 40, 61, 135

Haddenham, 161, 174
Hadrian, 19, 25
Hermenigild, 37-38, 94, 103
Historia Francorum, 32, 137
History of the Wars, 152
Holy Apostles churches, 82-83, 106, 107-114, 138

Holy Land, 8, 9, 13, 45, 106, 107, 115, 130, 134, 135, 137
Hospitius (hermit), 131

Île Agois, 133
Île Saint Maudez, 132
Illington, 173
India, 21, 65, 87, 160
Ireland, 15, 19, 133, 143, 147, 148, 152, 157
Irene, Byzantine Empress, 94-95
Islam, 9, 20
ivory, 65, 68, 79, 134, 170, 172, 173, 174, 188
Jarrow-Monkwearmouth, 139, 140, 161
Jerome, 63, 130, 160
Jerusalem, 40, 74, 77, 107, 115, 117, 134, 135, 160
John Cassian, 130
John Malalas, 33
Justinianic Reconquest, 19, 37-38, 47, 49, 51, 58, 60, 66, 72, 109, 110, 122, 152, 192, 193

Kellia, 130
Khazaria, 35-36
Krefeld-Gellep, 79, 92

La Cadière-d'Azur, 110
Lackford, 173
Langres, 116
Latin, 11, 15, 22-23, 157, 159
Lavoye, 79
Lavret, 133, 160, **colour plate 21**
Le Mans, 113, 117
Lechlade, 171, 172, **colour plate 28**
Léon, 66
Leovigild, 38, 94, 102-103
Lérins, 15, 132, 133
Life of Daniel the Stylite, 137
Life of St John the Almsgiver, 56, 151

Lives of the 'Jura Fathers', 130
Llandough, 160
London, 153, 163, 176-177
Lyon, 13, 15, 51, 57, 61, 98, 100, 111, 112, 117, 120, 126, 141, 159, 160

Maastricht, 92
Málaga, 38, 61, 124, 127, 129, 150
Mallorca, 66
marble, 42, 63, 118-119, **colour plate 4**
Marcellinus *comes*, 27
Marialba de la Ribera, 122
Marseille, 13, 15, 39, 47, 49-50, 51, 52, 53, 54, 57-60, 64, 72, 90, 95, 101, 111, 112, 117, 118, 119, 130, 132
Marzamemi shipwreck, 42, 119, 126
mausoleum of Galla Placidia, 123, 124
Mayen Ware, 15
Meols, 148, 153-154, 155, 161, **colour plate 19**
Mérida, 13, 61, 88, 120, 122, 124, 128, 137, 146
Metz, 117
Milan, 29, 98, 106, 107, 108-113, 130
Minorca, 67
Montcaret, 174
Monza, 109, 137
Murex Trunculus, 30, 87-88

Nantes, 110, 111, 112, 137
Naples, 38, 49, 51, 58, 61, 72
Narbonne, 34, 61, 120, 121
Narses, 38
Needham Market, 164
Nice, 61, 131
Niedernberg, 92
Niederstotzingen, 90
Nîmes, 61, 134

North Africa, 9, 20, 26, 37, 44, 47-51, 52, 53, 55, 64, 98, 110, 111, 115, 125, 146, 150, 186

Obolensky, Dimitri 16, 194
Odovacer, 12, 27-29
ogom stones, 157, 158
Ohrid, 17
oikoumenê, 21-22, 33, 138, 140, 160, 179, 193
Orléans, 61, 111, 137, 149
Ostia, 41
Ostrogotho, 35
Oswald of Northumbria, 179
Oxborough, 98, 164
Ozingell, 173

papyrus, 42, 59, 68, 151
Paris, 24, 61, 77, 82-85, 110, 112, 120, 146
Paul the Deacon, 135
Pedraza, 121
Pelagius, 155
Peloponnese, 17, 45
'Penmachno' stone, Gwynedd, 157
Pergamon, 12, 99
Perruson, 90
Persia, 25, 72, 87, 90, 95, 103, 151
pilgrimage, 69, 105, 107, 120, 134-138
Pirenne, Henri, 8, 9, 41
Pla de Nadal, 121
Planig, 90
Po Valley, 13, 65
Poitiers, 39-40, 61, 74, 135
Pope Boniface V, 140
Pope Gregory the Great, 55, 119, 137, 140, 141, 155, 178
porphyry, 10, **1**
Portable Antiquities Scheme, 153
Port-Cros, 15
Procopius, 30, 31, 32, 87, 101, 103, 152, 175, 176
Protet, 159

223

Provence, 26, 39, 72, 95, 101, 122
PRSW, *see* Byzantine pottery
purple dye, 30, 87-89
Putney, 176-177
Pyrenees, 32

Quintianus (hermit), 131

Rabbula Gospels, 120, 137, 174
Radegund, 39-40, 74
Raedwald, 169-170
Ravenna, 14, 29, 30, 38, 41, 49, 51, 52, 61, 70, 72, 73, 77, 81, 83, 98, 99, 100, 109, 110, 118, 121, 122, 123, 124, 139, 164, 184, 189, **colour plate 22**
Reask, 42, 147
Recceswinth, 76
Réoval, 40
'Rescript of Honorius', 20
Rhine, 11, 13, 14, 15, 20, 65, 68, 70, 90, 92, 111, 136, 143, 175, 176, 180, 183, 191
Rhône, 13, 42, 68, 111, 136, 143, 175
Riez, 110
Riom, 122
Robertsbridge, 164
romanitas, 7, 22-23, 98-99, 104, 157, 183, 185, 189-192
Romanization, 17-18, 97, 191
Rome, 11, 12, 20, 22, 23, 27, 29, 30, 38, 41, 42, 43, 46, 50, 52, 55, 57, 58, 61, 63, 70, 72, 98, 99, 100, 105, 106, 107, 108, 109, 113, 116, 117, 118, 120, 130, 134, 135, 137, 139, 140, 141, 143, 155, 168, 179, 186
Rosas, 52, 61
Roundway Down, 185

Saint-Blaise, 50

Salona, 50
Saltwood, 161, 165, 166
San Miguel de Escalada, 121
San Millán, 130
Sardinia, 50, 185
Sardis, 12, 43, 45, 88, 99
Sarragosa, 137
Sarre, 161, 164
Sea of Marmara, 12, 42, 59, 64
Ségobriga, 121, 122
Sens, 91, 92
'Seventh Century Transformation', 9
Seville, 38, 61
Sibertswold, 172, 174
Sichem, 107
Sicily, 9, 12, 38, 42, 50, 141, 152
Sidonius Apollinaris, 16, 23, 26, 88, 119
Sigibert, 38, 39
Sigismund, 31, 33, 35
silk, 10, 33, 56, 63, 84-93, 128, 139, 180
Siponte, 109
Sisenand, 101
Sitten, 91
Snape, 183
Sophia, Byzantine Empress, 40
South Cadbury, 144
St Albans, *see Verulamium*
St Cuthbert, 139
St Eulalia, 137
St Germanus of Auxerre, 15, 132
St Helier, Jersey, 133
St Honorat, Lérins, 132
St Ia, Cornwall, 159
St Just, Cornwall, 156, 159
St Just (Justus), 159
St Madron, Cornwall, 159
St Mammes, 40
St Martin of Tours, 20, 115-117, 130-132
St Maurice, Switzerland, 91, 92
St Menas flasks, 68-69, 71, 136, 138, 144, 148, 151, 153-154, 163, **colour plates 5, 19**

St Stephen, dedications to, 115-117
St Stinian, Wales, 159
St Symeon Stylites, 69, 108, 131, 135, 155, **colour plate 3**
St Bertrand-de-Comminges, 121
St Gallen, Switzerland, 13
Sts Cosmas and Damian, 116
Sts Gervasius and Protasius, 117
Sts Sergius and Bacchus, 116
Sudbury, 164
Sumaqa, 99
Sutton Hoo, 161, 165, 166, 167, 169-171, 176, 178-182, 186, 187-188, 192
Swintila, 38, 76, 101
Synod of Whitby, 140
Syria, 8, 45, 47, 48, 57, 59, 62, 63, 64, 69, 81, 87, 90, 106, 108, 123-129, 130, 131, 135, 143, 150, 151, 155, 169, 174, 182, 187, 190
'Syrians', 59-64, 65, 69, 72, 92, 111, 115, 116, 120, 127, 129, 131, 138, 151, 161, 175-176

Taplow, 161, 165-167, 171, 182, 186, **colour plate 27**
Tarragona, 38, 49, 64, 66, 121
textiles, 42, 47, 56, 64, 68, 73, 76, 78, 85-93, 182
Teynham, 164
Theodebert I, 50, 100-101
Theodebert II, 32, 36
Theodegotha, 35
Theodemer, 28
Theodora, Byzantine Empress, 77, 184
Theodore, Archbishop of Canterbury, 25

Theodoric I, 21, 28-31, 34, 35, 73, 82-83, 97, 103, 109, 121, 190
Theodoric II, 27, 88
Theodoric Strabo, 28, 29
Theodosian Code, 13, 87
Thessaloniki, 12, 17, 28, 98
Thrasamund, 35
tin, 150-151
Tintagel, 42, 144-150, 155, 160, 161, 190, **colour plates 15, 20**
Toledo, 116, 123, 124
Tongeren, 24, 133
Toulouse, 27, 61, 95, 118, 120, 121
Tournai, 80-82, 94, 104, 189
Tours, 16, 32, 40, 51, 61, 68, 88, 95, 96, 110, 115, 116, 131, 141, 149, 153
'Treasure of Bishop Desiderus of Auxerre', 168
Trethurgy, 147
Trier, 15, 98, 106, 108, 131

Upper Layham, 176

Valence, 101, 117
Verdun, 50
Verulamium, 15, 161, 163, 176, 177
Via Egnatia, 16, 18
Vienne, 61, 101, 113, 114, 117, 141, 159
Viviers, 101
Vouillé, 32
Vulfoliac (stylite), 131

Watchfield, 180
Westwell, 164
Wheathampstead, 164, 167
Whithorn, 148, 149, 160, 161
Wickhambreux, 164
Wingham, 164
Wymondham, 165

Xanten, 16

Ztathius, Lazi king, 33